W9-BCU-836

Down Mailer's Way

Robert Solotaroff

Down Mailer's Way

UNIVERSITY OF ILLINOIS PRESS
Urbana Chicago London

74-25495

To Sarah
and
to Ernest Wolf

Preface

TO take the long view, all of this began about two decades
ago when as an adolescent, eyeballs perspiring with curiosity about
what people really did in the wide world, I more or less memorized
The Naked and the Dead. The first formal effort was a seminar paper
on Mailer at the University of Chicago in 1965. Then, at the prompting of a friend who was then editor of the *Chicago Review,* I turned
the paper into an article. I needed the prompting because I had begun
to suspect that my breezy dismissal of *An American Dream* and my
claim that Mailer had embraced psychopathy were all wrong. I write
this small apology now as a way of suggesting how easy it is to deal
with Mailer in a relatively elegant fashion if one does not try to un-
ravel what is actually happening in his works. For example, in the
article (which was published in the June, 1967, issue of the *Chicago
Review*) I dispatched *An American Dream* in two or three pages.
When I finally finished absorbing the ideas in the nonfiction that
inform the novel and tried to show their workings—along with the
workings of Mailer's aesthetic and emotional imperatives—I found
that, try as I would to compress, it took more than fifty pages to fit
together what merited explanation. The critic who wishes to do justice
to this very didactic author's literary intentions can no more casually
demolish his ideas than he can take flight into impressionistic fluff
about Mailer's "wonderful spontaneity" or "fertile creativity" or
"stylistic daring-do," though all of this is true enough. Since Mailer
has always been driven by a desire to understand "how things work,"
we might take somewhat the same approach to his work.

I can think of no better way to begin a brief explanation of my
handling of this approach than to borrow these eloquent lines from
George Steiner:

> At Matthausen they tied together the legs of women in childbirth.
> In the Warsaw ghetto they gave each family one less residence permit
> than it had children, compelling each mother to select one of her
> children for immediate shipment to the ovens. We all now live under
> the imminent possibility of a mass death so complete that it will

go unrecorded, that there will be none left to mourn or remember. Either literature is about these things, or it is about nothing. That does not mean it must deal explicitly with the bestiality and menace which surrounds us . . . it means that literature, to be taken seriously, must recognize the hideous enlargement in the range of possible experience. . . .

Very few writers have had the nerve or insight to look at the new manner of man. They have acted as if all the ravenings and unknowns shadowing our time were exterior, as if the wounds and recoveries were merely of the flesh. . . .

Norman Mailer is among the honest men. He strives to know, at the peril of moral chaos, what it is that has been loosed upon the world and whether art can cope with it.

This was probably written in 1961 and thus falls near the midway mark of Mailer's publishing career. But it reaches back to inform his first major work to be published, *The Naked and the Dead* (1948), as well as it reaches forward to illumine his most recent works, *St. George and the Godfather, The Prisoner of Sex, Existential Errands,* and *Of A Fire on the Moon,* although the terms have changed somewhat. Mailer now stalks the psychic causes and effects of Vietnam, the riots, technological abstraction, Women's Liberation, Nixon's ability to prosper politically, and hundreds of other conditions and events instead of the camps, but his fundamental purpose is, as it was twenty-five years ago, to drive to the center of the American psyche and report what he finds there. Not all of what he finds there is the contemporary equivalent of camp guards and victims. There is no univocal decrying of the horror of modernity; he is too tough and resourceful a thinker and man to use, in Herzog's words, "the commonplaces of the Wasteland outlook, the cheap mental stimulants of Alienation, the cant and rant of pipsqueaks about Inauthenticity and Forlornness."

For all of his antics and controversies—perhaps in part because of them—Mailer, as much as any man in the country, occupies the kind of moralist-prophet role that Emerson, Thoreau, and Whitman did. The cosmic embrace of Emerson and Whitman has been hard for a perceptive man to come by in the last few decades, but Mailer has done his best. If he has found much that is horrific and cowardly in the collective mind, he has also unearthed a good deal of possibility, sometimes in places so improbable that his good news damages the work. In all, if there is any unifying strain in his diverse writings it follows from his fascination with growth and his commitment to trace the spoor of possibility wherever he finds it. In the more than two decades that he has been a writer of national and international prominence, Mailer's insistence upon a life which holds the promise of adventure and the possibility of self-development through that adventure has led him through such terrains as anarchism, revolutionary socialism, hipsterism, his own version of conservatism, and his own version of existentialism, which merges with his Manichean religion on one side and his gnostic biology on the other.

In part, this book is an attempt to track these paths, as Mailer repeatedly packed up and pushed on after his constantly receding psychic frontier. But only in part, for the first possibilities that a writer at his desk confronts lie within the infinity of unwritten linguistic combinations before him. Susan Sontag recently wrote that "if Norman Mailer is the most brilliant writer of his generation, it is surely by reason of the authority of his voice." To "voice," I would add Mailer's energy, insight, passion, and perhaps half a dozen other attributes, but none of these would have been realized with some consistency over the years had he not changed his style several times over.

All of which brings us to one of the paradoxes which any extended study of Mailer must take on: Why has Mailer's fiction never quite reached the plateau that *The Naked and the Dead* pointed toward? To repeat the dull litany about the decline of the novel does not begin to explain, for if the "well-made novel" is gone forever, hugely compelling fiction is not. Although Mailer's equipment is awesome, and although he has probably written more pages of glittering prose than any of his contemporaries, his fictional achievement does not approach Bellow's, or, to compare him to two contemporaries who have confronted hallucinatory extremes of experience (as Mailer has and Bellow has not), Mailer has not written a single novel as impressive as Ellison's *Invisible Man* or Burroughs's *Naked Lunch*. Yet Mailer could conceivably come out with a truly great novel next year or ten years from now.

This study also grapples with two of the more unusual products of Mailer's career—the wild system which he began creating in the mid-fifties and which is such a singular blend of integrity and opportunism, of profundity and hokum, and the author's sometimes breathtaking, sometimes bizarre manipulations of his own personae.

The great majority of the notes are at the end of the book, and there is a fair amount of commentary in the notes section. My hope was that one could read over a clean text without suffering the distraction of page numbers and sources within the lines or of a number above them. The latter so often creates that tic of obligation to flip to the back to make sure that nothing was missed, followed by the annoyance at finding only a citation. If you are interested enough to want more, or if you wish to follow up on a reference, there they wait for you. Occasionally I felt that some explanatory material would be of immediate assistance, so there are a few footnotes.

My debts are many. I would never have begun the project without the encouragement of Professors James E. Miller, Jr., and Robert E. Streeter of the University of Chicago, and I would never have completed it without the generous assistance of the successive chairmen of the English Department at the University of Minnesota, Robert Moore and William Madden. I also thank the Graduate School of the university for a summer grant which made possible the final revision and the colleagues who read parts or the whole of the manuscript and offered pages of badly needed suggestions: Chadwick Hansen; Donald Ross; and, especially, Edward Griffin, Charles Sugnet, and George T. Wright.

Minneapolis   **R.S.**
April, 1973

Contents

Yes, the world's a ship on its passage out, and not a voyage complete; and the pulpit is its prow.

HERMAN MELVILLE

A fictional technique always relates back to the novelist's metaphysics.

JEAN-PAUL SARTRE

Medical Kit of the Soul: *What is the strongest healing application?—Victory.*

FRIEDRICH NIETZSCHE

1
Within the Walls: The Political Solution

SINCE this chapter will wander about a good deal as I try to unknot the tangle of stale borrowings and exhilarating discoveries, obligations and assertions, shrewdnesses and gaucheries contained between the covers of *The Naked and the Dead,* it is perhaps perverse but certainly consistent to begin with a double reverse. The writer who Mailer has most consistently quoted and admired, and whom he has measured himself against, is, of course, Ernest Hemingway. Philip Young begins *Ernest Hemingway*—after twenty years still, in my opinion, the best study of that author's work—by referring to the dying hero of "The Snows of Kilimanjaro" as he remembers the room in Paris where "he had written the start of all he was to do." Young compares the hero to Hemingway and then very convincingly proceeds to analyze *In Our Time* as the start of all the significant work that Hemingway was to do. Although the start of most of what we value in Mailer—indeed, the apex of some of it—is in his first novel, it is, as Hemingway's great collection of stories was not, a flawed, transitional work.

Both works were published within a few months of the authors' twenty-fifth birthdays, but by that time Hemingway had in large part created the most influential style in twentieth-century American literature. One of the ways that *The Naked and the Dead* is transitional is precisely in terms of the extent of its stylistic and technical borrowings; again and again we can point to Dos Passos, Wolfe, Fitzgerald, Hemingway, and Farrell. But then, for all its faults, the novel is impressively memorable in its own right. Although the student works first collected in *Advertisements for Myself* are quite good for a teenager, their derivations are what most stay with us. The crude, precombat prelude to the novel, "A Calculus at Heaven" (1942), ends with two soldiers, who will be killed as soon as the sun rises a bit, talking a painfully stiff-upper-lip Hemingwayese:

3

The captain peered around the side of the window. "It's going to be one hell of a sun," he said.

"Yes," the Indian answered slowly, "sometimes you want to look pretty carefully at it."

"The Greatest Thing in the World," a story of a hungry drifter who escapes with five dollars from a crooked pool game, reads like a blend of the worst of Steinbeck and Farrell and some middling Albert Maltz, or, as Mailer tells us, the narrative told by a simple boy follows from a reading of *The Sound and the Fury* a month or two earlier. All of the stories are out of the social realism of the thirties and reflect many of the leftist stances of that period—even in the Faulknerian number, hoboes are cruelly beaten by townspeople and the boy's parents would probably not treat him so harshly if the father were not out of work in the depression. In fact, Mailer gives as one of the reasons for placing "A Calculus at Heaven" where he did, "The Pacific war had a reactionary overtone which my young progressive-liberal nose smelled with the aid of PM editorials."

But by the time he sat down to write *The Naked and the Dead* (in June or July of 1946), some strange fumes had worked their way into those conventionally leftist nostrils. To be sure, so much of *The Naked and the Dead* is clearly written by that talented, progressive Jewish boy from Brooklyn whose sweet, modest face looks out at us from the pages of the 1948 *Current Biography*. Gathered from pieces in *Cue* and the *New York Star Magazine* and from a publisher's release in the *Saturday Review,* the short biography is an implicit encomium to capitalism for rewarding with so much money and fame this nice boy who wrote a book which attacked capitalism. There are humorous reverberations in the fact that the reporter from the *Star*—the name only a few months old but the paper still very much Mailer's progressivist gospel, *P.M.*—wrote of the twenty-five-year-old who was to become the wild man of the late-night talk shows:

> His ears stick out from a head of brown curly hair. On his face, with the wide forehead, large blue eyes, and narrow, sensitive chin, it is still possible to see the traces of an earnest adolescent. How could so young a face have written such a book? *

As for the critique of capitalism, one of Mailer's intentions was to convince the reader that the American army of the novel was a

---

* The biography quotes the first two sentences of this and in the following two concludes: "Confident in manner, Mailer is said, nevertheless, to be self-effacing. He has taken up oil painting, of which he says: 'I have no talent at all and therefore can have no disappointments'" ("Norman Mailer," *Current Biography: 1948* [New York: H. W. Wilson, 1948], p. 410).

microcosm of American society. If we combine the authoritarian structure of the army with the civilian society as it is depicted in the Time Machine flashbacks and the memories and actions of the soldiers, then we get a pretty thorough run-through of the worst accusations of Farrell, Steinbeck, and Dos Passos; the society is largely characterized by spiritual and emotional barrenness, class prejudice, racism, economic and emotional exploitation, a collapse of sustaining democratic values, sadism, violence, crime, and a range of sexual ailments running from feelings of inadequacy to latent perversity. As for the political implications of the popular-front warning against the coming of fascism, the leaders of the army might be ponderous mediocrities or they might be brilliant, but since they invariably damage the men under them their effect is invariably perverse. As the novel's representative liberal, Lieutenant Robert Hearn, reflects, "By their very existence they had warped the finest minds, the most brilliant talents of [his] generation into something sick, more insular" than the leaders.

Since there is no escape from the enforcement of its values, the army would seem to be the worst possible version of American society that Mailer is to present in all his writing. A casual reading of *The Naked and the Dead* suggests that it offers no possibilities for growth at all; the most humane characters are killed or morally violated, and even the ones whose amorality best qualifies them for growth in the savage world of the novel are defeated. The only character who seems to succeed in having his basic ambition realized is Major Dalleson, the novel's model of bureaucratic mediocrity whose hope for the future runs no further than being demoted to nothing lower than captain when the war ends. That the book ends with Dalleson projecting ways to fill the time before the next campaign begins serves as an ironic commentary upon the worth of all of the endeavors that have filled the preceding seven hundred pages. In all, *The Naked and the Dead* seems, in moral terms, to be a wasteland vision of a dying world. In what were some of the author's earliest published comments about the novel, he replied to that charge in this way:

> People say it is a novel without hope . . . actually it offers a good deal of hope. I intended it to be a parable about the movement of men through history. I tried to explore the outrageous proportions of cause and effect, of effort and recompense in a sick society. The book finds man corrupted, confused to the point of helplessness but it also finds that there are limits beyond which he cannot be pushed, and it finds that in his corruption and sickness there are yearnings for a better world.

Nevertheless, however large Mailer's sympathies are, the book has the effect of belittling these yearnings since the author suggests that the characters are doomed to frustration in the peacetime world that awaits them. More importantly, this statement would make the novel's only triumphant assertions the flight down a mountain of a platoon pursued by hornets or the refusal of a large number of men to charge Japanese guns when a general attack is in progress. All of this goes against one of Mailer's later comments about the novel and, more to the point, what actually lies beneath the surface of *The Naked and the Dead*.

Several times in the past few years Mailer has come up with the idea that

> everybody, literate and illiterate alike, had in the privacy of their un-
> conscious worked out a vast social novel by which they could make
> sense of society. . . . the psychic fact was that as life presented
> new evidence, the book was altered in its details. When such large
> events as births, deaths, marriages, divorces, successes, failures, so-
> cial cataclysms and social revelations were sufficiently unexpected to
> indicate the conception one had of society—that conception so often
> forged by inferior art and entertainment—was faulty, then the out-
> lines of the novel would be drastically revised; in effect the Novelist
> was forever drawing up new social charts upon which the Navigator
> could make his calculations.
>   In its turn, the dream provided another sort of information for the
> Navigator. It ran simulations.
>   . . . It was possible that in the dream, one traveled through a
> scenario where one was his own hero, and in the dream one might
> learn how one would react to the death of the man with a crack in
> his voice, and conceivably have glimpses of reaction to one's own
> death as well? . . . So next day, the charts of the Novelist would
> be redrawn for the trip through the social world, new reefs to avoid
> laid in, new channels discovered and marked. Now subtle changes in
> the person might be evident. . . .

However fanciful this addition to Freud's dream theory may seem to us, Mailer was, in the novel, partially throwing off large gobs of second- or third-hand leftist stances by running simulations of sorts.*

---

* This refers to the advertisement for "A Calculus at Heaven":

In the year which had gone by since the war began, I had been indoctri-
nated like everyone else with the superheated publicities of the mass-
media. The nervous system of every American alive was being jammed
with propaganda, and it may be that "A Calculus at Heaven" is most interesting in the way it shows a young, fairly good mind throwing off large
gobs of that intellectual muck at the same instant that it is creating its own
special variety of the muck. [Norman Mailer, *Advertisements for Myself*

In the fifteen months that he wrote and rewrote the novel, he simulated by testing, beneath the sometimes off-key, more often quietly eloquent narration of the pains and frustrations which largely fills the book, the life views of three pairs of characters: General Cummings and Sergeant Croft, Lieutenant Hearn and Private Valsen, and Privates Goldstein and Ridges. This is not to say that these are the only views examined, but that they are the most deeply probed ones and the ones which most interestingly point the way toward Mailer's later development as a writer and as a man. Since the actions of each pair follow from a relatively consistent ethic, Mailer was able to present to the reader and to weigh for himself three fairly well fleshed evaluations of the possibility of a successful struggle against those forces which combine to undermine an individual's more fruitful conceptions of himself. As he wrote the novel, Mailer obviously came in good part to believe that the authoritarian ethic of Croft and Cummings offered the possibility not only of sustenance but, indeed, of psychic growth. The army only seems to be the worst possible version of American society; in actuality, the military world of *The Naked and the Dead* is a far more promising and healthier world than the one of *Barbary Shore*.

All six characters must be defeated, but for reasons which conflict. If the "good" characters must be defeated, since *The Naked and the Dead* is, among other things, a thesis novel attacking the sickness and corruption of American society in general and the American army in particular, then the "bad" characters should win, but Mailer arranged defeats for the novel's authoritarians because he did not want to seem to be praising the strength of fascism. Yet the novel also tries to be an allegory of the coming of fascism to the United States. What really complicated things and caused the author to lose control of the novel's symbolic lines was the fact that the values he consciously endorsed were against the grain of his deepest beliefs. This split is nicely caught in a comment made fifteen years after the novel was completed: "Beneath the ideology in *The Naked and the Dead* was an obsession with violence. The characters for whom I had the most secret admiration, like Croft, were violent people. Ideologically, intellectually, I did disapprove of violence. . . ."

(New York: G. P. Putnam's Sons, 1959), pp. 27–28 (hereafter cited as *Advertisements*).]

The social realism of the novel is quite a cut above the "muck" of the story, but it is finally no less foreign to the directions that Mailer's thought and style will take.

The author has said that he was an anarchist when he wrote *The Naked and the Dead* because of his dislike of collective action. Both by Mailer's statement and the fact that, as a whole, he did not believe that humane solutions could be reached by compromises between existing political powers, it would seem inaccurate to call the author a liberal. To state the same idea in a different way, liberalism obviously is contingent upon the assumption that a society has enough fundamental health to permit solution, and *The Naked and the Dead* is a biopsy of the profoundly sick body of America. Yet since the intellectual or ideological part of Mailer which opposed Croft subscribed to a number of beliefs which the novel designates as liberal, I shall (for the sake of economy as I try to pick my way through the conflicting positions in the novel) refer to this part of the author, and the novel as a whole, as the liberal Mailer and the novel's majority view. Correspondingly, those secret admirations and commitments which the preceding citation intimates will be described as belonging to the radical Mailer; this overall vision as it emerges in *The Naked and the Dead* is the novel's minority view. The categories are somewhat Procrustean, but ideologically the novel has almost as much jungle in it as Anopopei. Since the framework of the novel is, however, almost as clean as the contrasting ethical positions are prickly, we might reconnoiter before we plunge into the three life views and the two Mailers.

II

In its simplest sense, the design of *The Naked and the Dead* is dictated by the boundaries of the American conquest of the Japanese-held island of Anopopei in the South Pacific. The novel opens by focusing on one soldier in the hold of one of the troopships the night before the landing, a soldier who appropriately remains anonymous, submerged as he is in the common activity of anxiously sweating through the night with the six thousand others in the invading division. The book closes between three and four months later as the mopping up of the few remaining Japanese on the island is being completed and Dalleson is occupied with his plans for filling time before the Philippine campaign begins. In keeping with the idea of the army as a social microcosm, the narrative covers the campaign from two points of view, one representing the way the aristocracy of Division Headquarters under Major General Edward Cummings sees it, and the other that of the masses who fight the war, represented by the Intelligence and Reconnaissance Platoon of Division Headquarters Company under the command of Sergeant Croft.

In his preinvasion staff briefings, Cummings describes Anopopei as being shaped like an ocarina, and it is this ocarina that Cummings fully expects to manipulate with the eventual ease and control of any skilled musician. To continue the metaphor, the resisting difficulties of the ocarina are represented by the oppressive tropical climate, the dense jungle, and the five thousand defending Japanese under General Toyaku. Most of them are anchored in a formidable twenty-five-mile-long defense line—the Toyaku line—bounded by the ocean to the north and the ridge of mountains which bisects the length of the island to the south. Added to the resistances to Cummings's mastery are the physical limitations of his own soldiers and—what is far more important from Cummings's point of view—their emotional ones: the six thousand separate wills which might run counter to his own. But the soldiers are the fingers which must manipulate the island-ocarina if it is to be successfully played, and for the control of these fingers the general has formidable prerequisites which can more conveniently be discussed when we turn back to him in a few pages. Here the analogy must cease, for the soldiers have a resilient will of their own as fingers do not, and by the end of the novel Cummings is forced to reflect that "there were times now when he doubted basically whether he could change them, really mold them."

In a meaningful sense, it is not Cummings but Mailer himself who plays the ocarina of Anopopei. One of the strongest images I carried away from the last reading of *The Naked and the Dead* was of Mailer, in his own words "living like a mole writing and rewriting [the] seven hundred pages [of the novel] in those fifteen months," shut up in the rooms in Brooklyn and Cape Cod with *his* island. Sometimes the prose lapses; the control of the ideological framework of the war and of the postwar society that will follow is often shaky, as is the prewar America revealed in the Time Machine flashbacks. But when writing about many of the events which occur on his island, Mailer is, at his best, a sort of naturalistic Prospero as he conjures up such compelling passages as the long one in Part Two when the great storm is immediately followed by the platoon's agonized pushing of the antitank guns through the muddy jungle at night and their defense of the American flank against the nocturnal Japanese attack, or the platoon's entire reconnaissance mission in Part Three—particularly Martinez's solo scouting expedition, the climb up Mount Anaka, and the portage of the wounded Wilson's body. Here is Mailer truly at his best, over-whelmingly exhibiting what Norman Podhoretz has called the "phe-nomenal talent for recording the precise look and feel of things [that] is his most impressive single gift."

As one might expect in a war novel, Mailer's observing eye is primarily focused on human struggle, but whether writing about an action involving many men (like the pivoting of the American line in Part Two), the action of a smaller group (like the reconnaissance mission), or an individual effort (like Martinez's scouting of the pass to the west of Mount Anaka), Mailer is always able to lay out the particulars of mountains, slopes, valleys, streams, peninsulas, bays, jungle, kunai grass, path, and game trails in such a way that the reader is usually able to see both how his present location looks and precisely where it is on the island. (Mailer was in combat units only on the islands of Leyte and Luzon and saw combat only on Luzon. Neither island at all resembles Anopopei in size or shape; the embat-tled island of *The Naked and the Dead* is his own creation.) More is accomplished by this than the gratification of some readers' desire to master spatial relations. If Mailer sees one of the primary duties of the novelist to serve as the honest reporter of man's efforts to preserve or strengthen himself as he struggles against alien forces, and if the realities of war enabled him to turn Anopopei into an arena of almost constant struggle, then it is important that the reality of the arena be made as tangible as possible to the reader. In his arena Mailer creates test after test—the passive beset by the aggressive; Americans by Japanese; Japanese by Americans; Jews by anti-Semites; men by exhaustion, terror, despair, the unknown, the break-down of kidneys and bowels—and these are usually beautifully inter-related with the presence of mountain, jungle and stream, heat and storm.

All of this is reminiscent of the "scientific" naturalism of Zola, with the island the selectively constructed laboratory in which the sup-posedly objective scientist-novelist performs experiments with his characters as he tries empirically to ascertain natural laws. Consider-ing the tribute that the novel pays to Marxist social causality, it is not surprising that in discussing *The Naked and the Dead*'s naturalism most critics are not primarily concerned with Mailer's "realistic" transcription of speech and object or his willingness to treat "lower-class" characters. Rather, they focus on what they feel to be the irrevocable determinism of naturalism. Here Harris Dienstfrey speaks for a majority:

> *The Naked and the Dead* . . . is a book he would have written in one form or another even if the war had never occurred. Its characters, their strengths and weaknesses, and the possibilities for their change have all been determined, as though writ in stone, by the American life out of which they emerged. They funnel into one end of the island campaign that forms the immediate subject of the book and come out the other merely more of what they were at the start.

This is not the place to set about defining naturalism, surely an "ism" which is used as diversely and confusingly as romanticism or existentialism. C. C. Walcutt has devoted an extremely helpful book to this purpose, and we might borrow one observation concerning the determinism in Zola and those American writers who are generally considered to be naturalists—Frederic, Garland, Crane, Norris, London, Dreiser, Anderson, Hemingway, Farrell, Dos Passos, and Steinbeck. And this is that none of them has ever written a totally deterministic novel. Some independence of will is always present in some form to counter the idea that volition is only apparent, an inevitable effect of a social and/or biological cause. Among the tensions that Walcutt finds "contained in every piece of naturalistic writing"—and that we will find in *The Naked and the Dead*—he lists those "between hope and despair, between rebellion and apathy, between defying nature and submitting to it, between celebrating man's impulses and trying to educate them, between embracing the universe and regarding its dark abysses with terror."

When the freedom of a character in a novel is most severely curtailed, when the author makes him no more than the point upon which the vectors of his society, heredity, and unconscious converge, freedom still exists but is transferred to the author himself and to the reader. In a thesis novel which attacks the inevitable effect of certain social malignancies, the author is asserting his own free will in writing the book and tacitly demanding that the reader exercise his free will to resist, change, or eliminate these malignancies. With its attack upon American society and its warning of the coming of fascism, *The Naked and the Dead* is in part a thesis novel, but we need not look this far for assertions of free will. If the liberal Mailer will seek in the opening chapter of the book to establish his naturalistic assumptions by comparing a terrified soldier with Pavlov's famous dog, the radical Mailer will later give the character enough choice and courage to enable one critic very correctly to see in the soldier's characterization "the interweaving of necessity and freedom that Melville describes so vividly in the mat-making episode in *Moby Dick.*" Even the invocation of Pavlov is uncharacteristically Zolaesque; the novel contains little else that reminds one of quaint discussions of lesions or chemisms, and Mailer never consistently argues, even implicitly, that an act is the inevitable result of the unconscious. The deterministic, liberal Mailer causes the sound of a soldier's request to (in the best Frank Norris beast-leaping-forth manner) "work a spasm through Croft's fingers" and cause him to experience the crushing of a bird he held in his hand as an involuntary action. But the radical Mailer will turn with new fascination to weigh the possibilities of Croft's freedom, the uses to which it can be put as he struggles—as all of the characters struggle—against the obstacles Mailer creates.

In all, the use of causality in *The Naked and the Dead* tends toward the extreme of the deterministic spectrum opposite the one suggested in the preceding paragraph. Here, the pull between the author's conflicting ideas of the possibilities of the will is so severe that the novel is torn in half between them. Mailer keeps what I have suggested to be the novel's minority view—for only the radical Mailer can see real possibility—enough submerged so that he is able to patch things up and effect a rather shakily prevailing determinism. But it should be observed that the naturalistic tradition within which the novel is written, and upon which Mailer is so dependent, provides ample room for the emergence of experiential possibilities. We might then take issue with part of Dienstfrey's comment. As a whole, the characters do complete the novel "more of what they were at the start," but their possibilities are not so inevitably "writ in stone" as he would have them.

Let us first look at what is unquestionably right in his statement. By the end of the novel, Cummings and all of the surviving members of the platoon are forced to perceive their helplessness before external forces to a greater degree than they did before the invasion of Anopopei. A developing vision of man as Lear's "poor, bare, forked animal" before the storm of the external is captured in the titles of the book's four parts. The first part, "Wave," deals with the landing; "Argil and Mold" contains the early successes of the American forces as they advance within striking distance of the Toyaku line and the lethargy which they sink into at this point; "Plant and Phantom" is largely devoted to the platoon's reconnaissance mission but also contains the collapse of the Toyaku line; "Wake" is a sort of epilogue concerned with the mopping up of the Japanese resistance and the whole division's prospects for the future. All of this suggests an inevitable biological movement, with the soldiers reduced to aimless struggling organisms who ultimately have no more control over their fates than the kelp or plankton washed up on the beach.* Argil sounds like some sort of sea plant—it is not, of course—that is washed in and then molders. This seems to be what Ihab Hassan implies when he writes of how the soldiers' will to victory founders as they passively rebel against Cummings's proddings:

> Entrenched in their foxholes and duck-walked bivouacs, they refuse to respond to his will—it is no wonder that the main section of the novel is entitled "Argil and Mold." The image of the invasion army, "like a nest of ants wrestling and tugging at a handful of bread crumbs in a field of grass," describes it all.

To continue this parallel on a rather simple-minded level, the soldiers, particularly those of the platoon, are stirred to action in the third part and are either killed (they become phantoms?) or survive but become further dehumanized (plants?). Or is Mailer primarily suggesting that although the platoon's mission is in moral terms dreamlike and unreal, it is still filled with the biological reality of a plant? Finally, in "Wake," the platoon fades back into the anonymity with which the novel begins; the soldiers of the division have been reduced to no more than depersonalized killing machines, and they end the book waiting for the tide of war to sweep them kelplike to the Philippines. In a comment with which we shall have to deal, Mailer has asserted that the most profound influence upon *The Naked and the Dead* was a novel which was also concerned with the massive conflict of free will and determinism but which, thirty to one hundred years in advance, wholly transcended the "realistic" limitations of naturalism. "Wake's" final evocation of the pointlessness of human endeavor is much less grand but still reminiscent of *Moby Dick*'s

---

* This theme of men as phenomena in nature, not essentially different from all other natural phenomena in their ultimate passivity before vast natural processes, is, of course, a familiar one in naturalist literature. One of Mailer's early heroes was Steinbeck, and inasmuch as *The Naked and the Dead* is a biological epic it is reminiscent of *The Grapes of Wrath*. Could the friendship between Goldstein and Ridges be an ironic commentary on the upbeat, love-is-the-answer solution of Steinbeck's novel where Rose of Sharon suckles the dying man? If biological necessity was a literary loan when Mailer began *Naked*, he certainly made the concern his own as the novel and his career proceeded.

"then all collapsed, and the great shroud of the sea rolled on as it rolled five thousand years ago."

III

The influence of older naturalists such as Steinbeck, Dos Passos, and Farrell makes itself felt in *The Naked and the Dead* in more ways than through Mailer's emphasis on social causality, his attack on this determining society, and his evocation of the individual's ultimate helplessness before vast nature. The ten Time Machines which interrupt the narrative are reminiscent of the biographies in *U.S.A.*, and the fact that Mailer's biographies are written in the present tense, usually in a kind of semipoetry, picks up much of the feeling of *U.S.A.*'s Camera Eye intersticings. Further, the characters whose geographical and emotional pasts are filled in by the Time Machines were clearly chosen with an eye for their economic, geographic, and emotional differences. *U.S.A.*'s panoramic presentation of the diversities of America is imitated in *Naked*'s Time Machines with the biographies of a relatively religious Jew from Brooklyn and a reactionary Irish anti-Semite from Boston; a drifter from the Montana mines and a southern poor white; two characters from Texas, one an oppressed Mexican and the other a nearly psychopathic WASP; a social-register liberal and a Polish mobster from Chicago; and an affable Rotarian type from Kansas and a fascistic genius who is probably from Kansas or Nebraska. Much of the prose is in a flat Hemingway deadpan, and the monotonous, lower-class dialogue of the soldiers is perhaps overfamiliar to any reader of *Studs Lonigan*. And although Fitzgerald was not a naturalist, the evocation of the magical, upper-class world of money and glamour which appears in the description of Lieutenant Hearn's last summer at home before college is clearly derived from that author.

Derivative as the technique and much of the style are, *The Naked and the Dead* certainly offers no advance in exploring the possibilities of the novel. And for all the precision of Mailer's re-creation of the horrors and inanity of war, this aspect of the book does not strike me as being of a particularly different order from the attacks presented in the World War I novels of Hemingway, Remarque, and Barbusse. Only Dos Passos, in *Three Soldiers,* unequivocally argued that far from being a horrific crumbling of modern civilization, "war . . . was its fullest and most ultimate expression." This insight would have taught nothing new to the authors of what seem to me to be the two outstanding World War II novels, *The Naked and the Dead* and *Catch 22*. As Diana Trilling has written of Mailer's novel,

> it brings to a familiar subject the informing view of a new and radically altered generation. Our present-day belief that we stand outside the ordinary movements of historical evolution, the loss of faith in both the orderly and the revolutionary processes of social development, our always-increasing social fragmentation, and our always-diminishing trust in individual possibility—it is these changes in consciousness that separate Mailer's war novel from the novels that followed World War I, as does, too, its drastically accelerated sense of time. . . . The hot breath of the future—one might better say, the hot breath of our own expiring day—broods over the pages of *The Naked and the Dead* as foul and stifling as the surrounding jungle air.

This hot breath building in the waning democratic day is the fascism which General Cummings predicts will seize political control in the postwar years. The general sees the entire war as a consolidation of power, a preparation for the imminent time when a few strong men (ideally one strong man—himself) will subordinate the great mass of individuals to the machine. For the extraordinary man, Hitler is the interpreter of history, yet even the fascism of Hitler is decadent in its irrationality and inefficiency. If Cummings feels that the sanction to subjugate "efficiently" belongs to him by right, we might inquire about the standard upon which this right rests. He would seem to escape the ethical solipsism so familiar in this century of collapsing values, for he does not appeal to his own volition, to his value-creating will; instead, he attempts to ground his sanction in the external by appealing to a historical process standing outside himself. The question of whether historical process necessarily implies value would send us straying far from the real source of Cummings's appeal for justification, for it is an appeal to an entity both within and without, the same entity upon which such "moral" philosophers as Aristotle, Hume, and Dewey erect their values—the common nature of man. The morality of power which Cummings invokes, and which he feels will give postwar American society the same form as the army, is no random event in history, but rather the natural and therefore just culmination of "man's deepest urge . . . omnipotence." The last phrase is spoken by Hearn as he correctly interprets this speech of the general's:

> . . . from man's very inception there has been one great vision, blurred first by the exigencies and cruelties of nature, and then, as

nature began to be conquered, by the second great cloak—economic fear and economic striving. That particular vision has been muddied and diverted, but we're coming to a time when our techniques will enable us to achieve it. . . . There's that popular misconception of man as something between a brute and an angel. Actually man is in transit between brute and God.

Cummings then agrees with Hearn's interpretation and continues,

It's [man's deepest urge] not religion, that's obvious, it's not love, it's not spirituality, those are all sops along the way, benefits we devise for ourselves when the limitations of our existence turn us away from the other dream. To achieve God. When we come kicking into the world, we *are* God, the universe is the limit of our senses. And when we get older, when we discover that the universe is not us, it's the deepest trauma of our existence.

The general, then, posits the will to power as the monism through whose thrustings all human activities can eventually be explained. With the exception of the last two sentences, which are a blend of Freud and Rank, this is straight Nietzsche, and if it seems that I am exaggerating influences, it might be added that the last sentence of the first citation clearly derives from Zarathustra's "man is a rope stretched between the animal and the Superman." The general's conception of the highest expression of the will to power is the control of others; his aspirations reach beyond gaining high position in what he considers to be the inevitable war with Russia to achieving as much control of as many individuals as possible. If we belong to the group of Nietzsche buffs that Conor Cruise O'Brien has dubbed "The Gentle Nietzscheans," we might argue that Cummings (who does in his journal refer to Nietzsche's "arrow of longing") or Mailer has misunderstood the philosopher and that Cummings's desire to control others strikingly contrasts with Nietzsche's superman, who is primarily concerned with controlling himself and regards the need to direct others as a weakness. The general ultimately wants political control, but, as Werner Dannhauser has pointed out, Nietzsche urges men who wish to become supermen "to seek solitude, to flee from public life . . . from this point of view it might be maintained that the superman represents an apolitical solution to the total crisis of modernity." As for the political role of the superman, Nietzsche has predicted that the superman will refuse to rule the degenerate "last men" but will flee their moldering cities and live a wandering life. The Tough Nietzscheans might crack back with "Cummings and Mailer have perfectly understood Nietzsche. He has written of the right of 'society, the great trustee of life' to improve the stock and bring the emergence of supermen nearer by holding 'in readiness, without regard to descent, rank or spirit, the most rigorous means of constraint, deprivation of freedom, in certain circumstances castration.' As for the political role of the superman, 'Nietzsche does speak of the planetary rule of a new nobility, and the superman is Nietzsche's new idea of nobility.' "

But all of this is shadowboxing. We close with a fighter who is not yet at his full strength (will he ever attain it?) by observing that the man in transit is from the eighth page of the Modern Library edition of *Thus Spake Zarathustra,* the arrow of longing is from the ninth page, and the epigraph (from which the title of the third part of the novel is taken) is from the sixth, all of which suggests a penchant for instant, borrowed philosophy—so contrary to the relatively patient and distinctive accretions of the past twenty years—that will also find expression in *Barbary Shore.*

Mailer has often been praised for his sense of history at the present moment and a willingness, relatively rare among the novelists of his generation, to deal with large ideas. He was too willing as he wrote speeches (like the one cited a few pages earlier) in which that evil genius General Cummings effortlessly offers the neofascist line. To close with what is really telling about almost all of the general's expositions, one is increasingly struck by their tonal stiffness, their shallowness. The sense of Mailer as a good screenwriter for a bad movie, sweating in his determination to make the genius sound like a genius, often hovers close. It should be added, though, that the state-of-the-modern-world discussions are blended with an interpersonal struggle which, in spite of the ideological dialogue, is usually powerful and convincing. And the descriptive writing is often quite sharp. For example, Cummings makes a veiled homosexual overture to Hearn and sits "like a large and petrified bird, waiting . . . waiting for what must be indefinable." And when Croft sets out in Part Three to dramatize the general's theories, Mailer creates one of the most compelling stretches of writing of the past twenty-five years. But what are we to make of the spectre of the power-mad generals who are about to take over the United States? It's hard to know just how powerful "fascism" was twenty-five years ago precisely because it was already taking more subtle forms than the plotting of a coup d'état of the generals through force or election. The warning against Cummings is another unsuccessful borrowing, in this case the appropriation of popular-front appeals from the late thirties. In response to the complaint that the general is only a character used for dramatic purposes, I reply that the liberal Mailer made the appeal in the book, and the earnest young member of the Progressive Citizens of America said a few months after the novel was released:

> The chances are that there's not a single general in the U.S. army who's like him. But there could be! He articulates a kind of unconscious bent in the thinking of the Army brass and top rank politicians. He's an archetype of the new man, the coming man, the one who's really dangerous.*

We get the social and psychological origins of Cummings as we get those of nine other characters, in a Time Machine. Ralph Ellison, who learned to wing-shoot by reading Hemingway, once urged his interviewers to believe whatever Papa said in print because "he's been there." A close reader of the Time Machines can see that, on the whole, Mailer has quite simply not been there, either in actuality as he was on Leyte or with full imagination as he was on Anopopei. Often he borrowed stereotypes—the bleak life of a Montana miner, the easygoing Southerner with his love of women and liquor—and never did energize these Time Machines with the kind of sharp individual details which make life on Anopopei so convincing. And he often tried to cover up his imaginative and/or experiential shortcomings with an inflated, vaguely grand yet over-obvious style. The passage in the general's Time Machine which describes his discovery that the expression of his own deepest urge lay in the control of men is a typical example of this inflation. Here is Cummings as a lieutenant

* The immediately preceding paragraphs of the August, 1948, interview are of interest here:

> I never even thought of its being an anti-war book, at the beginning. But every time I turned on the radio and looked in the newspapers, there was this growing hysteria, this talk of going to war again, and it made me start looking for the trend of what was happening.
>
> It seems to me that you *could* get men to fight again. They came out of the war frustrated, filled with bitterness and anger, and with no place to focus their anger. They would begin thinking, "I don't give a goddam, I'll go into it, at least it'll be a change!" They would start remembering the good things about being a soldier, the furloughs with money in their pockets, how swell it was to be walking around in a uniform in a foreign city, and to be the most important men in that city just because they were in that uniform.
>
> That really formed the book—the feeling that people in our government were leading us into war again. The last half was written on this nerve right in the pit of my stomach. [Louise Levita, "The *Naked* are Fanatics and *the Dead* Don't Care," *New York Star Magazine*, August 22, 1948, p. 3 (hereafter cited as *Star* interview).]

in World War I having the most profound single experience of his life as he observes a successful American infantry charge:

> There were all those men, and there has been someone above them, ordering them, changing perhaps forever the fiber of their lives. In the darkness he looks blankly at the field, tantalized by the largest vision that has ever entered his soul. . . .
> To command all that. He is choked with intensity of his emotion, the rage, the exaltation, the undefined and mighty hunger.

At any rate, as his conversations with Hearn indicate, Cummings has learned to define his mighty hunger. In the dramatized present of *The Naked and the Dead,* his first step is to conquer the island quickly and impressively. For this, Cummings has formidable qualifications— six thousand men and considerable material under him; a knowledge of the strategies of war in terms of deploying the men and material to the right places at the right time which goes beyond solidity and reaches brilliance; the kind of courage that enables him to ride close to the front at a time when Japanese snipers are likely; great self-discipline; the ability to absorb vast numbers of variables and be able, at moments of crisis, to quickly devise and implement courses of action which synthesize these variables; and, above all, his will. It is with this will, supported by the authoritarian structure of the army and the simple physical fact there can be no fleeing from this structure—Anopopei *is* an island—that Cummings hopes to manipulate the fingers that will manipulate the ocarina of Anopopei.

It is not hard to see how these attributes, particularly the last two, appeal to Mailer. For all of Lieutenant Hearn's coldness and feelings of superiority, he is the character in the novel whose thought most resembles that of the author at the time of writing. The fascination which Cummings holds for Hearn interestingly anticipates Mailer's later conceptions of God (and sometimes himself) as a general, or his telling James Baldwin in the late 1950s, "I want to know how power works . . . how it really works, in detail":

> . . . he couldn't escape the peculiar magnetism of the General, a magnetism derived from all the connotations of the General's power. . . . The General might even have been silly if it were not for the fact that here on this island he controlled everything. It gave a base to whatever he said. And as long as Hearn remained with him, he could see the whole process from the inception of the thought to the tangible and immediate results the next day, the next month. That kind of knowledge was the hardest to obtain, the most concealed in everything Hearn had done in the past, and it intrigued him, it fascinated him.

Still, it is finally not too difficult for the liberal Mailer to defeat Cummings, first by having the soldiers slip into lethargy and then by letting the bumbling Dalleson virtually end the campaign while the general is off the island explaining the power of the Japanese resistance to his superiors. As Mailer said in 1948 and would say again in 1961, war consists of disproportions and has about it a fundamental absurdity which refuses reduction to the kind of intellectual control Cummings wants to exert. It was also easy enough for the author to believe that there was a point beyond which people could not be pushed, that they can find a certain strength in their weakness. But most of all, there is so much about Cummings that is distasteful. More important than his penchant for assuming false roles and his pretentiousness is the fact that his will to power expresses itself against others in an unequal struggle, with so much corrupt institutional power massed on his side. The liberal Mailer is thus able to undermine the lust for power which the radical Mailer endorses by tracing it to sicker past occurrences than the common loss of omnipotence. In a sense, Freud is placed beneath Nietzsche. A seductive mother and a threatening father have combined to displace the general's sexual energies, and his homosexuality is latent only because he was mugged before his surrender to an Italian could be consummated. Cummings's sexual abnormalities are used in other ways to help discredit his doctrine of growth through the amoral use of power, as the liberal Mailer points to the sickness of the individual from whom this doctrine emanates. Although Cummings's wife mistakes sexual violence for passion in the early months of their marriage, she soon perceives that "he is alone, that he fights out battles with himself upon her body." The same unhealthy relationship—at least for the liberal Mailer of the 1940s—between sex and violence is expressed in Cummings's contemplation of a howitzer with its "phallus-shell that rides through the shining vagina of steel, soars through the sky, and then ignites into the earth."

If Mailer can defeat Cummings without too much struggle, he has a far more difficult time defeating the will to power Cummings advocates when it is acted out by his double, Sergeant Croft. But Croft is more than a double of the general; he is an *extension* who completes Cummings's experience in somewhat the same way that Kurtz completes Marlow's journey into the heart of darkness. Since the masses will at first resist the dehumanization which Cummings feels to be so essential, they must be made afraid; it is the result of what Cummings feels to be an inevitable historical process that "the natural role of twentieth-century man is anxiety." All of this is anticipated in the army, which Cummings sees as "a preview of the future." He tells Hearn that a well-functioning army has "every man in it fitted into a fear ladder" and that even the hatred generated is of use since "the hate just banks in them, makes them fight a little better. They can't turn it on us, so they turn it outward." This is precisely what happens in the patrol behind the Japanese lines in Part Three. After Croft faces down an incipient rebellion, the exhausted men's only alternative is to pull themselves down into previously unexperienced states of agony as they drag themselves up Mount Anaka: ". . . they forgot about Croft. They had discovered that they could not hate him and do anything about it, so they hated the mountain, hated it with more fervor that [*sic*] they could ever have hated a human being."

The way in which Hearn is ground between Cummings and Croft offers another example of the way in which the general's theories find expression in the sergeant's actions. Cummings and Croft never meet, but they are connected through Hearn, the most formidable single human enemy that either of them faces. Cummings tells the lieutenant that in the power morality of the future (anticipated by the army) "a man who cannot find his adjustment to it [the power morality] is doomed" and "little surges of resistance," like Hearn's, "merely calls for more power to be directed downward, to burn it out." Since Cummings cannot ideologically or physically seduce Hearn, he reeducates the lieutenant to the realities of power by ordering him to pick up a cigarette butt, setting a court martial as the price of defiance. What Hearn calls his "crawfishing" might seem meaningless enough outside the context of their relationship, but to the lieutenant it is a humiliating epiphany of his own inability to get by on style if the authoritarian force does not wish to let him do so. Cummings cannot permit successful resistance by Hearn for several reasons. Obviously, it would indicate either that power was not all or that he did not have the personal force necessary for the realization of his great ambitions. And small as the victory over Hearn might seem, it *is* a victory. Reassured of the malleability of one, Cummings feels that he can find a way to control more fully the six thousand wills in the division and quickly overpower the Japanese resistance—from which promotion and the great victories of the future will follow.

As for the patrol to the rear of the Japanese lines, the general hopes that it will permit a second landing which will in turn effect a rapid conclusion of the campaign, but Cummings also suspects that Hearn, to whom he assigned the command of the patrol, will be killed on it. It remains for Croft to kill the lieutenant by leading him to believe that the guarded pass to the west of Mount Anaka is undefended, for Hearn threatens Croft's control of the platoon as he had threatened in a somewhat less direct way Cummings's power over the whole division. Mailer makes it very clear that Croft would not have had Hearn killed—at least not when he did—had the lieutenant agreed to lead the platoon up Mount Anaka when it was first discovered that the pass was guarded. It is at this point in the novel that Croft sets out to complete Cummings's ambition of forging a new, omnipotent self and clearly emerges as the actual hero of *The Naked and the Dead*. Armed with this victory over Hearn, Croft sets out to consolidate his power, as Cummings would put it—to demonstrate his control over the platoon, nature, and himself by leading the men up the mountain. Paralleling Cummings's humbling of Hearn with the gun of rank, Croft literally points a rifle at Hearn's lower-class counterpart, Private Valsen, when that disaffiliate stands between himself and climbing the mountain, between his innate understanding that the personality rises to heights only when it engages a cruel enemy and that enemy itself—the mountain.

After Mailer said in 1951 (three years after *The Naked and the Dead* was published) that he was on "a mystic kick" and that the strongest single influence on the novel was *Moby Dick,* he stated that he knew this while writing it and added, "I was sure everybody would know. I had Ahab in it, and I suppose the mountain was Moby Dick." Mailer would seem to be suggesting that Croft alone is Ahab, but then, at one point in the novel, Cummings thinks of himself as dominating the island like Mount Anaka, which implies dominating Mount Anaka as well. An attempt to compare and contrast the different meanings of Mailer's mountain and Melville's whale would not only take us far afield, but could easily become ludicrous. Shortly after *The Naked and the Dead* was published, Mailer admitted that he saw in the mountain and Croft's attempt to climb it a complex which he could not accurately define: ". . . death and man's creative urge, fate, man's desire to conquer the elements—all kinds of things that you never dream of separating and stating so baldly."

For all of the men who try to climb it, Mount Anaka means tremendous physical distress as they try to conquer the alien, resisting mass of nature. It is this distress which wipes out its first meaning to one soldier as all of the members of the patrol first see the mountain from the water: "Gallagher stared at it in absorption, caught by a sense of beauty he could not express. The idea, the vision he always held of something finer and neater and more beautiful than the moil in which he lived trembled now, pitched almost to a climax of words."

The same view of the mountain from the boat also appeals to Croft's most profound yearning, a more primal and intense vision of the future than Gallagher's vision of beauty:

> Croft was moved as deeply, as fundamentally as caissons resettling in the river mud. The mountain attracted him, taunted and inflamed him with its size. He had never seen it so clearly before. Mired in the jungle, the cliffs of Watamai Range had obscured the mountain. He stared at it now, examined its ridges, feeling an instinctive desire to climb the mountain and stand on its peak, to know that all its mighty weight was beneath his feet.

The power that Croft hopes to gain by conquering the mountain takes on more meanings than simple physical domination, and we would do well to observe them as they emerge from the climb itself. However, it should be said here that the fact that the climb only heightens the value of the mountain to Croft, as it does not to Gallagher, is at the heart of the radical Mailer's admiration for the sergeant.

To unify several perhaps indistinct observations, Cummings and Croft combine as the Ahab figure, driven by an implacable, amoral force to grow and to overwhelm whatever they feel opposes them. These two are the only contemporary spiritual pioneers Mailer can envision at this stage of his career; men who identify with the extant power structures and use them to burn out any opposition to their expanding sense of who they are or should be in the world. If we move through the biological process discussed earlier from the point of view of the lust for growth that Cummings articulates and Croft dramatizes, we can observe an antithetical process working, an example in the large structural elements of the novel of the double vision that Mailer brought to it. The landing in "Wave," which brings only anxiety to most of the soldiers, arouses in Croft a rushing sensation of power and a desire to expand this sensation through combat:

> For an instant he felt as though he were riding a horse at a gallop. . . .
> . . . Leading the men was a responsibility he craved; he felt powerful and certain at such moments. He longed to be in the battle that was taking place inland from the beach, and he resented the decision which left the platoon on an unloading detail.

Since expansion ultimately must be psychic and the value of physical combat must be measured in terms of how much it contributes to a new, stronger self, there are opportunities for growth at moments when physical assertion is impossible. At this moment, in the first example of the kind of premonition that will make so much of Mailer's later work bristle with psychic arcana, Croft intuits the death of an overcareful young soldier. The intuition is correct, and "Wave" ends with the soldier's death having "opened to Croft vistas of such omnipotence that he was afraid to consider it directly. All day the fact hovered about his head, tantalizing him with odd dreams and portents of power."

Mailer implies that only with Croft's discovery of his wife's unfaithfulness, that discovery which conclusively alienated him from "normal" relationships, did he experience such "numb throbbing excitement and the knowledge that his life was changed to some degree and certain things would never be the same." For Croft, Anopopei is an awakening of the dormant, the great opportunity to realize "crude unformed vision [of growth unto omnipotence] in his soul." This is the radical Mailer's interpretation of the biological process which informs the novel, one which suggests the survival-of-the-fittest naturalism of a Jack London novel. The weak fall off, but the strong are able to revert to the primitive beneath the surface—and Croft's primitivism has never been very far beneath—to adapt to cruel nature and its vast rhythms and grow through the adaptation.

As for Part Two, argil is not an organism, but white potter's clay. Will Croft, who always saw inevitable natural order in an individual's death and hinted in "Wave" an ability to intuit the operation of this order, prove to be the kind of clay that can advantageously mold itself to the irrevocable pattern in which men must grow or deteriorate? Or, to interpret in another way how the radical Mailer applies the part's title to Croft, will he be able to break through the deterministic mold of deterioration which the conditions of war seem to have cast for him and grow? With one crucial exception, Croft rises above the obstacles which terrify and deaden the other men in the platoon, but this exception is enough to balk the process of growth which he saw presaged for himself at the end of "Wave." He views the brutal struggle with the antitank guns as a contest—one which he wins—and as a whole displays great courage, self-control, and skill as he leads the turning back of the Japanese offensive. But his self-control wavers in the moment before the Japanese charge. As the Japanese mass for the attack, whispering out of the night, *"We you coming-to-get, Yank,"* Croft is for the first time in his life really afraid. Like his fictional descendant in *The Deer Park,* Marion Faye, Croft's drive toward growth is checked by the perception that other humans could powerfully affect his feelings. Croft tries to ease his way through this impasse which the Japanese have created for him by shooting a prisoner whom he has given a cigarette. But the memory of what he considers his shame persists.

Thus, Croft's progress has roughly followed Cummings's—early successes followed by inertia. Cummings's decision at the end of "Argil and Mold"—to have the platoon circle the island by boat, move through the pass in the mountain range which protects one flank of the Toyaku line, and scout the rear of the line—serves both Cummings's and Croft's desires for expansion. If successful, the expedition will permit the landing of American troops behind the Toyaku line, from which will follow a speedy conclusion of the campaign. It will also demonstrate to Cummings his intellectual, imaginative, and volitional control over events. For Croft it offers a chance to break through the impasse which his moment of fear and the lethargy of inactivity have thrown before him. And from the moment he sees Mount Anaka from the water, the patrol provides the possibility of conquering the mountain and all of the finally mystical fulfillment this victory would provide.

All of this fits in with the title as well as the contents of Part Three, "Plant and Phantom." I suggested earlier that the title implies an inevitable dehumanizing process. But if we interpret it in the context of the epigraph from which the title is taken, we find quite contrary possibilities suggested. The epigraph is: "Even the wisest among you is only a disharmony and hybrid of plant and phantom. But do I bid you to become phantoms or plants?" The lines are spoken by the noblest of living men, Zarathustra. After living for ten years in transcendent isolation on top of a mountain, Zarathustra descends, out of the overabundance of his being, to bring a new life to the deadened people in the lowlands beneath him. He tells them that the God they have created is dead; new horizons are open to them if they use their will to recombine their phantom (soul and reason) with their plant (body and passions) to achieve a new unity, a higher self.

If the patrol in "Plant and Phantom" is important as an application of Cummings's fear psychology, it is far more meaningful as the radical Mailer's inquiry and covert demonstration of the genuine possibility of a personal growth great enough to be called re-creation. The origins of this possibility lie deep within Croft's psyche, depths which emerge as Croft pursues his intuitive, unreflecting quest for a new unity of being. Two citations help us to perceive these depths. The first is from Mailer's narration of the first full day of the patrol, when all of the other men of the platoon are terrified by the expanse, silence, and "somnolent brooding resistance" of the unexplored land:

> Croft experienced it in a different way. The land was foreign to him, and spawned a deep instinctive excitement at the thought that no one had trod this earth for many years. . . . this country, unexplored, appealed to him deeply. Each new vista that the summit of a hill might furnish him was gratifying. It was all his, all terrain which he could patrol with the platoon.
>
> And then he remembered Hearn, and shook his head. Croft was like a high-spirited horse, unused to the bit, reminded he was no longer free by an occasional harsh pressure on his jaws.

The second citation is from the narration of the third day of the patrol. Hearn has been killed, his resisting effect removed, and Croft is leading the platoon up Mount Anaka:

> Croft had an instinctive knowledge of land, sensed the stresses and torsions that had first erupted it, the abrasions of wind and water. The platoon had long ceased to question any direction he took; they knew he would be right as infallibly as sun after darkness or fatigue after a long march. . . .
>
> Croft felt the nature of rock and earth, knew as well as he knew the flexing of his muscles how in an age of tempest the boulders had strained and surged until the earth had shaped itself. He had always a feeling of that birth-storm when he looked at land; he almost always knew how a hill would look on the other side. It was the variety of knowledge that felt intuitively the nearness of water no matter how foreign the swatch of earth over which he was traveling.

The two important facts about Croft that emerge here are his desire to explore and his understanding of the land before the exploration is completed—both of them connected with instinct. Mailer himself cannot decide whether the instinctive understanding of land is "innate or perhaps it was developed in all the years he had worked on land driving cattle, all the patrols he had led, all the thousand occasions when it had been important for him to know which route to take." But the seeds of this aptitude—indeed, of his whole personality—can be traced to the atavism which Mailer posits in Croft's Time Machine. In the beginning of the biography Mailer tries to explain how a Sam Croft came to be, what could have been the causes of the peculiar tensions, frustrations, and hungers that drive the Guardsman Croft to shoot a defenseless striker and, on Anopopei, crush a small bird in his hand and drag the platoon and himself up Anaka:

He is that way because of the corruption-of-the-society. He is that way because the devil has claimed him for one of his own. It is because he is a Texan, it is because he has renounced God.

He is that kind of man because the only woman he ever loved cheated on him, or he was born that way, or he was having problems of adjustment.

Most of this is the leveling, everything-can-be-explained liberal cant that much of Mailer has always despised. Still, the liberal Mailer tries to compromise the nearly psychopathic character by attaching some abnormalities shared by Cummings: latent homosexuality—Croft cannot stand to be touched by a man—and an ultimate sterility, symbolized by an unsuccessful, childless marriage. In both unions, the men tried to prove their omnipotence over their wives' bodies, and with Croft, as with Cummings, the liberal Mailer traces the urge to omnipotency to sick psychic origins—the last words of Croft's Time Machine, "I HATE EVERYTHING WHICH IS NOT IN MYSELF," suggest infantile regression. But all of this is brushed aside by the radical Mailer's admiration for what *he* feels to be the source of Croft's lust for growth and fury at having this growth obstructed—a reversion to earlier generations who possessed in full strength that need for adventure, conflict, and growth which Mailer will later place at the dead center of the American experience, the frustration of which is causing so much collective disease. Croft's "ancestors pushed and labored and strained, drove their oxen, sweated their women, and moved a thousand miles." But with all the American frontiers closed, Croft "pushed and labored inside himself and smoldered with an endless hatred."

Yet, as the prototype of the hipster, Croft instinctively knows what actions will minister to his ailments and enable him to break open the walls which have held his straining psyche encased. Anaka contains within its bulk all the frontiers that have been closed to Croft; his frontal onslaught of the mountain is also—to borrow some phrases from the author's 1957 defense of the hipster—a backward, inner movement, "the first wind of a second revolution in this century, [the Russian Revolution was the first] moving not forward toward [political] action and more rational equitable distribution, but backward toward being and the secrets of human energy, not forward to the collectivity which was totalitarian in the proof but backward to the nihilism of creative adventurers." *

* *Advertisements*, p. 363. This was written less than six months before Mailer decisively linked Croft's instinctualism with the demands of an existential God (see pp. 105–10).

In terms of the ongoing course of Mailer's career, the ultimate meaning of the mountain coincides with none of the meanings Mailer offered unless we interpret "creativity" as the ability to create a self which can free itself enough from the restrictions which external circumstance have inflicted upon it to be open to the blessings of the irrational. The discussion of whether a totally "new" self is possible or what it would mean if it were possible—just where does an altered self stop and a new self begin?—is finally as pointless as an attempt to define omnipotence in terms of external actions: Does it mean being able to do more or less than the Superman of the comic books? The discussion of the quest for an omnipotent new self only takes on meaning if we see it as Croft acts it out, as the attempt to create a new psychic synthesis which is omnipotent precisely in its ability to conduct forced marches into the secrets of the self, the discovery of which will free the energy and vision which will permit still further exploration. That the vision to be gained is one of the secret workings of the external world as well as of oneself is indicated by Croft's final reflections on his failure to climb Anaka: "Croft kept looking at the mountain. He had lost it, had missed some tantalizing revelation of himself. Of himself and much more. Of life. Everything."

These secrets are guarded by an archaic, presocietal terror of the unknown as well as by the deadening weight of societal value. What Mailer does by equating the expanse of alien physical terrain and psychic resistance is to multiply a hundredfold the experience of walking with one's eyes closed until one literally cannot force another step without opening them. Croft could push himself further into the unknown without encountering this resistance than any other member of the platoon, but his will is finally attacked:

> The closer he came to the crest of the mountain the greater became his anxiety. Each new turn of the staircase demanded an excessive effort of will from him. He had been driving nearer and nearer to the heart of this country for days, and it had a cumulative terror. All the vast alien stretches of land they had crossed had eroded his will, pitched him a little finer. It was an effort, almost palpable, to keep advancing over strange hills and up the flanks of an ancient resisting mountain [of his primitive self]. . . . He drove himself onward with the last sources of his endeavor, dropping at the halts with no energy left.
>
> But each time the brief respite would charge his resolve again and he could toil upward a few yards more. He, too, had forgotten almost everything. The mission of the patrol, indeed even the mountain, hardly moved him now. He progressed out of some internal

contest in himself *as if to see which pole of his nature would be successful.*

And at last he sensed that the top was near. . . . It spurred him on, yet left him exhausted. Each step he took closer to the summit left him more afraid. He might have quit before they reached it. [Italics mine.]

Although one pole of Croft's nature is the desire for growth (which is the same thing as more power over himself and all that is external to himself), it is impossible to be precisely sure what the other pole is. Perhaps it is Croft's vestigial attachment to a moral system which places limits on man's attempts to become a God or perhaps the archaic fear of the unknown; probably it is some combination of both. A number of men, Yeats among them, have defined the polarities of personality as the will to love and the will to control. Historically, the former pole is crystallized in the Judaic-Christian tradition, which asserts the ultimate limitations of the individual under an all-powerful and moral god and the value of other human beings. Obviously, the latter tradition—which we might call the Faustian one *— asserts only the value of the extraordinary individual with godlike possibilities, and in its purest form denies all other value but this. Cummings's articulations are an example of this tradition. Certainly, these were the two poles of Mailer's personality,† and the liberal one, which asserted Judaic-Christian values, predominated at least enough to prevent Croft from attaining the peak; in the next paragraph after the last one quoted, Croft accidentally kicks over a nest of hornets who drive the platoon down the mountain.

Robert Penn Warren has said that a true novelist doesn't find a subject, the subject finds him. If Mailer began the book intending to write a short novel about a patrol and was at first "annoyed at how long it was taking me to get to the patrol," the single great subject of his life found him when he did get to it. The pace of the novel as a whole is amazing for a work of seven hundred pages, but with Part Three one feels a massive acceleration which, in its much slower way, resembles that of the Saturn rocket—a process Mailer will describe

---

* I am using the word as it is used in the novel—as quite related to the amoral will to power. Later in his career Mailer will often designate as Faustian the desire to destroy nature. This is an immoral perversion of the will to power.

† In later years, Mailer will attempt to synthesize these views by dividing power into Devilish power and Godly power. The latter is not only compatible with love, it is a prerequisite.

with great detail and fascination more than twenty years later. So much of this energizing is generated by the sense of the author's growing excitement, and so much of it is propelled by the testing of Croft—still, after four subsequent novels, the most compelling character by far that Mailer has created. As Hearn grudgingly conceded, "That Croft was a *boy,* all right." Or as I suggested earlier, it all really begins right here. Croft had odd dreams and portents of power which will affect the rest of his life, and so did the radical Mailer as he explored in Croft the possibilities of this prototypical hipster—(in Edmond Volpe's words) "the existential hero who refuses to succumb to the dictates of an inherited moral and social code, who savors the freedom to exist in the present and to explore the extreme limits of personal power, who responds to the irrational forces in his being, and who creates his own meaning and identity through action." We shall be returning to Croft as he pits himself against the unknown, an action which will anticipate, among other things, the picture that Mailer will so frequently paint of himself—the writer peculiarly qualified by his courage to explore the buried mysteries of existence.

IV

At the same time that Croft is leading the agonized procession up Mount Anaka, an even more debilitating process is taking place. Four already exhausted men—Sergeant Brown, Corporal Stanley, and Privates Goldstein and Ridges—are, by carrying the wounded Wilson through jungle and kunai grass back to the landing beach, implicitly asserting the commitment to the Other that is at the heart of Judaic-Christian morality. All Stanley has to sustain himself in the portage is the most despicable version of ambition in the novel. The same kind of intelligence that instinctively leads him to tell potential benefactors whatever they want to hear calculates that there is no percentage in continuing the effort, so he pretends to pass out before the first full day of the litter detail is completed. Like Stanley, Brown sees himself as occupying a place in the army "society" as Ridges and Goldstein, the two survivors of the patrol held in the lowest opinion by the rest of the platoon, do not. Brown has equated his right to hold the position of sergeant with his ability to get Wilson back to the beach, but a final commitment to the maintenance of class status offers no more sustenance than Stanley's low-level ambition for advancement in the army society: Brown stays with Stanley; Ridges and Goldstein stagger on alone with the litter. As James Scott has written, Mailer has selected as his stretcher bearers two men of deep fundamentalist conviction—one a Christian and the other a Jew. Together they represent whatever is most stable and most enduring in western culture. Their almost primitive idealism, precisely because it was designed to sustain a defeated people, a political nonentity and a social minority, does succeed in that it keeps them harnessed to their burden where Stanley and Brown, nominal Christians, are incapable of real sacrifice.

His own involvement and excitement clearly deepening with each chapter, Mailer culminates this patrol into the self by alternating the narrative between the climb up Anaka and the portage of Wilson. The author thus simultaneously tests two extremes of behavior—the primitive morality of Goldstein and Ridges and the primitive amorality of Croft. For Ridges, there are two simple imperatives behind his need to continue staggering onward with Wilson—the belief that there is some divine purpose which orders the carrying of an obviously dying man and his sureness that he will be taking a long step toward damnation if he commits the sin of abandoning Wilson. With Goldstein, a more complicated process is sustaining him. Early in the portage, Mailer established a community of suffering in which the bearers' bodies responded to Wilson's screams. But with Goldstein's body growing numb to external stimuli as he burrows through successive layers of exhaustion and agony, his mind—simultaneously sharpened and dulled, "blunted and exposed, naked and stupefied"—is reaching toward a more profound identification with the wounded man. The process is triggered by the phrase "heart of nations," the residue of his grandfather's words to him that the meaning of a Jew lay in his willingness to be a scapegoat, to accept suffering so that the moral world would not collapse. The senile old man's lucidity had returned long enough for him to say: "Israel is the heart of all nations. What attacks the body attacks the heart. And the heart is also the conscience which suffers for the sins of the nations."

By rearranging the symbols, Goldstein enters into a sort of I-Thou relationship with Wilson in which the former's moral survival is integrally related with the latter's physical survival. Goldstein sees himself as the nation, the body. His suffering, indeed the suffering of all Jews, will have some meaning if the heart—Wilson—survives. While Wilson lives, Goldstein is able to believe in the possibility of transcendent value, of an order which makes sense in moral terms. But Wilson dies of his stomach wound when Ridges unknowingly gives him water—an ironic commentary on the efficacy of Christian generosity in the wasteland of Anopopei—and his body is lost in the rapids of a stream the bearers have to cross. Perhaps Mailer is attempting to suggest Eliot's "Waste Land" with Wilson's frequent pleas for water and the ironically hopeless way he gets all the water he could have wanted with those rapids which provide, in Scott's words, "rather than purification and catharsis, the ultimate symbol of the two soldiers' defeat in this venture." Whatever Mailer had in mind, the rush of water that carries Wilson's body away generates the novel's most explicit statements about the contemporary spiritual dryness—the collapse of those beliefs and values which have traditionally brought significance to human activity—reminiscent of the desiccated emotional landscape of Eliot's poem.

It is often with just such large statements, whether in the Time Machines or in the conversations in the general's tent, that the novel is least convincing, but with the meticulous and convincing description of the portage, Mailer created an objective correlative which justifies the summing up of the frustrations of the present and the meaninglessness of the past. There is no need here for instant Nietzsche or for the borrowings which mar so many of the Time Machines—the Wolfean rant to describe Chicago; the old men hawking up phlegm to create instant folksiness; demonstrations of and appeals for sympathy with instant liberalisms like Mexican boys from Texas don't have a chance, boys from Montana mining towns don't have a chance, and so on. Both emotionally and dramatically, Ridges has earned the right to challenge, for the first time in his life, God's ways, and though Mailer still uses big, abstract nouns more than he will in the future, he has earned the relative effectiveness of the following passage:

> . . . he had carried this burden through such distances of space and time, and it had washed away in the end. All his life he had labored without repayment; his grandfather and his father and he had struggled with bleak crops and unending poverty. What had their work come to? . . . Ridges felt the beginning of a deep and unending bitterness. It was not fair. The one time they had got a decent crop it had been ruined by a wild rainstorm. God's way. He hated it suddenly. What kind of God could there be who always tricked you in the end?
> The practical joker.
> He wept out of bitterness and longing and despair; he wept from exhaustion and failure and the shattering naked conviction that nothing mattered.

All of this can be said of the passage describing Goldstein's crushing perceptions. Goldstein's Time Machine is the most convincing of the ten, for Mailer has been there. His Brooklyn past was much more benign than his character's but he knew so well the world of dying candy stores and shy, untalented Jewish boys. Perhaps because the author grew up in what he has called "the most secure Jewish environment in America," the evocation of the meaninglessness of Goldstein's life multiplied by the meaninglessness of the martyrdom of millions is a bit abstract and lacks the electrified edge it would have had if the passage had been written a few years later:

> From time to time he would move his lips, scratch feebly at his face. "Israel is the heart of nations."
> But the heart could be killed and the body still live. All the suffering of the Jews came to nothing. No sacrifices were paid, no lessons were learned. It was all thrown away, all statistics in the cruel wastes of history. All the ghettos, all the soul cripplings, all the massacres and pogroms, the gas chambers, lime kilns—all of it touched no one, all of it was lost. It was carried and carried and carried, and when it finally grew too heavy it was dropped. That was all there was to it. . . . There was nothing in him at the moment, nothing but a vague anger, a deep resentment, and the origins of a vast hopelessness.

But neither is Mailer finally unkind enough to give so little to men who have so much fought the good fight. Although "the bitterness and frustration of losing Wilson" is only temporarily "encysted . . . by the stupor that had followed," both soldiers find with each other the friend they have been looking for.

V

Hans Morgenthau has lyrically argued that the lust for power and the longing for love can both be traced to the loneliness at the center of the human condition. In a "simulation" of a somewhat diluted version of the Hemingway code, Mailer tested with Robert Hearn and Red Valsen two characters who have tried neither to identify with the structure and intent of an army at war—and thus expand themselves through the conquest or control of the external—nor to preserve themselves through a love of some individuals and a moral God. Instead, each has committed himself to loneliness posited in ethical terms; that is, to the inviolability of the self. The most economical statement of this ethos is Red's "I won't take no crap from nobody," which is expanded upon by Hearn at the latter's level of articulation:

> "The only thing to do is to get by on style." He had said that once, lived by it in the absence of anything else, and it had been a working

guide, almost satisfactory until now. The only thing that had been important was to let no one in any ultimate issue ever violate your integrity. . . .

With their commitment to no more than what Podhoretz has called "style without content, a vague ideal of personal integrity, a fear of attachment, and a surly nihilistic view of the world," Hearn and Valsen are not sufficiently armed to stand in rebellion against Cummings and Croft. What has made this isolation necessary is the belief, which Hearn articulates and Valsen emphatically shares, that "everything is crapped up, everything is phony, everything curdles when you touch it."

Valsen's subscription to this view is clearly traceable to the way in which his intellectually formative years were shaped by the novel's most classic example of exploitation. The oldest son of a Montana ore miner who was crushed when a tunnel collapsed on him, Valsen's thirteenth through eighteenth years were ground out by sixty-hour workweeks in the mine. For five years, an attachment to his immediate family had meant this crushing series of weeks; a wife and family would mean marriage to a life of these weeks, waiting for a tunnel to collapse on him. As for power, flight is the only meaningful social gesture possible in a company town where all of the earnings eventually find their way back to the company. So Valsen frees himself for the ironic possibilities of the depression (being a dishwasher, hobo, truck driver, night clerk in a flophouse); he flees a company town for a company world. Although American society seen from its underside is not all that much more attractive than Anopopei, one could within some limits pick degrees of misery and exploitation without compromising one's self-respect. There is no flight from Anopopei short of getting seriously wounded or killed, and Valsen can only flee Croft's control by shooting him, a radical gesture which all of the pounding he has taken over the years will not permit him.

In Red's youth he rightly saw affection as a trap. Since affection for a friend on Anopopei usually means pain when the friend is killed or shame when he cannot be defended against injustice, it is no less a trap there. But since Red is not completely committed to the "everything is crapped up" view of life, throughout the novel he makes, in spite of himself, humane gestures that are expressions—as is his rebellion against Croft—of his opposition to the way that the natural rights of others as well as himself are being abused. The way that Red is doubled with Hearn reinforces his use as an inarticulate liberal, and the puncturing of his inviolability by Croft is, in the symbolism of the novel, a defeat for liberalism.

As a part of his commitment to style, Hearn flirted with such left-wing causes as Communism and the non-Communist labor movement but retreated from each as the shoddiness which he felt lay behind all human activity revealed itself—"a dilettante skipping around sewers" in his unspoken words. And it is also as a part of this style that Hearn tries to counter Cummings's interpretation of man and history with liberal precepts. All of this is more than the half-hearted attempt to assert the common dignity of the individual. As Cummings suggests, and the leadership of the patrol conclusively proves, Hearn's subscription to the liberal interpretation of individualism—the rights of all—has been only an attempt to hide from himself his endorsement of Cummings's interpretation—the rights of the powerful. Hearn discovers that he is finally not so empty as he (and several critics) thought, for a Faust with the same lust for power as Cummings and Croft lurks beneath the Quixote in search of the pure cause.

With the revelation of Hearn's final indifference to the sufferings of others, the proto-Marxist Mailer would seem to be striking out at the actual lack of sympathy of "liberal" intellectuals and suggesting that only a member of the exploited class, like Red, can identify with the sufferings of his own. But it is as a liberal, driven to vacillation by the typical liberal habits of being able to see some worth in all positions and being unwilling to undertake an extreme course of action, that Hearn is violated by Cummings. Of these limitations, Podhoretz has written:

> The trouble with Hearn and Valsen is their inability to transcend the terms of the given; they know perfectly well that these terms are intolerable, yet they cannot envisage any condition other than the ones before their eyes, and therefore they are reduced to apathy, cynicism, and despair. Croft and Cummings also know that the terms are intolerable, but the knowledge acts as a stimulus to their energies and a goad to their imagination. Though the laws of nature seem to prohibit a man from climbing the top of Mt. Anaka, Croft, who cannot bear to remain imprisoned within the boundaries of what has already been accomplished, dares to attempt the climb, while Hearn and Valsen shrug helplessly at the sight of the peaks: like liberalism, itself, they lack the vision and the drive to push toward the top of the mountain.

As a whole, this is quite acute and sharply sets the appeal that Croft has to the radical Mailer in an enlarged, more general perspective than the one I have offered. The only problem is that by the day Hearn is killed he does not shrug helplessly at Anaka; Mailer makes it quite clear that Hearn would have attempted the climb if he were alone, or alone with Croft, and possibly with the platoon if it were not for reasons which have nothing to do with the failure of courage and will. For the most part, *Hearn is no longer a liberal by the time he is killed.*

The original plan of the novel presumably called for the "good liberal" Hearn to be ground between the "bad" Cummings and Croft. We have already seen that the fact that Hearn endorses liberal principles and the other two fascistic beliefs creates a considerable problem for Mailer; as Podhoretz has suggested, the author is not completely ready to write off liberalism and must consequently defeat the authoritarians so it will not seem that he is endorsing fascism. If one of the purposes of the novel is to show that the army will inevitably crush a good man who stands against it, Mailer can reassure himself, when anticipating the charges that Hearn is not "good" but cold and detached, by proclaiming his own honesty in admitting the weaknesses of liberalism. But if Hearn becomes less admirable as a representative liberal than Mailer originally intended him to be, the confusion begins to accelerate when Mailer traces the liberalism to a lust for power which he consciously censures but unconsciously admires.

Cummings traces the liberal ineffectuality to "the desperate suspension in which they have to hold their minds." It is this suspension between what Hearn really values and what he thinks he should value that the lieutenant has been trying to sustain for the past decade. As Mailer suggests in *Naked,* and will explicitly state in *The Deer Park,* "there was that law of life so cruel and so just which demanded that one must grow or else pay more for remaining the same." Croft, Cummings, and, indeed, Mailer feel this at the deepest level of their beings. Hearn comes the closest of all the characters to formulating this inexorable biological law that rules Anopopei when, after his humiliation by Cummings, he says to himself, "he would have to react or die." If the reaction opposed to death is growth, one can only grow on Anopopei by asserting the will to power.

Mailer, then, brings Hearn into "Plant and Phantom" as a character who is ticketed to be destroyed but who possesses assets that fascinate the author—a will to power and a position that enables him to exert that power; a cold, logical intelligence; great physical strength; and considerable courage. Like Croft and Cummings, he enters Part Three having sustained a setback in "Argil and Mold," and doomed as the character is, Mailer cannot resist exploring Hearn's possibilities as the lieutenant seeks to react or die, grow or decline in the confrontation with Croft, nature, and the Japanese. And grow Hearn does. It would seem that his defeat by Croft is inevitably presaged at the end of the first full day of the patrol, when both characters are looking at Mount Anaka and see the great rocks of the peak, surrounded by the murky twilight, as a rocky coast besieged by ocean. Croft sees in the crashing coast the total struggle against which he has always wanted to pit himself; "the contest seemed an infinite distance away, and he felt a thrill of anticipation at the thought that by the following night they might be on the peak." At this point in time Hearn can only see in the rocks and the darkening sky "the kind of shore upon which huge ships would founder, smash apart, and sink in a few minutes."

By the next morning, while the other soldiers were panting hoarsely as they toiled up the slopes toward the pass,

> Hearn, however, was feeling good. His body had reacted from the preceding day's march, and was stronger now, the waste burned out of him. He had awakened with stiff muscles and a sore shoulder, but rested and cheerful. This morning his legs were firm, and he sensed greater reserves of endurance. . . . Everything smelled fine, and the grass had the sweet fresh odor of early morning.

And on this day Hearn further reacts; his lust for power leaps into high gear after he recovers from the terror of his first combat at the guarded pass to experience

> the unique ecstasy, of leading the men out of the field, he had been replaying those few minutes over and over again in his head, wishing it could happen again. Beyond Cummings, deeper now, was his own desire to lead the platoon. It had grown, ignited suddenly, become one of the most satisfying things he had ever done. He could understand Croft's staring at the mountain . . . or killing the bird. When he searched himself he was just another Croft.

Since Mailer's feelings about Croft are so divided, the symbolic strands of the novel (in terms of the possibilities and attractions of "moral" liberalism and the "amoral" radicalism of Croft and Cummings) become hopelessly tangled at this point. Probably, the liberal Mailer originally intended to beef up his cause by having Hearn grow, but the radical Mailer perceived that Hearn could only grow inasmuch as he became another Croft. Now, in a desperate attempt to keep the authoritarians from sweeping the novel before them,

Mailer has Hearn undergo an eleventh-hour conversion during the night of this second day, deciding to turn in his rank, resist Cummings in every way he can, and espouse the scapegoat philosophy of " 'It is better to be the hunted than the hunter,' and that had a meaning for him now, a value." (At this point a "moral" radical Mailer turns up as Hearn considers becoming a sort of Scarlet Pimpernel–type terrorist with a small band of fearless, devoted men if there is a fascist takeover.) The upbeat, fervent style of this scene has encouraged several critics to interpret Hearn as coming closer "than any other character to redeeming the wasteland of Anopopei." * This interpretation has the advantage of making *The Naked and the Dead* much more simple to deal with than my laborings imply, but neglects taking into account everything that Mailer is doing with Croft, Hearn's own will to power, and the fact that by the next morning Hearn decides that "the decisions of the previous night seemed unimportant." Always asserting the primacy of the gratifications of power, the radical Mailer has Hearn either change his mind about giving up his power or decide to savor it, Croftlike, for as long as he has it. "He was enjoying this, but if he was, so much the better. Quite *naturally* he assumed the point and led the platoon toward the pass." (Italics mine.) Since Hearn has not had enough leadership, become enough of a Croft, he cannot defend himself against the sergeant's animal cunning and is killed at the entrance to the pass in the next line of the novel.

Hearn's vacillations make perfect sense as those of a man who has seen the futility of the solution of isolation, is powerfully tempted by

---

* Ihab Hassan, *Radical Innocence: Studies in the Contemporary American Novel* (New York: Harper and Row, Inc., 1966), p. 148. In "Mailer: The Jew as Existentialist," *North American Review,* July, 1965, pp. 48–55, Paul B. Newman expands on Hassan's interpretation and claims that Hearn's self-sacrifice is enough to suggest to the rest of the men

> the possibility of their own redemption. Through Hearn they sense the tragic meaning of their own lives rescued, if only passingly, from the sterility of their isolation and their fear. Hearn's death as scapegoat is a reaffirmation of the values of empathy and sublimation—the fundamental virtues of the Jewish and the Christian heritage [pp. 54–55].

This is eloquent, but the facts of the novel argue against Newman's reading. The one soldier who suggests in the hour after Hearn's death that "the Lootenant was a good guy" is countered by Valsen's "They ain't a fuggin one of those officers is worth a goddam" and another soldier's "I wouldn't spit on the best one of them" (Norman Mailer, *The Naked and the Dead* [New York: Rinehart and Company, Inc., 1948], p. 605). As a fourth soldier says on the following page, the novel's true idealist is Croft.

the solution of power, but still has enough commitments to the appearances of morality to have misgivings about becoming a disciple of Cummings. But if the purple passage celebrating Hearn's sudden decision to oppose the general is at odds with what the novel seems to be saying about the weaknesses of liberalism, the greatest confusion comes when one tries to interpret just what is transpiring vis-à-vis Hearn and the mountain. This effort must be made, for the mountain is the dominant symbol in the novel, and each character's attitude toward climbing it finally serves as the same sort of index of the state of his psyche that the state of one's sex life will provide in the later novels. Here is Hearn's response when, in the last hour of the lieutenant's life, Croft suggests the climb:

> This morning, yes, it wasn't without its attraction. They could do that. But he shook his head firmly. "It's impossible." It would be crazy to lead the men up it, not even knowing if they could descend the other side. . . .
> . . . Hearn shook his head again. "We'll try it through the pass."
> Undoubtedly they were the only two men who would want to try the mountain.

Does all of this mean that Hearn is strong enough to attempt the climb but is held back by his consideration of the men, or is this consideration of others precisely the weakness which disqualifies one from such a total effort? And does whatever strength he has come only from amoral, will-to-power sources, or is Mailer suggesting that even if Hearn tried the mountain he could not go very far, not having the developed instinct of Croft? And how does all of this fit in with the fact that, with the pass apparently open, it would be a complete abdication of responsibility and reason to attempt the climb? Is obedience to responsibility and reason also a weakness? It is obviously unprofitable to continue this line of inquiry, since Mailer has clearly lost control of the novel's symbolic lines at this point. If he tried to be the objective scientist in describing Hearn's diversities, he became the sorcerer's apprentice as Hearn gradually moved out of his management.

VI

In search of possibility, but unwilling to accept the creative nihilism of the "second revolution," Mailer gradually moved toward affirmation of the Marxist assumptions of the 1917 revolution. The only Marxists who appear in *The Naked and the Dead* are an anonymous hobo who merits a few lines in Valsen's Time Machine and the members of the Harvard John Reed Club in Hearn's—all of whom are treated rather sarcastically. Still, the novel has a strong Marxist orientation with its generally prevailing social determinism, its emphases on class structure, class consciousness, and historical process, and its critique of the American ruling class as it is represented by the general and Hearn's father. Although Mailer thought of himself as an anarchist when he began the novel in 1946, the writing of the book and the political climate drove him to join the Progressive Citizens of America before he left for Europe in the fall of 1947, and the next eight or nine months in Europe provided enough examples of social and economic dislocation to push him further from his hatred of all organization and to stiffen his commitment to political action. (At least this is the way the nice progressive described the process in the August, 1948, *Star* interview.) He was a fellow traveler when he began, in 1948, the novel that was to become *Barbary Shore,* and it was as a fellow traveler that he campaigned for Henry Wallace in the presidential campaign of that year. By March of 1949, Mailer had quit the Communist-dominated Progressive party, announcing at the Waldorf Peace Conference that the state capitalism of Russia was no better than the monopoly capitalism of the United States.

This is one of the conclusions of *Barbary Shore,* published three years after *The Naked and the Dead* in 1951.* But the novel's obsessive concern with just how bad both capitalisms are seems primarily to have been the product of fairly intensive readings of Marxist literature from 1948 to 1950, particularly *Das Kapital,* Trotsky's *History of the Russian Revolution,* and the latter's polemics against the Soviet state. If Mailer's very impressive war novel is partially flawed by the author's occasional inability to keep contrasting ideas in balanced tension, *Barbary Shore* is choked primarily by his commitment to subordinate the plot and the characterization to an explicit, almost interminable exposition of an uncontested, unified set of ideas which purport to explain in general almost everything of primary importance in the present world and the world that is to come. From his first novel to his second, Mailer has moved from an interest in ideas to ideology, and an extreme ideology at that. As Irving Howe has observed, individuals and groups embrace ideology only when meaningful political action seems impossible, an insight which aptly applies

---

* "I started *Barbary Shore* as some sort of fellow-traveler, and finished with a political position which was a far-flung mutation of Trotskyism" ("Writers at Work: Interview with Norman Mailer," *The Paris Review,* No. 31 [Winter-Spring, 1964], p. 39).

to Mailer. In an attempt to help effect a society which permitted healthy growth, Mailer tried political action, found that futile, and turned to an ideology which, in Podhoretz's words, "brought the courage, vision, and uncompromising determination of Cummings and Croft into the service of freedom and equality rather than class and privilege."

The application of this ideology of courage, vision, and determination would seem to have produced a more optimistic novel than *The Naked and the Dead*. With the revolutionary socialism of *Barbary Shore*, Mailer offers hope for the future—his first explicit solution—while in the earlier novel the machines of society or indifferent nature inevitably frustrate the characters. This view is a myopic one; it disregards both Croft's near success and the hopelessness which grips the later novel. In the world of *Barbary Shore*, the inevitable economic and moral disintegration which followed the failure of the Russian Revolution to spread through Europe to this country has been so pervasive that the revolutionary can in no way even hope to slow down the process. The hope lies in an apocalyptic future.

There is much solemn talk in *Barbary Shore* of "theoretical equipment," and Mailer is nearly obsessive in parading his own equipment through the reflections of the amnesiac narrator, Lovett, and the speeches of the revolutionary, McLeod. What this equipment grinds out is the inevitability of a catastrophic war between the American economic bloc and the Russian one. If this war does not reduce civilization to barbarism, the wars that will follow out of the unalterable contradictions of capitalism will. The hope for the possibility of action which is both humane and effectual is contingent upon a war which is disastrous in just the right way. If the state deteriorates faster than the population after the first war, then the masses will finally be moved to a perception of the hopelessness of their condition sufficient to permit a few theorists to rouse them to socialist consciousness. The masses will at last seize the means of production themselves—exit unalterable contradictions, enter the socialist state (founded on justice and equality) and an "opportunity to discover of what we were capable and what we shall never achieve." And so *Barbary Shore* ends with Lovett having regained his lost revolutionary fervor and adding to his equipment through study as he banks on the odds that his chance will come. These odds are in fact so long, and Lovett's predicament so hopeless, that Chester Eisinger sees in *Barbary Shore*

the epitaph on the Communist novel in our period. . . . It lays Communism to rest as a meaningful cultural phenomenon and as a way to personal salvation. It records the failure of the social revolutionary in modern society, the victim of nameless terrors and alienation, who cannot make a vital relationship between his ideas and the society he lives in.

Podhoretz has written that *Barbary Shore* is " 'existentialist' in spirit" in that "everything seems to hang on the will of the people involved." With its emphasis on Lovett's choice to commit himself to the future and McLeod's choice to give "the little object" to Lovett, the novel provides an obviously important component to Mailer's later studies of self-creation. The last word is crucial. As Marxists who see the limitations of one's inner life as sharply defined by the economic base and social superstructure as the commodities one possesses, McLeod and Lovett (and Mailer) can finally only see the meaningfulness of choice as lying in its ability to effect a new society. This is in keeping with the majority view of *The Naked and the Dead,* in which most of the characters can only futilely think of changing the system. As the radical Mailer gradually emerges and rejects the concept of social determinism, his heroes will, with varying degrees of success, try to change themselves.

The author has already suggested the primary source of this re-creation with his hidden paean to Croft's instinct. Even Cummings, the character in *Naked* most concerned with intellectually controlling the problems of the present and discerning the possibilities of the future through cognition, had learned to count upon his instinct to make the right choice in moments of crisis. And what is his endorsement of the will to power but a commitment to the blessings of the irrational? If any irrational forces add to the workings of "the equipment" to influence Lovett's choice, they are not his own intuitive, guiding swells of feeling but the tortured explosions of other characters. All that emerges from the unconscious in *Barbary Shore*'s allegorical rendering of psychic America are feelings of aggression, narcissism, guilt, and terror which find expression in the sadism, masochism, nymphomania, homosexuality, hysteria, and near insanity which fills the novel. This absence of any healthy, informing instinct can, of course, be traced to Mailer's attempt to show the pervasive sickness of American society in the death throes of monopoly capitalism. Still, it is remarkable that a writer whose whole course of development can be seen as a movement from an unconscious primitivist to a conscious one should so exclude instinct from a novel. It is no less remarkable that Mailer should have so completely committed himself to an ideology which, brought up to date, suggests that the subconscious life is wholly the product of society and does not itself have depths untouched by social causality—sources of energy which can emerge and change the social determinants. For an understanding of these deviations from the general movement of Mailer's ideas, one must turn to the author's explanation of the profound effect that the huge success of his first published novel had upon him. My explanation is most partial, for there is little published evidence about Mailer's behavior from 1948 to 1951 besides his own comments and the hints *Barbary Shore* offers.

In *Advertisements,* Mailer has remarked about the confidence which *Naked* exudes, "it seems to be at dead center—'yes,' it is always saying, 'this is about the way it is.'" Even though the novel's world does not contain the familiar God Who anchors value, it is still the product of a writer who experiences a complexly mixed but more or less consistent and familiar pattern of responses to the people, objects, and institutions he contemplates; the world might be absurd in conventional moral terms, but it is not in emotional ones. Mailer's description of the radically altered, unfamiliar quality of the experience that followed his sudden prominence is reminiscent of Camus's discussion in *The Myth of Sisyphus* of the discovery of the absurd. The latter discovery is not an intellectual judgment—as was Mailer's positing of the collapse of values in *Naked*—but a profound emotional disorientation as one begins experiencing a completely different set of responses and the world steadily becomes strangely alien, subtly terrifying; "this divorce between man and his life, the actor and his setting, is properly the feeling of absurdity." Mailer not only faced life anew as a writer, "prominent and empty," with nothing to write about, since all of his preceding experience "seemed to have been mined and melted into the long reaches of the book"; he found that his interpersonal relationships were as violently altered by his new celebrity as was his economic status. A slave to the anxiety generated by the tension between his desire to use his sudden charisma to affect the self-esteem of others and the strictures of his conscience to avoid this kind of assertion, tortured by his asking with so many others if all his talent had been exhausted in *Naked,* in general "scared, excited and nervous," Mailer lived through several "overheated, brilliant, anxious, gauche, grim" years. Since "success had been a lobotomy to my past, [and] there seemed no power from the past which could help me in the present," Mailer's success blasted him into a strange, alien world: "This was experience unlike the experience I had learned from books, and from the war—this was experience without a name —at the time I used to complain that everything was unreal."

It is not surprising that no character in *Barbary Shore* experiences a surge of intuition which puts him in touch with what he feels to be the workings of history or nature; the author seems to have experienced precious few such surges in the years he was writing the novel. But the absence of the reassuring or the familiar can be pushed further.

War wounds have taken Lovett's memory; he even owes his new face to the unremembered army surgeons who reshaped his shattered one. The several good memories that come to Lovett are from experiences before the war. The ones during the war are usually nightmarish, and two of them—making love to a farmgirl at a sentry post while holding his machine gun and working at a machine in a factory as a prisoner of war—echo Cummings's assertion that the purpose of the war was to make man subservient to the machine. On the novel's allegorical level, Lovett's amnesia represents the sick, disoriented contemporary psyche which has lost its revolutionary animus and has been cut off from a healthy past, present, and future by the failure of the revolution to replace monopoly capitalism and its deterioration, in Russia, into state capitalism. The literal and the allegorical causes of the amnesia nicely fit together since, in the novel's argument, World War II was the result of capitalism's constant need for new markets. Although the war accelerated the deteriorating process of capitalism, the development of awesome weaponry augured that civilization would be destroyed in the subsequent wars before socialism could emerge, and so the war seemed to kill revolutionary socialism as a viable possibility. Further, Lovett's subordination to the machines during the war symbolizes the inevitable need of declining capitalism to replace men with machines in order to lower the manufactured cost and increase the surplus value of products.

If Lovett's amnesia represents the state of the contemporary psyche, then, as Podhoretz has said, "the weird unfamiliar world that we see through his eyes is in fact intended as a picture of the world we all inhabit," a world as filled in its own way with cancerous degeneration as the one of the tenth malebolge in *Inferno*. But all of the symbolic implications of Lovett's amnesia are the creations of an author who suffered a kind of experiential amnesia, one which was not caused by vast historical processes. Like Lovett, Mailer has suffered a lobotomy to his past; no power from the past could help him in the present; he, too, confronted a weird, unfamiliar world. Camus has written that

> a world that can be explained even with bad reasons is a familiar world. But, on the other hand, in a universe suddenly divested of illusions and lights, man feels an alien, a stranger. His exile is without remedy since he is deprived of the memory of a lost home or the hope of a promised land.

Small wonder then that Mailer embraced an ideology whose bad reasons offered both a promised land of the future and an explanation of the strange one of the present. As Howe has observed, ideology "represents an effort to employ abstract ideas as a means of overcoming the abstractness of social life."

But for all the flaws of Mailer's argument that capitalism could in no way adjust, economic conditions must worsen, and cataclysmic war with Russia must follow, *Barbary Shore* is not all that much mistaken about the state of American society. His vision of the terror at the center of so much of American life was revealed to be a prescient one by the hysteria of the McCarthyism that emerged in the half decade after the novel was completed. The best explanation of Mailer's attempt to combine the life he felt inside him and the one he saw outside him is his own; *"Barbary Shore* was really a book to emerge from the bombarded cellars of my unconscious, an agonized eye of a novel which tried to find some amalgam of my new experience and the larger horror of that world which might be preparing to destroy itself."

If *The Naked and the Dead* is pervaded by the fear that only the authoritarians can fight with purpose for the future, *Barbary Shore* would appear to be crippled by the terror that nobody can. By the time Mailer's third novel, *The Deer Park,* was published in 1955, he was at least able to posit the belief that it was possible for an individual to survive the wounds which society inflicted upon him and to grow. Now we must trace Mailer's course toward this reformulation as he heads away from the political, collective solution toward the individual one offered tentatively in *The Deer Park* and more unequivocally in "The White Negro."

2

Towards a New Formulation

IN the four or five years which followed the completion of *Barbary Shore,* Mailer groped with his fiction for more promising realms, but with his nonfiction he continued to wander through a bleak political terrain. Yet even in the socialist essays published in *Dissent* in 1954, the presence of a kind of revisionism which offers up fresh possibilities is evident. For example, in "The Meaning of Western Defense," Mailer again writes of the likelihood of disastrous war and "the insoluble contradictions of the Colossi"—the United States and Russia. But his interpretation of our contradictions is just enough altered to deny the deterioration of our economy and the impending war the inevitability they had in the thought of *Barbary Shore.* Though we need a war economy ("whose ultimate consumer . . . is the enemy soldier") to maintain prosperity, there remains the unspoken implication that the bullet might never find the soldier; we might simply keep our economy going by replacing the weapons. More important, the armaments *do* sustain our economy. Unlike *Barbary Shore,* "The Meaning of Western Defense" provides no demonstration of the irrevocable downward spiral of the American economy, and though the article shows that Russia is in an economic trap —caused by the inability to produce the consumer commodities necessary to raise the workers' energies enough that they can produce consumer goods along with heavy industrial products—it is a trap, an impasse, not a distintegrating process. Further, socialism is, in the nonfiction, still the name of Mailer's desire, but in keeping with the article's relative optimism it can come to America without the cataclysm envisioned in *Barbary Shore.* If the United States will relinquish its paradoxical defense of Western Europe,* then revivified so-

* Offered with the polite introductory comment (so typical of the pre-1956 Mailer) that he is not convinced of the worth of the argument and is offering it in all modesty, Mailer's reasoning runs this way: the Russians could successfully invade Western Europe at any time but—already drained by their undeveloped satellites—they must possess the West European industrial plant intact. Since we know we cannot defend the area, our cold war best interest

cialist countries might arise there which would stay independent of both the United States and Russia and "almost certainly revitalize the vigorous dissenting traditions of American political life," opening again "the faint perspective of a socialist world."

In an article written the following year, Mailer attacked what he felt were David Riesman's attempts to justify postwar America. Since he was bringing forward an opposing vision, one which emphasized what is wrong with America, "David Riesman Revisited" reads even more grimly than "The Meaning of Western Defense." In fact, Mailer admitted that Riesman's smooth rationalizations eroded one's socialist commitment, and the only constructive assertion offered was a feeble one:

> Yet, after everything else, there remains the basic core of socialism so deep in Western culture, the idea, the moral passion, that it is truly intolerable and more than a little fantastic that men should not live in economic equality and in liberty. As serious artistic expression is the answer to the meaning of life for a few, so the passion for socialism is the only meaning I can conceive in the lives of those who are not artists; if one cannot create "works" one may dream at least of an era when humans create humans, and the satisfaction of the radical can come from the thought that he tries to keep this idea alive.

As we shall see, Mailer had covertly suggested a quite different source of meaning for the nonartist two years earlier in "The Man Who Studied Yoga," a source much more overtly emphasized in the second draft of *The Deer Park,* which was completed a few months before this essay was written. The contradictions in Mailer's attitude toward socialism (which he was to renounce altogether in November, 1955) make themselves felt in the closing sentence of the essay, in which he quite heretically states that "as socialists we want a socialist world not because we have the conceit that men would thereby be more happy . . . but because we feel the moral imperative in life itself to raise the human condition even if this should ultimately mean no more than that man's suffering has been lifted to a higher level, and human history has only progressed from melodrama, farce, and monstrosity, to tragedy itself."

This desire for a historical movement from formless monstrosity to tragedy is an apt one for an author in search of a body of perceptions and emotions that will enable him to create a fictional world

---

would be to destroy the industries if the Russians attack. And since they know we will do this, they will not attempt force but try to gain control through peaceful means.

in which a genuinely embattled hero can convincingly struggle and grow. The components of a formula for growth were already fragmented throughout *The Deer Park,* though they were not to receive explicit formulation until 1957. Mailer's first two novels contain the seeds of these components, for the "solution" he was working toward from 1952 to 1957 is built upon the three pillars of courage, the ability to express violence, and hugely satisfying sex. Croft possessed the first two attributes in strength, but although he saw sex as a chance to control—as his hipster descendants will—it never gave him huge pleasure. In fact, sex was not at all to the 1948 Mailer what it was to become in the following decade. After twenty-five years, and the literary results of the Supreme Court decisions on pornography, it is amusing to read what was in 1948 the enticing comment that *Naked* was "virtually a Kinsey report on the sexual behavior of the GI." By current standards, the sex in that novel is not at all titillating, but this is why the reference to the Kinsey report is accurate; it catches the sociological flavor of Mailer's treatment of sex. In *Naked,* sex is a fact among other facts, certainly important enough to report, but still not much more than the nexus upon which social determinants converged. There is no anticipation in *The Naked and the Dead* of the view of sex as a reservoir of psychic energy that will emerge in *The Deer Park.* But if, as I suggested in the preceding chapter, the world of *Barbary Shore* is finally more hopeless and contains less possibility than that of the earlier novel, the seeds of Mailer's belief that sex is the primary human activity are in the book.

The war has cut Lovett (and the generation of intellectuals he represents) from more than the sustaining ideology of true Marxism; he has also been torn from those sane and nourishing relationships which are, in the symbolism of the novel, the interpersonal manifestations of Marxist thought. The only two good memories that come back to Lovett in the course of the novel are his prewar experiences of being obsessed with the Russian Revolution while he belonged to a Trotskyite study group and an affair in which he was able to make a girl love the pleasure her body gave her. Since together they represent the benefits of group interaction and the most complete blendings of two psyches (through successful sex), the two memories nicely complement each other. The dislocations and exacerbations that group and sexual relationships underwent in that war and which cemented the failure of the revolution are picked up in Lovett's memories of being one of a number of symbolically exploited slave laborers and of having intercourse by the machine gun. They are con-

tinued in the surrealist boarding house in Brooklyn, where occurs
what relatively little action the novel contains.

Although the war has precluded nourishing unity, the leveling co-
ercion of wartime conditions does not fully determine life in the
boarding house. In fact, the diversity of the inhabitants' sensibilities
is so great that it forms a sort of psychic microcosm of America.
What they all share are sexual maladjustments, disturbances which in
the allegorical scheme of the novel refer back to the failure of the
revolution and forward (or outward) to define one segment of the
collective American consciousness. For example, the allegory's symbol of the American masses, wooed by the revolutionary left (Mc-
Leod and Lovett) and the fascistic right (the FBI agent, Hollingsworth) is the vulgar, stupid, lazy, pettily ambitious landlady, Beverly
Guinevere. That she should indiscriminately fling her favors at anyone who seems to offer her anything; that she rejects, in McLeod, intellectual Marxism, which only criticizes her; that she should most
enjoy sex with a madwoman because the latter offers Guinevere the
most admiration (however sick it is); but that she should run off
with the fascist who beats her but promises the most security all
makes considerable symbolic sense. One of the critical comments
which most hurt Mailer when *Barbary Shore* came out was Anthony
West's assertion that "the choice of sexual inadequacy . . . to symbolize the relation between the individual and the government, shows
something beyond disorderly or careless thinking, something close to
a complete lack of emotional control." Mailer himself has, in the
1963 *Paris Review* interview, more or less admitted an inability to
coordinate consistently the characters' sexual desires and acts with
their political and social meanings, but his implication that a character's sexual nature is an index of the state of his entire psyche or
his treatment of sexual relationships as models of the interactions of
larger ideological or social groups is not in itself ridiculous in these
post-Freudian days. It is not as if Mailer tried to spin his allegory
of the fate of America from the way the characters walk, and the
vision of the American masses as a huge, collective Guinevere—an
insecure, alternately lethargic and frenzied slattern who will give
herself to the authoritarians—is not at all that improbable, especially
as the backlash of the seventies deepens.

But the very emphasis that Mailer places on so many different,
maddened visions of sexual gratification—like Guinevere's "million
dollar story" for Hollywood, in which a good sexual experience makes
worthwhile an abortion, an infanticide, two executions, and four

deaths—surges beyond any framework of political meaning and up-sets what balance the explicit ideology permits. The same disparity can be seen from a different angle if we consider the madwoman's giving herself to Hollingsworth. After a searing description of the struggles of the Jews in the German gas chambers, she tells Lovett: "There are no solutions, there are only exceptions, and therefore we are without good and without evil. . . . There is neither guilt nor innocence, but there is vigor in what we do or the lack of it." Her surrender to Hollingsworth because he seems to have vigor makes sense, and her role as the rememberer of the camps and, conse-quently, as the Cassandra of our own collapse is genuinely powerful —much too powerful for the allegorical meaning of the surrender of Trotskyism to the FBI to carry much weight with us.

To be sure, the superabundance of sexual abnormality can be ex-plained as a manifestation of the capitalistic cancer; while going over his equipment, Lovett attributes "the falling rate [of love]" to the growing rate of machinery. Still, the disproportionate space devoted to demonstrating Lovett's loss of sexual identity, Hollingsworth's sadism and homosexuality, the madwoman's willingness to give her-self to whoever promises to violate her most brutally, and Guine-vere's daughter's precocious deviations suggests that Mailer's interest in sexual disturbance ranges beyond its availability as a symbol and symptom of total social dislocation. It intrigues him in its own right. His fascination with sexual abnormality also suggests some ad-herence to the Freudian and particularly Reichian—but not Marxian —doctrine that sexual sickness is as much a cause as a result of social disease. This split in Mailer's novelistic objectives vis-à-vis his treatment of sex is borne but by a comment that he made twelve years after *Barbary Shore* was published:

> *Barbary Shore* was built on the division which existed then in my mind. My conscious intelligence . . . became obsessed by the Rus-sian Revolution. But my unconscious was much more interested in other matters: murder, suicide, orgy, psychosis, all the themes I dis-cuss in *Advertisements*. Since the gulf between these conscious and unconscious themes was vast and quite resistant to any quick literary coupling, the tension to get a bridge across resulted in the peculiar hot-house atmosphere of the book. My unconscious felt one kind of dread, my conscious mind another, and *Barbary Shore* lives some-where in between. That's why its focus is so unearthly.

Something should be said about this unearthly focus before we move on to track Mailer's path as he begins to study these psychic mysteries in their own right and to grope his way toward positing sex as a dynamism of re-creation. A great part of the success of *Naked* and the failure of *Barbary Shore* (beyond the disastrous effect that the ideology had upon the second novel) follows from the fact that in the first novel Mailer had, with the wartime setting, a situation which offered up numerous pairs of natural adversaries whose conflicts lent themselves relatively easily to dramatization. For example, the authoritarian mentality in the first novel is not characterized by a subtly diseased representative of a remote federal bureau; rather, it is dynamically objectified by Cummings and Croft, whose power and will to greater power are supported by the actual structure of the wartime world. And as I suggested in the preceding chapter, the realities of war enabled Mailer to turn Anopopei into an arena of almost constant struggle.

But as Mailer wrote in a symposium a year after *Barbary Shore* came out, "Today, the enemy is vague." The primary weakness of *Barbary Shore* is the vagueness of enemy and protagonist alike on the novel's literal level as Mailer tries to plumb in the allegorical one what he will in 1960 call the "subterranean river of untapped, ferocious, lonely and romantic desires, that concentration of ecstasy and violence which is the dream life of the nation." I really do not know if *Barbary Shore* has, as Mailer claims, "a kind of insane insight into the psychic mysteries of Stalinists, secret policemen, narcissists, children, Lesbians, hysterics and revolutionaries." Finally, these are precisely mysteries, and the successful novelist does not so much prove that the psychic depths are exactly the way he describes them as convince the reader that they are. For all of *Barbary Shore*'s premonitions about McCarthyism or the way in which Hollingsworth anticipates the revelations of the sick, banal mediocrity of an Eichmann, Mailer is usually unable to provide incidents which convincingly dramatize his perceptions. The strained and often bizarrely inverted narrative, the stilted conversations, and the improbable characterizations encourage no willingness on the part of the reader to accept the characters on their own terms,* and we certainly cannot

---

* The narrative is filled with lines like the following: "Later, my flesh roused like water over which blows the wind, I thought I listened to someone sobbing, and from my solitude I was marooned in equal grief." And though Lovett dreams this line of conversation on the same page, it's no less improbable than many others: "Lannie sang her songs, Hollingsworth giggled and McLeod sucking at the mordant candy-drop he must always pouch in his cheek, said from his great distance, 'Grieve not, m'bucko, for it's kismet, and that's the secret of it all' " (Norman Mailer, *Barbary Shore* [New York: New American Library, 1951], p. 207). Bruce Cook was right when he wrote,

accept an allegorical level so that we feel that we are participating in the collective dream life of a nation if we are constantly jolted by the unreality of the literal level. To cite a successful allegory as a contrast, Kafka's "Metamorphosis" is able to communicate powerfully such allegorical levels as the way in which the family injures and then destroys the moral life of an individual or the victory of the death wish in Gregor's regression because of the uncanny rectitude of all the thought, descriptions, and incidents in the story. Somehow, Mr. Samsa's throwing an apple into Gregor's back is just right; the idea of McLeod married to Guinevere or of Lovett as a revolutionary seems faked.

I do not bring in Kafka in order to pummel Mailer by comparing him with one of the few true geniuses of twentieth-century literature, but to clarify what was in three of Mailer's last four novels a striking disparity between what he wanted to do with his fiction and what he was able to do. For one thing, in trying to bring to the surface the buried realities of the American experience, Mailer faced, as Kafka did not, all the problems of writing in a mass society where the author can no longer assume that someone occupying such and such a place in the world is likely to have this or that kind of inner life. As we heave through the last half of the twentieth century, no honest and intelligent man is very sure about what's really out there in SuperAmerica; it is a large part of Mailer's great appeal that he so often has such fascinating conjectures. But, to speak only of what has found expression in the novels and not in the nonfiction or public life, what most sharply distinguishes Mailer's fiction from that of the other important writers of his generation has been the depth of his com-

---

"Ultimately it is Mailer's failure with language that defeats his fictional purpose in *Barbary Shore*" (Bruce Cook, "Norman Mailer: The Temptation to Power," *Renascence,* Vol. 14 [Fall, 1965], p. 210). When the novel came out, Irving Howe wrote: "Another trouble is that Mailer writes badly. His lumpy and graceless prose is strewn with quasi-intellectual chatter and stiff with echoes of radical jargon, 'Progressive' journalism and WPA living-newspaper skits. Once a writer has been exposed to such influences it is hard for him to develop a style . . ." ("Some Political Novels," *Nation,* June 16, 1951, p. 568). In an essay written about a decade later, Howe remarked that he had recently reread the excerpts in *Advertisements* of *Barbary Shore* "which I remember as a very bad novel . . . and they read astonishingly well, with a nervous jabbing accuracy" ("A Quest for Peril: Norman Mailer," in *A World More Attractive* [Freeport, N.Y.: Books for Libraries, Inc., 1963], p. 124). Parts of the novel, in much of the first half, do read very well in isolation, but it grows steadily more choked and claustral. One has to struggle to get through the last forty pages.

mitment to present to readers a world view which offers the possibility of victories or defeats in which much is gained. It is vastly easier to follow the collapse of a character's ambitions into the absurd than to show this kind of assertion working in the world. (So many of Kafka's great works are best read as the descent into absurdity, madness, or death—which is not to say that what Kafka did was easy.) And even with the structure of meaning that Mailer created with the metaphysical system which evolved in the fifties and sixties, it was so much easier to portray meaningful defeat than meaningful victory— with its protagonist defeated, *Why Are We in Vietnam?* is so much more convincing a book than *An American Dream,* in which the hero enjoys a qualified triumph.

But Mailer had no system which permitted meaningful assertion when he wrote *Barbary Shore,* and his imagination—not at all comparable with Kafka's but still impressive—was choked by the split between his conscious and very hopeless political solution and his unconscious fascination with the violence and sex from which his nourishing system was to come.

II

In *The Deer Park* (1955), his next attempt to communicate the collective malaise of America, Mailer chose in the locale modeled after Palm Springs, California, a much more believable metaphor for America than the boarding house in Brooklyn. Why shouldn't the actors, directors, and producers who appear in the novel profess adherence to conventional values while performing the acts of people who have lost all sense of traditional morality? The promiscuity of the movie community is, after all, such a vastly popular topic of conversation and fantasy that its depiction would seem to be a good way of mirroring a large part of the American fantasy life. Instead of having to create a largely original world—like the one of *Barbary Shore*— as a synecdoche of the tortured sickness hidden beneath the apparently solid, stodgy surface of the America of the 1950s, Mailer was able to use his great reportorial gifts to create with relatively realistic techniques a slice of society which quite probably did exist. All of this helps to effect a far more persuasive novel than *Barbary Shore,* but it never really seizes the reader by the shirt and pulls him into the underground river of the American unconsciousness. In his discussion of Mailer's attempts to "embody his keen if unstable vision in a narrative about people whose extreme dislocation of experience and feeling would, by the very fact of their extreme dislocation come to seem significant" (as a portrait of the amorphous "troubledness" of America), Irving Howe correctly observed:

> But in its effort to portray our drifting and boredom full-face, in its fierce loyalty to the terms of its own conception, *The Deer Park* tended to become a claustrophobic work, driving attention inward, toward its own tonal peculiarities, rather than outward, as an extending parable. Throughout the novel Mailer had to fall back upon his protagonist, through whom he tried to say that which he found hard to show.

I would add that much of the loyalty follows from the author's inability to really let his imagination go. Consider: had Mailer written a Hollywood novel in which the same characters performed roughly the same acts, but written it with the sensibility which produced *Why Are We in Vietnam?,* the result would have been a freewheeling, probably very funny novel. For better or for worse—and I think that by the time Mailer's career is over most readers will agree it was for the better—he freed his imagination and changed his prose style several times over in the twelve years between the publication of the two novels. Both processes were already occurring in the four difficult years when *The Deer Park* was written and then twice more rewritten, and both were related to Mailer's developing vision of the kind of person who could live the good life in spite of the wounds and swamps of the American existence. For example, the author has said that he added Marion Faye during the second draft because he felt the novel "needed . . . some sort of evil genius." Yet by the end of the third and final draft, Faye has been endowed with considerable moral grandeur, and he emerges as much the secret hero of *The Deer Park* as Croft was of *The Naked and the Dead.* Although the incidents of the third draft (completed in late July, 1955) are largely the same as those of the second (completed in April or May, 1954), the author's changing ideas in the intervening time about how he should lead his own life affected his conceptions of why one of his characters grew and another declined.

Mailer intended the second draft to be the final one, and it was agreed in May, 1954, that it would be published in February of the following year by Rinehart and Company. But when in November, 1954, the publisher demanded that Mailer delete the six lines which suggest that two characters are performing fellatio, Mailer refused, and the publication was halted. After having his book refused by six other publishing houses, it was accepted by the seventh (Putnam's), but, as Mailer wrote, between his disgust at the timidity of the seven

houses who rejected the novel and Stanley Rinehart's refusal to pay
the advance called for in the contract,

> the experience turned ugly for me. It took many months and the ser-
> vice of my lawyer to get the money, but long before that, the situa-
> tion had become real enough to drive a spike into my cast-iron mind.
> I realized in some bottom of myself that for years I had been the
> sort of comic figure I would have cooked to a turn in one of my
> books, a radical who had the nineteenth-century naïveté to believe
> that the people with whom he did business were 1) gentlemen, 2)
> fond of him, and 3) respectful of his ideas even if in disagreement
> with them. Now, I was in the act of learning that I was not adored
> so very much; that my ideas were seen as nasty; and that my fine
> America which I had been at pains to criticize for so many years
> was in fact a real country which did real things and ugly things to
> the characters of more people than just the characters of my books.

After some interesting, self-pitying comments about how this experience had forced him to perceive the changes in the publishing
business and the writer's place in it since the days of Maxwell Perkins,
Mailer more explicitly accounted for his rather sudden transition from
a well-mannered young socialist to the megalomaniacal, anarchistic
fauve of the *Village Voice* columns and *Advertisements.* How the
shrewd author of *The Armies of the Night* would have cooked to a
turn this humorless cockatoo, parading about and making his kicks
with his idiotically murderous marijuana and black swinger friends.
This is late fifties Mailer at his most impossible:

> . . . something broke in me, but I do not know if it was so much a
> loving heart, as a cyst of the weak, the unreal, and the needy, and I
> was finally open to my anger. I turned within my psyche I can almost
> believe, for I felt something shift to murder in me. I finally had the
> simple sense to understand that if I wanted my work to travel further
> than others, the life of my talent depended on fighting a little more,
> and looking for help a little less. But I deny the sequence in putting
> it this way, for it took me years to come to this fine point. All I felt
> then was that I was an outlaw, a psychic outlaw, and I liked it, I
> liked it a good night better than trying to be a gentleman, and with
> a set of emotions accelerating one on the other, I mined down deep
> into the murderous message of marijuana, the smoke of the assassins,
> and for the first time in my life I knew what it was to make your
> kicks.
>   . . . *The Deer Park* resting at Putnam, and new good friends
> found in Harlem, I was off on that happy ride where you discover a
> new duchy of jazz every night and the drought of the past is given a
> rain of new sound. What has been dull and dead in your years is
> now tart to the taste, and there is sweet in the illusion of how fast
> you can change. . . . I began to log a journal, a wild set of thoughts

and outlines for huge projects—I wrote one hundred thousand words in eight weeks. . . . this journal has the start of more ideas than I will have again; ideas which came so fast and so rich that sometimes I think my brain was dulled by the heat of their passage.

At any rate, the explosion of new ideas fizzled out by February, 1955, at which time he looked again at the second draft of *The Deer Park,* which Putnam's wanted to publish in that form. Nine months' distance from the book, and the experiences of the last three months, told Mailer that (in his own words)

> the style was wrong . . . I had been strangling the life of my novel in a poetic prose which was too self-consciously attractive and formal, false to the life of my characters, especially false to the life of my narrator who was the voice of my novel and so gave the story its air.

Mailer left the incidents unchanged, but his attempts to turn the style into a tauter, more muscular, more self-aware one which would fit the sensibility of his narrator demanded that he overcome his fear of creating a narrator whose personal force might be greater than his own. The author makes much of the role that personal courage played in the creation of this new voice for his narrator, and, as we shall see, the heightened emphasis that courage had for him from November, 1954, through July, 1955, makes itself felt in what changes in characterization are evident between the second draft and the third; the author is clearly working his way toward the position that courage is the primary virtue.* If Mailer said a few years later that "the final purpose of art is to intensify, even, if necessary, to exacerbate, the moral consciousness of people," † the change of consciousness he is

---

* The development of the new voice is described in *Advertisements* (p. 237):

> For six years I had been writing novels in the first person; it was the only way I could begin a book, even though the third person was more to my taste. . . . Yet the first person seemed to paralyze me, as if I had a horror of creating a voice which could be in any way bigger than myself. So I had become mired in a false style for every narrator I tried. If now I had been in a fight, had found out that no matter how weak I could be in certain ways, I was also steady enough to hang on to six important lines, that may have given me new respect for myself, I don't know, but for the first time I was able to use the first person in a way where I could suggest some of the stubbornness and belligerence I also might have. . . .

† A few moments later, Mailer elaborated upon this change of consciousness with ideas that we have seen before and shall see again:

> Well, ideally, what I would hope to do with my work is intensify a consciousness that the core of life cannot be cheated. Every moment of one's

trying to jar us into with almost all of his work from *The Deer Park* on is generated by the perception that it is possible for a man to re-make himself through a series of brave acts. But an act can only be brave if it is performed in an unfavorable context. With Sergius O'Shaugnessy, Charles Eitel, and Marion Faye—ex-pilot, blacklisted movie director, and pimp, respectively—Mailer presents three charac-ters who are forced to test their courage in a world which gives little moral support to the courageous.

The novel's title refers to a pleasure park of Louis XV for which, as an independent courtier tells us in the book's epigraph, pimps scoured the French nation to find girls who might satisfy the jaded tastes of "the infamous officials of such a place." Having chosen a Southern California desert resort frequented by the movie com-munity as his locale for America-at-play, Mailer renders it with a fine, careful eye. Desert D'Or symbolizes a break with the meaningful past; the shacks of the prospectors who were true adventurers are gone, and all of the buildings were constructed after the war and, like the people they serve, are not what they appear to be. "Stores looked like anything but stores . . . there was a jewelry store built like a cabin cruiser." Even the name of the resort—one of the first and most successful of Mailer's puns—plays upon this disparity. The original, grim name the pioneers gave was Desert Door; the new spelling catches both the appearance (Golden Desert) and the reality (Empty of Gold). All of this offers a proper setting for the members of the movie community, for their inner lives are illusions within hypocrisies. They help to establish the national image of morality through the marriage-is-ecstasy pap presented on the screen, yet they seem liberated enough to hunt out physical pleasure wherever they can find it—to be sexual adventurers. But most of them are actually crippled by caution and, without exception, they are the victims of the relationships which they feel they can control; even Faye, as we shall see, is defeated.

The radical inversions which mark their lives are caught in their conversation, which often reveals the hopeless confusion of the public and the private. Professions of impotence, desire, or affection are

---

existence one is growing into more or retreating into less. One is always living a little more or dying a little bit. That the choice is not to live a lit-tle more or to not live a little more; it is to live a little more or to die a little more. And as one dies a little more, one enters a most dangerous moral condition for oneself because one starts making other people die a little more in order to stay alive oneself. [*Advertisements*, p. 385.]

matters of public discussion. Of Munshin, a producer who is simultaneously endearing and predatory, Sergius says, "Like so many people from the capital, [he] could talk openly about his private life while remaining a dream of espionage in his business operations."

The world of *The Deer Park,* like those of Mailer's first two novels, is a dying one. Norman Podhoretz has set in the thematic framework of *The Deer Park* many of the perceptions of the growing discrepancies between consciousness and social forms that Mailer makes explicit in the opening pages of "The White Negro":

> What he [Mailer] sees in Hollywood is the image of a society that has reached the end of its historical term, a society caught between the values of an age not quite dead and those of a new era that may never crawl its way out of the womb. The defining characteristic of such a society is a blatant discrepancy between the realities of experience and the categories by which experience is still being interpreted —a discrepancy that can make simultaneously for comedy and horror. The reality is that the scruples, inhibitions, and conventions which were once effective in restraining the natural egoism of the individual no longer work very well because the values from which they drew their strength no longer command much respect. No one, however, is willing to admit this, and they all go on talking and sometimes acting as though what they "really" wanted were the things that people used to want when their psychological drives were still roughly in harmony with their professed values—when, that is, these values were powerful enough to create internal needs that became almost as pressing as the primary needs themselves. This situation reveals itself in every department of life, but it is in sex that its contours are most clearly defined, and therefore it is on the sexual affairs of his characters that Mailer concentrates in *The Deer Park.* What he gives us is a remarkable picture of people saddled with all the rhetoric of the monogamous while acting like some primitive tribe that has never heard of monogamy and is utterly bewildered by the moral structure on which this strange institution rests. It is a world of people who talk incessantly about being in love and craving "decent, mature relationships" but who are in fact tightly imprisoned in their own egos and who have no true interest in anything but self. For them sex has become a testing ground of the self: they rate one another on their abilities in bed, and the reward of making love is not so much erotic satisfaction or spiritual intimacy as a sense of triumph at being considered "good."

All of this certainly holds true for characters like Munshin and the actress Lulu Meyers, who are designed to represent the mainstream of the movie morality. But it does not fully apply to Eitel, for what has been aptly called "his trembling passage in Desert D'Or" is precisely his attempt to pull himself from his fifteen-year immersion in the moral morass of the movie community. Blacklisted because of his defiant refusal to give names to a House investigating committee, Eitel sees this exclusion from Hollywood as an opportunity to realize his buried creative powers. A half-dozen times in the past ten years, twice more in the fifteen months before the novel's "present," he had begun writing a screenplay—bearing a rather close resemblance to Nathanael West's *Miss Lonelyhearts*—which would deal realistically with the energy of evil. When, early in the novel, Eitel attempts to explain his inability to write the script for the movie which would justify the years lost on all the slick, dishonest films he had made, he complains that he feels emasculated, that he has not had a woman in three months. One cause for his abstinence in a place where so many women are so available is the pounding his vanity has been taking. When he perceived in the preceding year that he could not possess a young girl he desired, "he had begun to doubt himself. As he had grown older, he had become more sensitive to the small ways in which women refused his body even as they accepted it and this had made him fragile."

Eitel is conscious that his sexual needs reach beyond the vanity which Podhoretz posits as the animus to the characters' activities, for Mailer is reaching toward the formulation that more than offering up a revelation of the state of one's psyche, one's sexual activities are themselves decisive causes of growth or decline. In her lucid discussion of the mass sexual dream and the general moral deterioration which Mailer sought to mirror in the promiscuity of *The Deer Park,* Diana Trilling wrote, "Here is truly our jungle within walls, a miasma of desire fulfilled and yet always unfulfilled, as torturing as the burning, tangled, insect-infested jungle of *The Naked and the Dead.*" The analogy of the sexual backdrop and *Naked*'s jungle is an apt one, particularly when we consider that if the jungle meant only distress to, say, Stanley or Red, it meant to Croft an object to be overcome. Significantly, the possibility of writing his screenplay only comes alive to Eitel after he has performed well with Elena Esposito, the castoff mistress of Munshin with "the lusts of a bored countess" and skills commensurate with her lusts. For Eitel, sex

> was his dream of bounty, and it nourished him enough to wake up with the hope that this affair could return his energy, flesh his courage, and make him the man he had once believed himself to be. With Elena beside him he thought for the first time in many years that the best thing in the world for him was to make a great movie.
> Down one could go, very far down, but there was a bottom. Him-

self, wasted beyond wasting, and this girl he knew hardly at all [it is their second night together]. Together each of them would make something of the other.

The sentence which precedes this quotation ("Like most cynics he was profoundly sentimental about sex.") would seem to undermine the contention that Mailer is suggesting that one can grow through sexual adventure at the same time that he is attacking promiscuity. In fact, it does not; Eitel *is* being sentimental, for he only thinks of what sex will do for his courage and his work. He does not consider what his past failures in courage and creativity will do to his sex.

Perhaps some clarification would be helpful. In the rewriting of *The Deer Park*, Mailer is feeling his way toward a formula for re-creation which he will synthesize in "The White Negro" in 1957 and dramatize in the same or the following year in "The Time of Her Time." Simply stated, an individual can become better than his society and grow by bringing courage to a situation for which the result is in doubt. Usually, the achievement of a satisfactory result demands sexual success, violence, or a combination of the two. If one "makes it"—to use the terminology of "The White Negro"— if one behaves with enough courage to perform well, then one frees more of that buried, instinctual self which is the source of all energy. New psychic circuits are connected, some of the defeatist habits of the past are sloughed off, and one is armed with more courage, instinct, and freed instinctual power for the next confrontation. If, however, one "goofs," that is, if one remains imprisoned in the habits of the past and behaves like a frightened child, then the next confrontation must be faced with less courage and general psychic energy. Obviously, we are back to the will to power of Cummings and Croft, with the amount of movement from a lower state of being to a higher one dependent upon the amount of psychic power brought to bear. One new addition is the sexual emphasis; another is that the movement is two-way. The end *is* in doubt. The movement from a higher state to a lower one is just as likely as the growth from a lower to a higher state.

Now Eitel seems to perceive much of this:

. . . the core of Eitel's theory was that people had a buried nature—"the noble savage" he called it—which was changed and whipped and trained by everything in life until it was almost dead. Yet if people were lucky and if they were brave, sometimes they would find a mate with the same buried nature and that could make them happy and strong. At least relatively so.

But he has little perception of just how much bravery is needed or of the violence one might have to act out to stop the downward spiral of one's energies. He does not even realize that the instinctual nature is a quantitative entity and that its powers (or energies) have been diminishing all the time that it was dying. His view of the buried nature seems to be that of an essentialist; he sees it as a constant entity which will offer a man a refuge, a kind of cleft in the rock of the world if he can only get in touch with another nature like it. But the dynamic, existential view implicit in the novel is that the self is not only constantly changing but that it can only change for the better by some way struggling with the world which is trying to kill it. And one must "connect" with one's own nature before hoping to connect with another's.

These views were still evolving as Mailer wrote *The Deer Park*. If the book had been written by the Mailer who saw things as he did just two years later, Eitel's sex with Elena would not have been so good as it was during their first weeks together. The later Mailer would have felt that there had been too much capitulation, too many failures of nerve by Eitel in the past.* The way in which Eitel's pleasure declines when he finds himself unable to write the screen-play is consistent with Mailer's later thought. Although he attempts to mend with several weeks of sexual gratification, Eitel discovers when he finally begins the screenplay for the last time that he cannot stop seeing his characters through the cynical eyes with which he had viewed the figures in his commercially successful screenplays of the past. For as Mailer has said so often, the creation of an art work forces a man upon his life, and what the author calls Eitel's marriage to Hollywood had lasted too long. All of the times he had betrayed the artist in himself by settling for less than his best, all of the dishonest movies he had written and directed for the money, women, recognition, and commodities with which Hollywood rewards the right kind of corruption, catch up with Eitel as he finds himself unable to write his screenplay successfully:

* For example, he wrote in 1958 or 1959:

We want the heats of the orgy and not its murder, the warmth of pleasure without the grip of pain, and therefore the future threatens a nightmare, and we continue to waste ourselves. We've cut a corner, tried to cheat the heart of life, tried not to face our uneasy sense that pleasure comes best to those who are brave. . . . [*Advertisements*, p. 23.]

Mailer places more emphasis in *The Deer Park* on the blessings of sexual technique than he later will.

> The past was a cancer, destroying memory, destroying the present until emotion was eroded and the events in which one found oneself were always in danger of being as dead as the past. . . . most remarkable cancer! It not only erased the past and stunned the present but it ate into the future before he could create it.

After a few weeks of this paralysis, Eitel takes a long step toward permanent artistic perdition by agreeing with Munshin to write a maudlin version of the screenplay with a happy ending, a potboiler he dispatches with cynical speed and skill. Having discovered then that he is no longer an artist and "what was a commercial man without his trade," Eitel talks to the House committee. Although there are more contributing factors to Eitel's capitulation than his long failure of nerve, this is the primary one, and Eitel knows it. When he tries to ease his way out of the deteriorating affair with Elena by offering to marry and then divorce her—so that she will be left with something and his conscience will be eased—she refuses, and he reflects:

> The essence of spirit . . . was to choose the thing which did not better one's position but made it more perilous. That was why the world he knew was poor, for it insisted morality and caution were identical. He was so completely of that world, and she was not.

The primary virtues in *Barbary Shore* are intellectual; no action can be "good" unless it follows from a correct perception of the operative historical processes. Save for a few gaps which I will discuss shortly, Eitel's perceptions are acute enough, but Mailer has always believed that psychic expansion demands more primitive virtues than intellectual keenness. It is a sign of Sergius's immaturity that he had always thought that self-knowledge was all that was needed and so could not understand how Eitel could talk about his problems so clearly and yet be able to do nothing about them. This emphasis on the need to act out perceptions will become an obsessive strain in Mailer's writing and life. By May, 1956, he will write, "For where consciousness cannot be supported by the courage to make one's action, then consciousness lapses into despair and death."

With his emphasis on courage in *The Deer Park,* Mailer is returning to and continuing the radical, minority view of *The Naked and the Dead* which celebrated Croft. We are able to place in time Mailer's rediscovery of the possibilities of bravery. As Sergius grew into a tougher and more independent character in the third draft, Mailer was able to see the failings of his characters from a more exacting moral perspective than the dominating one of the first two novels, which made the characters so dependent upon external circumstances:

I was no longer telling of two nice people who fail at life because the world is too large and too cruel for them; the new O'Shaugnessy had moved me by degrees to the more painful story of two people who are strong as well as weak, corrupt as much as pure, and *fail to grow despite their bravery in a poor world, because they are finally not brave enough,* and so do more damage to one another than to the unjust world outside them. [Italics mine.]

In contrast to Eitel, Mailer intends Sergius as a sort of object lesson on the possibilities of living outside of the corrupt system, gratified by work and sustained by craft and courage. Sergius's origins, like Lovett's, are symbolic. Brought up in an orphan asylum and given only a fancy name by a father who left his son to institutional rather than parental guidance, he is like all contemporary Americans in lacking a past which could morally inform his behavior in the present. But then we are told that Sergius's interest (like America's) lies precisely in the openness of his future. The contradictions in his nature are great enough for him to contemplate in the course of the novel such disparate carers as those of a psychoanalyst, a high school coach, a writer, a movie actor, an FBI agent, and a disk jockey.

Because he "had been one of those boys for whom losing came naturally," he accepts the system, sees the armed forces as an opportunity, and literally fights his way into pilots' school. Working within the system, he is given a more gratifying machine than the ones Lovett had: "I used to believe I could control the changes of the sky by a sway of my body . . . for it was magic to fly an airplane; it was a gimmick and a drug." But reality closes in when Sergius finally perceives that the incendiary bombs he is dropping are burning children alive, not just forming pretty patterns beneath him. The result of this confrontation is a nervous breakdown. He partially recovers, receives a medical discharge, and settles with his gambling winnings in Desert D'Or to flee the world of "wars and boxing clubs and children's homes on back streets . . . a world where orphans burned orphans," where he was tricked into burning Korean children. Made impotent even before his breakdown, Sergius is in one way another Jake Barnes, sexually injured by an unjust world—as Mailer indeed thinks we all are. But unlike Jake, he is not willing at this point in his life to accept the fact that he will have to pay for everything he gets, and for Mailer one pays by struggling with danger or spiritually dying. Trading too much on his uniform and good looks and not enough on his courage,* Sergius does well enough in this false world

* It must be said that he regains his potency through the courage he shows in standing up to the tyrannical producer, Teppis, and getting invited to the

for a while. He picks up Lulu Meyers, regains his potency, makes love to her, is gathered into several entourages. But again reality closes in, or the false world turns out to be the real one after all, for he is dropped by the actress and, though he behaves well, is badly frightened by federal investigators. Sergius's subsequent attempts to reform himself—studying bullfighting with a *novillero* whose girl he has taken away, getting wounded by a bull in Mexico, teaching bullfighting on the Lower East Side of Manhattan—sound like a parody of Hemingway's cult of courage, but Mailer wants us to take them seriously. We are supposed to believe that those reflections he made after the interrogation—"of courage and of cowardice, and how we are all brave and all terrified each in our own way and our private changing proportion"—have been ballasted by brave actions. Correspondingly, Mailer wants us to accept, as the statements of a man who knows, Sergius's end-of-the-book philosophizings like "life is an education which should be put to use," or

> I had the conceit, I had the intolerable conviction, that I could write about worlds I knew better than anyone alive. So I continued to write, and as I worked, I learned the taste of a failure over and over again, for the longest individual journey may well be the path from the first creative enthusiasm to the concluded artifact.

Sergius is then intended as a double for Eitel, but one who is able to disaffiliate himself from the corrupting economic nexus—to act with enough courage and independence to grow into an artist. (*The Deer Park* itself, largely an imaginative reconstruction by Sergius, is supposed to be the manifest proof of his growth unto artistry.) While reading Eitel's defiant testimony, Sergius thinks that he felt as if he were speaking his own words, and a few pages later he feels that Eitel was a man like himself. Several years after his capitulation, Eitel stops to observe a boat while returning to his wife from some dreary midday adultery. He envies the seamen setting off to seek adventure and thinks it possible that Sergius is on the boat. We are supposed to conclude then that Sergius, who has symbolically refused to sell his life's story to the movies and has twenty fewer years of the cancerous past, is still ready for intellectual and experiential adven-

---

party on his own terms, then winning Lulu by again defying Teppis at the party. But Mailer makes it clear that more courage than this is needed as Sergius, intimidated by the FBI, is "reduced to heat rash and to panic, knowing I was weak and wondering if I would ever be strong" (Norman Mailer, *The Deer Park* [New York: New American Library, 1964], p. 277).

ture in a way that Eitel is not. For from this romantic readiness followed Sergius's Lower East Side resurrection.

I have spent this much space on relatively unadorned character summary because it is with these characters that Mailer's attempts, at this stage in his career, to propagandize his perception of the possibilities of courage catch up with him. With the possible exception of the satire on the movie community, the wonderfully subtle treatment of Eitel's doomed affair and the process of his cancerous realization and capitulation are the best things in the book. In a very contrived passage at the end of the novel, Mailer has Eitel confess to Sergius his inability to fight the good fight and urge the latter to try in his writing to capture the real world, "where orphans burn orphans and nothing is more difficult to discover than a simple fact." The irony of all this is that, in terms of believability, Sergius ends up in a very false and contrived world. Mailer finds the real world with Eitel, but the author does not want it; at this stage of his career, his desire to offer experiential possibility is stronger than the commitment to capture emotional stakes in all their intensity. But as his career proceeds, Mailer's unwillingness to permit his struggling protagonists to be defeated by the societal forces around them gradually ebbs. Although he is generally victorious, the hero of *An American Dream* suffers considerable loss, while the one in *Why Are We in Vietnam?* is conclusively defeated.

In the "optimism" of *The Deer Park,* Eitel is referred to as a nineteenth-century man, hindered by a certain lack of innate savagery as well as by his own past. He calls Sergius a twentieth-century gentleman when the ex-flier implies that he lives wholly in the present, and the astute if corrupt Munshin says of Sergius, "He'll kick you in the crotch if it's a fight to the death. . . . I sense ugliness in that kid." For all of this, and for all of Mailer's attempts in the third draft to strengthen the narrator's voice, Sergius remains a somewhat unconvincing, somewhat embarrassed wish-fulfillment that a nice enough fellow can remake himself.* Mailer cannot fully believe in

---

* Although Sergius is least convincing as a hipster artist, he is no miracle of persuasion throughout the novel. However much Sergius—"the frozen germ of some new theme" (*Advertisements,* p. 236)—finally unthawed and became believable for Mailer after three years, he by and large remains rigid to me. Another critic describes him as a "stick," "a grand lacuna into which whole chapters topple and vanish" (Marvin Mudrick, "Mailer and Styron: Guests of the Establishment," *Hudson Review,* Vol. 17 [Autumn, 1964], pp. 355, 358). While Sergius is not this vacuous, the quotation on page 71 (in which

Sergius because he has been heading from his first novel on toward the conviction that the enormous emasculating will of society can be resisted only by a descendant of Croft; not a nice fellow at all, but one who believes with a Hobbesian finality that "life is a contest between people in which the victor generally recuperates quickly and the loser takes long to mend, a perpetual competition of colliding explorers in which one must grow or else pay for remaining the same. . . ."

This quotation is from "The White Negro," whose hipster hero is anticipated in *The Deer Park* by the sadistic pimp, Marion Faye. Since Faye is wholly incapable of identification with any social or parasocial structure like the army, he is in one way closer than Croft to the hipster defined in the 1957 essay, but the sergeant is closer to the White Negro when we compare his unthinking, instinctual powers with Faye's emphasis on intellection. But then Croft had his identifiable, objective correlative of the primordial self he must conquer; he had his mountain. Faye is marooned with his all too rational will in amorphous, mid-century America. With his superior reason, Faye cognitively (not instinctually) knows that he can only conquer himself by expunging from his psyche all of the tendencies to obey the dictates of the society he hates so much. So guiltless as to be almost a pure psychopath, Faye still fears guilt and sympathy as a Trappist might fear sin, for both are the responses to the world's moral commands—proofs that he is not totally and finally his own man. This ideal is as unattainable as the peak of Anaka. Although he can will and carry out his sadistic acts, Faye's emotions are beyond his control; his eyes burn with pity for an addict to whom he has just refused money, and he is finally defeated when he feels relief that Elena, whom he has been driving to suicide, does not complete the act.

Though Faye has, as he reflects, his drop of mercy after all, he is too much of a thinking and not enough of a feeling creature. His hatreds, fears, and sadistic commands—which he does not even enjoy carrying out, as Croft does—are about all that emerge from the psychic areas beneath his cognitive control. The ultimate adventurer in the land of pleasure-seekers, Faye has almost no capacity for enjoyment. It is inconceivable that he could enjoy physical exertion as Croft does or the control of others like Cummings, and since his sexual relations and sadistic acts are merely a pleasureless demon-

---

the character tells us that he was able to discover emotions he never owned without really making the reader feel them) typifies his general inability to generate emotion and underscores Howe's contention that Mailer must tell us what he cannot show (page 54).

stration of his will over himself and others, he cannot experience, as Eitel does, a partial freeing of a hedonistic, primitive self. Determined to grow but unable to enjoy experience, Faye's goal of "making it" is strangely abstracted from actual possibility. In fact, the only justification he can find for his modus vivendi is that it will somehow separate him from all other life styles in mid-century America. He must drive Elena to suicide so that he can do "the other things," but what these things are and what benefit they will bring him Faye cannot tell us. Early in the novel he tells Sergius: "Nobility and vice—they're the same thing. It just depends on the direction you're going . . . if I ever make it, then I turn around and go the other way. Toward nobility. That's all right. Just so you carry it to the end." When Sergius asks Faye what is in the middle, the pimp replies, "Slobs . . . I hate slobs. . . . They always think what they have to think."

"Then I turn around and go the other way." By his own standards imprisoned in the sickening societal middle and determined to escape his prison, Faye is as clearly *The Deer Park*'s idealist as Croft was *The Naked and the Dead*'s.

In addition to the contentless purity of his own goals, Faye serves as Eitel's conscience, urging him to defy the committee and see if he can create anything better than the "crud" and "slop" he had been turning out for fifteen years. Faye's feeling for the director turns to hatred when he feels that the latter has spit on the artist in himself. Since Faye feels that love is "bullshit mountain" and that one must seek honesty instead of love, he tries with a mixture of sadism and patience to burn honesty into Elena and the call girl, Bobby. But since his idealism is so completely predicated on willed opposition, and since this opposition gives him so little pleasure, his nobility and vice are empty categories. Pure nihilism is grounded precisely on nothing. The only value Faye sees in social action is the destruction of society, and he has no feeling of a "nature" of his own that he must realize. Mailer does glancingly attach objective purpose to Faye's ambitions by having him fantasize that he is acting out the desires of the Devil who was actually "God-in-banishment . . . a noble prince deprived of true Heaven." Although this sentence anticipates an important turn in Mailer's later thought, it is, after all, only a sentence, tucked away in several pages of theological fantasies and not having enough force to give meaningful purpose to Faye's actions. Like a character from *The Possessed*, Faye's vision of creation is one of a destruction total enough to include himself and everyone else in the world. The closest that Faye comes to the undiluted solitude of self he longs for is when, one sunrise, he prays out of his inverted morality for an atomic holocaust:

> So let it come, Faye thought, let this explosion come, and then another, and all the others, until the Sun God burned the earth. Let it come, he thought, looking into the east at Mecca where the bombs ticked while he stood on a tiny rise of ground trying to see one hundred, two hundred, three hundred miles across the desert. Let it come, Faye begged, like a man praying for rain, let it come and clear the rot and the stench and the stink, let it come for all of everywhere, just so it comes and the world stands clear in the white dead dawn.

If Faye's nihilism is a dead end, his psychopathy is not. "The White Negro" will combine Faye's bravery, willingness to employ violence, and singleness of purpose with an actual purpose, the freeing of the buried noble savage of Eitel's theory. Even though psychopathy alone is obviously no experiential solution and must be rejected as such, Mailer's ambivalent feelings about it at this stage of his career are no less interesting than they were in *The Naked and the Dead*. The liberal Mailer finally gets Faye out of the novel and appears to punish him by having the pimp involved in an automobile accident which sends him to prison, but the radical Mailer's attitude is well expressed in Faye's last thoughts before he passes out after the accident: "it's all right. To make it, maybe I need a year [in prison] like that. More education." Though the books ends with Sergius's supposed regeneration, Faye unmistakably emerges as the novel's ultimate adventurer and actual hero. Perhaps the most important way that *The Deer Park* marks a watershed in Mailer's career is with his balking, as he did with Croft, at pressing onward with a character who is bent or driven to test the extremes of experience, with an adventurer who would be considered psychopathic in his disregard for conventional morality. This will not happen in the segments from Mailer's proposed thousand-page novel published in *Advertisements,* in *An American Dream,* or in *Why Are We in Vietnam?*

III

In a much different way, *The Deer Park* is as curious a novel as *Barbary Shore*. Mailer describes a fairly bizarre locale with considerable skill, his satire of the movie community is superb, and with Eitel, Marion, and Elena he has rather interesting characters, whom he depicts with considerable psychological subtlety, who do relatively interesting things. Yet the novel is strangely inert. If *The Deer Park* has, as a number of critics have observed, a claustrophobic quality, the claustrophobia seldom has the strident tension which manages almost singlehandedly to grip the reader's interest in *Barbary Shore* until all is ground down by the Marxist machinery. Part of this inertness is due to the point of view. Although *The Deer Park* is narrated by Sergius, it also employs the third person limited narrative. For more than half the novel we move into the consciousnesses of Faye and Eitel so that in Bruce Cook's words:

> *The Deer Park* is essentially a novel in the third person with a shifting point of view. . . . But over this third-person narrative, Mailer has imposed his own leaden reflections on the action presented through O'Shaugnessy. While he does provide him with a few rather pungent comments on the proceedings, Mailer's use of the narrator tends to slow the pace of the novel. Why did he choose to use it then? The moral passion which has always been strongest in his work, dictated the choice. He was moved by an irresistible necessity to comment on the proceedings and sit in judgment on his characters.

Mailer's sententiousness, so different from the usually noncommital surface of *Naked* which left so much up to the reader's intelligence, undoubtedly clogs the movement of *The Deer Park*. But I do not think that this is the primary reason for the use of the first person in the novel. In 1963, Mailer said that between 1948 and 1950 he perceived that it would be impossible for him to write a novel in the third person for many years. To quote the author: "I think I must have felt at that time as if I would never be able to write in the third person until I developed a coherent view of life. I don't know that I've been able to altogether." After his interviewer, Steven Marcus, observed that Thackeray could write in the third person because he felt like omniscient God Himself, Mailer replied, "God can write in the third person only so long as He understands His world. But if the world becomes contradictory or incomprehensible to Him, then God begins to grow concerned with his own nature. It's either that, or borrow notions from other Gods."

All of the four novels published after *Naked* are in the first person, and in *Barbary Shore* and *The Deer Park* the narrator is a confused young man who wants to write a novel—a literal and symbolic orphan who engages in similar relationships with older, wiser characters. Fred W. Dupee has written of the persistence of what he calls Freudian ideas in Mailer's fiction, "It is astonishing how often in his novels an authoritative older person is engaged in trying to assist some younger, more amorphous person to maturity." The most obvious examples of this are with McLeod and Lovett and with Eitel and Sergius, but we will see a more sardonic version with Rusty and D. J. in *Why Are We in Vietnam?* The "teaching" relationship is most intentional with Eitel's program to help Elena grow, it takes its most sadistic form with Faye's attempts to burn honesty into Bobby, and we can first place it in Mailer's fiction with Cummings's intellectual wooing of Hearn. Referring to *The Deer Park,* Dupee continues:

> But the Freudian ideas, like those of other derivation, often operate not to reinforce and clarify his [Mailer's] experience but to embarrass and devitalize it. The author himself seems frequently to approach his material as the learner, the disciple, the patient, eager to grow up.

As we add to these observations Mailer's comments about how he writes to discover the truth or how a novelist should discover in the writing something he did not know he knew, it becomes increasingly apparent that Mailer has projected himself into *The Deer Park* as an emerging novelist with the hope of better discovering the truth as he invents his fiction. Of course this is all an issue of degree—every true act of creation is also an act of discovery—but Mailer's desire to learn was so great that it undermined his control of *The Deer Park.* In trying to discern how an expanding life is to be lived, O'Shaugnessy-Mailer must choose between the sloppily generous, compromising liberalism of Eitel and the amoral will to power of Faye. (Although it is Eitel's sense of dignity and not his political beliefs that causes him to refuse to testify, he is generally associated with liberal positions through his emphases on the power of reason, the rights of others, and the need to make generous gestures.) Although Sergius slides Faye's way by cutting off Eitel after the latter agrees to testify, there is considerable indecision about the way Eitel should have behaved. On the one hand, he is too soft to fight his way into the mystery of growth "against all the power of good manners, good morals, the fear of germs, and the sense of sin." On the other, Eitel is condemned for not really caring enough about Elena and for lacking true generosity and loyalty to the weak. Another example of the intellectual confusion which attends Mailer's attempt to learn through writing is the way in which the growth of Sergius is schematically tucked away into the next-to-last chapter of the novel—a stunning disproportion when one considers how it is supposed to counterpoint the failures of Eitel, Elena, and Marion to become what they want to.

Mailer's double vision of the Hollywood sexual jungle provides still another example of the way he worked out his ideas as he wrote. If the liberal Mailer judges the jungle to be pleasureless and diseased, the radical Mailer endorses (in Marvin Mudrick's words) "the assumption that the Hollywood amalgam of forces—technical, personal, organizational—which alters, distorts, reshapes, imprisons the sexual consciousness of millions must itself be a reservoir of personal power, a sort of Catharist cell whose holy heretics practice rites forbidden and unimaginable to the laity." This would most apply to Eitel and Elena, but it would seem that their lovemaking is so rich because they are not completely of the movie community. But Lulu certainly is, and this description of Sergius's responses to her charms catches Mailer's fascination with the mystic rites as well as Sergius's callowness:

> I was able to discover emotions I never knew I owned, and I must have enjoyed it as much as Lulu. So I thought by virtue of the things we did I would put my mark on her forever. What she may have intended as a little dance was a track and field event to me, and I would snap the tape with burning lungs, knotted muscles, and mind set on the need to break a record. . . . Like a squad of worn-out infantrymen who are fixed for the night in a museum, my pleasure was to slash tapestries, poke my fingers through nude paintings, and drop marble busts on the floor. Then I could feel her as something I had conquered, could listen to her wounded breathing, and believe that no matter how she acted other times, these moments were Lulu, as if her flesh murmured words more real than her lips. To the pride of having so beautiful a girl was added the bigger pride of knowing that I took her with the cheers of millions behind me. Poor millions with their low roar! They would never have what I had now. They could shiver outside, make a shrine in their office desk or on the shelf of their olive-drab lockers, they could look at the pin-up picture of Lulu Meyers. I knew I was good when I carried a million men on my shoulder.

Further, what is the role of sex in Sergius's growth? Although he does have the affair with the bullfighter's mistress and, in New York, "a few girls who made for some very complicated romances," no more detail is given about the Mexican affair than the phrase offered about the later romances. What emphasis there is on the causes of his growth falls on the courage necessary to be a bullfighter and, much more emphatically, a writer. Yet Sergius-Mailer asserts at the end of the novel that new psychic circuits are connected through sex.

We shall shortly look at this crucial affirmation and here say only that it was added at the end of the third draft, after the decisive events of the November, 1954–July, 1955, period. If Mailer had gradually projected himself into the book as an inquiring novelist, he had changed enough in his three and one-half year struggle with it to finally perceive that his orphan should find his perilous home as a sexual adventurer, not a writer:

> Before I was finished, I saw a way to write another book altogether. In what I had so far done, Sergius O'Shaugnessy was given an opportunity by a movie studio to sell the rights to his life and get a contract as an actor. After more than one complication, he finally refused the offer, lost the love of his movie star Lulu, and went off wandering by himself, off to become a writer. This episode had never been an important part of the book, but I could see that the new Sergius was capable of accepting the offer, and if he went to Hollywood and became a movie star himself, the possibilities were good, for in O'Shaugnessy I had a character who was ambitious, yet in his own way, moral, and with such a character one could travel deep into the paradoxes of the time.
>
> Well, I was not in shape to consider that book. With each week of work, bombed and sapped and charged and stoned with lush, with pot, with benny, saggy, Milltown, coffee, and two packs a day, I was working live, and overalert, and tiring into what felt like death . . . there was only a worn-out part of me to keep protesting into the pillows of one drug and the pinch of the other that I ought to have the guts to stop the machine, to call back the galleys, to cease—to rest, to give myself another two years and write a book which would go a little further to the end of my particular night.
>
> But I had passed the point where I could stop. My anxiety had become too great.

But though the novelist never found a satisfactory home for Sergius in *The Deer Park,* he moved a long way toward finding one for himself.

IV

Mailer has written that an interesting American writer must venture "into the jungle of his unconscious to bring back a sense of order or a sense of chaos." As Ihab Hassan has said, and I tried to show, the prevailing effect of *The Naked and the Dead* is one of ordered chaos. *Barbary Shore* overwhelmingly exhibits the author's sense of chaos even though Mailer tried to hammer the moral bedlam of the novel into the framework of Marxist ideology. In *The Deer Park,* Mailer articulates for the first time the ordering law which prevailed on Anopopei and which is dramatized so much less convincingly here. Eitel has no desire to marry Elena after she is injured in the automobile accident with Faye, yet

> he knew that he would marry her, that he could not give her up for there was that *law of life so cruel and so just which demanded that*

one must grow or else pay more for remaining the same. If he did not marry her he could never forget that he had once made her happy and now she had nothing but her hospital bed. [Italics mine.]

I find these lines inscrutable. Do they mean that Eitel has recognized his failure to grow and will pay by making this marriage, or is he marrying Elena because he had once helped her to grow and now must do what he can to keep her from declining further? Whatever Mailer had in mind here, the quotation well exemplifies the undigested state of the author's ideas. The italicized line is the unifying thought of Mailer's intellectual career, yet it turns up in an incomprehensible passage.

To expand upon the idea once more, one grows or one declines according to the amount of courage and insight one brings to certain situations. As Mailer will later argue, the situation which not only offers but compels change is the sexual act. For example, in June, 1961, he wrote that "the orgasm is anathema to [the liberal] mind because it is the inescapable existential moment. Every lie we have told, every fear we have indulged, every aggression we have tamed arises at that instant to constrict the turns and possibilities of our becoming." The perception for which he had been reaching for four years and which he was to pursue for the next decade was finally articulated in the next-to-last sentence of *The Deer Park.* After Sergius has in a mystical moment asked God if sex is where philosophy begins, Mailer's God is kind enough to answer, "Rather think of Sex as Time, and Time as the connection of new circuits."

The last four paragraphs of the Putnam's edition of *The Deer Park,* the final and standard version, did not appear in the Rinehart edition, which ended with a variation of the fifth-to-last paragraph of the Putnam's version. These crucial paragraphs, introducing as they do Mailer's helpful God and his gnostic advice, probably were influenced by the author's use of drugs in late 1954 and all of 1955. The obsession with time surely follows from these experiments; anyone who has experienced the effects of marijuana or mescaline is familiar with accelerating or decelerating time. In fact, Mailer tells us in *Advertisements* that the last paragraph of the Putnam's *Deer Park* was written while the author was under the influence of mescaline, and he said in the *Paris Review* interview that his obsession with God began during this period of drug experimentation.

The Deer Park was originally conceived as the first of eight novels, all dealing with Sergius's wanderings through eight different worlds. We might better understand the cryptic last quotation if we turn to the prologue of the projected series. Written in 1952, not long after the three-year agony with *Barbary Shore* and at the beginning of what was to become the more than three-year agony with *The Deer Park,* the prologue was eventually titled "The Man Who Studied Yoga." A superb work of fiction, it gives some hint of the critical reputation Mailer might have enjoyed in the fifties had he been temperamentally able (or, as he would put it, cowardly enough) to write a few sympathetic novels about losers instead of struggling to create a fictional world of real possibility. "Yoga's" hero—or better, anti-hero—is Sam Slavoda, a self-accusing, washed-out radical who now lives in bourgeois comfort and is employed as a continuity writer for comic strips. Imprisoned in "flat and familiar dispirit," Sam hopes to write, "as a convenant of his worth, that enormous novel which would lift him at a bound from the impasse in which he stifles, whose dozens of characters would develop a vision of life in bountiful complexity." But the novel—a formless, sprawling wreck of notes, incidental ideas, and odd pages—will obviously never be written. Sam cannot write a realistic novel (let us say one in which a hero rises in the social order) because he feels that "reality is no longer realistic," adding "I don't know what it is." This is reminiscent of the complaint that Mailer had been making in the years before "Yoga" was written, and, like Mailer, Sam is in search of a hero. If Mailer later confessed his fear of creating a hero larger than himself from 1949 through 1955, Sam has been so atrophied by the formless, deadening malaise of American life that he can only project as a hero a man as numbed and futile as he is. Mailer could project a hero in 1952 and synthesize him from the elements in *The Deer Park* by 1957; Sam can only think that

> one could not have a hero today . . . a man of action and contemplation, capable of sin, large enough for good, a man immense. There is only a modern hero damned by no more than the ugliness of wishes whose satisfaction he will never know. One needs a man who could walk the stage, someone who—no matter who, not himself. Someone, Sam thinks, who reasonably could not exist.

Still contemplating the wreckage of his novel as he slips into sleep at the end of the dreary Sunday dramatized in the story, Sam is given an idea by the benevolently daemonic narrator: "Destroy time, and chaos may be ordered."

For one thing, the suggestion anticipates some destructions of time that Mailer had planned for the eight novels which were to be the eight stages of a dream that Sam was to have later that night. But the suggestion is more important as an element in the metaphysics of growth that will evolve in the fifties, one which we can perhaps see better if we add "consider Sex as Time and Time as the connection of new circuits" to "destroy time, and chaos may be ordered." Later in the 1950s Mailer will say that life is not chaos but that it is ordered by one's growth into more being or deterioration into less. His position in 1951 seems to be that existence can either be chaos or it can be ordered by growth. If the destruction of time will order chaos and growth will do the same, then it would seem that the destruction of time and growth are the same thing. Now, in "Advertisements for Myself on the Way Out," the late-fifties prologue to a still unpublished novel, Mailer suggests that there are two kinds of time, clock-time and growth-time:

> . . . when Time left to its own resources is excited into action neither by murder nor love, and so remains in step to the twitching of a clock [it is] . . . passive Time, Time on its way to death; but Time as growth, Time as the excitations and chilling stimulations of murder, Time as the tropical envelopments of love (even if murder is lusty in the chest and love a cold sweat on the hip), Time is then the hard of a hoodlum or the bitch on her back looking for the lover whose rhythm will move her to the future.

Blended images of lust and violence are here offered to evoke situations in which growth-time might flourish, in which it might murder the clock-time which seeks to murder us. This is still another way of saying that one can grow if one has enough courage to act out one's forbidden desires. When Mailer's God of growth urges Sergius to think of "Sex as Time," He is telling the latter to think of successful sex as growth-time, as a time when new psychic circuits will be connected. But "Sex as Time" could also mean bad, cowardly sex when nothing is risked. This sex would occur during clock-time, time on its way to death.

Sam Slavoda must destroy the objective, passive clock-time which has ticked away both the deterioration of the American radical spirit (a deterioration Sam laments) and the stale compromises and surrenders to security which have marked the decline of sexuality in his own life. He must open himself to subjective, active growth-time— those expanded, glitteringly illumined moments when one is free to change what is dead or dying in one's own psyche and be moved to the future through murderous love. "The orgasm . . . is the inescapable existential moment," the situation most pregnant with possibility for growth or decline. We are told that Sam suffers from ugly wishes whose satisfaction he will never know. We are not told just what these ugly desires are. Sam might long to murder, rape, or to engage in one of the lesser violences; the only profound wish we learn of is his craving for heightened sexual experience. He believes that his extraordinary amorous appetites have not been properly appreciated by his wife, Eleanor, but "his appetite for a variety of new experience . . . is matched only by his fear of new people and novel situations," and Sam remains monogamous but collects nude photographs. Hidden beneath the story's ironic, hopeless surface is an existential moment when Sam must decide if he will act out his desire for an orgy or be restrained by his fears of the unknown and the socially unacceptable.

On this Sunday in Sam Slavoda's life, two couples visit the apartment in the huge, bleakly functional Queens complex where Sam lives with his wife—a painter manqué as he is a writer manqué. Their two children are visiting their grandparents for the day. Although the Slavodas think themselves superior to the other couples, they have no particular justification for doing so. The three men are relatively gentle, saddened ex-radicals who somehow think themselves distinguished in their comfortable middle-class lives by their informed disillusion, and though the wives' social behavior is perhaps more distinctive, it is not radically so. Most important, all six share profound sexual yearnings. During the first showing of the pornographic movie which one of the couples brings, "a little murmur, all unconscious, passes from their lips. The audience sways, each now finally lost in himself, communing hungrily with shadows, violated or violating, fantasy triumphant."

By the second viewing, Sam wonders:

> Is it possible . . . that each of them here . . . will cast off their clothes when the movie is done and perform the orgy which tickles at the heart of their desire? They will not, he knows, they will make jokes when the projector is put away, they will gorge the plate of delicatessen Eleanor provides, and swallow more beer, he among them. He will be the first to make jokes.

Instead of the orgy, Sam keeps the film for the night, and in a wonderful encapsulation of safe bourgeois promiscuity, he and Eleanor make love on the couch as they watch it. Even if Sam was with companions who could have chanced an orgy, he would not have had the courage to risk the loss of what domestic and emotional security he has. And there is no chance of his being in such a group, for the basis of friendship among Sam and his acquaintances is a mutual willingness to mother the others. Instead of the creation of new psychic circuits which the orgiastic release of sexual violence might have permitted,

> self-critical Sam . . . makes love in front of a movie, and one cannot say that it is unsatisfactory any more than one can say it is pleasant. It is dirty, downright porno dirty, it is a lewd slop-brush slapped through the middle of domestic exasperations and breakfast eggs.

And instead of giving way to his instinct and freeing himself from the nagging cerebration that is the intellectual equivalent of clock-time, jargon-bound, psychoanalyzed

> Sam the lover is conscious of exertion. One moment he is Frankie Idell [the master rapist of the movie], destroyer of virgins—take that! you whore!—the next, body moving, hands caressing, he is no more than some lines from a psychoanalytical text. He is thinking about the sensitivity of his scrotum. He has read that this is a portent of femininity in a male. How strong is his latent homosexuality worries Sam . . . warm sweat running cold.

In my effort to show the first muted accents of what will become Mailer's battle cry for sexual adventure, I have no doubt shifted the actual emphasis of the story. Sam is so firmly strapped to the treadmill of his frustrating days that most readers never suspect for a moment that the orgy might take place, and even if Sam did try to fight his way into one, the tone that the narrator takes toward him is so consistently ironic and gently mocking that the logic of the story demands that his effort be a sort of Prufrockian social disaster. Still, beneath the ironic, superior tone, we can hear the radical Mailer's faint voice: "Why not an orgy? Let's at least try."

This voice was to get steadily louder, and by the end of 1955 sex was to Mailer "the sword of history . . . for only when sex triumphed could the mind seize . . . the hip of new experience." (As with the changes in the characterizations of Sergius, Elena, and Eitel, Mailer's growing sureness of the regenerative powers of sex would seem to have followed from his immediate experience).*

* To quote the preceding lines of the paragraph:

> Like all generals in command of an army of one, I started in the confidence of a secret weapon. I had marijuana. Mary-Jane, at least for me, in that first life of smoking it, was the door back to sex, which had become again all I had and all I wanted. Once again there was sanction to gallop on self-love—God's gift to women, wife, letters and history, marijuana my horse. So soon as I recovered from one bust-out, I was waiting to kiss off another; sex was the sword of history to this uncommissioned General, for only when sex triumphed could the mind seize the hip of new experience. [*Advertisements*, p. 278.]

Although no coherent explication of the importance of sex as an animus of re-creation was to appear until the summer of 1957, when "The White Negro" was published in *Dissent,* Mailer did, between January and April, 1956, argue that hip was a peculiarly American existentialism because of its emphasis on a mysticism of the flesh and add that, as such, it could touch off "the only revolution which will be meaningful and natural for the 20th Century . . . the sexual revolution." In fact, in the eight months following the completion of *The Deer Park,* one can see more relationships between Mailer's ideas and acts crystallizing than the one which affected his sexual theories. This paragraph from *Advertisements* offers an entry into these developments:

> Rewriting *The Deer Park* I had come to recognize by the time I was done that willy-nilly, in admiration for Hemingway's strength and with distaste for his weaknesses, I was one of the few writers of my generation who was concerned with living in Hemingway's discipline, by which I do not mean I was interested in trying for some second-rate imitation of the style, but rather that I shared with Papa the notion, arrived at slowly in my case, that even if one dulled one's talent in the punishment of becoming a man, it was more important to be a man than a very good writer, that probably I could not become a very good writer unless I learned first how to keep my nerve, and what is more difficult, learned how to find more of it.

By August, 1955, then, Mailer felt that courageous manhood was the immediate goal to struggle toward rather than, as he felt a year before, the ability to create art objects or maintain the socialist faith. Presumably, some of this nerve might be gained if Mailer proclaimed himself the psychic rebel he had come to feel himself to be. His first two declarations of independence from the proprieties of the literary world were an interview he held in November, 1955, while under the influence of marijuana, and a full-page advertisement he placed at his own expense in *The Village Voice* during the same month. The latter collected the most damning critical comments of the recently released *The Deer Park* and urged the paper's readers to buy the book. As for the interview, Mailer did not advertise his talking "with his brain full of marijuana," but he permitted publication without changing a word. The beginnings of the conception of himself as a younger, rougher, more aggressive and polemic Papa are suggested by his urging young artists "to keep the rebel . . . alive, no matter how attractive or exhausting the temptations" or his arguing that the role of the artist in our society "is to be as disturbing, as adventurous, as penetrating as possible." The title, "Sixty-nine Questions and Answers," was of course an intentional affront to conventional sensibilities—particularly back in 1955. But all of this was the barest skirmish compared to the tests of courage the author sought.

The months following the completion of *The Deer Park* saw, in Mailer's words, "my self-analysis . . . still going at locomotive speed, and since I was anxious above all else to change a hundred self-defeating habits which locked my character into space too narrow for what I wanted to become, I was at the time like an actor looking for a rare role. . . . At heart, I wanted a war." He found his war with the seventeen columns he wrote for *The Village Voice* published between January 11 and May 2, 1956. The role was that of General Marijuana (the appelation is Mailer's), the strategist who attempted to marshal his drug-induced insights in a way that would combine his desire to grow and society's need to change. The general reasoned that in order "to give a little speed to that sexual and moral revolution which is yet to come upon us" he would have to win great closeness of attention from his readers. This he sought to do by offending them. The first column certainly succeeds in doing this; the 1956 reader who might have read Mailer's comment eight years before, "I think it much better when people who read your book don't know anything about you, even what you look like; I have refused to let *Life* photograph me," * was now being told that he was probably frustrated in his ambitions and undernourished in his pleasures and shared a general animus toward Mailer as someone more talented than himself.

Part of this abrasiveness might follow from Mailer's general desire to alert his readers, part of it is probably an attempt to air accumulated rage, and part of it is certainly his desire to test his courage; we are again reminded of McLeod's comment that action gives ballast to theory. And the commitment to shock readers into wakefulness is not a temporary allegiance. Although Mailer's later writing will seldom so abound in insult, strains of the shrill, hectoring tone of the *Voice* columns turn up through 1962 or 1963. But for the origins of this commitment, we might again look back to the rewriting of *The Deer Park,* during which Mailer discovered how "the most powerful

* Correspondingly, the writer who railed in the late fifties at the old-maid conservatism of the literary establishment and so wanted to be the first novelist of his generation to produce two quality best-sellers said in 1948 that when he first heard that *The Naked and the Dead* had reached the top of the best-seller list, "I felt kind of blue the rest of the day . . . a lot of people I'd like to like the book are going to be set against it because it's a best-seller" (Levita, *Star* interview, p. 3).

leverage in fiction comes from point of view." If, in early 1956, Mailer was an actor seeking a role, he was also seeking an accompanying voice—a new, tonal point of view to sharpen, strengthen, and advertise his brave new role. Both in style and in content, many of Mailer's actions and writings during this period support John Aldridge's claim that "Mailer's sense of himself may very well depend on his ability to provoke and withstand attack . . . Mailer has made his private paranoid revision of Descartes: I offend; therefore, I am."

Mailer himself is undecided about whether these columns were beneficial to his personal and artistic growth. At one point in *Advertisements* he claims that "the column served as therapy . . . eliminating some of the sludge of the past." On the next page he writes, "If I do not finish the novel I have now in my mind it is likely that the better part was lost in that drug-gutting of my capacities which has become for me the real, if muted, theme of these columns for *The Village Voice.*" One's judgment about whether the columns contributed to his growth or decline as an artist is largely dependent upon one's evaluation of his later work, for the columns contain in some form most of the themes and attitudes that were to shape his writing for the next decade. The embattled god whose struggle we must continue on earth; the impending sexual revolution; the possibilities of creative nihilism or hipsterism but the horror of collective violence; the limitations of psychiatry and of the welfare state; the mystery of growth; the need to vote for a personality instead of an idea; man's nature and dignity following from his acting, living, loving, and destroying himself "seeking to penetrate the mystery of existence"; Mailer's aggressiveness, megalomania, anarchism and stylistic experimentation—they are all in some way asserted in the *Voice* columns. The presentation of the ideas is usually ill written and fragmentary, and most of them await the expansion, clarification, and synthesis they will receive in "The White Negro." This essay is the trunk of Mailer's existentialism from which later, even more exotic shoots will sprout, and we would do well to consider it in the larger context of Mailer's existential thought. But we might round off one part of the evolution of Mailer's fiction by reaching around "The White Negro" and examining one of the first two fictional pieces that lie on the other side of the essay—the segment of the projected novel, which Mailer still intends to write, called "The Time of Her Time."

The segment is much more crisply written than *The Deer Park,* though traces of the sententiousness remain; in reading both works, there were moments when I felt as if I were locked in a closet with Mailer while he shouted his ideas in my ear. Still, the greater part of "Time" crackles with energies that Mailer feels were given him through his hip insights. In fact, the segment dramatizes the primal hip conflict limned in "The White Negro." Two combative spirits struggle with each other, and the one with the preponderance of personal power emerges with even more power. Two sexual adventurers, an older and tougher Sergius O'Shaugnessy (who is willing to insult, strike, and forceably sodomize if he has to) and an aggressive nineteen-year-old girl literally collide as he tries to give her the physical pleasure which she has denied herself. The dominated hipster formula for growth is followed; one risks a great deal in a conflict, for if Sergius cannot give the girl an orgasm, he will sink closer to death. Success will enlarge the present and even balm the future years when he is beat (when he is no longer capable of restoring himself through sexual struggle) "because I had been her psychic bridegroom . . . had led her down the walk of her real wedding night. Since she did not like me, what a feat to pull it off."

Their first sexual combat is a draw; he performs well but she manages to keep her will intact. Their second meeting is a lull, winding "itself up with nothing better in view than the memory of the first night." It is only while waiting for her on the third night that Sergius really commits himself to his sexual project (the quotation from the preceding paragraph appears at this point). The climactic rematch is almost anticlimactic, for he suffers a premature ejaculation and implies that without her sympathy it would take him "weeks to unwind, and then years, and maybe never to overcome the knowledge that I had failed completely at a moment when I wanted very much to win." But she is sympathetic; he recovers and re-creates himself as a victor, going through a complicated series of physical and psychological maneuvers to give her, as he puts it, something that she can use. With a satisfied body but defeated will, her only retaliation is to accuse Sergius of latent homosexuality and flee before her conqueror, in his hipster's triumph, can tell her that she was a hero fit for him. Having then followed Mailer's progress from his relatively pessimistic socialist essays to the fiction of hard-won exultation, we might pause before we dip more deeply into Mailer's conqueror's philosophy.

3
The Formulation Expanded: Mailer's Existentialism

AT the beginning of *The Presidential Papers,* Mailer listed some—forty—of the topics discussed in the work, and quite a list it is, ranging from such relatively practical matters as totalitarianism, capital punishment, architecture, and the CIA to cannibalism, being and soul, digestion and the unconscious, the nature of dread, witchcraft, and the dialectic of God and the Devil. In the six or seven years preceding and the ten years following the publication of the collection, Mailer was so busy creating a web of interrelationships between apparently disparate entities that most of the forty topics relate in some direct way to each other, and all can be, and usually are, subsumed under the dialectic of God and the Devil. For since 1958 Mailer has, through his writings, interviews, and public appearances, been quite consistently committed to a belief in an existential God of goodness, courage, and expansion Who is locked in conflict with an equally powerful Devil of evil, cowardice, and surrender. The nature of this God's existence and of Mailer's continuing relationship to Him is so problematic that we would do well to postpone considering both for some pages, but it might be said here that this belief can be seen as a quite reasonable extension of the single ontological premise from which all of Mailer's post-1955 thought eventually follows. For as bizarre as it might sound, Mailer is an ontologist of sorts. Since he evades most of the vocabulary, problems, categorizations, and thoroughness which we normally associate with that branch of metaphysics, most serious students of philosophy would probably call him the illiterate half-brother of an ontologist. Yet he is a spinner of hundreds of ideas, most of which have ethical implications and all of which can be traced to the hypothesis that all being is in a Heraclitean flux—either expanding or contracting, growing into something better or deteriorating into something worse. (What is not Heraclitean is the distinction between being and matter—but more of that later.) Or, to reach back into

82

The Deer Park, there is that irrevocable law, cruel but just, which demands that all organisms grow or pay for remaining the same. When I refer to Mailer's ontological premise, it is this that I have in mind.

Phrases like *Heraclitean flux* and *ontological premise* might be pretentious, but they suggest the sense of self that caused Mailer to announce in *Advertisements* that he had a fair chance of becoming the first philosopher of hip and, indeed, implied that he might be the one to create the "neo-Marxist calculus aimed at comprehending every circuit and process of society from ukase to kiss as the communications of human energy." And although as the sixties proceeded and Mailer toned down hip's celebration of violence—indeed replaced "hip" with "existentialism," a more neutral term and one less immediately associated with himself—he presumed to bring Heidegger and Sartre up to spiritual date and wrote Platonic dialogues filled with words like *being, Being, soul,* and *spirit.* If by late 1967 he had eased his grandiose claims enough to suggest that he was at best "a good working amateur philosopher," he was only a few months later eager to have a graduate student—me—tell him why he was a systematic ontologist. In the preface to *Existential Errands* (1972) he wrote, as part of his attempt to justify the publication of his thinnest collection yet, a philosophical self-estimate which was only partially revisionary; the pieces were "written in a general state of recognition that if one had a philosophy it was being put together in many pieces."

On the one hand, many of his philosophical ambitions remind us of the appraisal of one of the actresses in his third movie, *Maidstone:* "His ego's as big as his ass." On the other, they suggest that although Mailer (so proud of his imaginative leaps) has never been a systematic thinker, he has quite consciously, since 1955, been following the lead that William Blake offers in "Jerusalem": "I must Create a System or be enslav'd by another Man's." Would that it were one man; here is a 1960 list of the American "regulators" who try to enslave our imaginations and desire for adventure and make us accept their conceptions of the world and of ourselves: "politicians, medicos, policemen, professors, priests, rabbis, ministers, *ideologues,* psychoanalysts, builders, executives and endless communicators." Each tries to impose his own "meaning" for, let us say, pouring someone a drink; the politician might argue that we have to grease each other's gears, the medico might recognize the social efficacy but lament the effect on the liver, the policeman might warn about getting drunk in public. But, to choose an example of Mailer's directly invoking his ontological assumption, he can say:

> If we pick up a bottle while listening to some jazz and we feel each of our five finger tips in relation to the bottle, the bottle begins to have a kind of form for us and we begin to feel each of our finger tips is receiving a different thing from the shape and the structure of the glass, and we then begin to think that maybe the very structure of this glass could conceivably contain some kind of hell within its constitution, some inorganic frozen state of imprisoned being [thus, actually a state of nonbeing] less being than us. I think it's a more interesting notion than just picking up a bottle and pouring out some whisky.

This conjecture appeared in that important 1958 interview in which Mailer first offered for print his notion of the aggressively embattled God, which he collected the following year in *Advertisements*. Toward the end of that book, Mailer wrote that he had started high on the mountain of literary acclaim and popularity and gone "down sharp while others were passing me." In the decade after this was printed, he published nearly three thousand pages, most of which were in eight new books, and as the sixties ended he was six months and two-thirds of the way into *Of A Fire On the Moon*—nine months to write a work four-fifths as long as *The Naked and the Dead.* Although the best of the works written during this climb back up the mountain never quite realized the tremendous promise of the twenty-four-year-old who completed *The Naked and the Dead,* their collective achievement made a back-of-the-paperback blurb like "the hottest writer in American letters" a very reasonable reflection of the response of a great many intelligent readers. During this decade, his sense that he was, or soon would be, a formidable philosophical force ebbed, as did the aggressive attempts to assert systematically the workings of human energy. This ebbing is particularly evident in the last book published in the sixties, *Miami and the Siege of Chicago* (1968). And although *The Armies of the Night,* published in the same year, is structured around two benign transformations—the individual one of Norman Mailer and the collective one of the American middle class—being, nonbeing, and the struggle between God and the Devil are almost completely left out. So baggy and expansive is the system that everything in both books can still be related to the ontological premise, but a great many contexts are badly distorted if we try to boil every passage down to his theories of nonbeing or expanding and contracting being. (This is not at all the case in

Deaths for the Ladies, The Presidential Papers, An American Dream, or *Cannibals and Christians;* the ontological urge has only half waned in the last book published before *Armies—Why are We in Vietnam?*) Since Mailer is true to his system in his fashion, the supernatural and the ontological very much turn up in *Of A Fire on the Moon* (1970) and *The Prisoner of Sex* (1971), but even here we usually find them encased in the sharp, empirical appeals of a good amateur philosopher rather than the somewhat abstract, ponderous terminologies of a man taking his formal philosophical capacities much too seriously.

But it is time to assert. The search for system encouraged Mailer to develop his own cutting edge into realities both within and without, to try to see, say, a whisky bottle as creatively as Cézanne saw those wine bottles of his great still lifes. It also further freed his always considerable ambitions and energies, though this is a chicken-egg problem: Did the search for system contribute to the great surge of energy of the sixties—three movies, more than ten pieces, and a mayoralty campaign in addition to the eight books—or were the philosophical assumptions a kind of spinoff from the raw energy? I would suggest that a spiraling interaction was the case—the greater the excitement with the possibilities of the "discoveries," the more sense of what he could do in fiction and nonfiction, the more the desire to trust the authority of those transforming senses, and so on. Certainly the system made it possible for him to once again get a novel written quickly—indeed provided the framework and almost all of the insights for *An American Dream*—and argues for a consistent view of the world, thereby defending Mailer against those critics who have called him modish, fickle, and opportunistic. Paradoxically, for a system, it demanded great control of the nuances of mood and situation and so drove Mailer to considerable stylistic experiment.

Of course, the best of systems is a mixed blessing. In his admirable introduction to his yet more admirable book *City of Words,* Tony Tanner wrote:

> But there is another side to this self-preserving creation of one's own "system," and we can go to another writer [than Blake] from the first part of the Romantic movement for a concise formulation of it. Thus Coleridge: "We have imprisoned our own conceptions by the lines that we have drawn in order to exclude the conceptions of others." That which *de*fines you at the same time *con*fines you. It is possible to be imprisoned in a system of your own choosing as well as in a system of another's imposing.

Since Mailer's system is at every one of its many turns designed to offer interesting possibilities for fiction and for life,* it is paradoxical that a writer could be imprisoned within the sharply defined possibilities that he has created (it is of course always easy for anyone to be paralyzed by the verbal and experiential labyrinth of possibilities before him). But imprisonment often seems to be the case with Mailer. Simply put, the system is at any stage of its development a collection of hopefully compelling alternatives which—again, hopefully—make possible heroic actions in life, heroic confrontations in fiction, and, most of all, a way for Mailer to get dramatic hold of any aspect of what so often seems to be the ambiguous, shapeless mass of American society. Anopopei provided the kind of believable arena that made telling conflict possible, and, by his existential God, Mailer will convince us that our smallest actions are victories or defeats, that absurd SuperAmerica is a vast arena of meaningful conflicts. Two months before he began writing *An American Dream* he said:

> . . . it's no little matter to be a writer. There's that Godawful Time Magazine world out there and one can make raids on it. There are palaces, and prisons to attack. . . . Sometimes I feel as if there's a vast guerilla war going on for the mind of man, communist against communist, capitalist against capitalist, artist against artist. And the stakes are huge. Will we spoil the best secrets of life or will we help to free a new kind of man? It's intoxicating to think of that. There's something rich waiting if one of us is brave enough and good enough to get there.

An American Dream is his most extended attempt to reveal some of those secrets which might free a new kind of man, but all of his writing could to varying degrees be regarded this way. Yet as well

---

* One cannot overemphasize the fictional benefits which Mailer hoped to reap through the system. This kind of opportunism seems to me to be totally justified if the consequent fiction is good enough; further, his fictional ambitions are usually blended with a very genuine social concern. The quotation above offers one example of this; or, immediately before he created his metaphysical whisky bottle he said that Hip

> opens the possibility that the novel, along with many other art forms, may be growing into something larger rather than something smaller, and the sickness of our times for me has been just this damn thing that everything has been getting smaller and smaller and less and less important, that the romantic spirit has dried up, that there is almost no shame today like the terror before the romantic. We're all getting so mean and small and petty and ridiculous, and we all live under the threat of extermination. [*Advertisements*, p. 382.]

written as the appeals might be, some of them seem to be less material for interesting conjectures, and still less for stirring exhortations, than for our response to the outlandish. One example of an unsuccessful attempt to dramatize our collective malaise (which I choose of many possible examples because we will look at it more closely at the beginning of the next chapter) is his telling us that so many New Yorkers responded with apathy to the threat of imminent extermination during the October, 1962, Cuban missile crisis because they knew at some level of themselves that they had so betrayed God in His struggle that they wanted the world blown up so that His judgment would cease. The style is soaring yet edgy, but we must be party-line, true-believer Manicheans to treat the conjecture with any seriousness, let alone experience the shock of eschatological recognition; it's nice to be told that we are that interesting, but it does seem a bit too silly.

Then there are the appropriations of the system for the fiction. The first truly Manichean efforts, "Advertisements for Myself on the Way Out" and "Truth and Being; Nothing and Time," are impossibly cloying and turgid, and we shall see a good many examples in *An American Dream* of Mailer's scorning stylistic and psychological subtlety for the easy formulations he can pull out of the system like premade strips of Linotype. The economic demands of his life—six children, four wives, three movies, a mayoralty campaign increasingly financed out of his own pocket, a high life style—have often encouraged Mailer to make the quick economic kill, and the system was always handy if any dramatic lacunae needed filling in. Consequently, if the system could encourage Mailer to think of himself as an agent of the Lord raiding upon the Devilish mass media, these forays seem more and more to show him playing the role of a hugely gifted public entertainer than an artist creating those visions of life which might restore us, however temporarily, to our better selves. This is not to say that Mailer has ever been fully whorish, for he has always written the best that he had in him at the time. It is just that he often refused to wait for a time when better writing came. Then even this writing was collected; as one reviewer put it, *Existential Errands* contains all of Mailer's recent prose save his checks. Of course it might be argued that this is the price one pays for being an intellectual answering service, that it is because Mailer so tried to dramatize possibility, to rank ontologically whatever seemed to be erupting at the present moment, that the machine mistakenly seemed to be an opportunistic Rube Goldberg contraption cranked up with pieces of Sartre, Kierkegaard, Marx, boxing matches, plastic, the

New Left, Apollo 11, Women's Lib, ecology, and so on and on.

With all of this said, Mailer's conception of himself as the last great romantic is still more stirring than comical, and his efforts are founded more on a largely honorable morality than on opportunism. Certainly it is fascinating to follow the course of his attempts to shore up with his ontological fragments the ruins of romanticism and to pick and choose among the often eloquent welter of *Advertisements, Presidential Papers,* and *Cannibals and Christians* in an effort to arrange some of the fragments into a coherent relationship. One way or another, it is always interesting to see a good mind genuinely excited by the objects of its contemplation, and since Mailer so often eloquently appeals to very deep longings and frustrations, his own excitement is particularly contagious. Some of the appeals are finally dangerous ones, in which he too much minimizes the amorality of the irrational, but, for convenience, I withhold comment on this until the next chapter. I also refrain from trying to place him within the romantic tradition even though to read him is, again and again, to come across positions that were held by Coleridge, Blake, Emerson, Whitman, Carlyle, and others. This is not to say that Mailer was directly influenced by the nineteenth-century romantics. He has been fond of dropping the names of existential philosophers; Blake is the only romantic that he has so far mentioned in print, and this was not until the Ontological Decade was almost over. He did not need to read the romantics to arrive at some similar positions; archetypes exist, and throughout the Ontological Decade Mailer often said things like "our feelings are a better guide to what goes on in these procreative matters than scientists" as if he were the discoverer of an idea which had never been voiced before. But he did draw directly from twentieth-century thinkers like Sartre and Wilhelm Reich, and I found it convenient to do the same.

The system is a fiction, but it is often an eloquent and sometimes a profound fiction; so are all visions of life fictions, but this carries us too far afield. We might merely say that it is so central to his work of the past fifteen years—of the past twenty-five, since it is simultaneously an immense revision and addition to *The Naked and the Dead*—that if we have any respect for Mailer's achievement we would do well to treat seriously what he felt was his peculiarly American existentialism for as long as we can, even to the point of contrasting it with the continental existentialism of heavyweights like Sartre and Heidegger. And even if we discard the rage for system, as Mailer finally did, there might still remain parts that we can treat seriously whenever we think of them or for which we can pay the highest tribute to Mailer by being guided by them.

II

Although the hipster hero celebrated in the 1957 essay "The White Negro" is not quite as dated as Mailer's 1958 claim that "there's a great danger that the nihilism of hip will destroy civilization," this vintage of the existential hero is nonetheless by now a very improbable figure. One wonders if ten, five, or any of them ever really existed. We would still do well to look at "The White Negro" closely. The extraordinarily well-written essay is of considerable interest in itself, and, whether by addition, revision, or rejection, the larger part of Mailer's later work follows from this first sustained attempt to formulate his existential positions. If "existentialism is based upon the supposition that to exist is to face up to the conditions of life which generate . . . anxieties about our very being . . . to exist is to realize man can be nothing," then the essay's opening considerations of the causes of our intimations of absurdity are stunning yet orthodox:

> Probably, we will never be able to determine the psychic havoc of the concentration camps and the atom bomb upon the unconscious mind of almost everyone alive in these years. For the first time in civilized history, perhaps for the first time in all of history, we have been forced to live with the suppressed knowledge that the smallest facets of our personality or the most minor projection of our ideas, or indeed the absence of ideas and the absence of personality could mean equally well that we might still be doomed to die as a cipher in some vast statistical operation in which our teeth would be counted, and our hair would be saved, but our death itself would be unknown, unhonored, and unremarked, a death which could not follow with dignity as a possible consequence to serious actions we had chosen, but rather a death by *deus ex machina* in a gas chamber or a radioactive city; and so . . . in the middle of an economic civilization founded upon the confidence that time could indeed be subjected to our will, our psyche was subjected to the intolerable anxiety that death being causeless, life was causeless as well, and time deprived of cause and effect had come to a stop.

Confronted with this collapse of nerve forced upon all of us by the lessons of the last few decades, that newly arisen, practical philosopher from the underside of society—the hipster—emotionally apprehends that

> if our collective condition is to live with instant death by atomic war, relatively quick death by the State as *l'univers concentrationnaire*, or

with a slow death by conformity with every creative and rebellious instinct stifled . . . if the fate of twentieth-century man is to live with death from adolescence to premature senescence, why then the only life-giving answer is to accept the terms of death, to live with death as immediate danger, to divorce oneself from society, to exist without roots, to set out on that uncharted journey into the rebellious imperatives of the self.

Embracing the fact that a more real life begins only on the far side of the acceptance of death,* the hipster insists that the way to this life is through growth; the animus to become more than one was, to accumulate more energy and perception, provides the only spring-board to value in an otherwise absurd world. He, of all men, must accept the possibility of death, for to grow he must let himself be driven by those imperatives, and the most rebellious one—the need for violent adventure—is dangerous. The intuitive hipster thus stands in extreme contrast to the more reflective conformist who has been numbed as much by the perception of his own murderous desires as by the imminence of death. The hipster, in Mailer's fond view, is instead a philosophical psychopath, totally committed to the gratification of his own desires and totally indifferent to the societal mores which forbid these gratifications. Such characteristics are common to all psychopaths, but Mailer argued that the hipster differs from the conventional psychopath—if such a term may be used—in his "narcissistic detachment of the philosopher, that absorption in the recessive nuances of one's own motive which is so alien to the unreasoning drive of the psychopath." He seemed also to argue that the hipster's superior capacity for intellectual and emotional detachment enables him to grow more than his unreflective counterpart. I say "seemed" because Mailer was finally unclear about the ways in which the hipster differs from the conventional psychopath and the possibilities of either one actually changing for the better.

Mailer never completely surrenders any of his idea complexes. They simply turn up late in a different context, in combination with other ideas. For example, in the opening paragraph of "The White

---

* The idea is a familiar one among existential thinkers. To place Mailer in heavier company, Karl Jaspers has said that "to philosophize is to learn how to die" (*The Way to Wisdom,* tr. by Ralph Manheim [New Haven: Yale University Press, 1951], p. 53), and Heidegger has urged us to rush toward death, to make our lives more authentic than the abstracted, second-hand ones of the mass of men by accepting the individuality of our deaths and basing the authenticity of our individuality upon the acceptance. The latter even defines man's being as *Sein-Zum-Tode* (being towards death).

Negro," Mailer implicitly argues that the meaning of Marxism has collapsed before the onslaught of the absurd. If it is no longer possible for one to believe that human happiness can be achieved by "mastering the links of social cause and effect," then we can no longer hope to reveal the historical importance of a period by discerning how much progress was made toward eliminating economic contradictions. Yet the historicity of Marxism, the emphasis placed upon historical process and the way that time accelerates or decelerates—to the Marxist inasmuch as it carries us toward the economic resolution—turns up later in "The White Negro" linked to a theory of individual possibility which is founded upon the workings of the nervous system. Grounding dynamic growth-time and deadening clock-time in biological and historical processes, the 1957 Mailer claims that we would be better able to realize ourselves in the horrific society in which we live if we did not possess historically antiquated nervous systems. They are antiquated because they were formed in our infancy and thus carry in the style of their circuits

> the very contradictions of our parents and our early milieu. Therefore we are obliged, most of us, to meet the tempo of the present and the future with reflexes and rhythms which come from the past. It is not only the "dead weight of the institutions of the past" but indeed the inefficient and often antiquated nervous circuits of the past which strangle our potentiality for responding to new possibilities which might be exciting for our individual growth.
>
> Through most of modern history, "sublimation" was possible: at the expense of expressing only a small portion of oneself, that small portion could be expressed intensely. But sublimation depends on a reasonable tempo to history. If the collective life of a generation has moved too quickly, the "past" by which particular men and women of that generation may function is not, let us say, thirty years old, but relatively a hundred or two hundred years old. And so the nervous system is overstressed beyond the possibility of such compromises as sublimation, especially since the stable middle-class values so prerequisite to sublimation have been virtually destroyed in our time, at least as nourishing values free of confusion or doubt. In such a crisis of accelerated historical tempo and deteriorated values, neurosis tends to be replaced by psychopathy, and the success of psychoanalysis (which even ten years ago gave promise of becoming a direct major force) diminishes because of its inbuilt and characteristic incapacity to handle patients more complex, more experienced, or more adventurous than the analyst himself.

Perhaps the most remarkable stance in "The White Negro" is not Mailer's argument that the hipster might break open the concrete surface of Eisenhower America or even the partial defense of "two strong eighteen-year-old hoodlums . . . beating in the brains of a candy-store keeper" by a man who had sympathetically characterized Joey Goldstein. Rather, it might be the possibility that the attempt "to divorce oneself from society" can actually be achieved. So much of Mailer has always believed that any individual alone on a desert island would bring with him the residue of all that family and society at large have inflicted upon him that he never asserted that the hipster could totally divorce himself. Rather, the hipster tries to become as freed from social imperatives as Marion Faye; how he tries is considered, and the possibility of success is forgotten or quietly buried.

Mailer has always been such a complicated man that one cannot bluntly assert that he celebrated the hipster because he unequivocally hoped to become one himself. Certainly the author, who could not explicitly endorse the hipster solution, was much less rebellious than the hero of the essay. And Mailer's need to turn out a first-rate piece of work was related to, but not identical with, the implicit celebration of rebellion in the essay. Rather, it would seem that most of him hoped (among other things) to so rebuild his own nervous circuits that he could fend off the threats and rewards of society much more easily than he had. Since he continued to want so many of these rewards, *Advertisements for Myself* is rebellious in a curiously opportunistic way, but what is more to our concern here is Mailer's obvious attempt to project the hipster as a kind of personal absolute who might exert a pull upon his own psyche to bend it toward the rebellious, the antisocial, the primitive, the creative.

More and more the essay seems to be a highly creative fiction— again, did any of Mailer's hipsters exist? Thus the claim for the diminishing success of psychoanalysis seems to be bluff as does (judging from what psychiatrists have told me—but of course they are suspect!) the replacement of neurosis with psychopathy. "Not a phony but a Faust," Hearn said. The claims might be "stretchers," but the fascination with force, whether as power in social spheres or energy in more individual ones, has been there throughout. Mailer wrote in *Of a Fire on the Moon:*

> If there is a crossing in the intellectual cosmos where philosophical notions of God, man, and the machine can come together it is probably to be found in the conceptual swamps which surround every notion of energy. The greatest mystery in the unremitting mysteries of physics must be the nature of energy itself—is it the currency of

the universe or merely the agent of creation? The basic stuff of life or merely the fuel of life? the guard of the heavens, or the heart and blood of time? The mightiest gates of the metaphysician hinge on the incomprehensibility yet human intimacy of that ability to perform work and initiate movement which rides through the activities of men and machines, and powers and cycles of nature.

These are gracefully posed questions; the 1957 ideologue, hammering out the foundations of his system, tries (as Mailer might say in one of his early-sixties poems) to drive to the short hairs: Just how does energy work, how might more of it be freed? Look to the absolute, to the philosophical psychopath for the way out of the emotional impasse in which Mailer claims we all find ourselves and out of which no psychiatrist can help us. With fanatic singleness of purpose, the hipster sets about making a new nervous system for himself. But how does it work? A year earlier, in one of his *Voice* columns, Mailer wrote that growth was finally a greater mystery than death. Here is an attempt to solve the mystery, to explain how sex might be time and time might be the connection of new circuits:

> The psychopath is notoriously difficult to analyze because the fundamental decision of his nature is to try to live the infantile fantasy, and in this decision (given the dreary alternative of psychoanalysis) there may be a certain instinctive wisdom. For there is a dialectic to changing one's nature, the dialectic which underlies all psychoanalytic method: it is the knowledge that if one is to change one's habits, one must go back to the source of their creation, and so the psychopath exploring backward along the road of the homosexual, the orgiast, the drug-addict, the rapist, the robber and the murderer seeks to find those violent parallels to the violent and often hopeless contradictions he knew as an infant and as a child. For if he has the courage to meet the parallel situation at the moment when he is ready, then he has a chance to act as he has never acted before, and in satisfying the frustration—if he can succeed—he may then pass by symbolic substitute through the locks of incest. In thus giving expression to the buried infant in himself, he can lessen the tension of those infantile desires and so free himself to remake a bit of his nervous system. Like the neurotic he is looking for the opportunity to grow up a second time, but the psychopath knows instinctively that to express a forbidden impulse actively is far more beneficial to him than merely to confess the desire in the safety of a doctor's room. The psychopath is ordinately ambitious, too ambitious ever to trade his warped brilliant conception of his possible victories in life for the grim if peaceful attrition of the analyst's couch. So his associational journey into the past is lived out in the theatre of the present, and he exists for those charged situations where his senses are so alive that he can

be aware actively (as the analysand is aware passively) of what his habits are, and how he can change them. *The strength of the psychopath is that he knows (where most of us can only guess) what is good for him and what is bad for him at exactly those instants when an old crippling habit has become so attacked by experience that the potentiality exists to change it,* to replace a negative and empty fear with an outward action, even if—and here I obey the logic of the extreme psychopath—even if the fear is of himself, and the action is to murder. [Italics mine.]

One of the most interesting struggles that runs through Mailer's career is his attempt to ground the intuitive in the factual, the mystical in the phenomenal, the psychic in the biological and the apocalyptic in the historical. If "incompatibles have come to bed" in hip thought, not the least incompatible of these matings is the explanation of the magical, expanded moments during which a man can change and become better than the society he lives in, in terms of the Freudian assumption that the Oedipus complex is finally the source of human neurosis—with the psychopath undergoing a far more radical cure than any the sternly moral Freud suggested. Mailer did not follow through and offer us the details of the marriage, but we can easily fill them in for ourselves. Presumably, the successful sexual act symbolically represents the possession of the mother, and the successful violent act works as a substitute for the killing of the father figure who stands in the way of incestuous gratification. Most of us have absorbed the father figure—who, of course, eventually extends to include the edicts of society—by identifying with him and thus creating the superego. Precisely because he has never made the identification, because he has no superego, the extreme psychopath does not have to overcome guilt as he nerves himself to perform his violent act. With the emphasis placed on raw animal courage, we are once more back to Croft, fighting his fear of the unknown as he tries to scale Anaka. (We also look ahead to the protagonists of *An American Dream* and *Why Are We in Vietnam?* as they nerve themselves to climb their respective Anakas. Although the celebration of sex and violence decreased considerably as Mailer's career progressed, the great concern with the courage of his characters and of himself continued unabated.)

Mailer added to the primordial linkage between hatred and love. The infant hates the father who blocks the path toward total gratification, but the psychopath also hates himself; he

murders—if he has the courage—out of the necessity to purge his violence, for if he cannot empty his hatred then he cannot love, his

being is frozen with implacable self-hatred for his cowardice. . . .
. . . At bottom, the drama of the psychopath is that he seeks love.
Not love as the search for a mate, but love as the search for an orgasm more apocalyptic than the one which preceded it. Orgasm is his
therapy—he knows at the seed of his being that good orgasm opens
his possibilities and bad orgasm imprisons him.

New energy is the goal, the possibility which both the hipster and
the unreflective psychopath seek. (The former also seeks perceptions
which will give him further energy and which seems to distinguish
him from the latter, though Mailer was not clear on this issue.) But
how does this relate to the symbolic incest and orgasm? Does the
value of a particular orgasm lie in its ability to serve as a surrogate
for the incest so that the mixture of frustrated desire and fear which
is blocking the energy is eliminated? Or does the symbolic passage
through the locks of incest enable the orgasm which—following Wilhelm Reich's theory—sets free the dammed-up energy?

Mailer tacitly chose the Reichian alternative; in fact, he has been
so influenced by his reading of that much maligned and very impressive thinker that we would do well to pause here to consider Reich's
explanations of the workings and nature of that sweet the hipster
seeks: energy. For Reich, energy is a bioelectric force in man. Its
basic unit is the orgone, eventually derived from the sun and present
in every organic cell and in some organic materials—a concept
which surely had a good deal to do with the formation of Mailer's
later theory of man's containing many "beings," some languishing,
some perishing.* This energy seeks release in orgasm, and when that
release is blocked, the energy is then fixated upon infantile conflicts.
Consequently, the psychoneurosis of the Oedipus conflict is now
charged with the misdirected energy. Thus strengthened, the neurosis
further inhibits sexual release, damming up still more energy as the
victim is plunged into greater anxiety and the emergence of different
physical maladies. For when energy is not released through the workings of what Reich calls the genital-sensory system, it is transformed
into aggression and moves to the cardiac sytem, where the aggression is felt as anxiety. Aggression is thus explained not in Mailer's
terms as anger towards one's parents or toward one's own cowardice,
but more basically as the first new form that energy takes when it
cannot find sexual relief.

* In *Of a Fire on the Moon,* Mailer grounded the hexes, intuitions, and
whammies which abound in his work of the sixties in the claim that we emit
electrically charged psychic forces. Could this also have been derived from
Reich?

Since Mailer by and large denies psychotherapy any real efficacy,* he prescribed in "The White Negro" the savage cure of acting out the anger as totally as possible. Reich's therapy has much more benign social consequences. Because of our fear of the dangers which the release of the aggression will bring upon us, we encase it in character armor. This armor is both physical and psychic in nature— physical in that it manifests itself as rigidities in different parts of the body as a defense against freeing that part in the orgasm which we have been taught is wicked, and psychic because it is caused by the erroneous ideas about sexuality given to us by repressive parents and society at large. Through physical and psychic therapy, the physician gradually cracks the armor, freeing the anger to express itself in socially harmless ways. (Hence Henderson's bellowing exercises in Bellow's *Henderson the Rain King*.) As the anger is dissipated, he encourages the patient's sexual activities, for orgasm is the cure for both the anger and Oedipus complex. With the body finally fulfilling its *natural* function of discharging accumulated energy, there will be neither the crippling anger (and consequent anxiety) which resulted from the lack of release nor the Oedipus complex, which drew its strength from the same source.

If Mailer disagreed with some of Reich's theories, he accepted enough to argue that orgasm sets free the dammed-up energy. For the hipster feels that

* The paragraph quoted on page 91 continues:

In practice, psychoanalysis has by now become all too often no more than a psychic blood-letting. The patient is not so much changed as aged, and the infantile fantasies which he is encouraged to express are condemned to exhaust themselves against the analyst's nonresponsive reactions. The result for all too many patients is a diminution, a "tranquilizing" of their most interesting qualities and vices. The patient is indeed not so much altered as worn out—less bad, less good, less bright, less willful, less destructive, less creative. He is thus able to conform to that contradictory and unbearable society which first created his neurosis. He can conform to what he loathes because he no longer has the passion to feel loathing so intensely. [*Advertisements*, p. 346.]

This is the first attack upon the technique of psychoanalysis. All of the earlier and most of the later criticisms are *ad hominem* thrusts at the cowardly, conformist, middle-class psychiatrist. Mailer will later write that "life seems to come from a meeting of opposites" (Norman Mailer, *Cannibals and Christians* [New York: The Dial Press, 1966], p. 281 [hereafter cited as *Cannibals*]), and it would follow that if psychoanalytic techniques are indeed as he describes them, there would not be the kind of opposing forces which would enable the emergence of new psychic life.

to be with it is to have grace, is to be closer to the secrets of that inner unconscious life which will nourish you if you can hear it, for you are then nearer to that God which every hipster believes is located in the senses of his body, that trapped, mutilated and nonetheless megalomaniacal God who is It, who is energy, life, sex, force, the Yoga's *prana,* the Reichian's orgone, Lawrence's "blood," Hemingway's "good," the Shavian life-force; "It"; God; not the God of the churches but the unachievable whisper of mystery within the sex, the paradise of limitless energy and perception just beyond the wave of the next orgasm.

(So wide are the differences among the thinkers mentioned in this sentence that a number of readers have misundertood Mailer. His lover's quarrel with Reich should be pursued here, though, and I offer in the notes at the end of the book a long note which treats the problems created by lumping together Lawrence, Shaw, and Hemingway.)

We must remember that Mailer, who said a year before he wrote "The White Negro" that if he were to go to an analyst he would go to a Reichian one, wrote that the orgasm which the hipster sought was "unachievable . . . just beyond the wave of the next orgasm." I have already referred to Mailer's claims that *he* is peculiarly qualified to ferret out the secrets of the self, and there was no chance of his reducing himself to a mere epigone, devoting his energies to restating or amplifying another man's system. But what follows from "natural" is far more important. In reply to the question of whether the orgasm serves as a surrogate for incest, Mailer accepts the Reichian schema enough to believe that the working out of the Oedipus complex is the means towards the end of freeing energy through improved orgasm. But precisely because Mailer also believed that total orgasm is unattainable, Reich's basic sexual theory is—within the vastly smaller world of "The White Negro"—subjected to a reinterpretation as radical as the transformation of Marx's theory of social upheaval by Mao's doctrine of permanent revolution.

It might be argued that the life views of both Reich and the Mailer of "The White Negro" are biological monisms. Reich posits a monism which acts best (or most naturally) in a circular manner— the energy builds up, is released, and the process then repeats itself. Mailer's monism (in its ideal or natural movement) describes a spiral—a man grows by freeing energy, but this energy must be put to the task of freeing still more energy. To make the same point in a way which better suggests its ethical implications, Mailer has liked to call himself a dialectician for some time, and, in fact, he has always been one. To the hipster (and Mailer), "incompatibles have come to bed, the inner life and the violent life, the orgy and the dream of love, the desire to murder and the desire to create, a dialectical conception of existence with a lust for power, a dark, romantic, and yet undeniably dynamic view of existence for it sees every man and woman as moving individually through each moment of life forward into growth or backward into death." Reich also sees each man and woman as growing toward the ability of having orgasm or dying away from the possibility. But the total orgasm is not only achievable, it is natural. The man or woman who cannot have it is unnatural. In terms of the circular process, the orgasm is the point at which the circle is closed. One is left wholly satisfied and ideally retraces the same course of accumulating energy and discharging it as economically as possible.

For Mailer one's nature is best expressed in the quest for the unattainable. It is worth repeating that we are describing the difference between an essentialist who can finally ground the value of a man's activities and thought in his ability to realize a fixed biological nature and a romantic existentialist who claims that man's nature is precisely to create new natures. The ethical problems of Mailer's 1957 position can be seen if we perceive that what makes his dialectic of growth so different from Plato's, Hegel's, or Marx's—all obvious differences admitted—is its endlessness. Not endlessness in time, for that comes with a particular individual's death, but in terms of a fixed goal which reached down to provide meaning and value to earlier, lower stages of the dialectic. There is in all four dialectics an emphasis on transcendent movement as there is not in Reich's. The movement in all but Mailer's is toward a conclusion—a realm of ideas, or the Prussian state, or the classless society—all of which argue (as does Reich's biological functionalism) for a basis by which an action, a state of consciousness, a historical stage, and so on, can be objectively evaluated. The fixed end permits an appeal to something outside the individual. In Mailer's endlessly spiraling dialectic, there is only the quest for the infinite ("the universe . . . being glimpsed as a series of ever-extending radii from the center") which is of course an infinite quest ("the hip argument . . . would claim that even in an orgasm which is *the most* there is always the vision of an outer wider wilder orgasm which is even more *with it*").

And the endlessness deepened as Mailer's career proceeded. Whether or not an individual's "time" ends with his death became an open question as the author's commitment to an afterlife began to emerge in 1958. Although the ethical imperatives of energy, God, and afterlife were grounded in his conception of Being, this Being is precisely something which tries always to grow into more Being. The attempts to explain systematically the workings of Being stopped after 1965, but, as I suggested, the fascination with energy continued, and the celebration of the endless romantic quest continued as well. Did not "immediate reflection" tell Mailer that the Apollo 11 moon-shot was a step toward expanding the holdings of God or the Devil out into the universe—toward the other planets, toward the stars? But let us return to that 1957 Vulcan on pot and the considerable heat that he generates as he hammers out his system.

III

As I look back to 1957, I seem to remember the purple cover of Walter Kaufmann's anthology *Existentialism from Dostoevsky to Sartre* sticking out from the back pockets of all my undergraduate friends who thought of themselves as beat. I would wager that Mailer's "White Negro" claim that the hipster's struggle to assert his own freedom enlarges our own possibilities and the system of value proposed in the 1957 essay derive in good part from Sartre's "Existentialism Is a Humanism," a 1946 lecture included in that anthology. In fact, I think that if one of the basement walls of Mailer's existentialism came from Reich, a good part of another was largely composed of rearranged building blocks from one of the lesser philosophical holdings of Sartre's thought of the 1940s. I say "rearranged" because Mailer really seemed to feel that he added something significant to continental existentialism.*

* Nietzsche had of course very comprehensively fused existentialism and biology seventy-five years before "The White Negro" appeared. It is curious that with all the references to Sartre, Kierkegaard, and Heidegger spread through Mailer's work, he never mentions Nietzsche after *The Naked and the Dead*. Once we throw out the God-Devil part there are considerable resemblances between Mailer's existential heroes and Nietzsche's superman, tapping his will to power as he extricates himself from a biologically bankrupt society and rises toward moral horizons which he has created. Since Mailer's aggressively embattled God had not yet appeared in 1957, it could be argued that Mailer created the hipster by applying the physical aspects of Nietzschean nobility to the lumpenproletariat whom Nietzsche so despised. If Mailer stopped reading this most intimidating of thinkers twenty-five years ago, indeed if he stopped with the first seven pages of *Zarathustra* (see p. 17), one suspects it was for the reason Freud gave in his autobiography: "Nietzsche . . . whose guesses and intuitions often agree in the most astonishing way with the laborious findings of psychoanalysis, was for a long time avoided by me on that

Although value or truth is for both thinkers located within and created by the isolated individual, they (value and truth) are not subjective for Mailer in the way that they are for Sartre. As the hipster winds his way outward in the spiral towards greater energy or inward toward failing powers, he is guided by two perceptions which are prior to a particular situation—his knowledge of the need to accumulate energy and his intuition of how this might be achieved —and one which follows it—his insight of whether he has succeeded or failed, "made it" or "goofed." Whether a man has gained or lost energy is a *fact* which could be objectively ascertained if we could describe the exact nature of his cells at the desired moment. Since this kind of knowledge is not attainable, only the individual in touch with his own deepest instincts can conclusively know if his store of energy has been increased or depleted. Because man's nature is to accumulate energy, the value of an action—its "goodness" or "badness"—derives from the energy which the actor has gained or lost. Morality is therefore solipsistic: "Hip abdicates from any conventional moral responsibility because it would argue that the result of our actions are unforeseeable, and so we cannot know . . . whether we have given energy to another, and indeed if we could, there would still be no idea of what ultimately the other would do with it." I use the word *solipsistic* in order to distinguish the morality of the hipster from that of Sartre. Because the latter argues that man's nature is to be free, the value of an act is created only by the fact that an individual freely chose to perform it. Although Mailer also emphasizes the importance of choice, there is another contingency for the creation of value—his natural need to grow. A valuable act, or one that frees new energy, must be seen as the actualization of the a priori potential of gaining greater energy. An act which does not realize this potential is bad. Sartre can only say that an act is bad if the actor sought to deny the freedom which made the act possible. This is, of course, a consequence of the common philosophical habit of positing an act as good if it realizes the particular philosopher's conception of human nature. Although Sartrean man cannot escape his nature (freedom), the attempt to do so can be called bad. Thus,

---

very account; I was less concerned with the question of priority than with keeping my mind unembarrassed" (*The Standard Edition of the Complete Psychological Works of Sigmund Freud*, tr. by James Strachey, et al. [London: The Hogarth Press, 1968], Vol. XX, 60). And if Mailer's ego is "as big as his ass," Freud's was vastly stronger—with, as admirable as Mailer can be, considerable justification.

Sartre is forced to admit in his famous closing comment in *Being and Nothingness* that, as far as his system has taken him, an aware, solitary drunkard is performing activities superior to those of an unsentient ruler of nations. But when Mailer claims that we were brought into this world to become more than we were, he is arguing that a man who has grown unequivocally is more than he was.

Mailer was at this time so convinced that he was or would soon become an original and important existential thinker that I might provide an example to clarify his belief that he had added the force of biological value to the fluidity and sensitivity to nuance of continental existentialism. Let us suppose that X chose to passively endure a beating by Y, who is smaller than himself. Sartre would have to argue that X's act was good. As men always do, he acted in the way he thought best and thus asserted the goodness of this act in this situation. Mailer would say that the act was probably bad because X's power to grow was probably diminished, though only X could know for sure. To this Sartre might reply that Mailer had by this statement created a new value; to respond the way Mailer had was "good." Mailer might then say that Sartre's rejoinder was "bad" because it dissipated his energy in sterile bickering. We might conclude this perhaps maddening discussion of Mailer's solipsistic relativism by turning to the great emphasis he placed and still places on context, a stress which formed the heart of his political existentialism.

Since it so powerfully attacks the traditional philosophical conception of man as *the* rational creature, context is a crucial idea in existential thought. As William Barrett has pointed out, there is no such thing as the pure Cartesian *cogito,* and there never has been. Man always thinks of something, to some purpose, in some particular experiential context:

> This I who thinks—according to Descartes and Kant—is a completely abstract being, who does not exist at any particular time . . . when I think, I am existing, and existence is inescapably historical . . . human consciousness is inexplicable except in terms of a concretely developing Self, which evolves by making its differences explicit and then attempting to unify them in a larger whole.

For Mailer, the truth or reality of a particular context lies in its ability to provide energy to a particular human being at a particular point in his life. For example, Sergius tells us that he was ready for Teppis's party and indeed proved that he was when he picked up Lulu and made love to her. The reality of the party was that it was a favorable context. But had he been flown to the party just as his breakdown began, it would have been a different party, a bad, un-favorable one, for he would not have been able to master the context. He might still have been able to have defied Teppis and run off with Lulu if the party had been given two days before or two days later, but its reality would have been somewhat different since he would have been slightly more or less able to call upon his energies, perceptions, and courage. Of course all of the others at the party would have differed slightly in themselves, and even the reality of an object —say, the swimming pool—would have been altered, since Sergius would have been responding to it slightly differently. Like his conception of morality, Mailer's 1957 theory of reality (which he was soon to enlarge) followed from his hypothesis that man's nature is to grow by accumulating energy:

> What domintes both character and context is the energy available at the moment of intense context.
>
> Character being thus seen as perpetually ambivalent and dynamic enters then into an absolute relativity where there are no truths other than the isolated truths of what each observer feels at each instant of his existence. To take a perhaps unjustified metaphysical extrapola-tion, it is as if the universe which has usually existed conceptually as a Fact (even if the Fact were Berkeley's God) but a Fact which it was the aim of all science and philosophy to reveal, becomes instead a changing reality whose laws are remade at each instant by every-thing living, but most particularly man, man raised to a neo-medieval summit where the truth is not what one has felt yesterday or what one expects to feel tomorrow but rather *truth is no more nor less than what one feels at each instant in the perpetual climax of the present.* [Italics mine.]

Howard M. Harper, Jr., has concluded from this passage that for Mailer "reality is the instantaneous sum of all human attitudes to-ward reality; it is subjective and created by man rather than objective and perceived by man." For Mailer to be consistent (and Harper to be correct) we must perceive that what the individual feels or what the collective response is refers not to a mere opinion or an attitude (as we normally understand that word). Rather, it refers to the pas-sions and perceptions at our deepest, most visceral level—to the to-tality of our inner life. A feeling in the sense of an opinion might be mistaken. We can then say that part of the reality of this individual at this point in time is that his opinions about the state of his feelings are mistaken. In that reality is created by men it is subjective, but only in this way. It is not necessarily true that something is or is not the case because someone thinks it. For example, Eitel originally thought that the primary reality of Elena lay in her possessing abilities that would enable him to grow into the person he had always wanted to be. But as he later ruefully perceived (along with McLeod in *Barbary Shore* and Mailer himself in *Advertisements*), "It's not the sentiments of men which make history, but their actions." And if the meaning of the present lies for Mailer in our collective ability to muster the energies and perceptions which have come to us from the past as we attempt to project ourselves toward the future, then reality is history-at-the-present-moment.

My attempts to follow through some of the implications of the difference between Mailer's conception of human nature and Reich's have carried us a good distance from the question of why Mailer did not accept more of Reich's schema. The latter believed that all psychic ills and most physical and social ones could be cured if our dammed-up sexual energy was released. In Christian essentialism, God has created our nature and its end—gaining heaven. In the biological essentialism of Reich, our benign nature has been (in Mailer's words) trapped and mutilated, but release promises what to most humans would be heaven on earth. Although Mailer has to varying degrees advocated sexual liberation, he no more believes that a society of happy, strifeless individuals can come about through improved sex than he thinks it could through the rational control of the sources of production. And when we recollect Mailer's 1954 comment that socialism sought to bring not happiness but a higher level of suffering, we can remember what a very strange socialist he was.

Norman Podhoretz has observed that as far back as *Naked*, Mailer believed "in the deepest reaches of his being . . . that the world is made up exclusively of stone walls and life consists in a perpetual crashing of the head against them." Reich promised heaven on earth, but as W. H. Auden has observed, purgatory is far more interesting than heaven. Correspondingly, although Mailer believes in the God that he grafts onto his existentialism in the year after "The White Negro," the primary source of this belief is the greatly increased interest He brings to the world around Mailer.

Committed as he is to his dynamic view of a strife-torn world of constantly struggling organisms, Mailer cannot accept the possibility of an orgasm which would bring an end to the turmoil. But his 1957 position about how much the hipster could actually grow was necessarily as unclear as his distinction between the hipster and the psychopath. In his search for orgasm, the psychopath becomes an embodiment of the extreme contradictions of the society which formed his character, and the apocalyptic orgasm often remains as remote as the Holy Grail, for there are clusters and nests and ambushes of violence in his own necessities and in the imperatives and retaliations of the men and women among whom he lives his life, so that even as he drains his hatred in one act or another, so the conditions of his life create it anew in him until the drama of his movements bears a sardonic resemblance to the frog who climbed a few feet in the well only to drop back again.

Mailer seems to be saying that the psychopath—stamped as he is "with the mint of our contradictory popular culture (where sex is sin and yet sex is paradise)"—cannot overcome the hatred and guilt with which he responds to his feeling that sex is evil and thus loses the energy which sex might have freed in him. But with an old Marxist's sense of the possibilities lying within contradictions, Mailer claims that there "has been room already for the development of the antithetical psychopath [the hipster] who extrapolates from his own condition, from the inner certainty that his rebellion is just a radical vision of the universe which thus separates him from the general ignorance, reactionary prejudice, and self doubt of the more conventional psychopath." The conventional psychopath does not feel guilt, since he is precisely a psychopath, but he does feel anger at what he considers bad. It would follow that since the hipster has enough consciousness to know that sex is not in itself bad, that the only evil is the loss of energy, he would be able to reap the benefits of the energy set free by sex. But it never does follow in "The White Negro." The only endorsement that Mailer gives to sexual adventure is the rather amusing one that it at least keeps the conventional psychopath in good physical health.* Although the third section of the essay distinguishes the psychopath genus from the hipster species, it slides from the good health

---

* Fred W. Dupee has seized upon this aspect of the essay with this witty comment:

> He quite possibly *over*-formulates Hip, schematizes it, makes its ways and words merely antithetical to those of its enemy the Square, reduces it to a kind of cross between a game and a form of hygiene. Hip makes for a livelier vocabulary, a more stylish way of carrying oneself, more and better orgasms. Thanks to Hip a bi-sexual Negro Mailer knows gets as much of a charge from a certain chick as out of a battalion of Marines. *There*'s a testimonial to Hip as conducing to fair play and a well-rounded life. Hip is *good for you*. ["The American Norman Mailer," *Commentary*, February, 1960, 128–32.]

While this is in "The White Negro," so is the emphasis on the hipster's commitment to growth.

recommendation to the relationship of psychopathy and Negroes and then closes with a discussion of the hip argot which arose out of Negro psychopathy. The discussion is interesting, but it does not tell us, nor did Mailer ever explicitly claim, that one is better off being a hipster than an ordinary psychopath or even a square. Unlike his contradictory claims about the psychopath's instinct—the psychopath knows what is good for himself; the ignorance, prejudice and self-doubt of the psychopath prevent him from knowing what is good for himself—this was not a slip; Mailer was attempting to pose as an objective reporter of hip philosophy, though he dropped this pretense when he defended hip (in the winter, 1958, issue of *Dissent*) against the attacks of Jean Malaquais and Ned Polsky. But however much he might have created the hipster's style, courage, and implacable commitment to accumulate energy, his admiration for these attributes is unmistakable. Tolstoy wrote "God is my desire" in the diary that he gave Gorky to read. By 1958, the name of Mailer's desire was to become a godly hipster.

Still, all of the overt endorsements of hip in "The White Negro" are not in terms of how much buried energy it actually freed but of its potential as a catalyst for radical social change. Time would prove that this potentiality had no more chance of actualization than the 1953 possibility of socialism's coming to America by way of western Europe. Scarcely more promising was Mailer's hope to jar large numbers of stagnating Americans into a more daring life style (and himself back into great prominence) by dynamically convincing them of the need to fulfill their languishing natures. As vigorous as Mailer's prose could be, the incentive behind the exhortation was bound to remain somewhat abstract. With his theories of God and afterlife, Mailer sought to bring to hip and to himself more excitement and considerably more purpose and incentive. As we shall see, these doctrines expanded but did not shatter the theories of truth, value, and purpose set forth in "The White Negro."

IV

The *Naked and the Dead* is clearly the book of a man who considered himself an atheist when he wrote it. His position is most clearly articulated with Goldstein's crashing perception that there was no God. A more sardonic alternative was offered seventy-five pages before Goldstein's realization when one of the soldiers struggling up Mount Anaka says "if there is [a God], he sure is a sonofabitch." Were Goldstein's insight not offered us, we could still have concluded from a consideration of the tone and incidents of the rest of the novel that atheism was one of the naturalistic assumptions which Mailer had borrowed. Nevertheless, a fascination with the nature of God developed during the writing of the third draft of *The Deer Park*, a fascination that was to become an obsession. That novel's kindly God, who offers advice about how to connect new psychic circuits without demanding a price for the information, will never be heard from in print again. Then, in May, 1956, in his "Public Notice on *Waiting for Godot*," Mailer finally found after all of the floundering of the preceding seventeen columns what he had been trying to write about:

> For I believe Beckett is also saying, again consciously or unconsciously, that God's destiny is flesh and blood with ours, and so, far from conceiving of a God who sits in judgment and allows souls, lost souls, to leave purgatory and be reborn again, there is the greater agony of God at the mercy of man's fate, God determined by man's efforts, man who has free will and can no longer exercise it and God therefore in bondage to the result of man's efforts.

This God does not appear in "The White Negro" or in the replies to Malaquais and Polsky, for He is more than the trapped God of our instincts—though this is indeed where He manifests Himself. But in a May, 1958, interview with Richard Stern, Mailer both amplified his conception of His nature and fused Him with the hipster's drive for personal growth. The God (Godot) of the 1956 pronouncement is a very passive one. As far as we can tell, Mailer is saying that His fate is wholly determined by man's efforts. His powers have faded, and his spiritual insomnia and agony have deepened in direct proportion to the amount that Vladimir and Gogo have failed. The God limned two years later is not passively atrophying; he is fighting with ruthlessness and imagination for his survival.

> . . . there is one single burning pinpoint of the vision in Hip: it's that God is in danger of dying. . . . I believe Hip conceives of Man's fate being tied up with God's fate.
> . . . the particular God we can conceive of is a god whose relationship to the universe we cannot divine; that is, how enormous He is in the scheme of the universe we can't begin to say. But almost certainly, He is not all-powerful; He exists as a warring element in a divided universe, and we are a part of—perhaps the most important part—of His great expression, His enormous destiny; perhaps He is trying to impose upon the universe His conception of being against other conceptions of being very much opposed to His.

With his suggestion that we cannot divine the vastness of this God's involvement in the universe and that we are only a part of His vision, Mailer is admitting the existence of eternal agents and would thus seem to be retreating from his claim made in 1957 that man creates reality. But he does not do this any more than he suggests, as Sartre, for example, has, that there are two orders of reality—a human one and one belonging to the physical order which has no fundamental relationship to man. No, for Mailer there is only one inclusive, constantly changing reality, and man does create it. It is just that Mailer has decided that the actions of a God, a Devil, and perhaps other superhuman beings alter reality, as might the actions of animals and certain things. The actions of any being (synonymous with soul) ultimately alter the beings of God and the Devil, and beings may or may not inhabit the body of a human or—in the gnostic animism which has developed in the past decade—a sardine or a piece of driftwood. (A being or soul is "anything that lives and still has the potentiality to change, to change physically and to change morally.") * But the actions of a man with a soul are a much more powerful vector in the force field of reality than those of lesser organisms, and the total reality of the universe is altered by a man's actions just as surely as the meaning of a conversation is affected by the slightest change in the nuance of the voice of one of the speakers.

Nietzsche could only say that God was. Heidegger concedes that God *is* but does not *exist*—that is, He is not subject to the contingencies of existence. Mailer claims that He both is and exists. He is eternal only if He succeeds in remaining eternal, if enough of the beings that metaphorically compose His body do not die. Because He is subject to that same just, cruel law of growth or decline, His embattled future is as uncertain as man's. Mailer has many times in many ways expressed his intuition that life is war; in the preceding quotation, he expands the battlefield until it includes the universe.

---

* "The Metaphysics of the Belly," *Cannibals*, p. 287. In "The Political Economy of Time," Mailer writes:

Suppose I define soul by saying it is a sort of creature, doubtless invisible, which has a purchase on eternity. It also has an individual life, a *personal* life, which is contained in itself, and this personal life is carried through its metamorphoses. . . . Its desire is to live. So long as it is a healthy soul, its nourishment comes from growth and victory, from exploration, from conquest, from pomp and pageant and triumph, from glory. Is this sufficiently simple for you? It lives for stimulation, for pleasure. It abhors defeat. Its nature is to become more than it is." [*Cannibals*, pp. 340–41.]

The last sentence sums up Mailer's view of life as well as any nine words could.

God is a warring general in this vision of total conflagration, and we are perhaps his most trusted foot soldiers. If we are indeed "the seed, the seedcarriers, the voyagers, the explorers, the embodiment of that embattled vision" of His, then we affect His reality—and thus all reality—as surely as Cummings's individual "truth" was altered by the actions of the soldiers on Anopopei. For the fundamental reality of both generals at any moment in time is the one common to all beings—the amount of effectual power they possess as they seek to shape the total reality of the future more along the lines of their own desires. Thus, in Mailer's post–"White Negro" thought, total reality is the total power of all beings to grow. Although Mailer is egalitarian in celebrating the potential of each individual, his philosophy is no less power-oriented than Cummings's.*

Just as Mailer retained his basic conception of reality but enlarged it to include other creators of reality besides man, so the closed energy-economy of "The White Negro" has been expanded in the author's later thought. In the all-human world of the 1957 essay, he tells us that the hipster is a sort of child fighting for the sweet of new energy, one who knows that there is not enough sweet for everyone. His enlarged universe is a warring one because the same classic equation for war holds. There is no essential difference between the situation in Canaan in 1300 B.C. and in the universe in 1972; we might arbitrarily say that $2x$ number of beings are seeking to gain sustenance in a territory that only offers it to x number. Mailer suggested some of the logistics of this universal war in the Stern interview and repeated them almost to the word a decade later. Sometimes God makes excessive demands upon us to achieve His ends and sometimes we make exorbitant demands upon Him. Here is an example of the latter process from the 1958 interview:

> In Hip . . . the attitude would be . . . that if taking drugs gives
> one extraordinary sensations, then the drug-taker is probably receiv-
> ing something from God. Love perhaps. And perhaps he is. . . . If
> the hipster is receiving love from God he may well be draining some

---

* In the dialogue "The Political Economy of Time," written in 1963 and reworked for *Cannibals,* Mailer says that souls are "His present tense. His moral nature exists . . . not in the soul but in the Vision. . . . Vision is the mind of God; soul, His body; and Spirit is what He has left behind. Literally. It is His excrement" (*Cannibals,* p. 365). God's vision is implied in the quotation on page 106 and more explicitly stated in the second one on page 109 and in the following paragraph. Spirit is all that which is not soul or vision: an inanimate object; an animate object that can no longer grow; a mood.

of the substance of God by calling upon this love . . . which the drug releases. And in draining the substance of God he's exhausting Him, so that the drug-taker may be indulging in an extraordinarily evil act at the instant he is filled with the feeling that he is full of God and good and a beautiful mystic.

Whether the general gains energy at the expense of his private or vice versa, this sort of internecine strife certainly does not help the cause of the army of growth and expansion. The point is to get the energy at the expense of the opponent or opponents, for if there is an embattled God then there must surely be a Devil against whom He is pitted. Our proper task is then to war against the Devil, to reclaim energy from him. In a passage from a column originally published in the April, 1963, *Commentary,* Mailer fused his ontological and theological premises:

> . . . if there is any urgency in God's intent, if we are not actors working out a play for our salvation, but *rather soldiers in an army which seeks to carry some noble conception of Being out across the stars, or back into the protoplasm of life,* then a portion of God's creative power was extinguished in the camps of extermination. If God is not all-powerful but existential, discovering the possibilities and limitations of His creative powers in the form of the history which is made by His creatures, then one must postulate an existential equal to God, an antagonist, the Devil, a principle of Evil whose signature was the concentration camps, *whose joy is to waste substance, whose intent is to prevent God's conception of Being from reaching its mysterious goal.* If one considers the hypothesis that God is not all-powerful, indeed not the architect of Destiny but rather the creator of Nature, then evil becomes a record of the Devil's victories over God. [Italics mine.]

And so, throughout the sixties Mailer placed superhuman intent behind the premise that what promotes individual growth ("the noble conception of Being") is good and what hinders or destroys it is evil. The inner instinctual voice which enables us to flower if we are able both to listen to it and to act out its commands—to be what Mailer calls authentic—must then eventually derive from God. Institutional knowledge, so pounded into us by endless reiteration that we cannot hear our instinct, effects the purpose of the Devil—"a monumental bureaucrat of repetition." * God created phenomenal nature to permit

---

* With the flight of Apollo 11 in 1969, Mailer was—between the technology of the space program and the courage of the apparently prosaic astronauts—confronted anew with the possible creativity of institutionalized, corporate America. See pages 242–47 for the reconsidered views of God and His relation to man and technology.

as much expansion by as many beings as possible, but (to take an example of the fusion of the Marxian and the Manichean which better explains the workings of the energy-economy) "if the world, through the eyes of Marx, is the palpable embodiment of a vast collective theft—the labor which was stolen from men by other centuries—then one need not retire in terror from the idea that the power of the world belongs to the Devil, and God needs men to overthrow him." Every lie which deadens people from the perception of the actual conditions of their lives is Devilish; every act or statement or object which drives the reality home is Godly. To take one of hundreds of possible examples from the writings of the sixties, fallout shelters were an example of the former. They did not actually protect us from the nuclear assault, but their presence convinced some that they were safe and so further deadened the will to perform those protesting acts which might help change American foreign policy. A small example of a Godly act would then have been Mailer's standing in City Hall Park in New York and refusing to take shelter during a 1962 civil defense drill in order to advertise the futility of the shelters. The beauty of any man-made or natural object is the result of the struggle between the resistance of the medium and the energies which worked it, and so the stone, language, paint, and other materials which compose the object are fulfilling their divine purpose. But plastic—never a part of the struggling continuum of nature, effortlessly rolled out in sheets—is the material of the Devil.

It might be asked whether Mailer thinks that the Devil is simply whatever God is not—an absence—or whether the author believes that a thinking, purposing malevolence is literally out there. According to a 1967 interview, most of the time he is not sure. When the *Playboy* interviewer inquired about a recent comment that God is the Devil in exile, Mailer replied:

> I don't know if the Devil is finally an evil principle of God—a fallen angel, a Prince of Darkness, Lucifer—a creature of the first dimension engaged in a tragic, monumental war with God, or whether the Devil is a species of nonexistence, like plastic. By which I mean every single pervasive substance in the technological world that comes from artificial synthesis rather than from nature. Plastic surfaces have no resonance—no echo of nature. I don't know if plastic is a second principle of evil just as much opposed to the Devil as it is opposed to God—a visitor from a small planet, if you will. So when I talk about the Devil these days, I don't really know whether I'm talking about a corrupter of the soul or a deadening influence.

To push closer to the heart of the matter, does Mailer mean to say that his God objectively exists apart from our thoughts and actions, or is it the case, as Samuel Hux has suggested in an ambitious study,

> that we are indeed the "seed" of this divinity in Mailer's cosmology; that this God is not all-powerful and is a "warring element" because his is finally the expression of our "infinite craving" translated into a "craving for the infinite"; that this God is created by man, and made in the image of man; that he is, finally, some envisioned composite Truth formed by the composite of all the truths we create in each "enormous present"; that this God is the ultimate sum of all our acts, all our "enormous presents"; that he is, I am suggesting, the human desire to become God, the *En-Soi-Pour-Soi,* or in Sartrean terms again, he is a futile expression of man as a "useless passion."

While this is quite provocative, the theory that Mailer's God is the expression of our futile attempts to become God would have much more credence if it only concerned the man who wrote the majority view of *The Naked and the Dead,* but the Mailer who believed that life was fundamentally absurd and who defeated the two Gods-to-be (Cummings and Croft) has for more than fifteen years been laid to rest by the creator of an evolving vision of order. The easy equation of Sartre and Mailer takes no account of the minority Mailer who, as I observed earlier in the chapter, in no way sees man's efforts to realize his nature condemned to a Sartrean futility.

The man who was inspired for close to a decade by the possibility that he was in the process of making a mighty addition to continental existentialism is very much the same man who was at the same time railing in *The Presidential Papers* and *Cannibals and Christians* against the art and life of the absurd. We could get a better sense of the workings of Mailer's rage for biological order by using Sartre further, by contrasting Mailer's assumptions about the workings of phenomenal Nature with the ones that Sartre laid out in the forties. For the latter, Nature is finally obscene in that superabundance which is a constant reminder that man had no essential place among its naturally flowering forms. Animals and things *are,* but only man, with his projecting, purposing *pour-soi*—"that hole of being in the center of Being"— exists. Sartre's Being includes being which is (*être-en-soi*—human bodies, animals, rocks, trees) and being which is not (*être-pour-soi*— that human freedom which alienates man from Nature because it is peculiar to man). On the other hand, Mailer's man is integrated into Nature because, in his scheme, Being is composed only of that which exists, that is, of the totality of beings. The fundamental distinction in his natural order is not between man and everything else but between Being—that which can change for the better, or grow—and nonbeing. The latter category can be used either for God's purpose of facilitating the growth of a being or a number of beings (and thus Being as a whole) or to fulfill the Devil's intention of creating less Being, or it might not be used at all. (This is true if the Devil is being and not a species of nonbeing; Mailer does not confront the problem of how the Devil could be a being who grows through the diminution of nonbeing.) For example, a piece of driftwood might fulfill the first possibility by housing a soul and offering it sanctuary while it regained its strength or the third possibility if no souls occupied it. If a ship sank, and a man tore a woman from the driftwood, seized it himself, and left her to drown, it would fulfill the second possibility; the man's being would presumably be seriously weakened. Far from claiming that the natural order is ridiculous in its irrelevance to man, there might be no *essential* difference between a man, a sardine, and a piece of driftwood. They can all offer sustenance to a soul or being, or they might all be uninhabited. If all three are inhabited, the beings are all bending their particular powers toward growing so that they can more fully insinuate their being upon the environment around them.

The examples of the last few pages have been drawn from Mailer at his most ontologically ambitious; that is, from the dialogues "The Metaphysics of the Belly" ("part of a longer manuscript on Picasso which was worked on in June and early July of 1962") and "The Political Economy of Time" (written in 1963 and reworked for *Cannibals and Christians,* which was published in 1966). Both dialogues, particularly the latter, serve as the culmination and the end of Mailer's attempt to capture by systematic terminology and definitions what he called in *The Presidential Papers* the underworld of magical connections. The fictional summary of the Ontological Decade (about 1956 through 1966) comes with *An American Dream,* in which the hero can smell impoverished souls from Negro hash-houses in vomit or listen to an obviously ensouled umbrella, and in which, right on schedule after searing sex, the torch-singer heroine can announce that some people have souls, some are only spirits, and the people with souls can't live with the people with spirits. Happily for his writing—particularly for his fiction—the systematic urge waned as the sixties proceeded, and comparisons which gave him the biological edge on Sartre would have seemed to him a good deal less relevant than they would have a few years before. Although his obsession with the workings of energy continues, his compulsion to place everything on the rungs of his ontological ladder has also ebbed. For example, here is his 1970 response to an account of the workings of homeopathic magic in Frazer's *The Golden Bough:*

It was the magic of savage metaphor, the science of symbol, it married spiders' legs to the music of the fingers and the useful frenzy of the rat to the sensors in his hair. It made a wedding between the spiraled-in will of insects forced to focus on a point of tether and the loss of any will-to-escape in the slave. It was pretty, poetic and nonsensical, it was nonsensical. Unless it were not. What if some real exchange between insects, trees, crops, and grains, between animals and men, had lived with real if most distorted power in the first hours of history? What if that Vision of the Lord which had gone out to voyage among the stars had obtained the power to be carried up by the artwork of a bounteous earth exquisite in the resonance of all psyches in its field?—what if radio, technology, and the machine had smashed the most noble means of presenting the Vision to the universe.

There is no distinction between organisms with souls and those which are merely spirits; rather, there was a time when all organisms communicated, and God was strengthened by the psychic interaction. One wonders about the state of things in all those millennia between the first hours and technology, and if God's being has been wasted, how do our beings compare with those of the primitives? Mailer would have taken on questions like this five years before.

But to turn back for the last time to the system builder, the 1957 claim that the hipster was able to employ his philosophical detachment in order to know precisely what forces drove him was necessarily modified by the 1958 fusion of hip and the embattled, existential God. Since religious quests were primarily associated with those disaffiliates who called themselves beat and not hip, Mailer was forced to suggest that the hipster's attempts to manifest God's Vision and increase His Being (along with his own being) were guided by an unconscious that

has an enormous teleological sense, that . . . moves toward a goal, that . . . has a real sense of what is happening to one's being at each given moment—you see—that the messages of one's experience are continually saying, "Things are getting better," or "Things are getting worse. For me. For that one. For my future, for my past. . . ." It is with this thing that they move, that they grope forward—this navigator at the seat of their being.

The epigraph of most of Mailer's work of the past twenty years could be the same as that of Forster's *Howard's End:* "Only connect."

The American neoprimitivist has been at least as concerned with the linkage between a man's baffled, mistaken, or glutted consciousness and his informing unconscious as with that between individuals or social classes. (Of course, being Mailer, he is very interested in the connections between any two or two thousand things he can think of.) To apply existential parlance to the need to yield to the unknown in ourselves, Mailer would say that the man who is brave enough to act out the promptings of the Navigator (the communicating part of the soul, being, or unconscious), during those moments of grace when the latter chooses to speak, is behaving with authenticity. Of course, two thinkers' theories of authentic behavior will differ just as much as their conceptions of the most fundamental conditions of existence vary. Since Heidegger believes that one aspect of the human *Dasein* is to be a being-towards-death, since death is our primary possibility, he urges us to "rush toward it," to act and think in anticipation of our death, for "when, in anticipation, resoluteness has *caught up* the possibility of death into its potentiality-for-being, Dasein's authentic existence cannot be *outstripped* by anything." But Sartre defines man as "a being having freedom within the limits of a situation." Since death is not a situation in which a man can express his freedom, Sartre must reject Heidegger's concept of being-towards-death:

> Thus we must conclude in opposition to Heidegger that death, far from being my peculiar possibility, is a contingent fact which as such on principle escapes me and originally belongs to my facticity. I can neither discover my death nor wait for it nor adopt an attitude toward it, for it is that which is revealed as undiscoverable, that which disarms all waiting, that which slips into all attitudes . . . so as to transform them into externalized and fixed conducts whose meaning is forever entrusted to others and not to ourselves. . . .

So, while Heidegger claims that authenticity can only be achieved by adopting a resolute attitude toward death, Sartre must say that "although there are innumerable possible attitudes with which we may confront this unrealizable which 'in the bargain' is to be realized, there is no place for classifying these attitudes as authentic or inauthentic since we always die in the bargain."

I have brought up the relationship of authenticity and death in Sartre and Heidegger because it is on this issue that Mailer most decisively separates his post–"White Negro" existential thought from that of the two Europeans:

> . . . the reluctance of modern European existentialism to take on the logical continuation of the existential vision (that there is a life

after death which can be as existential as life itself) has brought
French and German existentialism to a halt on this uninhabitable
terrain of the absurd—to wit, man must lead his life as if death is
meaningful even when man knows that death is meaningless. This
revealed knowledge which Heidegger accepts as his working hypothesis and Sartre goes so far as to assume is the uncertainty upon which
he may build a philosophy, ends the possibility that one can construct
a base for the existential ethic. The German philosopher runs
aground trying to demonstrate the necessity for man to discover an
authentic life. Heidegger can give no deeper explanation why man
should bother to be authentic than to state in effect that man should
be authentic in order to be free. Sartre's advocacy of the existential
commitment is always in danger of dwindling into the minor aris-
tocratic advocacy of leading one's life with style for the sake of style.
Existentialism is rootless unless one dares the hypothesis that *death
is an existential continuation of life, that the soul may either pass
through migrations, or cease to exist in the continuum of nature*
(which is the unspoken intimation of cancer). But accepting this
hypothesis, authenticity and commitment return to the center of
ethics, for man then faces no peril so huge as alienation from his
own soul, a death which is other than death, a disappearance into
nothingness rather than into Eternity. [Italics mine.]

Although there is much in the critique of Sartre and Heidegger with
which we might differ, Mailer has clearly offered to us the marrow of
his existentialist ethics and the bridge between the ethics and his
gnostic biology. If the premises of Heidegger's and Sartre's philosophy
are as Mailer defines them, then it would seem inevitable that an individual, beset as he is by all of the weaknesses within and the bullying
forces without, should reply to the Europeans' urgings to be authentic,
"Why should I? What's in it for me?" But if he can be convinced that
the fundamental fact of his existence is that he is engaged in a struggle to maintain his purchase on eternity, then he can be enough driven
by his fear of a "disappearance into nothingness" to act in what Mailer
would call an authentic manner. Since our being's, our soul's, "desire
is to live, to gain nourishment from conquest, from pomp and pageant
and triumph, from glory," an authentic act is any one that nourishes
our energies, which keeps our chance for reincarnation open if we do
not deteriorate too badly in any particular avatar.

To say "grow," "amass energy," "connect with your nourishing unconscious" is finally about as helpful as offering for advice the suggestion someone once offered me, "be happy." Among other things,
An American Dream is an attempt to dramatize the workings of authenticity in all of their concrete complexity, and we will turn to that
quite curious novel in a few pages. We might here consider the origins

of what was for about eight years Mailer's version of the fire and brim-
stone sermon—grow or go to hell. In "The White Negro" Mailer had
not yet cast his thought across that lonesome valley and found something on the other side. All of the opportunities that death offers us lie
on this side of our lungs' last breath; since death is the ultimate danger,
the total negation of possibility, we can best demonstrate our courage
and free or accumulate energy in the face of this threat. By the following year (for I think that "Advertisements for Myself on the Way
Out," was written in 1958), Mailer had clearly decided that the death
of the immortality-seeking soul was the greatest threat. A now nearly
godlike Marion Faye broods about Hell as "the onanisms of connec-
tionless Time, the misery of the lone chance in one out of the billion
of billions to be born again," and the dead narrator is whirling through
space with the terrifying thought that he has not grown enough in life
and was ". . . already on the way out . . . a fetor of God's brown
sausage in His time of diarrhea, oozing and sucking and bleating like
a fetal puppy about to pass away past the last pinch of the divine
sphincter with only the toilet of Time, oldest hag of them all, to spin
me away into the spiral of star-lit empty waters."

For Dostoevsky's Father Zossima, hell was the condition of being
unable to love, but consistent with Mailer's subordination of love to
growth,* hell is the condition of being unable to grow. Since Faye's
Hell offers a chance in billions for future life, it is a more promising
residence than the narrator's cosmic toilet. Nevertheless, all of
Mailer's later utterances about hell will deny that one chance. The
author's final position, or at least the stance consistently taken
through the sixties, is that of the last quotation; hell is precisely the
condition of having no more chance to exist and grow (remember the
hell of the imprisoned being of the whisky bottle). Because it can no
longer grow, the soul is no longer a soul but a spirit, suffering "some
unendurable stricture of eternity," having existed only inasmuch as it
knows forever that it has failed—though we cannot accurately refer
to the spirit as existing because, to Mailer, to exist is to engage in a
struggle for possible growth.

In the earlier discussion of Mailer's conception of truth and value,
I quoted a passage from "The White Negro" which celebrated man,
the maker of value, as being "raised to a neo-medieval summit."
When Mailer also placed a God and a Devil on this summit where

* That is, "the soul can only love what offers it growth. It loves most what
offers it the happiest, richest growth. It detests sickness, dying, death" (*Canni-*
bals, p. 341).

value was created, man's solitary eminence ceased, but with this very addition of the divine and the satanic, a new and far more persistent neomedieval strain arose. Viewed through the lens of Mailer's eschatological vision, every man's life becomes a sort of ontological morality play as he struggles to maintain or strengthen his being—his purchase on future life and being. Acts of violence or passivity, courage or cowardice, sex or abstinence expand or diminish the state of the soul in his biological salvation story, and they add their ontological status to the ethical force field around them. In 1969 Mailer could still write that

> he is still sufficiently a Manichean to believe that if Saturn V goes up in perfect launch, it will not be the fault of the guests. No, some of the world's clowns, handmaidens, and sycophants and some of the most ambitious and some of the very worst people in the world have gotten together at the dignitaries' stand. If this display of greed, guilt, wickedness, and hoarded psychic gold could not keep Saturn V off its course, then wickedness was weak today.

As for the nature of God's existence, there must be a good many days when he feels that his God has no more objective reality than Hux believes Him to have. But what appears in print is heavily weighted on the side of a God whose existence is in some way independent of human actions and thoughts. For one thing, I see no other way of interpreting the statements in the Stern interview and the one in *Playboy* of the occasional unreasonability of God toward us and us toward God. Further, all of Mailer's intuitions of order argue for some organizing external truth which we might call God, even if we call God a principle. Yet I think that his God is far more personal than that. I do not think that he would have the interviewer in the dialogue "The Political Economy of Time" accuse him of creating "a philosophy of hugely paranoid proportions" if he did not intend the preceding statements about God, the Devil, spirit, and excrement to be interpreted as the expressions of extreme positions.

Some arguments which help to show the singleness of Mailer's vision might also be brought to bear. There is first what can be called the cult-of-the-charismatic-leader strain that runs through his social thought, for if Mailer is a democrat about social adventure who argues that every man should get a chance to see how he would fare in a dramatically dangerous situation, he is also enthralled by the hero who influences the masses from on high. His existential politician is one who dramatically communicates to the populace the intuition which caused him to perform a certain act as well as the context (particularly the opposing forces) and the very act of choosing itself. Does it not seem likely that Mailer would believe as literally as he possibly could in the most dramatic and charismatic leaders conceivable, in God and the Devil? It is even more likely that a man who frequently refers to himself as a club fighter or an old rifleman, who hooks with his fists while he talks, who delivers crushing blows to the "cancerous" walls of whatever Hilton hotel he happens to be staying at, who can intuit from Liston-in-the-ring versus Patterson-in-the-ring a Manichean struggle of God against the Devil, Sex against Love, The Syndicate against the Liberal, and the Magician against the Artist should believe as much as his rationality will permit him in the most concrete possible existence for the greatest fighter in the most widespread and decisive war in history. No, most of the time Mailer thinks or tries to think that something purposeful is out there. In ethical terms, and probably even in biological ones, we did not simply spring into being *ex nihilo*.

V

Yeats has said that he did not ask us to believe his system of gyres and two-thousand-year cycles and phases of the moon but to understand that it offered him images for his poetry. Mailer does ask us to accept his system but to understand that he speaks in metaphors. The equations offered in his longest and most arcane dialogue, "The Political Economy of Time," "are not mathematical, but metaphorical; and therefore full of science. . . . I am thus trying to say my equations are a close description of phenomena which cannot be measured by a scientist."

His metaphors usually have in common their eschatological intent. Through them we can better discern how our soul fares *vis-à-vis* our attempt to grow or enough maintain ourselves so that we retain our option on incarnation. A soul (or a being) is probably a metaphor for certain bioelectric or biochemical substances; other names could be used. Yet the substances *are* potentially eternal; they *do* maintain an individual characteristic throughout each incarnation; their strength *is* always waxing or waning. The entities—soul, spirit, the Navigator, the Novelist, the Eater, the Censor—are metaphorical. The states—growth, adjustment, insight, incarnation, death—are not.

But to turn to the scientific aspects of metaphor, the modern scientist has no desire to contemplate the metaphorical aspects of, let us say, a disease or a protein molecule:

The scientist will describe the structure and list the properties of the molecule (and indeed it took technological achievements close to genius to reach that point) but the scientist will not look at the metaphorical meaning of the physical structure, its meaning as an architectural form. He will not ponder what biological or spiritual experience is suggested by the formal structure of the molecule, for metaphor is not to the present interest of science. It is instead the desire of science to be able to find the cause of cancer in some virus: a virus—you may count on it—which will be without metaphor. You see, that will be equal to saying the heart of the disease of all diseases is empty of meaning, that cancer is caused by a specific virus which has no character or quality, and is in fact void of philosophy and bereft of metaphysics.*

The word *science,* of course, derives from the Latin word for "to know," but the scientific explanation of a disease—that it is caused by this virus and manifests itself in those symptoms and can be cured by that drug—does not offer the most important kind of knowledge to Mailer. To say that cancer tells us that the cells have rebelled, that the soul has died, that we have lost our chance for future life is to state a metaphor which contains the most profound knowledge of the biochemical events which have made future incarnation impossible. With his metaphorical approach, Mailer feels that he is harking back to the good old days before experimentalism set in, when science was illumined by moral vision. For science had begun

> with the poetic impulse to treat metaphor as equal to equation: the search began at the point where a poet looked for a means (which only later became experiment) to measure the accuracy of his metaphor. The natural assumption was that his discovery had been contained in the metaphor, since good metaphor could only originate in the deepest experience of a man; so science still remained attached to poetic vision, and scientific insight derived from culture—it was not the original desire of science to convert nature, rather to reveal it. Faust was still unborn when Aristotle undertook his pioneer observations.

We have here the familiar theme of the ability of the deepest part of a man (the God-given soul, being, unconscious) to discern the secrets of Being. For Being—the totality of beings—is the same thing as nature, or at least of those parts of nature which can still grow

---

* *Cannibals,* pp. 310–11. The next sentence of the quotation states as well as any one in all of Mailer's writings his commitment to biological order: "All those who are there to claim that disease and death are void of meaning are there to benefit from such a virus, for next they can move on to say that life is absurd."

and so are not the property of the Devil. Mailer obviously includes himself among the pre-Aristotelian visionaries who, like Heidegger's pre-Socratics, were willing to let Being be and who stand in juxtaposition to those modern scientists driven by the Faustian, ultimately Satanic urge to dominate nature. Although Mailer does not discuss the Devil in the pages I have just treated, the interrelatedness of Mailer's vision easily permits us to see how the scientists are instruments of the Devil.

All of the beings that collectively compose nature can accumulate energy. Obviously, anything that can grow cannot be completely controlled, and so "the devil hates nature so much he cannot bear to look at it. He must name what he sees before he sees it. Or instantly after. He must dominate nature because it does not belong to him. That is why he cannot bear to contemplate it."

To contemplate fully a being at the present moment is to perceive that it is an entity whose future is open. When the Devil names an object before or after he sees it, he is attempting to disregard this capacity for development, for transcendence, which is precisely what makes a being a being. The Devil's attempt to escape the dynamic possibilities of the enormous present is what Mailer is referring to when he writes that the former is the repository of all the past, which deadens our capacities to respond to the options of the present. (In contrast, Mailer writes that the future of God is not written; He is both the embodiment and provider of possibility, of souls or beings.) A disease or a tension is trying to tell us what has been wrong in our past and what we must do in the present to have a better future. The scientist who masks the symptoms with a drug only interrupts the process of communication. The disease will now affect ten organs instead of one, though this is probably Mailer's metaphorical way of saying that our distress will be much more severe. The doctor or the scientist has been fulfilling the Devil's purpose by deadening our capacity for the authentic, truly pragmatic action which we must take. And so our souls are lost, says the radical moralist.*

Save for a few instances when he parodies himself, and which we shall come to in good time, Mailer, then, wants us to take his metaphors as seriously as possible. But how moral is the moralist? Does *he* believe all of this Manichean folderol? Again, Mailer likes to see him-

---

* But, confronted with Apollo 11 in 1969, Mailer offered along with the expected attacks on mood-numbing technology the possibility that we have so betrayed God's need for us that He has settled for a new mechanized man to further His purposes.

self as the last great romantic; for his romanticism, altruism, literary and economic ambition he believes as much as he can. But how much can he? *He* and *believes* are intricate words; given enough imagination and industry one could spend the rest of one's life defining them, particularly when the "he" is Mailer. What he says about himself is always clear enough, but as Wilfrid Sheed has observed in his review of *Cannibals and Christians,*

> he is a highly intelligent man as well as an egregiously sly one. And much of the very best Mailer-criticism actually originates with Mailer himself. Such of it as doesn't, he is apt to keep in circulation anyhow by feeding it back to us in his own words, so that he is the ringmaster to the whole Mailer criticism industry, down to dictating the precise terms in which he is to be discussed (e.g. the way one always talks about his "talent").

So Sheed's very shrewd observation is transformed and circulated; Mailer speaks in his very next book of darting out at night, in his sleep, to paint improvements on the sarcophagus of his image. At night, indeed; in the same book, *The Armies of the Night,* he tosses back into circulation Sheed's comment about having a heavy, sodden heart. Good old Norman, carrying on valiantly in spite of his heavy, sodden heart.

From the *Voice* columns on, Mailer has increasingly become the impresario of his own personae. When I try to dive behind the personae and contemplate what might be happening inside his head as he watches, say, a boxing match, I think of Portnoy in bed with The Monkey and the Italian whore—he's so *busy.* Is one part of his mind deeply engaged by the fight, a second part watching the first part, and a third part considering and then rejecting an article about the conflict between the first two parts? Can one measure the belief of a man who tells us that he "had long built his philosophical world on the firm conviction that nothing was finally knowable"? Some rough estimate can be made. In the July 28, 1972, *Life,* he wrote that

> once, how many years back, he had thought to himself, "The world's more coherent if God exists. And twice coherent if He exists like us." And had come to live as well with ideas of a Devil whose powers might be equal or sometimes prevail as in the bullets of assassins which found the mark. . . .

How many personality shifts back from "comfortable middle-aged Aquarius," now safe for *Life,* was the shrill, hungry, self-proclaimed rebel who told Richard Stern, back in 1958, that we were the seeds of God's embattled vision and that we had gotten so petty and trivial we needed the concepts of hip to make our life worth living? The difference between 1958 and 1972 is that between a man desperate to believe these metaphors which offered so much possibility for his life, writing, and the world and one who seems to enjoy his career and life very much indeed and who seems to offer the metaphors still more apologetically than the time before. It was tempting to portray the Mailer of, say, 1961 in Camus's terms—as a Sisyphus happily pushing his ontological rock up the hill. But more and more, Sisyphus-Mailer seems to look back over his gleaming shoulder and regard us in amazement for taking him seriously. Is the sweat sprayed on at his desk? Crudely put, I think that Mailer's belief in his metaphors was far more intense and occupied more minutes of his days between 1958 and 1966 than from 1967 to the present.

Freud justified his theories of the death wish and aggression by saying that

> it was only tentatively that I put forward the views I have developed here, but in the course of time they have gained such a hold upon me that I can no longer think in any other way. To my mind, they are far more serviceable from a theoretical standpoint than any other possible ones; they provide that simplification, without either ignoring or doing violence to the fact, for which we strive in scientific work.

The coherence that Mailer sought could not merely explain how things worked; it had to offer explanations that were, for him, heroically meaningful. More and more of Mailer seems to feel that the Manichean bifurcation might do damage to social facts; if God was once the name of his primary desire, He more and more seems to be a long shot who only runs occasionally on a track that Mailer feels less and less interested in visiting. As for the intensity of the rest of Mailer's beliefs, John W. Aldridge made of Mailer one of T. S. Eliot's Elizabethans when he wrote in his review of *Cannibals and Christians* that "Mailer has the capacity to feel his ideas as if they were passions, and to endow his passions with some of the practical force and symmetry of ideas." Perhaps this is true half the time (how inflamed was Mailer by his idea that the NASA ballyhoo of the space venture would give strength to all confidence men?), and I would wager that more and more it is in writing, when he has found the exact verbal equivalent for the metaphysical metaphor, that it lives most incandescently for him. For all of Mailer's boxing the former light heavyweight champion on television and his other television antics—even for his three movies and mayoralty campaign—one increasingly thinks of him as a very skillful writer who has developed a playful streak rather than, as one might have ten years ago when he seemed more of a social phenomenon, the still-talented author of *The Naked and the Dead* who had stabbed his wife but still had a messiah complex.

As Mailer has mellowed, and a fair part of the country has passed him heading in the direction he left, we can no longer think of him unqualifiedly as a personality of extremes.* Still, he presented in most of his writing of the sixties the farthest extremities of individual solitary possibility that he could at all believe in. The options he offered were solitary in that the isolation of the individual was emphasized; he must finally act as an individual—alone. Yet the possibilities were collective in that they apply to all men. Put differently, Mailer was making the familiar existential claim that what is universal is not so much human nature as the human condition. Perhaps the best indicator of the nature of his belief in such doctrines as transmigration, animism, and contesting supernatural orders are the two words which follow his 1962 statement that God's intentions might be such that it is better for a particular man to rape than to masturbate: "Maybe, maybe." Maybe existence is as exciting and meaningful, maybe the future is as open as I hope it is; maybe I can effect a revolution in the consciousness in my time. Maybe I reconcile my desire for order and my desire for a world of dynamic conflict; maybe I can become a household word and write great novels besides. We'll see how he fares.

* For example, the first *Life* installment of *Of A Fire on the Moon* was sandwiched between an account of the Woodstock festival (which is not quite to the point) and the Charles Manson murders (which most certainly is). The ante for notable antisociality has gone up considerably.

4
A Tour Through the Land of Maybe; or, Self-Reliance Revisited

WE remember that Mailer's most explicit endorsement of the hipster in "The White Negro" was not so much for his individual possibilities as for his potential as a member of a revolutionary vanguard that would finally break open the bleakly conformist surface of Eisenhower America. If Mailer convinced few people that the hipster, as he described him, actually existed in any significant number, he persuaded even fewer that his bravery, psychopathy, and self-knowledge could tear society apart. At the present time, more than a decade and a half after "The White Negro," the leaden facade of conformity that Mailer saw all about him in the fifties has quite obviously been shredded by Vietnam, assassinations, the race revolution, the sex revolution, and a younger generation that has so surpassed Mailer's marijuana with LSD, his magic with spells about the Pentagon, and his politics with theories of permanent revolution that the fauve of the fifties has since 1964 called himself a left conservative and has let melt away such extreme arguments as the ones that justify murder.

In the four months that followed the publication of "The White Negro," there occurred the two events—the launching of Sputnik and the eruption of violence at Little Rock—which Mailer felt blew open the stifling inertia he had sensed through the fifties. These designations were made in "Superman Comes to the Supermarket," the glittering piece on the 1960 Democratic National Convention and the first of those sorties into journalism that have often enough blended intriguing speculations and arresting insights, images, and metaphors with a style simultaneously tough and lyrical (with many long, skillfully controlled sentences which somehow fuse the most disparate elements) to make Mailer the unquestioned king of the New Journalism and, in the opinion of some, the best journalist in the country (though he claims this soubriquet annoys him; he likes to think of himself as the best novelist). The piece's mixture of speculation, journalism, and autobiography points the direction that so much of his writing of the

124

next twelve years will take; it also contains several important shifts in his intellectual career. The statement that America was not too hip but too beat for the Russians to occupy is not simply gallows humor, for it is an attempt to quietly bury hip as a possible social movement. And although Mailer remained throughout the sixties true to Marxism in his fashion and continued to argue for the creativity buried in the masses—particularly in the Negroes—he added a new social alternative in "Superman" by suggesting that a truly heroic president could turn the stagnating population back toward its historic quest for growth and adventure.* Neatly combining his new existential politics, which in decidedly non-Marxist fashion moved the animus for sweeping social change from the bottom of society to the top of the political structure, with his megalomania, Mailer had already decided or was soon to decide to run for the New York mayoralty.

Nevertheless, hip's celebration of violence did not die so easily for Mailer. About ten weeks after he finished "Superman Comes to the Supermarket," or in mid-November, 1960, he told two interviewers from *Mademoiselle* that

> there weren't enough White Negroes around and so the organized world took on my notion of the White Negro and killed the few of us a little further. And I betrayed my own by writing that piece. It's even remotely conceivable that I would have done better to have kept silent. I advanced my career at the expense of my armies.

All of which would sound like General Marijuana at his most melodramatic as he postured for the two ladies from the fashion magazine had he not been arrested twice in the past six months and, much more to the point, had he not stabbed Adele Morales Mailer, his second wife, in the back and abdomen with a penknife about a week after the interview. It is not merely ghoulish interest that makes one want to look at the interview closely; the writings that precede and

*Mailer did, in one of his 1956 *Voice* columns, suggest that Hemingway should be the Democratic candidate for president that year, but it is mostly couched in "practical" suggestions—Hemingway's good war record; he would speak simply; people would distrust him less since he had no previous political career. The most optimistic arguments are, "there might be a touch more color in our Roman Republic" and "with all his sad and silly vanities, and some of his intellectual cowardices . . . Ernest Hemingway looks like the best practical possibility in sight" (*Advertisements*, p. 312). The identification that Mailer made with Hemingway is particularly interesting here, since it was at this time that Mailer began dropping hints to friends that he was available for the presidency.

follow Mailer's statements are at least as closely related to them as his extreme act:

INTERVIEWERS: Does the hipster try to kill his will?

MAILER: He tries to keep his will. But he remains tender.

INTERVIEWERS: You mean he feels tender as he grinds the heel of his boot into the face of the dying man!

MAILER: May I say this? If we are going to be extreme let's put it on record that you were extreme first! People always think I start these things but I don't. If you're going to grind your heel into the face of a dying man I still insist on the authority of my existential logic: let the act finally be authentic. If you're going to do it, *do it*.

INTERVIEWERS: You mean enjoy it?

MAILER: The poor soul is going out of existence. You might as well enjoy yourself! If you're going to grind your boot in his face, don't do it with the feeling, "I'm horrible, I'm psychotic, I should be in a bughouse." Do it. There are very few people who grind their feet into the face of anyone else, because when you get down to it people are much tougher, much more capable of defending themselves than anyone ever believes.

. . . if it's gotten so bad that one of America's better writers is talking about somebody grinding his heel into someone else's face, then let us consider this moment. Let's use our imaginations. It means that one human being has determined to extinguish the life of another human being. It means that two people are engaging in a dialogue with eternity. Now if the brute does it and at the last moment likes the man he is extinguishing then perhaps the victim did not die in vain. If there is an eternity with souls in that eternity, if one is able to be born again, the victim may get his reward. At least it seems possible that the quality of one being passes into the other, and this altogether hate-filled human . . . in the act of killing, in this terribly private moment, the brute feels a moment of tenderness, perhaps for the first time in all of his existence. What has happened is that the killer is becoming a little more possible, a little more ready to love someone.

. . . [And most ominous of all] I don't like myself well enough to follow my instincts as I should. I think I've not had the courage to be authentic. . . .

There is nothing new here in Mailer's existential thought. The point is rather that the application of a phrase like "existential thought" to stances like these is a grotesque abstraction from the actions which the stances endorse. The shared commitment which most enables us to designate a disparate group of thinkers as existentialists is precisely their opposition to abstraction, to definitions which appeal only to one's mind and not to one's experience, to philosophers who (to borrow Kierkegaard's metaphor) write in castles but live in doghouses, to philosophies which do not primarily deal with the realities of life as we live them but are filled with empty universals about experience without ever treating the particulars. Here one does not have to be an existential thinker to want the particulars of how one existentialist was driven to assert in action the worst potential of his thought.

The "objective" particulars of the stabbing are simple enough. On the evening of November 19, 1960, Mailer gave a party at his new apartment on West 94th Street in Manhattan—"a combination of a birthday party for my friend Roger Donogue, and an unofficial kick-off for the Mayoralty campaign." He got into several fights with crashers on the street and then, early in the morning of the next day, he walked over "with a funny look on his face" to his wife as she was preparing for bed and stabbed her. As for the "subjective" particulars, the Ringmaster has not offered much information about his motives, but he did say, "I felt somehow it was phony. . . . It wasn't me." After all of the literary and extraliterary gymnastics that Mailer has put his "image" through, it's hard to say with even relative sureness who Mailer was at any time, particularly in this climacteric of his hipsterism. His comments of the interview offer up as motives the tension between his contempt for his own authenticity and his guilt at betraying the hipsters on the one hand and the implicit assertion that he still was a hipster, that he could find in himself the authenticity to kick a man's head in if the rebellious imperatives of his own self demanded it.* Given the particularly wild state of Mailer's ego at this time, it was certainly easier for him to believe that he had betrayed the hipsters than to accept the fact that they had never quite existed. And must not a man who so declaimed the blessings of authenticity shut up if he did not finally put up? The victim was no arbitrary choice; she was the partner of an obviously complicated marriage. Nothing is more intricate (or private) than a complicated marriage, but Mailer so encourages this sort of conjecture, and the act is so important, that we might press on for a bit. Brock Brower argues that Mailer had tried to totally dominate his second wife and that he had "moved out with her to the pot scene and the sexual anomy of mere orgiastic linkage." By 1960, his explanation goes,

> he had manipulated her until she was almost a living projection of his Hip dares. "Norman finally got his Frankenstein monster," several people have said of that union, and possibly, on that soul-sick

---

* INTERVIEWERS: Are you naturally a hipster or do you have to work at it?

MAILER: I think you're charming. (Laughter) ["An Interview with Norman Mailer," *Mademoiselle,* February, 1961, p. 161.]

and arctic November morn in 1960, he tried to do what Dr Franken-
stein felt compelled to do out on his own icy verge: destroy his own
creature.

As my notes suggest, there are some flaws in Brower's overall account; here, it is most improbable that Mailer attempted at all to
slaughter the monster for the good of mankind. If she had become as
liberated as Brower suggests, it seems more likely that Mailer wanted
out of the competition. Small wonder then that he might say in 1965
that he did not know if the orgasm or the family was more important
or that the sexual emphasis in his writing through the sixties had
gradually swung from orgasm to procreation.

One of the more vivid images that I carry around followed the
sound of someone mightily breaking wind in an undergraduate recita-
tion section fifteen years ago. Most of the class turned around to see
a tackle on the football team fiercely pointing his finger at the mousy,
terrified girl next to him—245 pounds silently shouting, "It wasn't
me, it was her fault." So much of Mailer continued to protest in the
next four years that the divine energy economy might justify murder,
that while he was struggling to kick his addiction to Seconal in 1956
she was

> . . . lying in bed in hate
> of me, the waves of unspoken flesh
> radiating detestation into me because
> I have been brave a little but not nearly
> brave enough for you, greedy bitch,
> Spanish lady, with your murderous
> Indian blood and your crazy purity
> hung on courage in men as if it were
> your queen's own royal balls. . . .

It was her fault; *she* made me stab her to prove my bravery. These
lines are part of "A wandering in prose: for Hemingway: Summer
1956," written in March, 1961, "about a week before the marriage
was finally lost," * and published in 1962 in Mailer's interesting collection of verbal doodlings, *Deaths for the Ladies (and other disasters)*. The title suggests the intricate mixtures of defiance and self-

---

* Norman Mailer, *The Presidential Papers* (New York: Bantam Books,
1964), p. 64 (hereafter cited as *Papers*). The preceding lines are interesting:
"One got out of Bellevue, one did a little work again. The marriage broke up.
The man wasn't good enough. The woman wasn't good enough. A set of psychic stabbings took place." When *Papers* came out in 1963, an unsympathetic
but clever friend said to me, "Yeah, he wasn't good enough to kill her and she
wasn't good enough to die."

hatred which are precisely what makes the collection interesting. On the one hand there are all those lines about cunnilingus, fellatio, the dreariness of married life, the *gallante* telling some lady "Your curse I mean your flow don't smell too bad," how cancer began when "he" refused to strike his mother for visiting him thirty-six hours after he had stabbed his wife, and above all that line offered once by itself and repeated to a cowardly director to explain to him the workings of the world:

> So long
> as
> you
> use
> a knife,
> there's
> some
> love
> left.

By now Mailer had moved into the beginnings of the marriage with his third wife, Lady Jeanne Campbell, and there are a good many lines which attack the rich, the English, and everyone who tries to put a good man down. But there's so much self-hatred—the God of love left me because I was not good enough; there's Loathesome, who squashes something every time he moves; authority deprives Mr. M of depravity; and, several times, doing the limbo bit is good enough for me. Perhaps most relevant to the novel that will follow are the good number of lines about suicide, particularly the one in which the ledge on the window of the nineteenth floor tells you that one nerve screams before you fall.

Mailer has suggested that the primary personal value of these lines lay in their ability to keep him writing at a time when he could do very little composition and that the writing helped him to stave off alcoholism by pushing off for a few hours the moment when he would pick up the bottle. But one thinks of more subtle benefits than these; one thinks of Hemingway saying that his typewriter was his psychiatrist or of the original Hemingway hero, Nick Adams, waiting in the last story in which he appears until the time comes when he can "get rid" of his father's suicide by writing about it. A number of critics have written of fiction as therapy; one of them was Norman Mailer with his critic's hat on, about six months before he began *An American Dream,* writing of Philip Roth's *Letting Go:*

> . . . Roth is not writing a book with a vision of life; on the contrary, one could bet a grand he is working out an obsession. His

concentration is appropriated by something in his life which has been using him up in the past. Virtually every writer, come soon or late, has a cramped-up love affair which is all but hopeless. . . . But the obsession is opposed to art in the same way a compulsive talker is opposed to good conversation. The choice is either to break the obsession or to enter it. The compulsive talker must go through the herculean transformation of learning to quit or must become a great monologuist. Roth tried to get into the obsession—he gave six hundred pages to wandering around in a ten-page story—but he did it without courage. He was too careful not to get hurt on his trip and so he does not reveal himself: he does not *dig.*

But what writer has the courage to take on an obsession, indeed, to revel in the revealing? Why, the same one who wrote, about seven months before he began *An American Dream,* that "for every great writer there could have been a hundred who would have been equally great but lacked courage" or who said about a turn his writing had taken those seven months later:

> To have your hero kill his wife in the first instalment of an eight-part serial is like taking off your clothes in Macy's window. What do you do next? But finally I realized I was the one man in America who could do it. The clue to me is, I figure I've got as much physical courage as the next guy, but I'm profoundly afraid of being a moral coward.

This was offered for the readers of *Life* a few months after *An American Dream* was released in book form, and we might attribute some of the braggadocio to his desire to drum up some sales from low-*Life* readers. Perhaps he originally projected a novel "about someone a little bit like me, who'd had an active life—but someone less successful—who takes a trip across the country with a girl to Las Vegas, and gets caught up in the second Liston-Patterson fight." But what opportunities to work through obsessions the murder offered.

Let us step back for a moment. When Marion Faye was thrown out of his mother's house "he found his trade ready to hand." When Norman Mailer decided around the middle of 1963 that he had to make a good deal of money in a short time, that the only way to do it was to write a novel, and that the novel could only be written by meeting magazine deadlines, he found his subject ready to hand—in fact, within his own skin: "someone a little bit like me!" Stephen Richards Rojack was born about three years before his creator, but both were Harvard graduates; both had recently "felt weak without a drink" for the first time in their lives; both were television celebrities; in the dramatized year of the novel, Rojack had discovered he was capable of suicide; in the same year, the talking ledges appeared in *Deaths for the Ladies;* both men seem to be stockily built five-foot-eighters who like to box; both felt they wandered in a wasteland after great early success; both joined the Progressive party in 1948; and, most importantly, both are (in much different ways, however) professors "of existential psychology with the not inconsiderable thesis that magic, dread, and the perception of death were the roots of motivation." Then there is the tangle of relationships which, if unsympathetically observed, certainly helps to justify Anatole Broyard's claim that Mailer's "career seems to be a brawl between his talent and his exhibitionism. Like Demosthenes, who exposed himself during his speeches to hold his audience, Mailer has made his life a blurb for his books." Cherry Melanie, Rojack's Beatrice, is a physical ringer for Mailer's fourth wife, Beverly Bentley, whom he married the year he began the novel and whose picture was on the original cover of the paperback edition. Judging from the one picture that I have seen of Lady Jeanne, whom Mailer divorced that same crowded year, she remarkably resembles Deborah Caughlin Mangaravidi Kelly, whom Rojack does not stab but strangles to death. If the resemblance is slighter than it seems, I would still guess that the sounds of Deborah's upper-class, British-style putdowns came from echoes still in Mailer's ears. Adele Morales Mailer does not make the book as a character, but of course she made the book possible.

Although the evidence that Deborah was murdered is considerable, the police are forced to drop charges because the official medical report concluded that she had died from a suicidal leap from a window some hundred or more feet above the East River Drive. Obviously, the fix is in, or as Police Lieutenant Roberts, Rojack's interrogator, puts it, "You have a big brother somewhere." But where is he? What mysterious demands will be made upon the killer? Here is Rojack in a cab on his way from the police station to the Lower East Side hideaway where Cherry awaits him:

> . . . I lay back on my seat and felt something close to nausea because mystery revolved about me now, and I did not know if it was hard precise mystery with a detailed solution, or a mystery fathered by the collision of larger mysteries, something so hopeless to determine as the edge of a cloud, or could it be, was it a mystery even worse, something between the two, some hopeless no-man's-land from which nothing could return but exhaustion? And I had a sudden hatred of mystery, a moment when I wanted to be in a cell, my life burned down to the bare lines of a legal defense. . . . I knew . . . I would not be permitted to flee the mystery. I was close to prayer

then, I was very close, for what was prayer but a beseechment *not* to pursue the mystery, "God," I wanted to pray, "let me love that girl, and become a father, and try to be a good man, and do some decent work. Yes God," I was close to begging, "do not make me go back again to the charnel house of the moon."

When Mailer wrote this in January, 1964, he was far from father-less; he had four daughters by his first three wives, and Beverly Mailer was about seven months pregnant with the first of their two sons, Michael. Further, he certainly thought he was doing good work with this novel, and mystery was his business. Still, there is so much that argues that Rojack's plea—indeed the whole attempt to work out the attack of his wife and the waste of abilities—follows in good part from Mailer's probably quite conscious attempt to work through some of his actions and obsessions. He has said of the stabbing: "Let me say that what I did was by any measure awful. It still wasn't insane." So is it awful to justify the killing of a helpless shopkeeper or the alternative of rape instead of masturbation; so is it awful to fall into so perverted a romanticism that one can argue for the tenderness one might feel for the man whose head one is kicking in. Mailer never decisively repudiated the system which at its outer reaches could justify such acts, but then, after *An American Dream,* he never again made such extreme pleas for violence. Compare the 1970 equivalent—"Hell's Angels were possibly nearer to God than the war against poverty"—with the earlier equivalents.

I would bet my financial equivalent of a grand that in the novel Mailer was "not only trying to sell dictatorial theorems, he was also trying to get rid of them." This is Mailer writing of the movement in the novels of D. H. Lawrence from the worship of women to the desire to murder them, then—freed of murderous desires through "the dialectic by which writers deliver themes to themselves"—back to the worship of women in *Lady Chatterley.* He is also writing of a movement from the writer who defined women as sexual objects to be conquered in "The White Negro" and "The Time of Her Time" toward the one who wrote of the idyllic equality in the sex between Rojack and Cherry. *An American Dream,* written by a man in his third marriage in three years, is among many things a plea which might go something like this: Free me from self-hatred; from suicidal temptations and the temptation of suicide itself; from guilt, dread, and the dictatorial extremes of the system which helped to drive me to stab a wife, to insist on reading obscene poems at a YMHA be-tween the stabbing and the sentencing, to insist that rape might be better than masturbation; free me from crazy, destructive mysteries which mask themselves with the demand to prove that I'm not a moral coward. Let me be freed by the dialectic, freed from the most murderous extremes of the system or of that part of the self which produced that part of the system, by pushing the system to its extreme in print. Release me from the suicidal need to show courage by having enough courage to write of a wife murderer who gets away; let me do it courageously under the pressure of deadlines; let this book be not merely the working out of a compulsion, let me so transform this grappling with the system with fine writing that the book is a work of art that justifies the time and energy I spent on the system. And, since I am finally myself, let me also make a great deal of money and regain my reputation. The dedication to wife and son in this new family is not merely seven words after the title page, for though I think that Herzog is a fool, his plea is my plea: "I owe God a human life."

This is one way of looking at the book (before we actually look at the book) which is both fancy and simplistic—for Mailer is still exposing himself with the gleeful self-accusation of an exhibitionist—but I think that it is part of the truth. A more certain and less romantic approach confronts the very romanticism of the book. We remember that in *Advertisements* Mailer lamented the drug dependence, exhaustion, need for immediate success and general lack of courage which prevented him from letting Sergius become an actor and himself from beginning *The Deer Park* yet again, but this time to "travel deep into the paradoxes of time" with his ambitious yet moral protagonist. Since this is late-fifties Mailer, I am fairly sure that "the paradoxes of time" refers to the mysterious interrelationships between growth-time and clock-time. By the time that he began writing *An American Dream* in September, 1963, he had, of course, worked out a sort of metaphysics of growth, and if he applied it to one man's attempts to strengthen his being against many of those forces in America which might seek to weaken it—perversity, war, police, Mafia, politics, mass media, racial terror, high society, big business, and so on—he might have a novel which was simultaneously sharply focused and endlessly reverberating. A good deal of ingenuity and eloquence has been expended in attempts to make *An American Dream* something altogether different from a fictional rendering of Mailer's ontology. For example, Leo Bersani has argued that the many attacks upon the banalities of plot and language in the novel are irrelevant, since the narrator and hero, Stephen Rojack,

by taking the risk of abandoning himself to the fantastic suggestiveness of every person, every object, every smell encountered during
the thirty-two hours he writes about . . . discovers fantasy as a
source of imaginative richness in himself instead of fearing it as an
ominous signal from mysterious, external powers. He moves, in other
words, from fantasy as a psychological illusion about the world to
the use of fantasy as a somewhat self-conscious but exuberant display
of his own inventive powers. Every menace becomes the occasion for
a verbal performance, and his fluttering nervousness about being
deprived of his "center" is rather humorously belied by the incredibly
dense and diversified self which his language reveals and created.
Nothing in the book . . . except the virtuosity of the writing itself
indicates a way out of the nightmare which Rojack seems to be
telling. The nightmare would be nothing more than a nasty story if
Mailer, like his critics, had allowed it to separate itself from the
virtuosity, from, especially, the metaphorical exuberance which is,
I think, a way of mocking and outdoing the dangerous inventiveness
of a magic-ridden world. This means of course that the *playfulness*
of the novel is by no means a frivolous attitude toward "dirty" or
"ugly" events, but rather the natural tone of a man for whom events
have become strictly literary-novelistic situations to be freely exploited for the sake of a certain style and the self-enjoyment it perhaps unexpectedly provides.

Curiously, this much better describes what is happening in Mailer's
next novel, *Why Are We in Vietnam?*, than it does the role of the
narrator in *Dream*. D. J. is playful, not just in the wide sense in which
we always play roles, but playful as "putting us on," as we might say,
or "guying us," as Henry James might. But we are to believe that
since Steve Rojack was kept by his weaknesses and society's temptations from writing the twenty volumes of metaphysics which would
prove that "God was not love but courage," he is offering the narrative as one example of the workings of this metaphysics of courage
which is precisely the way out of the nightmare. He can reveal as
much of the workings as he does because, after years of spiritual dalliance, he has been forced to risk his social position and his present
life to maintain his option on future life. When one considers the
terms of this Maileresque religion, the appelation of Saint Stephen,
which Christopher Ricks sarcastically applied to Rojack, is more apt
than he suspected. Mailer has said that "in order to be profoundly
religious, to become a saint for example, one must dare insanity."
The novel asks us to believe that Rojack's frantic quest for authenticity, bred by his terror of dying forever, drove him into many
demonic areas of American life and his own psyche. Like Prufrock's
Lazarus, Rojack arises from the dead to tell us all, not to mock and

outdo "the dangerous inventiveness of a magic-ridden world." "The fantastic suggestiveness of every person, every object, every smell encountered" is not at all the fantastic display of his inventive powers, but his uncannily accurate responses to the actual nature of the people, objects, and odors about him. Rojack might create the metaphors which explain these entities, but Mailer wants us to believe that these metaphors, like the ones in the dialogues in *Cannibals,* are more filled with truth about what is "out there" and in us than the laborious recordings of conventional science.

Saint Stephen does have his whimsical moments in some small incidents—the telephone conversations with the producer of his television show and his department head at the university—but we are to take these as his quite correct responses to the very few frivolous intrusions into his most serious struggle. But the whole of the book has a bizarrely playful side to it; this follows not from Rojack's novelistic invention but from Mailer's zany intrusions. Dwight Macdonald once wrote in one of his *Esquire* film columns how distracting it was to see one of those movies which are studded with "guest stars" in cameo roles. Mary Magdalene runs backward from the cross and turns; the audience gasps, "It's Shelley Winters!" Macdonald even improved on this by remarking that it was like seeing a crazy uncle run into the room dressed up as Napoleon. One gets something of this feeling all through *An American Dream.* For example, we see that groupy of pugilism Stephen Norman Rojack Mailer deepening in concentration as he prepares to take out his opponent in a boxing exhibition turned ugly, then toughing out the threat of a retired top-ranking boxer; Stephen Mailer beats up the best black singer in the world for (among other things) making the two mistakes of calling him fat and threatening him with a knife. Jim Brown got to do his run in *The Dirty Dozen;* Norman Rojack, who was too small to play varsity football at Harvard but was a gutty house football player, heaves his first-second-third wife out the window and runs toward East River Drive where she has landed:

> There was one instant when the open air reached my nose and gave me a perfect fleeting sense of adventure on the wind, of some adventure long gone—a memory: I was eighteen, playing House Football for Harvard; it was a kickoff and the ball was coming to me, I had it, and was running.

Three years after he completed the novel, Mailer played the lead in his movie *Beyond the Law*—Francis X. Pope, a tough, Irish, New York police lieutenant with a knowledge of good and evil. But he really could not wait that long. Here is Rojack bending over his dead wife, the goal line in his psychic touchdown:

> "Are you the husband?" a voice asked in my ear. Without turning around, I had an idea of the man who spoke. He was a detective, and he must be at least six feet tall, big through the shoulder and with the beginning of a gut. It was an Irish voice oiled with a sense of its authority, and in control of a thousand irritations. "Yes," I said, and looked up to meet a man who did not correspond to his voice. He was about five-eight in height, almost slim, with a hard, clean face and the sort of cold blue eyes which live for a contest.

Five-eight, cold blue eyes which live for a contest, wants to be six feet, wants to be Irish, wants to have a hard, clean face, wants to be slim— "It's Norman Mailer!" we gasp.

One of the attributes of the nonfiction of the sixties that I did not mention is the frequent display of humor. The comic gift that Mailer showed in the early fifties with Guinevere's story for Hollywood, "The Man Who Studied Yoga," and "The Patron Saint of Macdougal Alley" does not really surface again in the fifties. The antics of the movie moguls are well rendered in *The Deer Park,* but Mailer was too concerned with their power and the damage they do to play up their comic possibilities; compare the novel with the play of *The Deer Park* which he finished in 1967. Personal and social concerns turn the parodies in the *Voice* columns into concrete, and the monolithically serious Mailer was too busy with his rebellion and new freedoms to court a laugh for the rest of the decade. But by the second paragraph of "Superman Comes to the Supermarket" (with its political definition of "the man in the street" as "the quixotic voter who will pull the lever for some reason so salient as: 'I had a brown-nose lieutenant once with Nixon's looks,' or 'that Kennedy must have false teeth'"), it is clear that Mailer was already occasionally tiring of what in 1968 Dwight Macdonald called "the Messianic-*cum*-Superman nonsense he has too often in the past indulged himself with." With everything else in *An American Dream,* with the working out of obsessions while he seriously played Superman and the Messiah, Mailer was also tiring of those most unfrivolous assumptions of the system. Sometimes he quite simply let his frivolity go. To the temperance cry of "Ireland sober is Ireland free," Joyce replied, "Ireland sober is Ireland stiff." Mailer capering is Mailer serious; one can almost hear the giggle above the cantus firmus of "This isn't just anyone being frivolous; this is happening in *my* psyche where one can also find working the course of

American history at the present moment." There's more of this—for example, Mailer's silently offering himself once again as the presidential candidate (he's so *busy* in the novel!)—but most of the book is not comical-serious but serious-serious, as he tried throughout to dramatize the workings of that architectonic science of expanding energies which reaches down to lend meaning to all human activities. The novel can be approached from many points of view; I have chosen first to consider Mailer's attempts to translate the insights of the nonfiction into fiction and then to judge his success. Let us then close with the novel as Mailer did, in a sense, by turning to *The Presidential Papers,* that collection published the year he began the novel which is in so many ways a wild yet fascinating propaedeutic for the transfigured world of *An American Dream.*

II

In a frequently quoted section of "Superman Comes to the Supermarket," Mailer wrote:

> Since the First World War Americans have been leading a double life and our history has moved on two rivers, one visible, the other underground; there has been the history of politics which is concrete, factual, practical and unbelievably dull if not for the actions of some of these men and there is a subterranean river of untrapped, ferocious, lonely and romantic desires, that concentration of ecstasy and violence which is the dream life of the nation.
>
> . . . this myth, that each of us was born to be free, to wander, to have adventure and to grow on the waves of the violent, the perfumed, and the unexpected had a force which could not be tamed no matter how the nation's regulators—politicians, medicos, policemen, professors, priests, rabbis, ministers, *idéologues,* psychoanalysts, builders, executives and endless communicators—would brick-in the modern life with hygiene upon sanity, and middle-brow homily over platitude; the myth would not die.

The quickest way to justify *An American Dream*'s considerable improbabilities of plot and characterization or the accounts of murder, sodomy, and incest which crowd its pages is to pick up the title with one hand, the quotation above with the other, and argue that Mailer attempted a dream vision of a collective unconscious driven half insane by the frustration of the myth of adventure. And so he did, but he got far more mileage out of the title and contents than that. The Manichean system which informs the book demands the existence of two American dreams, one which is of authenticity and one which is not, and the novel attempts to render the sick American unconscious precisely through the collision of these two collective dreams.

With the exception of "A Program for the Nation" and "She Thought the Russians Was Coming," all of the articles, columns, open letters, and commentary that were gathered together to form *The Presidential Papers* were written in the three years which separated the August, 1960, completion of "Superman" and September, 1963, when Mailer began writing the first installment of *Dream* for *Esquire*. This was a period of assimilation for Mailer as he set down in print for the first time the ideas about dread, magic, the Devil, and authenticity which gradually fell into coherent relationship with each other. As he related these ideas to the state of the American unconscious, there several times appeared the suggestion of a collective nightmare, one which stands juxtaposed to the dream of perfumed adventure as a sort of black reflection. Thus, Mailer explained in this eschatological way why so many New Yorkers responded with apathy to the threat of imminent extinction during the Cuban missile crisis of October, 1962:

> Which of us could say that nowhere in the secret debates of our dreams or the nightmare of open action, in those stricken moments when the legs are not as brave as the mind or the guts turn to water, which of us could say that never nor nowhere had we struck a pact with the Devil and whispered, Yes, let us deaden God, let Him die within me, it is too frightening to keep Him alive, I cannot bear the dread. . . .
>
> We sat in apathy because most of us, in the private treacherous dialogues of our sleep, had turned our faith away from what was most vital in our mind. . . . We had drawn back in fright from ourselves, as if in our brilliance lay madness, and beyond the horizon dictated by others was death. . . . We had been afraid of death as no generation in the history of mankind has been afraid. None of us would need to scream as eternity recaptured our breath—we would be too deep in hospital drugs. . . . We had turned our back on the essential terror of life, We believed in the Devil, we hated nature.
>
> So we watched the end approach with apathy. Because if it was God we had betrayed and the vision with which He had sent us forth, if our true terror now was not of life but of what might be waiting for us in death, then how much easier we might find it to be blasted into eternity deep in the ruin of ten million others, how much better indeed if the world went with us, and death was destroyed as completely as life. Yes, how many of the millions in New York had a secret prayer: that whomever we thought of as God be exploded with us, and Judgement cease.

With all that has been written about the different relationships between courage, growth, authenticity, God's Vision, and the struggle for being, it should furrow no brows if I were to refer to the myth of growth and adventure "on the waves of the violent, the perfumed, and the unexpected" as the Dream of Being or the Dream of Authenticity. If Mailer were much more simpleminded than he is, if courage and adventure were always associated with God and his soldiers, and if cowardice and passivity always dominated the actions of the Devil and his soldiers, then we might make use of the preceding quotation and designate the inner life of the latter as the Failure of the Dream or the Nightmare of Judgment. This sort of simplistic reduction is made impossible by the fact that God is locked in battle with an equally strong opponent as well as by the realities of individual and collective behavior. Such a formidable opponent as the Devil cannot be paralyzed before danger, and neither can his soldiers—all those who suppress the expression of the God-given talents and the Dream of Being in themselves and others. (Obviously, all of the regulators listed a few pages earlier qualify as soldiers of the Devil.) However, we must realize that Mailer did not want to use his polarizing system to turn everything into God-Devil, black-white, Free World–Communist World simplicities, but rather designed it as a tool for bringing value, drama, and insight to human complexity. In the same way, perhaps his insistence on making courage the primary virtue is not as ominously childish as it seems. If we regard courage as an absolute and all acts which do not realize this condition as degradations, as being in some degree cowardly, then we might perceive how an act of a soldier of the Devil might be brave by normal standards but cowardly by Mailer's, Since he has defined bravery as "doing something that engages grave risk without the certainty that you're going to win," then true bravery would consist of acting in a dangerous situation with a dependence on nothing more than one's own resources. The cowardice of a soldier of the Devil is not paralysis before danger, precisely because the Devil has found some way to lessen the sense of danger to him. All of these ways are in some sense magical.

In "Ten Thousand Words a Minute," that long piece on the first Liston-Patterson fight which is a kind of nonfictional twin to *An American Dream,* Mailer defines magic as the agent of *both* God and the Devil "which entered . . . [one's] brain before an irrevocable battle." The apparent slip of attributing magical powers to both God and the Devil is resolved when Mailer implicitly distinguishes between the white magic freed by self-reliance and the black magic invoked by swearing obedience to a sovereignty higher than oneself:

> Patterson was the champion of every lonely adolescent and every man who had been forced to live alone, every protagonist who tried to remain unique in a world whose waters washed apathy and compromise into the pores. He was the hero of all these unsung romantics who walk the street at night seeing the vision of Napoleon while their feet trip over the curb, he was part of the fortitude which could sustain those who lived for principle, those who had gone to war with themselves and ended with discipline. He was the artist. He was the man who could not forgive himself if he gave less than his best chance for perfection. . . . Liston came from that world where you had no dream but making it, where you trusted no one because your knowledge of evil was too quick to its presence in everyone; Liston came from that world where a man with a dream was a drunk in the gutter, and the best idealism was found in a rabbit's foot blessed by a one-eyed child. Liston was voodoo, Liston was magic, Liston was the pet of the witch doctor; Liston knew that when the gods gathered to watch an event, you kept your mind open to the devils who might work for you. They would come neatly to your eye and paralyze your enemy with their curse. *You were their slave, but they were working for you. Yes, Liston was the secret hero of every man who had ever given mouth to a final curse against the dispositions of the Lord and made a pact with Black Magic. Liston was Faust. Liston was the light of every racetrack tout who dug a number on the way to work. He was the hero of every man who would war with destiny for so long as he had his gimmick:* the cigarette smoker, the lush, the junkie, the tea-head, the fixer, the bitch, the faggot, the switchblade, the gun, the corporation executive. [Italics mine.]

Mailer has admitted that his dichotomy might be wrong, that Liston might have become the soldier of God and Patterson of the Devil in this archetypal confrontation "where decision is rare and never clear." But the schema still holds. The man of God, the soldier in His war for expanding Being, is a solitary figure wholly dependent upon his courage and the discipline he has exercised in developing his innate (read God-given) powers.* In Patterson's case, these are

* Since Patterson's powers were a part of Being and since Liston knocked him out in the first round,

> the world quivered in some rarified accounting of subtle psychic seismographs, and the stocks of certain ideal archetypes shifted their status in our country's brain. Sex had proved superior to Love still one more time, the Hustler had taken another pool game from the Infantryman, the Syndicate rolled out the Liberal, the Magician hyped the Artist, and . . . the Devil had shown that the Lord was dramatically weak. [*Papers,* p. 255.]

"the forces of the past which had forced their way into the seed which made him [and which] now wanted no less than that he be extraordinary . . . great . . . a champion of his people." Because he is armed with his gimmick, the soldier of the Devil needs courage less, for the end is less in doubt for him. Stated differently, one is a soldier for the Devil whenever he hopes to gain power from the totemizing of things. This is why Mailer felt that he betrayed Patterson when, a few hours before the fight, he had spun a lighter at the Playboy Club to see who would win. It is also why the executive in "Responses and Reactions II," the stunning piece on dread first published in the February, 1963, *Commentary,* wants to kill himself. Suicide beckons not because he is neurotic or because a pure, Freudian *thanatos* has erupted but because he has just perceived that the sense of secure identity can only come to him if he touches things. By killing himself he hopes to save his soul before it falls into permanent bondage to the Devil.

Presumably, the Playboy Club was "the place for magic" because it was "bossland," a haunt of people who, like the hunters in *Why Are We in Vietnam?* take for granted the fact that they enter into any battle with an enormous armament advantage. Like Marx, Mailer deplores the subordination of the self to the things which were originally created to free the self. But as a sort of supernatural gloss to the thought of his early idol, he argues that this flight from authenticity aids an external force which is engaged in a cosmic war.

We are now able to postulate the two dreams locked in a literal death struggle deep in the American psyche. One of them is indeed the Dream of Being, of preserving our purchase on eternity through the growth gained by self-reliance, courage, and what might be called creative discipline. (Patterson would be one exemplar of this; Rojack trying to get through the evening without a drink or nerving himself to meet all challenges is another.) The other vision is the Dream of Power, that pact with the Devil which is struck when we exchange reliance upon the self for reliance upon other things or other people. Since the goals of this dream are usually some combination of money, recognition, or power over others—the rewards which society has to offer—we can say that the effects of the Dream of Power are more likely to be publicly evident than those of the Dream of Being, and since the area of conquest for the soldiers of the Devil lies more in the public arena than in the self, we can easily perceive a reason different from the one offered on page 110 to explain why "the power of the world belongs to the Devil, and God needs men to overthrow him." Authentic action might also yield one money or acclaim or power, but these easily visible manifestations of success need not accompany the man who is enjoying the private success of realizing the Dream of Being. If the tokens of public success have been gained by a soldier of God, they have been the result of his exercising the same faculties that have brought private success to his unknown counterpart. Patterson could not have amassed wealth and fame nor Kennedy great admiration and power had not these two existential heroes performed lone acts of will and courage:* "Kennedy's most characteristic quality is the remote and private air of a man who has traversed some lonely terrain of experience, of loss and gain, of nearness to death, which leaves him isolated from the mass of others."

During the early sixties, Mailer embellished his explanation of how one might fight off the Dream of Power and enact the Dream of Being by freeing the white magic of instinctual power. The brave acts which most enable us to expand properly spring—and here Kierkegaard, whose name Mailer has dropped a dozen times in as many years, makes himself felt—from total desperation, from the

---

* All of this is situational. Like William Blake, the only British Romantic that he has quoted in print, Mailer argues that most of us are alloys of the Godly and the Devilish, with the proportions of the mixture shifting with our response to each significant situation. Thus Mailer wrote that the God-Devil, talent-magic, self-reliance–dependency dichotomy he intuited from Patterson versus Liston "spoke . . . from the countered halves of my own nature" (*Papers*, p. 261). The Devilish part of Patterson might at any time opt to serve the Dark Prince of Entropy, and Mailer would have said that the Devilish part of Kennedy was behind the Bay of Pigs invasion. And the Dream of Power means power unfairly earned and used. In 1956 the pre-Manichean Mailer responded to the question "Whom do you hate?" with "People who have power and no compassion, that is, no simple human understanding" (*Advertisements*, p. 271). Since then he has had much to say about how power is unfairly earned. Of course, his fascination with energy—that is, with all forms of power—is so complete that one of the best one-sentence descriptions of his career is this observation by Alfred Kazin:

> Mailer is a chronicler of American power in the grand realistic mode that made the novel in this country; which is why people are interested in him even when they don't approve of him, and why his novels—of war, *The Naked and the Dead;* of orgy and McCarthyism, *The Deer Park;* of sexual hate and social skill, *An American Dream*—always revolve around images of the power of concentrated intellectual force, of the power to move other bodies, above all, their minds. ["Imagination and the Age," *The Reporter,* May 5, 1966, p. 34.]

sense of having come to an experiential dead end. And they are executed in what Mailer has called, borrowing a Zen phrase, the purity of no-concept.* Since the thinking mind is excessively attuned to those societal demands which estrange us from our instincts, it is not surprising that conceptualization should be absent when we are engaged in those acts which are authentic because they help us to grow. Perhaps a quotation from the *Mademoiselle* interview will make the relationship between authenticity and the purity of no-concept more graphic. Mailer then defined the emotional quality of the authentic as

> the moment when our aesthetic and theological and ecclesiastical sense of meaning and the beatnik sense of kick, the hipster sense of cool, all came together. It's that moment, the Spanish moment of truth, where one feels that it's no use arguing about anything because this is the way it is really and this is what we must do.

This 1960 idea was somewhat altered in the next few years; the cool hipster dropped away, and Mailer several times suggested that an accurate sense of the theological was more often accompanied by dread than by cool. Certainly Stephen Rojack had had little dread or magical cool until his twenty-second or -third year. The first link in the chain of events that brought him to his thesis that "magic, dread and the perception of death were the roots of motivation" was his being given the command of a recalcitrant platoon in World War II as

> a stiff, overburdened, nervous young Second Lieutenant, fresh from Harvard, graduated a year behind Prince Jack. . . . I had gone into the Army with a sweaty near-adolescent style, Harvard on the half shell ("Raw-Jock" Rojack was the sporting name bestowed on me in House Football) and I had been a humdrum athlete and, as a student, excessively bright: Phi Beta Kappa, *summa cum laude,* Government.
>
> Small wonder I was thus busy working to keep some government among the hard-nosed Southerners and young Mafiosos from the Bronx who made up the double nucleus of my platoon, working so busily that death this night first appeared to me as a possibility considerably more agreeable than my status in some further disorder. I really didn't care much longer whether I stayed alive. When I

---

* It is a basic tenet of Zen that there is no need for cognition if "the whole man" has focused his attention on a particular task, act, or sensation. Mailer writes "There would be very few problems in life if our organs could perform two or more complex highly differentiated functions equally well at once" (*Cannibals,* p. 278). A Zen proverb which would say essentially the same thing would go, "A man should not urinate and sing at the same time."

steered us up the hill therefore to get pinned down in a long bad line, one hundred feet from the summit, a modest twin dome, a double hill with a German machine gun on one knoll and a German machine gun on the other, I was so ready to die in atonement I was not even scared.

It was Rojack's ignorance of the theological which helped him to free as much of the white magic of the unconscious as he did. His having been excessively bright but a humdrum athlete neatly suggests that over-dependence upon the intellectual and neglect of the instinctual brought him to such a desperate situation that he was ready to embark upon radically different, authentic action. And since Rojack had no theological sense, no perception of how one can gain or lose the chance for eternal life, he was able to experience the peculiar relief of having nothing to lose by dying. As Rojack entered into the realm of authentic action by preparing to do what quite simply must be done, he felt "danger withdraw . . . like an angel, withdraw like a retreating wave over a quiet sea, sinking quietly into the sand." He then ran up the hill toward the guns that were firing at him. His freedom from fear and his willingness to do what must be done opened him to the blessings of the Navigator at the seat of his unconscious, instinctual self—referred to as *it* by Rojack—that donor of white magic who guided each of his two simultaneously thrown grenades to within a few yards of each emplacement. Rojack's flow of talent continued as, with a kind of mystical ease, he then shot three of the four surviving Germans. But *it* deserted Rojack as he confronted the last surviving German, dying but still holding his bayonet, with eyes that contained

all of it, the two grenades, the blood on my thigh, the fat faggot, the ghost with the pistol, the hunchback, the blood, those bloody screams that never sounded, it was all in his eyes, he had eyes I was to see once later on an autopsy table in a small town in Missouri . . . eyes of blue, so perfectly blue and mad they go all the way in deep into celestial vaults of sky, eyes which go back all the way to God is the way I think I heard it said once in the South, and I faltered before that stare, clear as ice in the moonlight, and hung on one knee, not knowing if I could push my wound, and suddenly it was gone, the clean presence of *it*, the grace, *it* had deserted me in the moment I hesitated, and now I had no stomach to go. . . . I fired. And missed. And fired again. And missed.

In the last chapter of the novel, we learn that the eyes on the autopsy table belonged to an old man who was dying of cancer when he suddenly perished from peritonitis. For Mailer, cancer is entropic growth—that leap of the cells into the creation of nonbeing, the unspoken intimation that our purchase on eternity has been lost, that we have ceased to exist in the continuum of nature. What was in the eyes of both the dying German and the dead Missourian was the perception that their being had died before their lives had ended; they knew there would be no more life for them.

Before the confrontation with the German's eyes, Rojack presumably believed that all death was nothingness. Consequently, he was able, at least once, to overcome his fear of dying. But Mailer-esque religion passed from the German's eyes to Rojack's, and with it, dread.* The talent which partially authentic action had freed in Rojack retreated before the demand for a still more authentic act, for there are levels to the authentic, and Rojack had just touched bottom. In civilian life, the most difficult authentic action would be the one which is most foreign to our normal sense of "the good" but which is ordered by the most fundamental demand of one's being—it must survive. Thus, the command to kill might be ordered not by "that religion which is called Judeo-Christian" but, to turn again to "Ten Thousand Words A Minute," by

> an older religion, a more primitive one—a religion of blood, a murderous and sensitive religion which mocks the effort of the understanding to approach it, and scores the lungs of men like D. H. Lawrence, and burns the brain of men like Ernest Hemingway when they explore out into the mystery, searching to discover some part of the

* Although Mailer has dropped Kierkegaard's name a number of times and even referred to *The Concept of Dread* in *Why Are We in Vietnam?*, his use of the term markedly differs from the Danish philosopher's. For the latter, dread was "the dizziness of freedom which occurs when the spirit would posit the synthesis, and freedom then grazes down into its own possibility, grasping at finiteness to sustain itself. In this dizziness freedom succumbs" (*The Concept of Dread*, tr. by Walter Lowrie [Princeton: Princeton University Press, 1946], p. 53). Perhaps the term is more clearly expressed in his *Journals:*

> . . . dread is a desire for what one fears, a sympathetic antipathy; dread is an alien power which takes hold of the individual, and yet one cannot extricate oneself from it, does not wish to, because one is afraid, but what one fears attracts one. Dread renders the individual powerless and the first sin always happens in a moment of weakness." [*The Journals of Kierkegaard*, tr. and ed. by Alexander Dru (London: Oxford University Press, 1951), p. 402.]

Mailer's emphasis is not on the dizziness of freedom (which might occur to someone who has no consciousness of the supernatural) but on dread as the reponse to the awareness of the presence of God and/or the Devil, which might or might not leave one powerless.

secret. It is the view of life which looks upon death as a condition which is more alive than life or unspeakably more deadening.

Judaic-Christian "morality" would certainly insist that Rojack kill the German soldier, and so would the more primitive religion (which anthropologists seem to have missed but Mailer somehow unearthed). It is not easy to kill a man when you know, as Rojack knew, that you are speeding his journey into a condition unspeakably more deadening than life, but the operative law of the novel is the construction of the same absolutist who ominously said, three years earlier, "If you're going to grind your heel into the face of a dying man . . . let the act finally be authentic. If you're going to do it, *do it.*" Whether Rojack could not kill the German because he was unwilling to speed the latter into nothingness or whether he was simply stunned to learn that a potential eternity of life or a certain eternity of death hung on his acts, his courage balked before the perception that "death was a creation more dangerous than life." He could not be fully authentic, he could not *do it,* and that free exercise of talent which is the blessing of authenticity fled with his courage.

The novel would be a vastly easier one to deal with if we could flatly say that with the murder of his wife Rojack was ripped from the sane, everyday world of midtown duplexes; of roughly recognizable cause and effect; of academic career, television show, parties, charity balls, liberalism, and the workings of the Judaic-Christian code (all with concomitant imagery) to Harlem; to the Lower East Side and Waldorf penthouses; to the world of magic, dread, existential God, Devil, curses; to the primitive imagery of swamps, forests, grottoes, seabeds, jungles, deserts, split heavens, and dark, whistling winds. The murder did tear him from any dependence on the first world, which indeed exists to protect us from the terror of the second. But from that moonlit night in his early twenties when he first sensed the workings of the second world to that moonlit night two decades later when he killed his wife, he had tried, as the saying goes, to have the best of both worlds. For example, he had tried to preach the commandments of the murderous and sensitive religion from the easy security of an academic lectern. There were times when he realized that this could not be done; the last quoted phrase in the preceding paragraph is Rojack's, uttered in his explanation of why he had surrendered that place in Congress which had largely been provided for him by what he alone knew was an act of only partial bravery in the battlefield. The possessor of so solid an image—the

handsome, twenty-six-year-old, intelligent, war-hero congressman—
Rojack was too often torn from his image, from the world of rational
politics, by the primitive message of the German's eyes, by the moon
which acts in the book as the herald of the dreadful presence of the
second world:

> Where many another young athlete or hero might have had a vast
> and continuing recreation with sex, I was lost in a private kaleido-
> scope of death. I could not forget the fourth soldier. His eyes had
> come to see what was waiting on the other side, and they told me
> that death was a creation more dangerous than life. I could have had
> a career in politics if only I had been able to think that death was
> zero, death was everyone's emptiness. But I knew it was not. I re-
> mained an actor. My personality was built upon a void. . . . I
> wanted to depart from politics before I was separated from myself
> forever by the distance between my public appearance which had
> become vital on television . . . and my secret frightened romance
> with the phases of the moon. About the month you decide not to
> make a speech because it is the week of the full lunar face you also
> know if still you are sane that politics is not for you and you are not
> for politics.

We learn of only two acts performed by Rojack during his one-
term Washington stint. One was his 1948 bolting the Democratic
party for the Progressive ticket, so that he ran more for sure defeat
than for reelection. This ultimately nonpolitical act was an authentic,
second-world one, performed so that he would not separate himself
from his instinctual self forever. The other act was his seduction of
Deborah Kelly, mentioned in the first paragraph of the book, wherein
Mailer takes pains to let us know that his hero has acted out the
stuff of American fantasy life and will probably continue to do so;
Deborah would have been bored by a diamond as big as the Ritz,
and the seduction came as the conclusion of a double date with his
fellow congressman and war hero, Jack Kennedy. (In the original
Esquire version, Mailer really let his zany obsession with the Kennedys go and told us that "We even spent part of one night on a long
double date, and it promised to be a good night for me. I stole his
girl.") But to return to the serious-serious—for I think Mailer largely
intends us to take the seduction that way—Stephen was no soldier of
Being but just a copulating scoundrel of inauthenticity. We might
reach back to one of the novel's hip locutions, being "with it," as
Rojack was with *it* and could therefore throw grenades with such
accuracy and shoot the first three Germans with such ease. Like any
authentic act, the sexual one demands total absorption in its possi-

bilities; the only way to be with it in sex is to be only with the sexual act, but that Devilish 1946 version of Saint Stephen was agog with Deborah's Bourbon, Hapsburg, banker, financier, priest antecedents and with her father who

> had made a million two hundred times. So there was a vision of treasure, far-off blood, and fear. The night I met her we had a wild ninety minutes in the back seat of my car parked behind a trailer truck on a deserted factory street in Alexandria, Virginia. Since Kelly owned part of the third largest trucking firm in the Midwest and West, I may have had a speck of genius to try for his daughter where I did. Forgive me. I thought the road to President might begin at the entrance to her Irish heart. She heard the snake rustle in *my* heart; on the telephone next morning she told me I was evil, awful and evil, and took herself back to the convent in London where she had lived at times before.

Well, Stephen, you'll have to earn our forgiveness. However wild your tumble was, your primary concern was not to make love but to gain power; your immediate goal was not to free the white magic of the being but to move closer toward one of the ultimate goals of the American Dream of Power, the presidency. The black magic, the gimmick, you sought was the support of the Kelly millions and connections, to be gained by possessing Deborah near a manifestation of the Kelly power.

But Rojack's pursuit of the Dream of Power and his invocation of black magic have gone much further than this political purpose, since Deborah and the Kelly fortune are, in the prevailing symbolism of the novel, the choicest gifts of the Devil. To understand the workings of this symbolism, we must briefly turn to Deborah's father, Barney Oswald Kelly, whom one critic has quite accurately called the Devil's vicar. Religious metaphors fit Kelly well. First, he functions in *Dream* as the priest-general of such Devilish forces of power and magic as his daughter, her maid, Ruta, the CIA, and the Mafia. Alfred Kazin's description, "the money man inside the golden room," describes in secular terms how fully Kelly has realized that historic, American, Faustian Dream of Power which Mailer feels is religious— even if it is the religion of the Devil. And Kelly has risen to the golden room by acting out a sort of Maileresque *Pilgrim's Progress* in reverse, with the white magic of authenticity constantly spurned and black magic constantly invoked.

By the time Kelly was twenty-three, he had parlayed the three thousand dollars of life's savings stolen from his miserly father into a million and the chance to court and marry Leonora Caughlin Mangaravidi, the heiress of a family high in international society. As a part of what Mailer calls his biological view of history, he argues that the primary function of marriage is to produce the most remarkable possible offspring. Clearly, this was not Kelly's first purpose. Just before the climax of the novel, he tells Rojack that his wife spooked him but that he needed the Caughlin connections. When she didn't conceive, he feared that the marriage would be annulled, and there he was, without her, "upstart, whereas with her—I adored the life she opened, Leonora's friends were the patch for me. Money which cannot buy into the most amusing world is cabbage, stinking, stifling cabbage, that much I knew at twenty-three." So reproduction also took on great importance for Kelly, but his purpose was antithetical to adding to the forces of the army of Being. A child is needed to secure his position in that world of weighted advantage and accustomed ease which Mailer usually associates with the Devil. Far more than the charm of stylish acquaintances, Kelly sought in this world the black magic of the Caughlin connections. During the last half of the Ontological Decade, Mailer liked to think that the magical intercessions of God and the Devil might be operative anywhere, but surely they affected the actions of mighty men (like himself?). Kelly speaks for his creator when he tells Rojack that

> God and the Devil are very attentive to the people at the summit. I don't know if they stir much in the average man's daily stew, no great sport for spooks, I would suppose, in a ranch house, but do you suppose God or the Devil left Lenin and Hitler or Churchill alone? No. They bid for favors and exact revenge. . . . There's nothing but magic at the top.

The cosmic heavyweights *must* be present when two such different men as Patterson and Liston meet to decide who is the terrestrial champion at pounding one's opponent into unconsciousness, or of coming as close as possible.

We are far from Fitzgerald's romance of the rich; Kelly did not seek, as Gatsby did, to rise out of human struggle, to be high above the sweating poor—high where clothes never soil, flowers never wilt, pleasures never fade. Kelly, like Mailer, wants a dynamic Heraclitean world, but he was unwilling to exercise authentic self-reliance in his pursuit of pleasure, to "make his own kicks" as Mailer claimed he first made his in his revolt from that world of genteel hypocrisy which he often calls Devilish when the Manichean mood is upon him, as it so often is in print.

We might push further. These lines appear in a fragment of a novel included in *Papers:* ". . . God has hegemony over us only as we create each other. God owns the creation, but the Devil has power over all we waste. . . ." Although this is taken from a passage dealing with digestion and excrement, it illuminates the nature of Kelly's devilish desires—as indeed, almost everything of the Ontological Decade illuminates everything else. Hegemony or power which encourages others to free their own powers, to be authentic, is godly power. The possession of this power is the primary requisite for Mailer's existential politician. But if the Devil has power over all we waste, whether in ourselves or in others, then Kelly is doubly guilty of an alliance with the Devil. For he has not only wasted the possible benefits of self-reliance; he has, even before conception, subordinated the child's being to his own social advantage. There is really no need to continue arguing that Deborah is the product of a satanic pact, for Mailer is quite explicit about this. Kelly referred to himself as Napoleon, but it was to a higher general that he directed his plea for a child. It is no acccident that the ambitious Kelly bound himself to the more evil of the primitive powers at just the same age that the vacillating Rojack backed away from the older religion in Italy:

> "Well," B. Oswald Kelly said to himself, "Napoleon, the armies must occupy the womb." And we did. My troops made one do-johnny of a march. . . . I drilled my salt into her, I took a dive deep down into a vow, I said in my mind; "Satan, if it takes your pitchfork up to my gut, let me blast a child into this bitch!" And something happened, no sulphur, no brimstone, but Leonora and I met way down there in some bog, some place awful, and I felt something take hold in her. . . . That was it. Deborah was conceived.
> . . . you strike a bargain with the Devil, the Devil will collect. That's where Mephisto is found. In the art of collection. Trust me: Leonora was in bad shape after the birth, gutted, all of that. I didn't care, I had the infant—that was my connection to good luck.

By this time, the reader knows very well that Kelly's force is the power of the Devilish half of primitive blackness. Sixty pages before the appearance of the preceding quotation, Rojack reflects that Deborah is the Devil's daughter; thirty pages before, he is over-whelmed by a vision that he is dead and "was in the antechamber of Hell" as he waits in the lobby for an elevator to Kelly's door. Upon arrival he is greeted by the family crest, which "includes a lion and serpent—both forms taken by Satan in *Paradise Lost*—and his motto, starkly honest as Kelly can afford to make it in our time, is *Victoria in Caelo Terraque.*" (There is also on the shield a naked child—the contribution from the Kelly family shield to the symbols from the Caughlin and the Mangaravidi coats of arms which symbolizes the sacrifice of Deborah to Satanic powers.)

With his place on the isle of the socially blessed secured by black magic, Kelly was off to the Riviera, where magical traffickings with another satanist, "the Devil's little gift," not only made his instinct for the stock market infallible but gave him enormous leverage in unheroic confrontations:

> Lying in bed I could feel the potential of a given stock as much as if I were bathing in the thoughts of a thousand key investors. I could almost hear the sound of the mother factory. . . . And there were other spookeries. One time a bugger started to give me a hard time, pompous little promoter. As he was walking away, I said to myself, "Drop, you bugger," and he had epilepsy right at my door. Wondrous sort of power.

By 1946, then, Kelly had made his first two hundred million, and by the time he talked to Rojack in 1962, this prince of the Devil was able to describe himself with some accuracy as "a spider," with "strings in everywhere from the Muslims to the *New York Times.*" He connects the traditional penthouse splendor of the Waldorf, where he lives, with the New Vulgarity of Las Vegas, where he also lives; he is, in short, an embodiment of that totalitarian force that Mailer calls The Establishment.

The whole movement of *Dream* leads toward the confrontation between Rojack and Kelly, between the pilgrim committed to his quest for future substance and the prince of that Devil whose joy it is to waste our substance. If the power that Kelly has over Rojack at the time of this confrontation is so considerable that the latter must seek to exorcise it, the power was made possible by his daughter, who acted as an extension of Kelly's decreative purposes just as Kelly had been an extension of the Devil's. For Rojack, nine years of marriage to Deborah had meant having his courage, the sine qua non of the independent self, so repeatedly punctured that his relationship with her had become "the armature of my ego; remove the armature and I might topple like clay." It had meant swimming in the well of her intuitions until he had "come to believe in spirits and demons, in devils, warlocks, omens, wizards and fiends, in incubi and succubi." It had meant having Deborah so effectively seize the center of his psyche, "ready to blow the rails," that by the ninth year Rojack would "certain nights go leaden with [that] dread" which is a terror of disappearing into an eternity of death. Although the elements of good and evil were mixed in Deborah, she had opted for evil, for destroying being (or substance). As she once told Rojack, she despised being evil, "it's just that evil has power."

All devotees of black magic destroy the beings of themselves and others or, as Mailer put it in another context, take more out of nature than they put into it. The unfortunate victim of the bitch, whom Mailer listed among the devotees of black magic in the quotation on page 140, is any male with whom she has had intercourse—in this case, Rojack. By the ninth year, which he spent separated from Deborah, Rojack wanted to

> evacuate my expeditionary army, that force of hopes, all-out need, plain virile desire and commitment which I had spent on her. It was a losing war, and I wanted to withdraw, count my dead, and look for love in another land, but she was a great bitch, Deborah, a lioness of the species: unconditional surrender was her only raw meat. A Great Bitch has losses to calculate after all if the gent gets away. For ideally a Great Bitch delivers extermination to any bucko brave enough to take carnal knowledge of her. . . . And Deborah had gotten her hooks into me, eight years ago she had clinched the hooks and they had given birth to other hooks.

However much Rojack might once have justified the marriage—he loved Deborah, he needed her clan's vast connections to become a senator, then he would be a soldier of God with enough power to raid Devilish enclaves—it had become a "devil's contract," a surrender to the cowardly and the decreative within and without: *

> She had, at her best, a winner's force, and when she loved me (which may be averaged out somewhere between every other day to one day in three) her strength seemed then to pass to mine and I was live with wit, I had vitality, I could depend on stamina, I possessed my style. It was just that the gift was only up for loan. The instant she stopped loving me . . . then my psyche was whisked from the stage and stuffed in a pit. A devil's contract, and during all of this last year, not living with her and yet never separated, for though a week might go by or two weeks in which I hardly thought of her at all, I would nonetheless be dropped suddenly into an hour where all

---

* An instructive and amusing example of political independence was provided by Mailer during his 1969 mayoralty campaign. The high-powered political adviser Adam Walinsky insisted that on television Mailer "must look the same as the other guys.

"Walinsky made a grave error: Norman Mailer wasn't put on earth to sing in a chorus. 'Kiss a cocksucker,' he spat into the stunned silence, 'and you'll end up one.' The meeting quickly and nervously broke up" (Joe Flaherty, *Managing Mailer* [New York: Coward-McCann, Inc., 1970], pp. 132–33).

of my substance fell out of me and I had to see her. I had a physical
need to see her as direct as an addict's panic waiting for his drug. . . .

Mailer intended Deborah to be much more than another one of
the castrators who have clawed their way across so many male
psyches on so many pages of American literature. If Rojack is, among
other things, the collective psyche, Deborah is lifted beyond being
even a Great Bitch; she is the Bitch Goddess of Success, the embodiment of the Dream of Success, wrapped in gorgeous robes but having
for the man who finally takes her hand (as Rojack does) a deadly
touch, "soft now as a jellyfish, and almost as repugnant—the touch
shot my palm with a thousand needles which stung into my arm
exactly as if I had been swimming at night and lashed onto a Portuguese man o' war." The ideal meaning that Deborah had for Rojack
was similar to the one she had for her father. She was to serve as a
clasp which would secure both of them to a world of the glamour of
Fitzgerald's rich, for which Gatsby and Dick Diver had sacrificed
their great natural talents, and the power of Mailer's rich, for which
Kelly and Rojack had sacrificed theirs. Deborah had been Rojack's
gimmick for success just as she had been her father's; if Rojack had
been the object of her black magic, she had been the source of his.
"You were their [the devils'] slave but they were working for you,"
went part of the quotation from "Ten Thousand Words a Minute."
Rojack is driven close to the deadest of ends on the Mailersque road
system of being because the black magic of Deborah's personal force
is no longer carrying him—the melodramatic phrase "the hunter
became the hunted" is appropriate for many turns of this psychedelic
morality play of a novel. His being seems to have been so atrophied
by this dependence that it can no longer regenerate. Instead, it hopes
through suicide to break out of the downward spiralling of its energies
before its purchase on eternity is lost forever. Or, considering Deborah's symbolic meaning as the embodiment of the wrong kind of
success, suicide now appears to be the only way that Rojack can tear
himself from the Dream of Success (which he chose when he married
Deborah) and redeem some part of the Dream of Being.

And so, almost two decades after he had first encountered dread
under the full moon in Europe, Rojack stands under another full
moon on a balcony ten stories above Sutton Place, prepared to jump.
In the apartment behind him are the remains of a just-ended cocktail
party and its sleek host. Beneath him is the melange of "gin-and-

tonics, anchovy paste, pigs-in-blankets, shrimp cum cocktail sauce, and last six belts of bourbon" which Rojack has just vomited onto the awning of a second-story balcony. All of it—the food, the locale, the host and the party—are a neat encapsulation of where too much of Rojack's life has gone. Since it is part of Mailer's mythology of profound metaphor that the food we eat contains souls and spirits which can be either good or bad for us, the upheaval of the very food of his wasted social life, of spirits bad for one's salvation, has brought Rojack to a moment when his authenticity is tested even more severely than it was by the German's eyes:

So I stood on the balcony by myself and stared at the moon which was full and very low. I had a moment then. For the moon spoke back to me. By which I do not mean that I heard voices, or Luna and I indulged in the whimsy of a dialogue, no, truly it was worse than that. Something in the deep of that full moon, some tender and not so innocent radiance traveled fast as the thought of lightning across our night sky, out from the depths of the dead in those caverns of the moon, out and a leap through space and into me. And suddenly I understood the moon. . . . The only true journey of knowledge is from the depth of one being to the heart of another and I was nothing but open raw depths at that instant alone on the balcony, looking down on Sutton Place, the spirits of the food and drink I had ingested wrenched out of my belly and upper gut, leaving me in raw Being, there were clefts and rents which cut like geological faults right through all the lead and concrete and kapok and leather of my ego, that mutilated piece of insulation, I could feel my Being, ridiculous enough, what! I could feel lights shifting inside myself, drifting like vapors over the broken rocks of my ego while a forest of small nerves jumped up, foul in their odor, smelling for all the world like the rotten, carious shudder of a decayed tooth. Half-drunk, half-sick, half on the balcony, half off, for I had put my leg over the balustrade as if I were able better to breathe with one toe pointing at the moon, I looked into my Being, all that lovely light and rotting nerve and proceeded to listen. Which is to say, I looked out deep into that shimmer of past death and new madness, that platinum lady with her silver light, and she was in my ear, I could hear her music: "Come to me," she was saying, "Come now. Now!" and I could feel my other foot go over the balustrade, and I was standing on the wrong side of the railing, only my . . . fingers to hold me from the plunge. But it was worse than that. Because I knew I would fly. My body would drop like a sack, down with it, bag of clothes, bones and all, but I would rise, the part of me which spoke and thought and had its glimpses of the landscape of my Being, would soar, would rise, would leap the miles of darkness to that moon. Like a lion would I join the legions of the past and share their power. "Come now," said the moon, "now is your moment.

What joy in the flight." And I actually let one hand go. It was my left. Instinct was telling me to die.

When Mailer has Rojack tell us that the moon spoke to him and that new madness lay before him, he is not condemning his hero as a psychotic. Far from it. Rojack's madness is lunacy in the ancient sense; the moon has inspired him with holy madness, with the ability to apprehend pure truth. Throughout *Dream* the moon functions as the triggering device which enables Rojack to hear his being, the proclaimer of the pure truth about himself: "I looked into my Being . . . and proceeded to listen." The moon is also a symbol of all Being, the continuum of nature of which Rojack's being, enfeebled by its "rotting nerve," is only a part. (Mailer confusingly uses the spelling of the totality [Being] to refer to Rojack's part [being], a practice inconsistent with the distinction he will make several times in "The Political Economy of Time." The dead legions in the caverns of the moon are the disembodied beings in the repository of Being who will return to seek out new forms to inhabit.) To say that Rojack's most extraordinary acts in Europe, New York, and Las Vegas occur while he is influenced by the moon is only to observe that the truly extraordinary act can only come about when a man is in either enjoyable or literally dreadful contact with his being.

If Rojack's apparent madness is actually inspired sanity, insanity is what Mailer called "psychotic autonomies" in his June, 1963, "Responses and Reactions" column—here, the lead and concrete and kapok and leather of Rojack's ego, that piece of insulation which had been mutilated once before in Europe and is once again so shredded that he can "connect." Probably the foul-smelling forest of raw nerves refers to that part of his being which has become so diseased that it can no longer be called being. He had not been aware of how far gone his being was until this moment because the ego, that part of himself which had wanted Deborah and all she represented and which had responded to all that she and society at large offered and commanded, had prevented his being from emerging to tell him what *must* be done.

The passage in which "psychotic autonomies" appears is worth quoting for several reasons. Written six months before the above quotation, it sharply states the juxtaposition of society and instinct or being, and it helps to show how completely the thought of the nonfiction organizes the thought in *Dream*. (Among other things, society is referred to as "insulation" in both passages.) It is also the most lucid statement that Mailer has made since "The White Negro" about what might actually happen inside the psyche to enable the

imprisoned instinctual life to be set free by courageous action. Unlike
the explanation in that essay, however, it in no way follows from
Freudian assumptions about the Oedipus complex:

> The logic in searching for extreme situations, in searching for
> one's authenticity, is that one burns out the filament of old dull
> habit and turns the conscious mind back upon its natural subservi-
> ence to the instinct. The danger of civilization is that its leisure, its
> power, its insulation from nature, so alienate us from instinct that
> our consciousness and our habits take on an autonomy which may
> censor even the most necessary communication between mind and
> instinct. For consciousness, once it is alienated from instinct, begins
> to construct its intellectual formulations over a void. The existential
> moment, by demanding the most extreme response in the protagon-
> ist, tends to destroy psychotic autonomies in the mind—since they
> are unreal, they give way first—one is returned closer to the reality
> of one's personal strength or weakness. The woman in search of a
> child goes on a pilgrimage in which her end is unknown—she may
> find the Baal Shem or she may not, but her commitment is com-
> plete, and the suggestion intrudes itself that on the long miles of her
> march, her mind, her habits, and her body were affected sufficiently
> to dissolve the sterilities of her belly and prepare her for a child.

So, for all of the mood music of the platinum lady with her silver
hair, what we have with Rojack on the balcony is the most simplified
and therefore the most extreme situation in the existential gospel as it
is preached by Mailer-Rojack on the mount. To decide in a paragraph
or two whether Rojack has searched out this extreme situation would
demand the dialectical skill of a Sartre, particularly when we begin
attributing his presence on the balcony to possible unconscious moti-
vations. What immediately concerns us is that whether searched for
or not, the instinct has told Rojack of his strength and weakness. It
has let him know that the weakness is so pervasive that he can best
preserve strength for the struggle for new life by killing himself.

One feels Maileresque dread in the presence of Maileresque super-
nature. Since the supernatural part of Rojack is counselling him,
dread pours in; "but it was worse than that." Nevertheless, as filled
with numbing dread as a man might be, he must still act in the
existential moment of faith; not the secure faith of the stodgy, un-
doubting believer but Mailer's version of the Kierkegaardian leap
of faith, with no assurance of where the leap will end and much
less assurance than God provided Kierkegaard's early model of re-
ligiosity, the Knight of Faith. Like Kierkegaard's later models of
religious authenticity, Rojack must also face the possibility that he
is mad, or will soon go mad. Thus, Rojack says later in the book:

"Do you know psychosis? Have you explored its cave? I had gone out to the end of my string. It was stretching behind me—I could feel it ready to snap." When the being speaks, one must act quickly. Hesitation, the implicit demand that the soul repeat its command, is dependence on a precedent, a Devilish gimmick. In the April, 1963, "Reactions and Responses" column, Mailer quoted with total approval the maxim of the hassidic Rabbi Pinhas, "The soul teaches incessantly . . . but it never repeats."

Rojack cannot give himself to faith; a doubting question enters into what should be the purity of no-concept. To continue the quotation of *Dream* from the point at which I stopped:

> Which instinct and where? The right hand tightened in its grip. . . .
> "Drop," she said one more time, *but the moment had gone.* Now if I dropped, all of me passed down. There would be no trip.
> "You can't die yet," said the formal part of my brain, "you haven't done your work."
> "Yes," said the moon, "you haven't done your work, but you've lived your life, and you are dead with it."
> "Let me be not all dead," I cried to myself, and slipped back over the rail, and dropped into a chair. I was sick. . . . This illness now, huddling in the deck chair, was an extinction. I could feel what was good in me going away, going away perhaps forever . . . my courage, my wit, ambition and hope. Nothing but sickness and dung remained in the sack of my torso. [Italics mine.]

Having followed Rojack's descent this far, we shall, for a few pages, leave him suspended over the spiritual bottoms. He will rise, of course; much of what was good about him had not gone away forever, but simply ebbed. What follows in the remaining 250 pages of *Dream* is a tale of exorcism and rebirth as Rojack frees more and more of the white magic of his being by tearing from his psychic flesh the clenched hooks of Deborah's black magic. To be sure, this reduction takes no account of the hundreds of different ideas and images which—for better or for worse, depending upon how one likes one's fiction—cram these pages.

There are probably a fair number of readers who liked much of the novel and tried to like more of it by pushing a symbolic reading in such a way that the supernatural is expunged from it. For example, Kelly's pact with the Devil could become the decision of any man who has chosen to suppress reliance upon his instincts for the more assured benefits of society. As the manifestation of this pact, Deborah could become any child whose individual possibilities are sacrificed for the parents' ambitions. Indeed, she could be and so she is in the novel, but she is also someone who has chosen to raid upon the power of God rather than that of the Devil, both of whom Mailer believes in as much as he can.

Particularly since Women's Liberation has gone to work on Mailer, there is little need to argue that he is seriously suggesting that some men should kill their wives. Around this time, Mailer was fond of saying that, well, he was sorry about it, but things in the individual psyche might have gotten so bad that murder might be the only solution for salvation. Or, to expand Rojack's plight and the primitive cure he undertakes to the collective level—and so partially answer in advance the question which forms the title of Mailer's last novel—

> the only explanation I can find for the war in Vietnam is that we are sinking into the swamps of a plague and the massacre of a strange people seems to relieve this plague. If one were to take the patients in a hospital, give them guns and let them shoot on pedestrians down from hospital windows you may be sure you would find a few miraculous cures. So the national mood is bound to prosper from the war in Vietnam. For a time.

Vietnam cannot cure the plague—that rapid, collective weakening of Being in America—but only deepen it, because Mailer believes the war to be such a Devilish, cowardly one. As such, it would kill far more American souls than it would save, for since 1958 the arguments justifying violence have followed from his eschatological premise. But how these last two words could dignify the monstrous; how easy it is to get so absorbed with the Ringmaster's gestures that we forget what hoop we're jumping through. Kate Millett's claim that Mailer was opposed to the German genocide of the Jews because the Jews were dispatched with gas and the poor Germans never got a chance to tear them apart with their hands pretty well typifies the way she distorts early-sixties Mailer. But, by Mailer's logic, if heroic genocide which added to Being were somehow possible, why then we would have to be authentic, wouldn't we? Even if inauthenticity (or humanity) would keep us from the act, we would have to retain our membership in the new sensibility by doing our verbal thing, particularly if the liberal Establishment (that is, the most reasonable conduit of what is actually totalitarianism, the New Fascism) remembered things like mass graves and gas chambers and suggested that such games were dangerously irresponsible;

> if the liberal Establishment is right in its unstated credo that death is a void, and man leads out his life suspended momentarily above

that void, why then there is no argument at all. Whatever shortens life is monstrous. We have not the right to shorten life, since life is the only posesssion of the psyche, and in death we have only nothingness. . . .

But if we go from life into a death which is larger than our life has been, or into a death which is small, if death comes to nothing for one man because he swallowed his death in his life, and if for another death is alive with dimension, then the certitudes of the Establishment lose power. . . . If we are born into life as some living line of intent from an eternity which may have tortured us or nurtured us in death, then we may be obliged to go back to death with more courage than we left it. Or face the dim venture of going back with less.

That is the existential venture, the unstated religious view of boxers trying to beat each other into unconsciousness or, ultimately, into death. It is the culture of the killer who sickens the air about him if he does not find some half-human way to kill a little in order not to deaden all. It is a defence against . . . that plague which comes from violence converted into the nausea of all that nonviolence which is void of peace.

We have turned again to the novel's nonfictional twin, "Ten Thousand Words a Minute." Since all of this is couched in the polite tones of an interesting suggestion, we might reject Mailer's invitation to apocalyptic romance by prosaically insisting that whatever boxers fight for, it is not for Maileresque Being. However, it is more important to perceive that with the poor, half-human killer, suffering from the sickness of his culture, we are back to the really dangerous sentimentality of the advocate of head stomping in the *Mademoiselle* interview. So are we also in *An American Dream,* where Mailer tries to reconcile his desires to continue challenging the "liberal Establishment" and to retrench his celebration of violence by having Rojack ready to kick in the heads of his dead wife and the beaten black singer. But here the novel's central "moral" premise—Rojack's back is against the wall of eternal death; he is clawing to preserve his being; the murder, sodomy, lying, beating, voodoo that he engages in are what he must do—does not ask this.

Novel, article, and interview should be seen in the perspective not only of Mailer's career but of the last decade. When "Ten Thousand Words a Minute" was written in 1962, we could talk much more easily about Mailer's heroic need to present extreme alternatives. After the assassinations, ten more years of Vietnam, Newark, and Chicago; after the Manson family murders, many of us who know very well that undischarged aggression usually turns to anxiety and that it feels better to be angry than to be anxious still decline the invitations to really let our ids go, whether in action or in imagination. Those of us who do not sagely speak of the practical necessity for violence while we are on our way to a good restaurant have had enough of extreme alternatives, and so, increasingly, has Mailer. This is not to say that Mailer will never again approve in print the possibilities of murder. Previously unpublished work from the period which saw the culmination of his hipster stances will appear—perhaps in the next collection which might also have grocery lists, deposit slips, and letters to his children—but I do not think that he will write again of the blessings of violence with the same intoxication.

Whether or not boxers are engaged in that existential venture which is a venture for more existence, Rojack certainly is as, an hour or so after we left him on the balcony, he stands over his kneeling wife, his arm gripped about her neck. Deborah has just tried to further weaken him by unfavorably comparing him with her most recent lover and then literally to damage his genitals after he struck her. This is relevant, but not as relevant as her cumulative effect upon him and his recent failure of will on the balcony, for the sickness of Rojack's suppressed violence is greater than that of any boxer, who is at least able to discharge some of it. The sustained effort of containing his violence has built until it was "like carrying a two-hundred-pound safe up a cast-iron hill" until cancer beckoned. Mailer's existential boxer was sickened by nonviolence that was void of peace; Rojack is driven on by a vision of the peace that will come if he voids his violence. Of course his conscious, socially obedient mind is still active; it speaks after the strangling Deborah taps his shoulder, pleading with him to release his hold: "Hold back! you're going too far, I could feel a series of orders whip like tracers of light from my head to my arm, I was ready to obey, I was trying to stop. . . ." But Rojack does not make the mistake(!) of listening to this voice as he did on the balcony. For the emergence of the being, with its command to do what must be done and its promise of the benefits that authentic action will bring, is too strong:

> I had the mental image I was pushing with my shoulder against an enormous door which would give inch by inch to the effort.
> [Here Deborah taps his shoulder and he eases his grip] . . . the door . . . began to close. But I had had a view of what was on the other side of the door, and heaven was there, some quiver of jeweled cities shining in the glow of a tropical dusk, and I thrust against

the door once more and hardly felt her hand leave my shoulder, I was driving now with force against that door: spasms began to open in me, and my mind cried out then, "Hold back! . . ." but pulse packed behind pulse in a pressure up to thunderhead; some black-biled lust, some desire to go ahead not unlike the instant one comes in a woman against her cry that she is without protection came bursting with rage from out of me and my mind exploded in a fireworks of rockets, stars, and hurtling embers, the arm about her neck leaped against the whisper I could still feel murmuring in her throat, and *crack* I choked her harder, and *crack* I choked her again, and *crack* I gave her payment—never halt now—and *crack* the door flew open and the wire tore in her throat, and I was through the door, hatred passing from me in wave after wave, illness as well, rot and pestilence, nausea, a bleak string of salts.

His hatred drained and his being freed, Rojack is "with *it*" in both the conventional meaning of the slang phrase and the Maileresque application: ". . . my flesh seemed new. I had not felt so nice since I was twelve. It seemed inconceivable at this instant that anything in life could fail to please." And so, in the next hour or so Rojack enjoys the windfalls of authenticity, as he will several times in the remaining hours of his often grim, often joyous saturnalia.

With the gimmick of his narcotic, the drug user is able to suppress the social, unimaginatively utilitarian self that sees all objects as one of a group which might or might not be useful so that he is able to apprehend each color, odor, form, and so on, in its distinctive oneness. But Rojack's freeing force is not the black magic of a drug but the courage which has beaten back the numbing power of his social self and thus released the white magic of his being. Most of us have, at one time or another, tried to decide what color we saw when our eyes were closed, but the creatively responsive Rojack has only to close his eyes "and a fall of velvet rain red as the drapery in a carmine box" pours into his retina. Washing his hands and dressing turns the bathroom into a garden of sensuous delights:

My hands were tingling in the water. . . . As I put down the soap, its weight in my palm was alive; the soap made a low sticky sound as it settled back to the dish. I was ready to spend an hour contemplating that sound. But the towel was in my hand, and my hands could have been picking up the crisp powder of autumn leaves as they crumbled in my fingers. So it went with the shirt. Something was demonstrating to me that I had never understood the nature of a shirt. Each of its odors (those particular separate molecules) was scattered through the linen like a school of dead fish on the beach, their decay, the intimate whiff of their decay a thread of connection leading back to the hidden heart of the sea.

Yes, I returned this shirt to my body with the devotion of a cardinal fixing his hat. . . . Speak of a state of grace—I had never known such calm.

So it continues as Rojack hears the pitches of silence, enjoys his steps as a ballerina might, and looks in the mirror to discover his face to be as handsome as any he has ever seen. If nothing could fail to please, sex would be particularly pleasurable, so the Navigator draws him down the stairs to the room of Ruta, Deborah's maid. What follows is a scene that Elizabeth Hardwick has described as "particularly loathsome and ridiculous." To disagree partially with so elegant a critic as Miss Hardwick, I feel that the scene is too ridiculous to attain to the loathsome. But I'm much more interested in the way such a judgment very reasonably follows Miss Hardwick's claim that Mailer's primary purpose in the novel was to reveal "the excremental, the sadistic, the hideous" as a way of frightening us into self-knowledge. Again, the unifying axis of the novel is Rojack's quest for authenticity, or Mailer's attempt to show how a self can and must project itself into "loathsome" acts which are not loathsome because they enable the self to achieve a higher self. Perhaps the comment of Mailer's which best illustrates how the plot of *An American Dream* is structured was made about fourteen months before he began writing the novel:

> Postulate a modern soul marooned in constipation, emptiness, boredom and a flat dull terror of death. A soul which takes antibiotics when ill, smokes filter cigarettes, drinks proteins, minerals, and vitamins in a liquid diet, takes seconal to go to sleep, benzedrine to awake, and tranquilizers for poise. It is a deadened existence, *afraid precisely of violence, cannibalism, loneliness, insanity, libidinousness, hell, perversion, and mess, because these are states which must in some way be passed through, digested, transcended, if one is to make one's way back to life.*
> . . . The love of death is not a mass phenomenon; it exists for each of us alone, our own private love of death. Just as our fear of death is also ours all alone . . . these morbid states . . . can obtain relief only by coming to life in the psyche. But they can come to life only if they are ignited by an experience outside themselves. . . . A dramatic encounter with death, an automobile accident from which I escape, a violent fight I win or lose decently, these all call forth my crossed impulses which love death and fear it. They give air to it. So these internal and deadly emotions are given life. In some cases, satisfied by the experience, they will subside a bit, give room to easier and more sensuous desires. [Italics mine.]

As we have seen, Rojack enjoyed a sensuous banquet once his deadly, murderous emotion was aired. Now he is driven by the easier and more sensuous desire for sex itself, not vicarious sex mixed with murder (refer to the simile comparing his desire to continue choking Deborah and "the instant one comes in a woman against her cry that she is without protection"). If the desire was intense enough to inspire Mailer to writing of the purplest hue, part of the intensity derives from the large portion of perversity in the desire. Having overcome his fear of violence, Rojack must now overcome his fear of perversion. This is one way of explaining why Rojack performs with a truly inspired efficiency, sodomizing Ruta, pulling her hair, and calling her a dirty Nazi. But Mailer is even more *busy* than Rojack. While dramatizing Rojack's sodomy without fear, he gets to work in two of his favorite metaphorical premises—one must raid upon the power of the Devil to advance that of God, and the anus is the very symbol of the decreative, the Devilish—all the while running a peep show for any heavy-breathing readers. Thus Rojack, now in constant touch with his being, "had a desire suddenly to skip the sea and mine the earth, a pure prong of desire to bugger, there was canny hard-packed evil in that butt, that I knew." Indeed, Rojack refers to his alternating plunges between the anus and the vagina as "a raid on the Devil and a trip back to the Lord." One of the smells that comes from Ruta to Rojack by way of his olfactory antennae is "the mono-maniacal determination to get along in the world," and as he continues sodomizing her "a host of the Devil's best gifts" come to him until he feels "like a thief, a great thief." The gimmicks he received from a woman who as a child made a pact with the Devil so that she could stay alive in wartime and postwar Berlin were "mendacity, guile, a fine-edged cupidity for the stroke which steals, the wit to trick authority." At the same time, Mailer is advancing the plot in a way that will enable him to celebrate further the blessings of primitivism, all of which should deeply appeal to the frustrations and fantasies of a good many readers.

In other words, Rojack's being, loving whatever would help it to expand, led him to Ruta's room so that he could get, through Mailer's metaphorical osmosis, the wherewithal to stand off the police until his release was granted. This is the typically baffling explanation of how a college professor turned murderer could have behaved with the coolness and wit that Rojack displayed with the police until, in even more baffling fashion, he is freed because Deborah was associating with spies, and the CIA does not want an investigation.

Thus, Rojack is freed from the workings of that legal code which arose from the Judaic-Christian religion and tried under the edicts of that older, bloodier religion. The initial premise of the former legal code is an eye for an eye, with the implication that under the law all eyes are equal, but just as one of the bases of Mailer's attacks upon the welfare state is that it treats all men as equal, his eschatological premise is that though our conditions are the same, our particular realizations of the possibilities of the condition are not. One individual has more or less being than another. We are back to the existential venture of the two boxers—it might be perfectly all right for A to kill B because the former gained being through the act and so added to all Being. Rojack's situation was so desperate that he had to murder to create, to kill Deborah before he could have the affair with Cherry.

Several impressive critics have been bothered by Rojack's escape from retribution for the murder. For example, Philip Rahv (who, in a sarcastic comparison with Dostoevsky titled his review "Crime Without Punishment") complained that "only in a hipster's fantasy is society so easily cheated of its prey and only in his fantasy can the self become so absolutized, so unchecked by reality, as to convert itself with impunity into the sole arbiter of good and evil." Of course the majority of murders in the larger American cities go unsolved, but Rahv is not concerned with statistics; he is interested in justice, and so, in his grimly romantic way, is Mailer. Rojack is society's prey throughout the novel, and he ends it having experienced what Mailer intends to be a most bitter and painful loss. We must perceive that the punitive arm of society is not the police but the hooks of dependence and cowardice which Deborah has set in him and which are still being manipulated by her father. Rojack is not at all the sole arbiter of good and evil, for he is bound by the workings of our old friend—now expanded into cryptic ontology—that so cruel and so just law. In its different forms, it is the moral law operating in all of Mailer's novels except *Barbary Shore*. Saint Stephen must wholly overcome Kelly to gain Cherry, but since he does not act with quite enough courage, she is killed. Since Rojack did behave fairly well with her, he is left with some of his powers, but the task of further re-creating himself lies before him at the novel's end.

But what windfalls can be gained by killing an emasculating wife! Because Rojack bested Deborah in a more or less fair fight—she is of the same height as Rojack, strongly built, and of enormous strength during the struggle in which she tried to knee him and tear off his genitals—some of her powers, one of which was the ability to cast spells, passed to him. This black magic, the reward of a successful raid upon the Devil, must be employed in the expansion of being, for the raid, like the murder, will only be justified if Rojack grows. Since Rojack's attempt to win Cherry is, like all struggles for love, a quest for more being, his use of black magic is as justifiable as his use of violence was—if he does indeed manage to grow. The Devilish is transformed into the Godly, for in Mailer's system, as in all teleological ones (to somewhat dignify the prevailing logic of the book), the end does not merely justify the means but reaches down to impart value to it, and so, when Rojack is locked in silent contest with the Mafioso nightclub manager that Cherry has just defied, we are to approve of his calling upon the powers won only a few hours before as an example of newly gained creative forces:

> Tony and I were now alone. We avoided each other's eyes and stood there side by side in a contest: his presence against my presence, two sea creatures buried deep in the ocean silt of a grotto, exuding the repellent communications of sea creatures. Tony's oppression was muddy, a sea stench of wet concrete. I could feel him burying me beneath it. So I called on Deborah. How many times talking to Deborah had my hand gone to my throat—doubtless she had been drawing an imaginary razor down one ear and up the other. Small wonder she believed in miracles. Now I in turn put my hand in my pocket to feel my pocketknife and took it on a small mental trip into my palm where figuratively I opened it, reached across and made a slash into Tony's neck deep across the apple. "That's the way," said Deborah in my ear, "At last you're learning. Put some salt in the wound."
>
> "Where do I find salt?" I asked of her.
>
> "From the tears of anyone this man has been able to oppress. There's your salt. Rub it in."
>
> So I called for some distillate of sorrow, and so powerful was the impression returned that my fingertips felt a grit of white crystal with which they could travel to Tony's neck, and there some part of my mind must have rubbed it in.
>
> I could feel his discomfort.

Verbal magic is also employed in Rojack's besting of Tony, but the preceding lines capture the tenor of the scene and, in fact, of many other passages in the book. But what are we to make of the quoted passage in terms of literal experiential possibility? In *The Deer Park,* Sergius told us that he grew, but he never really told us how. Here, Rojack tells us how but leaves us sinking into the quagmire of trying to decide how we are to take the explanation. To turn only to the scene with Tony, we are no doubt supposed to accept the fact that one Stephen Rojack was able to perform better with Cherry because he was strengthened by his victory over this Devilish oppressor of the weak. We may, in fact, see the victory as a middle term in a familiar Maileresque process of expanding powers whereby the more one does, the more one is able to do. (Rojack was able to stand off Tony because he had been able to kill Deborah, which enabled him to steal Ruta's "gifts," which enabled him to stand off the police, which enabled him to hold his own with the ex-prizefighter who was baiting him at the nightclub. "Putting down" Tony helped him to perform well with Cherry, which enabled him to beat up Shago Martin, the black with the knife. The powers gained from Shago were then used in the climactic struggle against Kelly.) But is the psychic throat slitting only a metaphor for the irrevocably mysterious powers which a man can call from himself if he is brave enough? Or is Rojack supposed to be so inspired, with so much of his being at work to perform any act that will further free it, that he can actually call upon powers which we could employ if only we were brave enough and desperate enough to find our way to them? In this case, the joke is that there is no joke. Mailer thought that Patterson was oppressed by the Don Capos shooting psychic bullets into his legs; in the 1968 siege of Chicago, Mailer was "having psychic artillery battles with the Mafia at the next table"; in the year *An American Dream* came out in book form, Mailer was applying "long, mad stares across parties to whammy any man, or lady, he has picked out for his next bout of logomachy." Mailer is arguing in *Dream* that this is a part of the magical world that exists if we are brave enough to get to it.

This is one of the more charming growths in Mailer's garden of extreme possibilities, and here we must add the repeated adverb that follows that far less charming suggestion that rape might be better than masturbation—*maybe* one can smell the state of another's being; *maybe* we do exist in an immensely subtle field of bio-electric charges which we can consciously affect with our own emanations. In the *Realist* interview containing the rape-masturbation comment, Mailer admitted that his view of history was essentially biological and added that as time went on he more and more found the essential meaning of sex to lie in its procreative possibilities. What Mailer called his obsession with procreation found its way into the novel he was to begin less than a year after the interview. As

Richard Poirier has perceived, "Perversity is in many ways the sub-ject and the villain of the book, or at least the evidence of villainy." The leader of the perverse forces in *Dream* is of couse Kelly, who not only viewed procreation as a means of furthering his Dream of Power but tried to lure Rojack onto the same bed on which he had seduced and impregnated his daughter.

Mailer has suggested in several ways that one's being is aided by creating a gifted baby. In keeping with the general barrenness of his past life, Rojack was childless. His one real chance to win Deborah back from Kelly's destructive influence lay in the developing embryo which he had planted within her, but his chance ended with mis-carriage because, as Rojack admits, he had not been good enough. Just as Cherry stands in antithesis to the Kellys in the novel's creativ-ity-attrition pairings, so the act which most contrasts with Kelly's conception of Deborah for social leverage and later seduction of her is Rojack's removal of Cherry's diaphragm so that they can make a baby. It is in keeping with Rojack's inspired condition that he knows that conception has indeed occurred. After all, their commitment is so total, the white magic of both emerges with such strength, that Cherry experiences her first natural orgasm and Rojack, as he tells us, discovers for the first time what sex is all about. As the culminat-ing human activity, it is all about increasing his being and that of his partner and creating a remarkable new being. Or, as Mailer, whose thought can always be traced back to what he feels to be the biological realities, said shortly before he began writing the novel, "One has to keep coming back to one notion: How do you make life? How do you *not* make life?"

We are to feel that the demands of the system of justice under which Rojack is being tried are severe in the extreme. He must totally overcome Kelly to keep Cherry, but he is not quite brave enough; this would mean wholly conquering the cowardly and de-creative in himself, and this he could not quite do. When Rojack mauled Shago, he beat back part but not all of his profound terror of Negroes. Although Rojack walked toward Shago and his drawn knife at one point in their confrontation, he later attacked the singer when his back was turned. For what he has achieved, Rojack gains some of Shago's powers—in particular, a voice which speaks through the medium of Shago's umbrella and tells Rojack, "Go to Harlem . . . if you love Cherry, go to Harlem—there is time!" But Rojack's responsibilities flood over him; he must be in Harlem to expiate the element of cowardice in the attack of Shago during the same hours that he must confront Kelly.*

He goes to Kelly's, and the climax of the book comes when he must pace two round trips on the twelve-inch-wide wall of the terrace outside the millionaire's thirtieth-story suite. He manages one circuit, and when Kelly tries to push Saint Stephen to his death with Shago's magical umbrella, Rojack seizes the talisman of the powers won from Shago, strikes Kelly with it, and leaps back down onto the terrace. Although Rojack perceives that he has to traverse the parapet once more to fully free himself from the destructive hold the live Barney Oswald Kelly and the dead Deborah Kelly Rojack still have upon him, the confrontation with Kelly snaps his resolve, and he flees the Waldorf. Rojack had realized during his first night with Cherry that he would have to be very brave to keep her. He was not nearly brave enough; it is part of Mailer's underworld of magical connections that Shago—now so totally a victim of "white shit," not just beaten by Rojack but so beat that he can no longer withstand the primitive challenges of Harlem—is killed there, and a friend of Shago's blames Cherry and kills her and the talismanic child she is carrying. Rojack would have had to have been very brave indeed to have completely freed himself from the nets and coils of his own and his country's past, and we leave him at novel's end about to drive to Yucatan and Guatemala.

How are we to interpret his self-imposed exile? It is tempting to compare Rojack to that other woman-killer who confessed the crime to his beloved but stood off the police and to make of Guatemala a counterpart to the Siberia of Rodion Romanovitch Raskolnikov, but Rojack needs no place to permit the expiation that will eventually enable him to rejoin the society that he wronged. Subject as he was, as we are, to that cruel, just law of growth or decline, it was to free himself from New York society that he killed Deborah; it was to follow the Dream of Being that he renounced the Dream of Power. To understand what Mailer had in mind when he sent Rojack off to Central America, one should turn not to Dostoevsky but to this comment from the *Realist* interview—to the last sentence in particular:

* Rojack must also expiate for his collaboration in the parts of society which, in Cherry's words, enabled the Devil to take all the hate in the country and pipe it into Shago. The singer is in several ways the precursor of the hero of Mailer's next novel, so we will look at his plight more closely there.

. . . tropical people are usually more sexual. It's easier to co-habit, it's easier to stay alive. If there's more time, more leisure, more—we'll use one of those machine words—more support-from-the-environment than there is in a Northern country, then sex will tend to be more luxuriant. Northern countries try to build civilizations and tropical countries seek to proliferate *being*.

We could also turn to Saint Augustine's "The Devil Hath established his cities in the North." According to the novel, the American Southeast, where Cherry's brother learned to move in small-town political circles by having incest with her older sister, or the American Southwest is still too far north. For on his way to the land of proliferating being, Saint Stephen stops off for a month at Las Vegas to win back at the tables the $16,000 debt that Deborah had incurred (she had a substantial independent income—of which Rojack had no knowledge—but spent lavishly to build up the debts which would further distract him from the Dream of Being). The resort was one of the best symbols Mailer could have used for decreative, homogeneous SuperAmerica, expanding at a cancerous rate as it increasingly alienates man from sustaining nature. It is Desert D'Or ten tasteless, destructive years later. Outdoors, ones sees not by the sun, but at night by immense towers of neon. Man can no longer stand very much sun, so he spends most of the day protected from it in sealed, air-conditioned rooms in which one

caught the odor of an empty space where something was dying alone.
Lived in the second atmosphere for twenty-three hours of the twenty-four—it was life in a submarine, life in the safety chambers of the moon. Nobody knew that the deserts of the West, the arid empty wild blind deserts were producing again a new breed of man.
Stayed at the dice tables. I was part of the new breed. Cherry had left a gift. Just as Oswald Kelly once went to sleep knowing which stocks would be on the rise by morning, so I knew . . . when to go down on the pass-line and when to bet the Don't Come. . . . In four weeks I made twenty-four, paid my debts, all sixteen plus the loan for the car, and got ready to go on.

Rojack is a part of the new breed only for the month that he stays in Las Vegas. He is not good enough to pull down those neon towers that he had envisioned as he ejaculated into Ruta's Devilish anus—what man is? Nevertheless, Rojack is a promising variant of a new breed—the wandering, saintly knight, the persistent seeker of the holy grail of being who raids upon the Devilish and moves on to continue his quest elsewhere. Drawing upon the gift he has earned from Cherry, Saint Stephen raids upon the money which is the commodity this land of the decreative has to offer. The money won, he mystically communes with Cherry away from the air-conditioned Sodom, on a telephone out in the desert under the full moon of judgment. The moon now shines more benignly upon him than it did in New York. His being purged of the resort's deadly residue, Rojack is ready to continue in the more primitive, sustaining ambiences of Central America his quest for the other city, the one with its cool underwater lights shining in tropical dusks that he saw as he strangled his wife and made love to Cherry—the Heavenly City of Being.

III

Aesthetically, *Dream* seems best to hold together if one regards it as a relatively conventional allegory; that is, a morality play acted out in the heated theatre of Rojack's mind. Like Dante, the narrator of that most celebrated of all dream visions, Rojack must relinquish his allegiance to the temptations of the Devil and once again align himself with the will of God. Thus, we could answer Philip Rahv's complaint of the improbability of Rojack's engaging in thirty-two hours "in feats of strength—consuming vast quantities of alcohol, fighting, making strenuous love to two different girls, not to mention murder—that would lay low not one but several younger men" with a less haggling reply than "such an astonishing release of energy for a short period is indeed possible for a forty-two-year-old in good physical condition." After all, no critic has ever troubled himself with the improbability of a historical personage getting a ride on the back of a mythological animal or with how little sleep the thirty-five-year-old Dante got during his one-week pilgrimage down to a confrontation with Satan and up to a vision of God. And are not, as John Corrington has observed, Rojack's steps always "tending toward the encounter with Barney Kelly, even as Dante's moved inexorably toward that moment of confrontation with Satan in the depths of Hell"? And would not Rojack's telephone call to the dead Cherry more or less correspond to Dante's vision of God?

It would seem, then, that Rojack could escape some of his critics by fleeing into the protective conventions of this literary form. We can, in fact, make *Dream* even more conventionally consistent if we regard all of the interrelationships between God, procreation, self-reliance, Cherry Melanie, the vagina, and the soul on the one hand and those with the Devil, sodomy, incest, dependence, Kelly, Ruta,

Deborah, the Mafia, the mass media, spirits, the Dream of Power, big business, Las Vegas, and New York society on the other as no more than two sets of symbols for the creative and the decreative in Rojack's own psyche. The only problem with this—and it is an enormous one—is that all of these forces are far more than symbols in a character's mind; this is somehow supposed to be the reality, however transfigured, of how big business, for example, works.

Since it is so difficult for anybody (and impossible for myself) to keep the novel's different levels of reality in some consistent focus, we might break the hybrid of the dream-allegory into its separate parts. To turn first to the argument that it is ridiculous to subject the free flow of a dream vision to the logic of nineteenth-century fiction, there is no doubt that Mailer has in the novel tried to capture the sleeping consciousness of America. I am impressed with Mailer's total vision of the nether levels of American psychic life, but this is precisely the total vision built up from all of his work of the past fifteen years, particularly from the nonfiction. When I first read *An American Dream* in the eight installments in *Esquire* back in 1964, I found the novel a disappointing, windy, silly bore. After spending a good deal of time with his other works, particularly *The Presidential Papers,* I found it fascinating at last reading to follow Mailer's attempts to transplant the insights of the nonfiction into a novel. For it is obviously one thing to tell the reader what is going on in the American unconscious and then, let us say, return to a description of Kennedy's appearance and life style, and another to develop a continually believable narrative through constantly evolving interaction of the fictional elements—most of which the novelist must invent and not report—while progressively compelling the reader to *feel* that he is plumbing the world of his deepest self.

Although *An American Dream* made fine sense as an exposition of ideas, I still found it impossible to emotionally accept most of it, even as a narrative occurring on some other level than the one we usually call "realistic." One thing that made it difficult to keep the book in focus as a vision germinated from a nonrealistic logic was its collection of tones, a melange like that in no dream vision I have ever heard of. This is not to say that Mailer must, to take a few examples, approximate the blendings of words and languages which Joyce used in *Finnegan's Wake* to suggest the complexity and creativity of the unconscious, or the incredibly evocative limpidity of Hermann Broch's language in *The Sleepwalkers,* or the uncanny suggestiveness of the way in which Kafka matter-of-factly describes the most bizarre events. A writer can do anything if the print on the page somehow offers us a body of experience that we are able to value. It is just that the strange mixture of tones Mailer offers up makes it much harder for him to impose his sense of the real upon us, and the problems of convincingly dramatizing his system at length are, from the start, awesome.

Mailer has said, "When I wrote the novel, I had decided to take a pretty conventional movie story, or movie melodrama, and make it into a realistic novel." Obviously, Mailer did not mean the realistic novel of, say, Farrell or even James, but something more like the psychological romance wherein, as Hawthorne said in the Preface to *The House of the Seven Gables,* the writer "may so manage his atmospherical medium as to bring out or mellow the lights and deepen and enrich the shadows of the picture," but the book "sins unpardonably so far as it may swerve aside from the truth of the human heart." Mailer cannot, as Hawthorne urged, make moderate use of his privileges; the system is most immoderate, as it must be for Mailer to charge with romantic voltage that urban swarm, simultaneously gray and infinitely variegated, for him to use the opposition of God and the Devil to turn New York into a romance ground where heroism for the highest stakes can take place. Perhaps we can better appreciate the vast demands that extended fiction makes upon the system if we think not of an article which offers the interesting suggestion that Liston-in-the-ring is an agent of the Devil but of a 270-page novel which follows Liston after he leaves the ring. Can he go home and Devilishly confront his wife because she has her curlers on? Eat Devilishly? Have Satanic looks at television? Be tempted to buy a house which looks heavenly?

Rojack's sensibility must be transfigured for him to experience 270 pages of Manichean world, and there is no place in this sensibility for recognizable slices of New York, which Mailer could have set up as convincingly as he did Sam Slavoda's Queens, the Miami of the 1968 Republican convention, or a dozen other milieus. Just as no part of his New York can exist in the compelling but untransfigured way that parts of it did in Bellow's *Seize the Day, Herzog,* and *Mr. Sammler's Planet,* there is no place in *An American Dream* for the shock of recognition of evil that comes to Herzog when he discovers that mothers do kill their squalling babies by hurling them off walls and that acts as horrific as this probably occur every day in New York. For how can one confront such evil heroically? No, one meets Barney Kelly after midnight and walks ledges. Another way that the mode within which Mailer is working robs him of his greatest strengths follows from his attempt to combine allegorical romance and social criticism. It is 1962, Jack Kennedy is still in the White House, but it cannot even be the sharply observed Kennedy of some of *The Presidential Papers;* it must be Prince Jack, who was quite a cut below Stephen Mailer because he did not have enough respect for the dark, primitive religion but was still somehow allied with Barney Kelly. Mailer must bend his fanciful but still sharp sense of history at the present moment, and the result is a sort of crazy house of history; when Kelly announces that "Jack" has just called, it is again like having that uncle dressed as Napoleon run into the room.

Allowing for the hazy boundaries between novel and romance, we can still see that Mailer has with his great eye, intellectual force, and social concerns the gifts of a novelist, but that the quest for apocalyptic struggle where clearly demarcated good and evil exist is the desire of a pure romancer. This is why the system seems less outlandish when it is trained on the sharply limited conflict between two men, as in the Liston-Patterson fight, than on the multiplicity of value, appearance, vocation, and so on, which is so much more the province of the novelist than the romancer. It is, of course, possible to capture gradations of human subtlety while invoking absolute values, to disect a society set in a precise moment in history while writing sub specie aeternitatis; all one has to be is Dante. Translated to the more modest realm of *An American Dream,* we might say that the mixed modes within which Mailer was working presented great problems; still, all he had to do was to write well enough. This he did not do.

His strategy was usually to try to push his happenings to the profundity of the dreamlike by employing a style, usually baroque in construction and feverish in tone, to record in detail Rojack's super-sensitized responses. Sometimes these passages caught the luxuriant sensuousness or strident tensions that Mailer sought—Rojack's body of feelings as he kills Deborah, particularly those he experiences after the murder. But often these passages are damaged by an annoying coyness or an even more jarring breakdown of tone. Chapter One ends with "She was dead, indeed she was dead." After Deborah tries to tear off his penis, "That blew it out." He cannot bury Deborah's teeth in Central Park, "Not Central Park, not by half." Rojack would have made "a champion sight" getting a cab for the beaten Shago. These might be idiosyncracies which only I happen to find annoying, but there are times when any reader should wonder what Mailer might have had in his mind. When reporting what are supposed to be the vastly important doings on the balcony where he was contemplating suicide, Rojack says, "I could feel my Being, ridiculous enough, what!" Surely a writer may parody himself in any appropriate place in any appropriate way. Mailer had been so serious about the system for so long that it was fine to hear about the academic flap with Rojack's voodoo seminar or a faculty wife's parodic versions of the relationship between food, transmigration, and soul, particularly since within the logic of the novel she belongs to the world which plays with such ideas and has not, like Rojack, been forced to act upon them. But to have Mailer more or less ask us, with Rojack on the balcony, if we're really taking all this nonsense seriously and then to drive on with all apparent seriousness is dizzying. Can we really justify this by saying the logic of dreams is a contradictory one?

The problems that dramatizing the system presented were so great that my tolerance was roughly a critical equivalent to Mailer's recent articulation of his perception that he could not reasonably expect everybody to take woman's procreative role with the high romantic seriousness that he did:

> Let woman be what she would, and what she could. Let her cohabit on elephants if she had to, and fuck with Borzoi hounds, let her bed with eight pricks and a whistle, yes, give her freedom and let her burn it, or blow it, or build it to triumph or collapse . . . let her travel to the moon, write the great American novel, and allow her husband to send her off to work with her lunch pail and a cigar.

Let Mailer bring Cherry into the plot in the most fantastical way; let the style switch from Nightclub Ominous to Rose-petal Romantic mixed with a sermon on authenticity. They are in the act; the Navigator says:

> . . . "choose now!" and some continent of dread speared wide in me, rising like a dragon, as if I knew the choice were real, and in a lift of terror I opened my eyes and her face was beautiful beneath me in that rainy morning, her eyes were golden with light, and she said, "Ah honey, sure," and I said sure to the voice in me, and felt love fly in like some great winged bird, some beating of wings at my back, and felt her will dissolve into tears, and some great deep sorrow like roses drowned in the salt of the sea came flooding from her womb and washed into me like a sweet honey of balm for all the bitter sores of my soul and for the first time in my life without passing through fire or straining the stones of my will, I came up from my body rather than down from my mind, I could not stop, some shield broke in me, bliss, and the honey she

had given me I could only give back, all sweets to her womb, all come in her cunt.

Let Mailer carry on with his rising continents of dread; surely the melodrama in this is redeemed by the eyes golden with light, the great winged bird escorting us into honied release, all in that headlong melting sentence. This is the stuff our sexual dreams are made of. But should this girl with the golden eyes wave a syntactic wart at us as she says, "But I'm a lousy singer, I fear"? Should her song be described as "some rich sausage her voice was ready to stuff"? All right, the power of evil in the novel is so strong that Cherry is right to feel that once she had a natural orgasm she would die, but why have her say in so stilted a fashion, "I know that's special and doubtless very crazy of me, but that's been my little fear"? Far from following Hemingway's famous advice and keeping the metaphysical base of the novel seven-eighths under the surface, Mailer tried to force the emotional reality of the world of heightened romance upon us by refusing to let the characters have very much living space of their own as he repeatedly pulled strings that jerked different characters into reciting his metaphysic. The strain on Mailer's stylistic powers is immense: How does one make a torch singer say something like the following and not have her sound like a sort of idiot savant?

> ". . . I always end up with something like the idea that God is weaker because I didn't turn out well."
> "You don't believe everything is known before it happens?"
> "Oh no. Then there's no decent explanation for evil. I believe God is just doing *His* best to learn from what happens to some of us. Sometimes I think He knows less than the Devil because we're not good enough to reach Him. So the Devil gets most of the best messages we think we're sending up."

Rojack responds with, "When did you begin to have ideas like this?" and so the lovers' discussion outlandishly continues. In trying to write of his God, Mailer sinned by swerving aside from communicable truths of the heart.

Not only must the language somehow charge with dramatic force the pulp-fiction characters—sexy playboy, castrating wife, sexy torch-singer, available maid, heartless financier, and shrewd detective—but it should somehow transform to more palpable characters and milieus a "nonrealistic" logic of events and some linguistic mixture of texture and pitch which we might in some way associate with the dreamlike. All of this is thrown out the window when Rojack confronts the police. The goings-on in a big-city police station have such dramatic possibilities, and Mailer is so anxious to play a "real" Lieutenant Roberts that he drops the metaphysics and the gaggle of tones that goes with it and lets the sharp eye which helped make so much of *The Naked and the Dead, The Deer Park, Why Are We in Vietnam?*, and *The Armies of the Night* so outstanding record what it might see. Mailer could always do this sort of thing very well indeed, and so he does it, with the parting-of-the-psychic-veils sound of the rest of the novel replaced by a terse, hardboiled prose sometimes reminiscent of James Cain. Except for that uncanny "It's Norman Mailer!" feeling, the scenes in the police station are fine. Our sense of the real is being satisfied, and we even stop wondering where we are, for the logic and tone are very, very far from Pop Fiction Transfigured. We're tolerant; all right, we'll start a new book. But just when we have settled down to watch with enjoyment Raskolnikov take on Porphyry—admittedly, both played by Norman Mailer—Rojack is freed through that device that so reeks of pop fiction—Deborah's traffickings with spies and the CIA's opposition to an investigation. It is typical of the difficulties involved in trying to perceive the level of reality on which *Dream* is to be taken that Deborah's dabblings in foreign intrigue would fit in quite well with her love of power, the most integral part of her largely serious characterization.

Much the same problem of focus occurs if we try to excuse the pulp-fiction characters by arguing that their primary importance lies in their functioning as symbols of the choice of either good or evil in the allegorical struggle going on in Rojack's mind. In a true allegory, each significant character and event symbolizes some shift in the psychological and/or eschatological process which the protagonist is undergoing. Most of the characters do fall into the good-evil antitheses I observed earlier, but then we come to Lieutenant Roberts, Rojack's interrogator. Surely he is on the side of the good—the brave, disciplined man fighting the hard fight—but he is robbed of of the object of his struggle by the deus ex machina of Deborah's foreign intrigues. Of course *some* explanation can always be worked out. It can be argued, for example, that although he is good, the short prison sentence that he offers to Rojack for a speedy confession is bad—in other words, that Being will be more increased by Rojack's victories than by Roberts's—but this is too tenuous to pursue, and I am left with the feeling that Mailer did not worry about the jarring contrast between the level of reality on which Roberts exists and the one, with all of its allegorical reverberations, of the other characters.

Roberts was a type for whom Mailer has expressed much admiration, Mailer wants to play him, and so he's included in the novel.*

Confronted with the immense problem of turning American society into a romance ground for an extended period, Mailer used whatever elements of allegory or dream vision that appear in the book as a pretext for throwing up his hands, for writing whatever he wanted to write without being bound by *any* strictures of verisimilitude. In his attempt to have it both ways, there is present in *Dream* neither the pervasive logic of a nonrealistic form nor the consistency of a realistic one. To those who would argue that the book's strange mixture of microscopic reportage and ridiculous happenings, of claims for cosmic vision and blowhard braggadocio, is a perfect approximation of the collective malaise of America. I can only reply that the book falls between the two horses of the seriousness with which we're to take Rojack's efforts and the melodramatic silliness of his opponents. In what seems to me this fascinating failure of a novel, the tone used to deride decreative America swims up to drown the model of creativity.

For the villains of the book are often silly to stupefaction; "Don't I know it, honey one," "I mean, *figure-toi,* pet . . ." and "I got this nifty little Caesar giving birth to you, pet, so don't complain" offer some idea of what is supposed to be the tony style of Deborah's upper-class, talent-devouring evil. The power that comes from her father's body would be a great deal more convincing if he didn't

---

* In his second movie, *Beyond the Law* (1968), Mailer played the lead—Police Lieutenant Francis X. Pope. According to Joseph Haas, Pope sums up the plot of the movie in this way: " 'It was a long night. I found a girl, I almost lost my wife, I kissed corruption and I kicked it . . .' and Farbar, as a vice-squad detective, provides the tagline, '. . . in the ass' " ("Notre Dame Meets Norman Mailer," *Panorama*, April 6, 1968, p. 3). In April, 1968, Mailer offered the following as the "message" of the movie:

> Enforcing order is one of the most complex problems society faces and yet, it has to be done or you have anarchy. All of these policemen in the movie—and they're not bad cops, but the average run of cops—are concerned with their idea of the right way to enforce order. Because order is necessary, some men must judge other men even though they may not be better than those who are judged. I'm fascinated with the complexity of the problem; the actual living conditions that policemen must confront every day are so morally complex it staggers the imagination. [*Ibid.,* p. 4.]

The last time Rojack sees Roberts, the latter weeps at how a policeman's standards and quality crumple under the frustration he undergoes.

keep telling us how his wife's friends were the patch for him or how "our mutual antipathy was so perfect a room was spoiled if the other had been in it five minutes before." Perhaps this is supposed to be a put-on, with Kelly mocking Stephen before he invited our saint to "get shitty," to get into bed with him and Ruta. By this time, one really doesn't care, and besides, there's the Ringmaster in 1969 announcing to a *Look* reporter that *An American Dream* is his most skillful novel and continuing:

> I don't think the rich have ever been written about with that insight. Scott Fitzgerald was right when he said that the rich are indeed not like you and me. Being rich is a problem. How can you know if somebody really loves you or not if you are rich? It's hard enough even for me.

The way in which Mailer's normally crackling conversation turns into near gibberish here recapitulates the muddled result of his attempt to transform the workings of "the very rich" into his romance of evil power. I suspect that he was enough aware of the novel's stylistic failings to prime the critical pump with special vigor before *Dream* even came out in book form. Here is Conrad Knickerbocker passing through the Ringmaster's hoops:

> He told me recently that writing the first, serial version of "An American Dream" last year against deadlines for Esquire forced him to create a structure much tighter than those of his previous novels. Since the Esquire version, he has rewritten perhaps 40 per cent of the book, fleshing out scenes and adding them, sounding every sentence, he said, 10 times for timbre.

Whether or not Mailer intentionally sought to free his own life of the most extreme dictates of the system, he freed himself from the desire to use his metaphysics as the unifying axis of his next novel. He also found for *Why Are We in Vietnam?* ways to combine successfully the desire to play and the desire to offer serious social criticism, to combine verbal exuberance with moral judgment. And, perhaps most important, if he never got far enough from the protagonist in his fourth novel to profit by a fruitful conflict in their psyches, he will not make that mistake in his vastly more successful fifth novel.

5
The Devil Gains a Charming Recruit

IN its general development, Mailer's fictional style has evolved from a conglomerate of borrowed styles (*Naked*) through the sometimes awkward constrictions of *Barbary Shore* and *The Deer Park* to the much more individual tones of the two segments in *Advertisements* and the last two novels. Each of the last four works is written differently, but we can say that in each Mailer sought to achieve an effect which was simultaneously baroque and freewheeling. The mixture of puns, mock dialects, and obscenities which characterizes the tone of *Why Are We in Vietnam?* is—except for Shago Martin's rants—such a sharp departure from anything Mailer had written that the novel surely came as a shock even to those readers who had decided that *An American Dream* was not overwritten after all. Had we absorbed William Burroughs's *Naked Lunch* and known how impressed Mailer was by that great work when he began writing *Vietnam* in late 1966, we need not have been surprised at all, but more of that later. Mailer offered a different explanation for the novel's stylistic departures when he wrote in 1967 (shortly after *Vietnam* appeared) that his style changed for every project because he had learned that "the clue to discovery was not in the substance of one's idea, but in what one learned from the style of one's attack." Although Mailer has believed since the early 1950s that style is the sharp cutting edge which permits entry into the resistant body of reality, his perception of the American reality has shifted slightly in the three years between the time he began writing *Dream* and the time he began writing *Vietnam*. To assert dogmatically that Mailer has become more pessimistic about the nation's present state and its probable one in the future is to oversimplify. Although the first three and one-half pages of *Cannibals and Christians* seethe with his biopsy of the deepening madness, Mailer closes the fourth with this declaration of uncertainty:

Yet every year the girls are more beautiful, the athletes are better. So the dilemma remains. Is the curse on the world or on oneself?

179

Does the world get better, no matter how, getting better and worse as part of the same process, or does the world get better in spite of the fact that it is getting worse, and we are approaching the time when an apocalypse will pass through the night?"

Whether or not we feel the professional Jeremiah inflating himself here, we still notice a willingness to entertain more desperate conjectures. For example in *Papers,* written before *Dream,* Mailer claimed that the secret fear of every American is that he is going mad. In a section of *Cannibals* which was written after *Dream* and before *Vietnam,* he admitted that he had decided that the nation is indeed going mad or, as he put it not six months after the novel was published:

He came at last to the saddest conclusion of them all for it went beyond the war in Vietnam. He had come to decide that the center of America might be insane. The country had been living with a controlled, even fiercely controlled, schizophrenia which had been deepening with the years. Perhaps the point had been passed.

An American Dream is filtered through the voice of a man who had become mad with creative inspiration; *Why Are We in Vietnam?* is narrated by a human amplifier for the madness of America. But there is so much energy and charm alongside the madness—perhaps even within it—that the narrative voice is ten times more authoritative and engaging than Rojack's. Perhaps Mailer's most impressive achievement is his offering us a 1967 version of Whitman's prairie rooster sounding his virile, barbaric yawp over the rooftops of the world while arguing at the same time that the rooster rages with a hectic fever. Although the collective madness steadily increases, the narrator is able to revel in it. The girls are prettier, the athletes better, but aren't we all going down the toilet nonetheless?

To make the same point somewhat differently, for all the differences of tone, character, and setting, the bulk of both of Mailer's last two novels is closely related to a problem which has obsessed the author for two decades. What will happen to the talent of America? Will it grow into more or deteriorate into less? The difference in the two novels' conclusions is that if *Dream* could be subtitled "The Man Who Got Away," *Vietnam's* would have to be "The Boy Who Never Really Left Home." Finally, the narrator and protagonist of the latter novel could not extricate himself—as Rojack could—from the destructive forces bearing down on all Americans, and we leave him at the end of the novel having confused God with the Devil, eager to fight in our most Devilish war in Vietnam. Or as

Mailer was to write a few months later in *The Armies of the Night,* what is best in America (the promise of our youth) has been corrupted by what seems to be second best (our technology).

The narrator is the eighteen-year-old Ranald Jethroe Jellico Jethroe, who refers to himself as D.J., the son of a high-ranking executive in one of those immense, interlocking, conglomerate corporations. The novel is D.J.'s "broadcast to the world" made from his Dallas home the night before he and his buddy Tex Hyde leave to fight in Vietnam. Most of the broadcast deals with the hunting trip made two years before in the Brooks Range of Alaska by D.J., Tex, Rusty Jethroe (D.J.'s father), two of Rusty's underlings, and several members of the Moe Henry and Obungekat Safari Group.

D.J. claims to be "Disk Jockey to the world," with mental associations of such prodigious speed that "old McLuhan's going to be breaking his fingernails all over again." To get some idea of the static and sound effects in the broadcast, we might consider a long paragraph which, uncrudely put, tells us that the helicopters in the Brooks Range have made the behavior of grizzlies unpredictable and that Big Luke (the head guide) is afraid of having some of his clients clawed to death. Crudely, or (as Mailer would say, because it tries to give the feeling of the actuality) existentially, the helicopters are "Cop Turds" disturbing the "general fission of the psychomagnetic field . . . now the psychomagnetic field was a mosaic, a fragmented vase as Horace said to Ovid. . . ." One of the hunting party is classified as a "high-grade asshole" and two others as "M.A.'s"—middle-grade assholes. The Cop Turds are "exploding psychic ecology all over the place," a grizzly is referred to as "a grizzer" or the "Grizzly Express," and the reader is benignly referred to as "man" or less benignly as "Suck-Mouth." Here is D.J. putting Big Luke's fear in his version of mythic context:

> . . . Big Luke knows he's getting away with too much, he's violating the divine economy which presides over hunters, and so he would lose a client, he would mar the record of a life, this is Yukon, man, heroes fall, listen to Big Luke folklore, Big Ruby Lil, the great whore of Saskatchewan, never failed to please a client, giants and pygmies they all came—Luke could tell the tale—until the day she pressed her luck, took Yukon hashish—what?—to speed the passing of the hours, and behold an auditor from Manitoba rolled in her comfortable soft brown slightly charred (from thirty years of peter burn) sweet whore's old Cadillac of a cunt, it was thus big and roomy (the secret was that her clients used to let the fatigue of a lifetime shoot, fire or seep out into those homey cunt walls—

she was medicine, man) well, the audit got it up but he could not let it go, there was a knot of congested fatigue in his heart, he was afraid he would blast himself if he ever blew it into her, so Ruby Lil tried everything, she even, after four hours, sucked his dick, and Ruby Lil had not done that for twenty years, she was a Mexico-Eskimo Queen, man, she put down the taste of semen, but she even did the rim on that auditor with the eyeglasses from Manitoba, yet she failed, so he never got the first drop to say sayonara to his dick, no floods of seed left the comptometer of his nuts, and Ruby Lil declined and was diminished to a dyke.

Then Mailer, playing with the idea of the solipsistic narrator spinning his coils of thought, has his narrator say in the next paragraph that this was not Big Luke's thought but "D.J. on the edge of masturbating in the Alaska night, with the excitement of going for griz in the morning, and holding off, holding off, cause a handful of spit on a sixteen-year-old dick puts a worm on the trigger and you slip off your shot."

Mailer wrote in *Armies* that in the army he had

come to love what editorial writers were fond of calling the democratic principle with its faith in the common man. He found that principle and that man in the Army, but what none of the editorial writers ever mentioned was that that noble common man was as obscene as an old goat, and his obscenity was what saved him. The sanity of said common democratic man was in his humor, and his humor was in his obscenity. And his philosophy as well—a reductive philosophy which looked to restore the hard edge of proportion to the overblown values overhanging each small military existence. . . . "That Lieutenant is chickenshit," would be the platoon verdict, and a blow had somehow been struck for democracy and the sanity of good temper.

We might then regard the obscenity of the broadcast not simply as a gleeful neonaturalistic display by Mailer, but also as the attempt to gain sanity by a boy who "suffers from one great American virtue, or maybe it's a disease or ocular dysfunction—D.J. sees right through shit." But as we shall see, there is so much shit about him that his perceptual apparatus is fouled, and even his supreme obscenity cannot preserve his sense of proportion. Since he sees so much rottenness about him, he might be one of the sanest Americans who is eager to fight in Vietnam. But he is still mad.

D.J.'s ranting sometimes makes the book harder to stay with than *An American Dream,* but one of the reasons that *Why Are We in Vietnam?* is a much better novel and easier to hold in one's mind is Mailer's creating, as he did not in *Dream,* a narrator whose sensibilities differ enough from his own to enable the preservation of one constant, if complex, focus. Although the author uses his narrator to attack many of his own enemies, the divergence between Mailer's opinion of D.J. and the latter's opinion of himself is both crucial and gaping. D.J. claims to be a genius—a mighty and unflawed product of the culture which produced him. Mailer has said about the book:

> I'm afraid it's saying that America enters the nightmare of its destiny like a demented giant in a half-cracked canoe, bleeding from wounds top and bottom, bellowing in bewilderment, drowning with radio transmitters on the hip and radar on his ear. He has a fearful disease this giant . . . greed. Vanity . . . the Faustian necessity to amass all knowledge, to enslave nature. The first vice of the giant is arrogance. Half the people in this country think they are possessed of genius.

The name of the moment, as of so many conversational moments of the late sixties, is Marshall McLuhan, already referred to by D.J. and in fact the villainous subject of Mailer's comment. For the bellowing D.J., delightedly drowning in the electronic gadgets which are most of all an extension of his arrogant, Faustian greed, is a disciple of the celebrated Canadian. He borrows what Mailer doubtless feels to be McLuhan's egomaniacal sureness and insane optimism as he describes himself as America's "own wandering troubadour brought right up to date, here to sell America its new handbook on how to live, how to live in this Electrox Edison world, all programmed out," derisively telling all of us squares, fools, and cowards "out there in all that implosion land" how the good life is to be lived. With "implosion land" we are hard upon McLuhan's eager welcoming of the new implosive order, in which the miracles of electronic media will bring back to the self the "wholeness, empathy and depth of awareness" which have been lost since Gutenberg caused our fall from communal, medieval Eden by inventing the printing press. With our transmitters on the hip, radar in the ear, and TV in the eye, with our central nervous system miraculously extended by computers—to temporarily combine the horrified Mailer and the approving McLuhan—we will heal our shattered psyches and the divisions between us and join as contented and integrated inhabitants in the "huge seamless web" of McLuhan's global village.

Mailer buys none of this. McLuhan argues that the simultaneity of electronic circuits will free us from the slavish identification with the linear processes of machinery. Mailer perceives no particular difference between what mechanical "aids" have done for man and what electronic ones will do. They are only heightened causes of the same sad, dehumanizing process:

> The twentieth century may yet be seen as that era when civilized man and underprivileged man were melted together into mass man, the iron and steel of the nineteenth century giving way to electronic circuits which communicated their messages into man, the unmistakable tendency of the new century seeming to be the creation of men as interchangeable as commodities, their extremes of personality singed out of existence by the psychic field of force the communicators would impose. This loss of imagination was a catastrophe to the future of the imagination. . . .

To apply the effects of the linear, mechanical technology and the electronic, simultaneous one to a particular medium, Mailer brushes aside McLuhan's claim that television brings to the viewer the revivifying total involvement that has been denied the newspaper viewer. For him, they are equally dishonest and thus equally dangerous. Newspaper reporters "help to keep America slightly insane" because the demands of this medium will not permit them to communicate any "notions which are not conformistically simple, simple like plastic is simple, that is to say, monotonous." Mailer calls any such systematic attempt to flatten the psyche by robbing a situation of its particular reality totalitarianism or fascism. And television, "corporation land's whip . . . at home," is at least as powerful a tool for totalitarianism as the press:

> Fascism is not a way of life but a murderous mode of deadening reality by smothering it with lies.
> Every time one sees a bad television show, one is watching the nation get ready for the day when a Hitler will come. Not because the ideology of the show is Fascistic; on the contrary its manifest ideology is invariably liberal, but the show still prepares Fascism because it is meretricious art and so sickens people a little further.*

The implicit debate between Mailer and McLuhan is reminiscent of Kierkegaard's shrieking "What about *my* life?" to Hegel's advice that one should not worry about the miserable conditions of one's own time or condition because they will all be resolved in a future historical synthesis. Mailer tells us that TV is destroying present and future; McLuhan urges us to disregard the incredibly shabby quality of most TV fare and consider what the medium will bring us in the wondrous future. He would say we only discuss the form of tele-

* This too easy equation between liberalism and fascism is discussed later in the chapter.

vision; television as material cannot be considered until the next technological advance.

For Mailer, content and form are inseparable; dishonesty of content will be accompanied by a misuse of form. In a passage from *The Armies of the Night* which helps to explain D.J.'s often solipsistic, disconnected responses, Mailer attributed the radicalism of the marchers on the Pentagon to

> their hate for the authority—the authority was the manifest of evil to this generation. It was the authority who had covered the land with those suburbs where they stifled as children while watching the adventures of the West in the movies, while looking at the guardians of dull genial celebrity on television; *they had had their minds jabbed and poked and twitched and probed and finally galvanized into surrealistic modes of response by commercials cutting into dramatic narratives, and parents flipping from network to network—they were forced willy-nilly to build their idea of the space-time continuum (and therefore their nervous system) on the jumps and cracks and leaps and breaks which every phenomenon from the media seemed to contain within it.* [Italics mine.]

If you will pardon two more quotations which realize contrasting responses to a central American reality, both moral and perceptual, here is McLuhan on the rigged TV quizzes:

> Any play or poem or novel is also rigged to produce an effect. . . . But . . . So great was the audience participation in the quiz shows that the directors of the show were prosecuted as con men. . . . Charles Van Doren merely got clobbered as an innocent bystander. . . . Regrettably, [the investigation] simply provided a field day for the earnest moralizers. A moral point of view too often serves as a substitute for understanding in technological matters.

And here is part of the next paragraph from *Armies:*

> The authority had operated on their brain with commercials, and washed their brain with packaged education, packaged politics. The authority had presented itself as honorable, and it was corrupt, corrupt as payola on television, and scandals concerning the safety of automobiles . . . the real scandals as everyone was beginning to sense were more intimate and could be found in all the products in all the suburban homes which did not work so well as they should have worked, and broke down too soon for mysterious reasons.

The Canadian encourages enlightened passivity—the future will be fine if we leave it to the electronic circuits; all we can do is understand what is happening. Mailer believes that we must break from any Faustian gadget that tries to enslave a nature which would nourish us if we used it properly. Far from preaching passivity, he bellows at us that everything in this country will soon get much worse if everyone does not act more bravely. The violent disagreements between McLuhan and Mailer can finally be traced to their divergent conceptions of human nature. McLuhan seems to regard this creature who is about to enter the electronic millennium as a tabula rasa receptive to the messages which the media imprint through the senses. Mailer follows the biological implications of his dynamic ontology far enough to claim that "each cell in each existence labors like all of life to make the most of what it is or can be."

But the radicals who had their nervous systems remade by television were protesting the war in Vietnam; D.J. closes the book by enthusiastically crying, "Vietnam, hot damn." Mailer will argue in *Armies* that the protesters are urban middle class in origin. Although D.J. is from the Dallas upper middle class, the ferocity of his commitments is much closer to small-town America than that of the protesters. To understand how the television culture which McLuhan tries to smooth over could have helped to shape the maddened and egomaniacal components of D.J.'s sensibility, we must turn to *Cannibals and Christians,* a collection which informs the meaning of *Vietnam* in much the same way that the ideas set out in *Papers* largely guided the shape *Dream* took.

When Mailer described the ideology of the mass media as liberal, he could have as easily used the word "Christian"—had he applied his own definition of the word. Not that Mailer's Christians invariably profess a belief in the divinity of Christ—most of them do not; it is simply that "in a modern world which produces mediocrities at an accelerating rate" they are by theory opposed to any destruction of human life. We should not let those two words *by theory* slip by too easily, but emphasize the distinction between the humanitarian positions which the Christians think about and profess and the more murderous feelings which reside deeper within them; otherwise, the involvements of Christians in our venture in Vietnam and, in the novel, of the Christian hunters in Alaska are contradictory. Some Cannibals will admit that they enjoy taking human life, but no Christian will. If we are Mailer's Christians, "we believe man is good if given a chance, we believe man is open to discussion; we believe science is the salvation of ill, we believe death is the end of the discussion; ergo we believe nothing is so worthwhile as human life. We think no one should go hungry." In short, we are liberals.

Opposed to the Christians (who have somehow acted out their

views in such a way that they started every war in the last two decades and further poisoned our waterways, air, and food) are the Cannibals. All Cannibals believe that "there is too much on earth and too much of it is second rate." They would save the world "by killing off what is second rate." Like the Christian, the Cannibal is not without contradiction. For example, he has a profound rage at the destruction of nature but often destroys it himself. This paradox is typical of those that alienate the Cannibal from the whole-hearted endorsement of his classifier, Norman Mailer. For example, of the Cannibal premise that the plague poisoning our surroundings and our lives is to be associated with collectivism, Mailer has said: "I am not so certain they are wrong. The essence of biology seems to be challenge and response, risk and survival, war and the lessons of war." But most of the Cannibals are not brave enough to face the implications of the survival-of-the-fittest ethic that has always strongly appealed to Mailer. War against whom? Response against what? The Cannibals' choice of adversary often reflects a stupidity and/or sickness which separates them from the rest of the natural order. After all, they are Cannibals:

> . . . they believe that survival and health of the species comes from consuming one's own, not one's near-own, but one's own species. So the pure cannibal has only one taboo on food—he will not eat the meat of his own family. Other men he will of course consume. Their virtues he will conserve in his own flesh, their vices he will excrete, but to kill and to eliminate is his sense of human continuation.
> . . . What characterizes the Cannibals is that most of them are born Christian, think of Jesus as Love, and get an erection from the thought of whippings, blood, burning crosses, burning bodies, and screams in mass graves.

The Christian's desires are not very much less murderous, but he either dams them up deep inside himself (where, since Mailer is faithful to Reich in his fashion, they cause ailments running from headaches to cancer) or they express themselves in such pious acts as devastating South Vietnam "for the good of the inhabitants." But how has it come to pass that the fervor of the believers in Jesus has taken such a debased form and the self-professed bleeding hearts endorse so much violence with so much righteousness? Or why is it that if they forgo violence they suffer so much from the proscription? Since the thematic movement of *Vietnam* is, in its simplest form, the process of D.J.'s rejection of Christianity and his embrace of Cannibalism, we would do well to turn to Mailer's account of the formation of those two huge, tormented groups which largely constitute contemporary, plague-ridden America.

Mailer has always believed that the presence or absence of good art enormously affects the psychic life of the nation's inhabitants. Thus, his history of America's descent into the plague begins with the failure of writers to produce "the novel which would ignite a nation's consciousness of itself." In the absence of such a great novel,

> the American consciousness . . . ended by being developed by the bootlicking pieties of small-town newspaper editors and small-town educators, by the worst of organized religion, a formless force filled with the terrors of all the Christians left to fill the spaces left by the initial bravery of the frontiersman, and these latterday Christians were simply not as brave. That was one component of the mud [the nation's consciousness and culture was dragged through]. The other was the sons of the immigrants. Many of them hated America, hated it for what it offered and did not provide, what it revealed of opportunity and what it excluded from real opportunity. The sons of these immigrants and the sons' sons took over the cities and began to run them, high up in the air and right down into the ground, they plucked and they plundered and there was not an American city which did not grow more hideous in the last fifty years.

But the despoilation of the cities by the rapacious sons of the embittered immigrants was, compared to what would follow, a small contribution to the acceleration of the plague. Let us resume Mailer's apocalyptic account of the evolution of the Cannibal-Christian dichotomy, of the effect of the television culture that McLuhan smooths over, and of the most recent turn the plague was to take:

> Then they spread out—they put suburbs like blight on the land—and piped mass communications into every home. They were cannibals selling Christianity to Christians, and because they despised the message and mocked at it in their own heart, they succeeded in selling something else, a virus perhaps, an electronic nihilism went through the mass media of America and entered the Christians and they were like to being cannibals, they were a tense and livid people, swallowing their own hate with the tranquilizers and the sex in the commercials, whereas all the early cannibals at the knobs of the mass-media made the mistake of passing on their bleak disease and were left now too gentle, too liberal, too programmatic, filled with plans for social welfare, and they looked and talked in Show Biz styles which possessed no style and were generally as unhealthy as Christians who lived in cellars and caves.
>
> Yes, the cannibal sons of the immigrants had become Christians, and the formless form they had evolved for their mass-media, the hypocritical empty and tasteless taste of the television arts they beamed across the land encountered the formless form and the all

but tasteless taste of the small-town tit-eating cannibal mind at its worst, and the collision produced schizophrenia in the land. Half of America [the Christians] went insane with head colds and medicaments and asthmas and allergies, hospitals and famous surgeons with knives to cut into the plague, welfares and plans and committees and cooperations and boredom, boredom plague deep upon the land; and the other part of America [the Cannibals] went ape, and the motorcycles began to roar like lions across the land and all the beasts of all the buried history of America turned in their circuit and prepared to slink toward the market place, there to burn the mother's hair and bite the baby to the heart. One thought of America and one thought of aspirin, kitchen commercials, and blood. One thought of Vietnam.

Three metamorphoses are outlined here. The first is that of the big-city cannibal who evolves into the liberal, emotionally constricted Christian. (I shall continue to use the lowercase initial letter to refer to the two types who existed before the mass media dislocated their sensibilities and the uppercase to refer to the new types that came into being after the dislocation.) The other two metamorphoses concern the common small-town mind, which was a mixture of the God-fearing Christian and the mildly cannibalistic. Some of these minds went the way of the old city cannibals and professed liberal doctrines even if they did not always act in accordance with their statements; the rest became the new, electronically maddened Cannibals.

II

Having rejected the America of aspirins and kitchen commercials, of repression and commerce, for blood and hearty endorsement of Vietnam, D.J.'s personal development parallels the last of the three collective ones. The buried beasts of American history with whom D.J. signs his murderous pact are largely contained within his best friend, Tex Hyde. Tex is also D.J.'s alter ego; since D.J. several times refers to himself as Dr. Jekyll, Mailer leaves no doubt that he is characterizing in Tex the archetypal cannibal of our time—an amalgam of the most ferocious ingredients of the American melting pot:

> Tex is half-German and half-Indian on his father's side, Redskin and Nazi all in one paternal blood, and . . . Tex Hyde's mother is jes old rawhide Texas ass family running . . . fifty-two shacks right back to the Alamo. . . .
>
> Well, Tex Hyde, he's a mother fucker . . . and he nothing but D.J.'s best friend. . . . Listen to Halleloo [D.J.'s mother]. Her tone is full of hell now. . . . "Tex Hyde is the son of an *undertaker,* I mean think of that, a Montesquiou Jellico Jethroe a-whopping around with a Kraut mortician's offspring, and all that bastard Indian Hyde blood in the background, firewater and dirty old Engine

oil, . . . it's just the sort of dirty vile polluted cesspool Eenyen blood like Mexican—you know just a touch of that Latin slicky shit in it, vicious as they come, and mated up, contemplez-vous, to fatty Bavarian oonshick and poonshick jawohl furor lemme kiss your dirty socks my leader, can you imagine? the filthiest of the Indians and the slimiest of red hot sexyass Nazis fucking each other, mating and breeding to produce Tex Hyde . . . that boy growing up there comes out like a malevolent orchid in a humus pile, or a black panther, that's what he is, black panther with all his black panther piss, . . . he's got my son who's just as beautiful as George Hamilton and more clean-cut swearing by him . . . I think they took the vow of blood, cut their thumbs and ran 'em around the rim of some debutante's pussy, after the way these kids now live there ain't much left for them but to gang fuck tastefully. . . ."

When Halleloo's pungent lament is finally concluded, D.J. tells us that this is not the way she talks, just the way she thinks. It is also the way Mailer thinks. By this I am not referring to the language in which Halleloo thinks but to Mailer's disapproval of the way the boys live. Mailer has always been opposed to purposeless promiscuity, and there is no stronger condemnation of the ways of plague-ridden America than the evocation of "gang-fucking with style" or D.J.'s boasts of "closet fucks"—surprising Dallas mothers who are "cliff-hanging menopause types" in a bathroom and there enjoying "a two minute red-hot steaming ass blubberwet slap-dizzy oceanic cunt fuck." In fact, Tex is not above trying to lure Halleloo into a bathroom on the very night that D.J. is making his broadcast to the world. It is a bit comical that Mailer claims to have soured on the sexual revolution which he predicted in the late fifties and, to an unmeasurable extent, helped to bring about. His invocation of the dark gods of mystery only helped to drive them further away. For since he has argued that development through sex is directly proportional to the amount one fights against his sense of sin, it grieves him that so few of the youth have a sense of sex as sin. As he wrote in *Armies,* he had no interest in flirting with young girls who were "innocent, decent-spirited, merry, red-cheeked, idealistic, and utterly lobotomized away from the sense of sin . . . they conceived of lust as no more than the gymnasium of love." D.J., neither innocent nor idealistic, with no desire for love, does seek danger—one of the matrons in the bathroom might try to kick his scrotum in. But this is really of the same order as his telling some sexually free but socially proper Dallas deb that her vagina smells like a Mexican's urine. It's all entertainment. D.J.'s mother thinks that her son is morally anesthetized, and so does Mailer.

The sex "plus ghoul surgery on corpses . . . derives from their encounter with all the human shit and natural depth of their Moe Henry hunt two year ago." The natural depth resulted in a blood pact between D.J. and Tex, which is to say, on one of the novel's symbolic levels, between D.J.'s conscious mind and the most violent and primordial part of himself, but the pact did not itself cause D.J. to seek out quick sex with near madwomen in bathrooms or perform ghoul surgery for secret powers. It took the collision of the pact and all the "human shit" D.J. reencountered after the pact was made.

D.J. would not have gone on the hunting trip to the Brooks Range if his father had not been (as the narrator might put it) a minion of the Great Plastic Asshole. For D.J.'s favorite theory "is that America is run by a mysterious hidden mastermind, a secret creature who's got a plastic asshole installed in his brain whereby he can shit out all of his corporate management of thoughts." The anus and plastic have long been two of Mailer's favorite symbols of the decreative, and they are here linked with a force which is the psychic equivalent of plastic —the corporate mentality. To Mailer, it is both a symptom of the plague and a cause of deeper plague that America has denied the dynamic hero the leadership of America and turned it over to the faceless committees of big business and government. The result has been disastrous because "committees do not create, they merely proliferate, and the incredible dullness wreaked upon the American landscape in Eisenhower's eight years has been the triumph of the corporation."

The preceding line was written in 1960 when Mailer was arguing that one potentially heroic leader, John F. Kennedy, could lift the nation out of the purposeless dullness into which it had fallen. But *Why Are We in Vietnam?* was written late in 1966; in the six-year interim, the terms of Mailer's diagnosis changed from dullness to plague, from frustration to madness, and the corporate mind which contributed so heartily to the acceleration of the plague is, as Joseph Epstein has pointed out, much in ascendence. (In fact, Mailer will in a few months write that "the American corporation executive . . . was after all the foremost representative of Man in the world today.") We might turn to Epstein's trenchant comments about the workings of all those corporate types who have to say the expected with quality:

> Mailer's grasp of the corporate mind, and his altogether devastating caricature of Rusty Jethroe as an embodiment of that mind in action, are among the most impressive aspects of his novel. . . . Nothing quite so much characterizes this mind, as Mailer neatly delineates it, as its will-to-power and its insistence on dominance and control.

The corporate type, far from being a mere cipher, is frequently cunningly intelligent on behalf of his own ambitions and stalwart in defense of his own ego. At top form, the corporate style can be flexible, incisive and ruthless.

The Croft who toiled up Mount Anaka on a quest which inspired his creator's sympathies was also characterized by his will-to-power. He, too, was cunningly intelligent on behalf of his ambitions and stalwartly defended his conception of his own worth, and so was Rojack, once his quest for being truly got under way. But the entity over which Croft and Rojack sought dominance was ultimately themselves; the ambition which drove their quests onward was the desire to become more than they were, to be able to do and feel more than they had before. The desired end of Rusty's considerable will and energies are not the freeing of more will and energy, but the final concern of every corporative mind—status. So much of *Vietnam* is devoted to an abrasively funny diagnosis of the American malady that the Dream of Being makes only a brief (though glittering) appearance. Yet we are back to the distinction between the Dream of Being and the Dream of Power. Far from being a soldier in God's holy war to expand Being, Rusty's ultimate concern is to be treated with more deference by others, even though he despises most of the men whose approval he seeks.

Although Rusty heads a new division in a vast corporation,* the primary meaning the hunting trip has to him is the possibility it offers of enabling him to move up a rung on the status ladder. For the head guide for the trip is the Great White Hunter, Big Luke Fellinka, and "all the minions of the Great Plastic Asshole were slobbering over the

---

* The company is Central Consolidated Combined Chemical and Plastic (4C and P); the division is for "Four C-ing the cancer market—big lung subsidiary." The product is a plastic cigarette filter "trade name Pure Pores . . . the most absorptive substance devised ever in a vat—traps all the nicotine, sucks up every bit of your spit. Pure Pores also causes cancer of the lip but the results are inconclusive, and besides, fuck you!" (Norman Mailer, *Why Are We in Vietnam?* [New York: G. P. Putnam's Sons, 1967], pp. 30–31 [hereafter cited as *Vietnam*]). Rusty's job is a neat metaphor for the corporation man's fatal disassociation with nature. In a 1964 interview Mailer said:

A fibre-glass hull can go through storms which would spring a leak in a wooden hull. Then, one day, in a modest squall, the fibre-glass splits completely. Or abruptly capsizes. That is because it is a material which is not even divorced from nature but indeed has not ever been a part of nature. Plastic is the perfect metaphor for 20th century man and for the curious, stupifying, bewildering nature of so much modern violence. ["Talking of Violence," *20th Century*, Vol. 173 (Winter, 1964–65), p. 112.]

bear grease on Big Luke's boots." D.J. tells us that the inestimable value Big Luke had to the corporate types lay not in his great marksmanship or his knowledge of the woods or even in his having fought a grizzly with his bare hands, but in a personal force so great that "if you even a high-grade asshole and had naught but a smidgeon of flunky in you . . . it would still start in Big Luke's presence to blow sulfur water, steam and specks of hopeless diarrhetic matter in your runny little gut, cause he was a *man!*" And Rusty is, in D.J.'s analysis of the corporate structure, a high-grade asshole—one who takes orders only from the decreative force informing the corporate mind, the Great Plastic Asshole, or, in Mailer's more familiar cosmology, the Devil. The status of an executive who has held his own with Big Luke is thus considerably enhanced. But Rusty has to do more than avoid betraying any trace of the flunky in word or act; he must return to Dallas with a bearskin, even though Big Luke tells him at the beginning of the trip that bear are scarce and he might have to settle for caribou. For Rusty is "the cream of corporation corporateness":

> . . . let Rusty travel all that round trip 6,000 plus miles, spending 6,000 plus dollars on D.J. and himself . . . and present himself at 4C and P with a deer's head and no bear. Rusty and his status . . . can now take a double pine box funeral—they'll never got off his ass at Combined Consolidated, no, no, the office staff will wet their little pants waiting for Christmas so they can send him an anonymous set of antlers off some poor ass spavined Texas buck twice the antlers in width of measurement and holding four more points than the one he air-freighted back from Alaska . . . Rusty knows a piss cutter when it scratches his scrotum—thank you very much, Mr. Luke Fellinka, but no thanks on that deer.

In addition to being an executive with a life style reminiscent of Lyndon Baines Johnson's, a onetime third-string All-American football player, a formidable outdoorsman, and a lover of considerable if occasional powers, Rusty is a Maileresque Christian. This is not to say that Rusty does not have murderous desires; the Christian only professes not to have them. We can best distinguish the Cannibal from the Christian by discerning what the ultimate concern, the central desire, of each type is. Mailer's Christians are above all "the commercial. The commercial is the invention of a profoundly Christian nation —it proceeds to sell something in which it does not altogether believe." The Cannibal's ultimate desire is not to sell; it is to destroy whatever he feels to be second rate. Rusty's profession is of course a highly commercial one, but so is his avocation—selling himself as the corporate man's man to any potential buyer. When D.J. dismisses

Rusty as "the highest grade of asshole made in America and so suggests D.J.'s future: success will stimulate you to suffocate," he is also rejecting the species of Christianity that hails a Rusty Jethroe as a corporate knight.

D.J.'s final rejection of his father's life style is precipitated when they break off from Big Luke and the rest of the hunting party to look for bear by themselves. Temporarily freed from his servile underlings and Luke's judging eye, Rusty begins "shedding those corporation layers, all that paper ass desk shit and glut . . . and he's free of Luke the Fink with his Washington up your ass connections, he's being bad Rusty and it's years, man, he wants to holler hallo for a grizzer any size big ass beast." As his layers peel in the magnificent, apparently unspoiled surroundings, Rusty displays surprising pockets of information and response. With none of his usual posturing and executive role-playing, he points out to D.J. the local flora; he warns his son of the dangerous three seconds when a hunter steps from light to shadow. The superchauvinist even tells his son of the worst thing he ever saw—an eagle killing an already wounded deer—and proclaims it "a secret crime that America . . . is nonetheless represented, indeed even symbolized by an eagle, the most miserable of the scavengers, worse than a crow." In short, he is so much more than usual what a father should be that D.J. loves him.

Then they are charged by a huge grizzly who, like so many animals of the Brooks Range, has been maddened by the helicopters of the overplentiful hunters. Both Jethroes get shots off, but it is D.J. who maintains enough self-control to slam his bolt home and break the bear's charge by sending another bullet into its jaws when it is less than ten yards from the hunters. It is also D.J. who suggests tracking the spoor of the badly wounded and extremely dangerous animal down a ledge and into the thicket into which it fled. This the badly shaken Rusty clearly does not want to do; he would now much rather "holler hallo" from a distance. It is also D.J. who insists on walking close to the dying bear to see if this embodiment of primordial power could tell him anything that would help him to live as he should. The bear's eyes tell D.J. of the existence of some kind of ethical natural order: ". . . when D.J. smiled, the eyes reacted, they shifted . . . they looked to be drawing in the peace of the forest preserved for all animals as they die, the unspoken cool on tap in the veins of every tree, yes, griz was drawing in some music of the unheard burial march. . . ."

Showing more and more of the white feather, Rusty is too frightened to permit the bear the good death which it has earned by its good fight: ". . . Rusty—wetting his pants, doubtless, from the excessive tension—chose that moment to shoot, and griz went up to death in one last paroxysm, legs thrashing, brain exploding from new galvanizings and overloadings of massive damage report, and one last final heuuuuuu, all forgiveness gone." Stunned by his father's cowardice and insensitivity, D.J. gives Rusty one more chance when they return to camp and Big Luke asks who got the bear:

> . . . D.J., in the silence which followed, said, "Well, we both sent shots home, but I reckon Rusty got it," and Rusty didn't contradict him—one more long silence—and Rusty said, "Yeah, I guess it's mine, but one of its sweet legs belongs to D.J." Whew. Final end of love of one son for one father.

D.J.'s rage at being betrayed by his father's obsession with status is so extreme, his desire to kill Rusty so strong, that he and Tex slip out of camp that night, hours before dawn, and head deeper into the wilds of the Brooks Range. Or, stated in terms of D.J.'s psychic movement, he turns away from the Christian in himself and—between the wilds and Tex—heads into the wilder parts of himself. Although they experience some of the vaulting emotions which always lift Mailer's heroes as they move into unexplored areas, they are still

> half-fouled with the emanated nauseas of medium assholes and Rusty high-grade asshole, disillusioned with Big Luke's Cop Turd copping out on the big game hunter's code and oath, and just in a general state of mixed shit, for the walk up to here has done them only a minim of good. They have not cleaned the pipes, not yet. They are still full of toilet plunger holes seen in caribou, and shattered guts and strewn-out souls of slaughtered game meats all over the Alaska air and Tex feels like he's never going to hunt again which is not unhorrendous for him since he's a natural hunter. . . .

The toilet plunger holes and shattered guts—the result of the hunters' devilishly excessive armament, reported earlier in scrupulous, mock-epic detail—deepens the association of the hunting trip and the American involvement in Vietnam, a fusion which was begun with the references to the Hail-the-Cop-Turds and the perception that the two yes-men, Medium Assholes Bill and Pete, were playing McNamara and Rusk to Rusty's LBJ. We might cement the association by again consulting Mr. Epstein:

> Rusty, in his obsessive need for victory in landing a bear, disaffects his son, so America in its obsessive need not to lose face in Vietnam has disaffected some of the best of its young people. The style of

these Texans is characterized by mindless destruction, awe of technology and a mania for status, but these elements are not absent from the American venture in Vietnam. Mailer . . . has created a powerful metaphor for his own nation's intrusion in another land, and through the force of this metaphor shown that intrusion to be the wretched affair it is.

Now—to borrow from a less earthy radio format than D.J.'s—let us return to the boys to see why the rejecter of the symbolic carnage in Vietnam should be so eager to join it at book's end. In an attempt to cleanse their fouled psyches (one which recalls the purification ceremonies in the first part of Faulkner's "The Bear"), the boys decide to proceed without rifles, knives, binoculars, packs, sleeping bags, food, or compass. But before they have walked two hundred yards, they return to take everything but the guns, knives, and compass from the cache they have left behind them. And they discover that they have not exceeded the terms of the pact necessary to purify themselves of that hunting party which is a paradigm of the society they are trying to flee:

> . . . mixed shit does not flow in again to the reservoir of their heart because celestial mechanics is built on equations and going with nothing into the forest is not necessarily more loaded with points of valor than going with rudimentary bag and forage yet without arms into mountain snow. September, and that land ahead is white as a sheet!

So, still feeling freed of the mixed shit, Tex and D.J. move further into the mountains. They confront a huge, starving wolf, but they emanate through psychic waves such a total determination to defend themselves that the wolf is frightened off. The mood changes as the day wears on; the sight of a fox whining and crying because a squirrel will not climb down from a tree to be eaten moves them to such mirth that they stop to pummel each other. But as soon as the horseplay stops

> (1) the King of Mountain Peak M.E.F. shit, (2) Mr. Awe and (3) Mr. Dread—that troika—that Cannibal Emperor of Nature's Psyche . . . Mr. Sender, who sends out that Awe and Dread is up on their back clawing away like a cat because they *alone,* man, you dig? why, they just dug, they all *alone,* it's a fright wig, man, that *Upper* silence alone is enough to bugger you, whoo-ee. . . .

In other words, they have confronted Mailer's God and, as is usually the way with his characters when this happens, they experience dread and awe; as D.J. realizes, God always wants more from man

than man is willing to give. The M.E.F. refers to the Magnetic-Electro
fief of the dream, not to be confused with the e.m.f., the entire electro-
magnetic field in which the M.E.F. struggles. At our best, the dream
to which we are fief is the collective Dream of Being or, to reach back
to the preceding chapters, God's embattled vision. But we are not all
at our best; many of the desires expressed and simulations run in our
dreams are cowardly, Devilish ones—we reach back again to the
Dream of Power. Both visions seek to realize themselves in the totality of the world, but here the context is electronically conceived. The
context is the e.m.f. or what McLuhan might call the technological
configuration. But all humans contribute to the M.E.F. In one of the
early-sixties poems in *Deaths for the Ladies,* Mailer wrote of staying
up to listen to the dreams of the sleeping New Yorkers. Five years
later, dream communication became a major thematic element in a
very good novel:

> D.J. your disc jockey is telling you, where you going when you sleep?
> well, hole, there's only one place you go, and that's into the undis-
> covered magnetic-electro fief of the dream, which is opposed to the
> electromagnetic field of the earth just as properly as the square root
> of minus one is opposed to one . . . when you go into sleep, that
> mind of yours leaps, stirs, and sifts itself into the Magnetic-Electro
> fief of the dream, hereafter known as M.E. or M.E.F., you are a part
> of the spook flux of the night like an iron filing in the E.M. field
> (otherwise glommed as e.m.f.) and it all flows, mind and asshole,
> anode and cathode, you sending messages and receiving all through
> the night. . . .

Mailer ingeniously fuses the actual magnetism of the Arctic Circle,
the fact that the best of the M.E.F. is in a sense God's voice, and the
apparently unspoiled nourishing purity of the Brooks Range to suggest that the M.E.F. runs toward the North Pole and one can hear it
(or God's voice) quite clearly in the crystalline air of the mountains.
D.J. and Tex experience dread because they sense that the voice
of God is near; they are in awe of His presence and in dread of the
demands He might make upon them. Almost twenty years earlier,
Mailer had written of another violent, baffled Texan who pushed
against his fears into wild, foreboding surroundings in an attempt to
discover what D.J. now perceives is near—"a secret . . . some mystery into the secret of things." Croft is denied any revelation of the
mystery; D.J. is not. It comes to him and Tex as they wake up in the
middle of the night with their fire nearly out and a wolf lurking
nearby. They drive off the wolf by rebuilding the fire and watch the
glittering green and red wash of Aurora Borealis:

And they each are living half out of their minds. For the lights were talking to them, and they were going with it, near to, the lights were saying that there was something up here, and it was really here, yeah God was here, and He was real and no man was He, but a beast, some beast of a giant jaw and cavernous mouth with a full cave's breath and fangs, and secret call: come to me. They could almost have got up and walked across the pond and into the north without their boots, going up to disappear and die and join that great beast. In the field of all such desire D.J. raised his hand to put it square on Tex's cock and squeeze. . . .

The lights, in a sense the glittering crown of the M.E.F., function (like the moon in *Dream*) to reveal the mysteries of growth and decline to anyone who has been enough moved to hear their message. Tex now desires D.J. as much as D.J. does him. Each perceives that he can gain the other's powers through triumphant sex—as Rojack got Ruta's cunning and Cherry's magic at the gaming tables—but since each is as desirous of maintaining his own powers as gaining the other's,

> Tex Hyde he of the fearless Eenyen blood was finally afraid to prong D.J., because D.J. once become a bitch would kill him, and D.J. breathing that in by the wide-awake of the dark with Aurora Borealis jumping to the beat of his heart knew . . . Tex was ready to fight him to death, yeah, now it was there, murder between them under all friendship, *for God was a beast, not a man, and God said, "Go out and kill—fulfill my will, go and kill,"* and they hung there each of them on the knife of the divide in all conflict of lust to own the other yet in fear of being killed by the other and as the hour went by and the lights shifted, something in the radiance of the North went into them, and owned their fear, some communion of telepathies and new powers, and they were twins, never to be near as lovers again, but killer brothers, owned by something, prince of darkness, lord of light, they did not know; they just knew telepathy was on them, they had been touched forever by the North and each bit a drop of blood from his own finger and touched them across and met, blood to blood, while the lights pulsated and glow of Arctic night was on the snow, *and the deep beast whispering Fulfill my will, go forth and kill.* . . . [Italics mine.]

At this point in time, the blood union between the two boys primarily symbolizes D.J.'s movement towards authenticity. The Jekyll and the Hyde, the mind and the wilder passions, are connected, and he is ready to act out the being's command to kill. But whom should he kill? Precisely what acts will fulfill the will of the immanent God?

If Mailer's God of growth is speaking, as I think He is, then D.J. should—like Rojack—kill the decreative both within and without. If some enemy of Being, a Deborah or an Oswald Kelley or a Rusty Jethroe, were before D.J. at that moment, the boy might have tried to kill him, but he must wait until morning for enemies, and he must reinterpret anew God's message (or his being's, or the M.E.F.'s, or that of his unconscious).

As we have already seen, God never repeats; constant reiteration would give the hearer a gimmick, a devilish advantage. To once more tread familiar ground, one's sense of reality is finally one's sense of God's dictates, one's perception of what must be done to aid in the struggle for Being, but the most persistent accusation that Mailer levels at the mass media is that it distorts our sense of reality. As D.J. returns to camp the next morning, his perception of God's command and his capacities for joy and creative sex are necessarily altered by the dream messages of the minions of corporate-TV culture now fouling the M.E.F. throughout

> North America, that sad deep sweet beauteous mystery land of purple forests, and pink rock, and blue water, Indian haunts from Maine to the shore of Californ, all gutted, shit on, used and blasted . . . and those messages at night—oh, God, let me hump the boss' daughter, let me make it, God, all going up through the M.E.F. cutting the night air, giving a singe to the dream field, all the United Greedies of America humping up that old rhythm . . . the ionization level rises . . . comes down again like a cloud, and intercranial communication is muffled, no mean matter, cause at Brooks Range, on the edge of the great snow-white parabolic reflector [of the valley where the boys camped], sitting in the silent resonant electric hum of the still, there is a rub in the air like your hair on edge or coitus all interruptus with electric coils of gas in your bowel, pain in your balls, and hate in your ding, yes, discomfort as the ionization layer settles back and the hills is full of static charge.

Enough of the pieces of Mailer's complex parable are before us now. The world is indeed a McLuhanite global village, with everyone's sensibilities powerfully affected by the total electronic configuration. Or, in the terms of the novel, the best of the M.E.F. is thrall to horrors of our daytime world, of the e.m.f. The collapse of ideals which created the dependence upon electricity is now being amplified and programmed into the ears of every "tuned in" listener, and it is very hard not to be tuned in; as Mailer complained in *Cannibals,* one can scarcely go anywhere and escape the sound of an electric motor.

The power of this electronic nihilism is so great that two years after his temporarily purifying experience in the Brooks Range (where he escaped for a few hours the effects of the electronic morality), D.J. sees himself not as a soldier of Growth but as an amplifier of that hopelessly debased morality pouring through him.

When D.J. heard God's command, he was neither Cannibal nor Christian. In their purest form, the members of these types are finally cowardly and inauthentic, and D.J. experienced an authentic moment. To recall Mailer's account of the formation of the two diseased species, the impact of the electronic nihilism upon a passionate small-town mind such as D.J.'s creates either an acceptance of the corporate Christianity of his father or the acceptance of the buried beasts of American history; that is, an acceptance of the worst of Tex, of himself, of blood shed unheroically. Having rejected his father, D.J. chose Cannibalism and, with it, Vietnam. Some Americans fight in Vietnam for Christian reasons; they want to bring democracy to Southeast Asia, to halt communism, and so on. This will not stop them from enjoying carnage any more than concern over status stopped the hunters in the novel from enjoying blowing animals apart. But the Cannibals are more open about the joy they find in slaughter, and one of these bloody revelers will be D.J., whose perceptions have been so shifted by our new electronic morality that he goes to Vietnam for the sport of it—to quote again the last words of the novel, "Vietnam, hot damn." The issue is not so much D.J.'s becoming a Cannibal rather than a Christian as his succumbing to the new electronic morality, for all of the members of both groups succumb in varying degrees. The novel grows yet darker when we remember that Mailer began his description of the two types by writing, "We are martyrs these days," with the implication that almost all of us are martyrs. It steadily grows harder for any of us to be more a soldier in the holy war for Being than a decreative force.

In the preceding chapter I suggested several times that the heroic Godly figure ultimately depends upon his courage, not some advantageous gimmick. Because America's advantage in the war is so immense, our whole endeavor becomes a perfect metaphor for Devilish effort. We are in Vietnam because we are plague-ridden and murder seems to offer relief from the plague, but we would not be plagued if we were not cowardly. The war which springs from the devilishness of our cowardice is fought in a corresponding fashion. In *The Armies of the Night,* Mailer cited what was for him an obscene statistic and then proceeded to explain in a number of ways why our adventure in Vietnam was such a misadventure:

> Next to every pound of supplies the North Vietnamese brought into South Vietnam for their soldiers, the Americans brought in one hundred thousand pounds. . . . All wars were bad which undertook daily operations which burned and bombed large numbers of women and children, all wars were bad which relocated populations (for the root of a rich peasant lore was then destroyed) all wars were bad when they had no line of battle for discernible climax—an advanced notion which supposes that wars may be in part good because they are sometimes the only way to define critical conditions rather than blur them) certainly all wars were bad which took some of the bravest young men of a nation and sent them into combat with outrageous superiority and outrageous arguments: such conditions of combat had to excite a secret passion for hunting other humans.

Indifferent to any arguments for or against the rectitude of our Vietnam effort, D.J. is a pure Cannibal after his kicks; he merely wants to hunt human beings, to, in a sense, eat his own kind.* Had he been able to avoid the collective madness of America—the mixed shit of the e.m.f. and M.E.F.—he might have gone off to Vietnam to fight for the outnumbered Viet Cong, or perhaps he would have fought in the war on the American side but in a Godly way, as Rojack used Las Vegas for good purposes, or as Mailer, in the fall of 1968, used a television variety show as the platform to announce to mass America that because we were burning babies in Vietnam all of the pornographic novels ever written were not as obscene as one moment in the mind

* Mailer offers in *Armies* a lyrical explanation of the lobotomizing effect of technology on the small-town mind, one which does not employ the Cannibals-Christians terminology. The passage—in Book One, Part IV, Chapter 3— closes: "technology had driven insanity out of the wind and out of the attic, and out of all the lost primitive places: one had to find it now wherever fever, force, and machines could come together, in Vegas, at the race track, in pro football, race riots for the Negro, suburban orgies—none of it was enough— one had to find it in Vietnam; that was where the small town had gone to get its kicks" (*The Armies of the Night* [New York: New American Library, 1968], p. 153).

Rusty tells D.J. that "my grandmammy . . . used to be a witch, so evehbody claims. She used to tell me when I was a little three-year-old . . . that I must never sleep under a pioneer tree, cause it is full of sorrow and alone and bats piss on it at midnight, therefore it stands by itself getting messages, all kind of special messages, and if you sleep under it, you witched by it, you get the messages too" (*Vietnam*, p. 130). With the death of this potentially creative insanity, D.J. is off to fight with the technological, decreative insanity of the American effort in Vietnam.

of the American commanding general there. Or D.J. might have been one of the stormers of the Pentagon in October, 1967. But filled as he is with the demons of mindless violence, he ends the novel as a part of the obscenity.

III

All of the preceding is in *Why Are We in Vietnam?*, but says little of the shift in Mailer's novelistic ambitions since *An American Dream* or—except for the structural ingenuity and the way in which the social criticism is compressed into an onrushing narrative—why his last novel is by far the best one since *The Naked and the Dead*. Here, two statements that Mailer made in much different courts are helpful. The first, made in 1960 in a New York City courtroom shortly after the stabbing, followed the recommendation of the court doctor that the defendant was "having an acute paranoidal breakdown with delusional thinking and is both homocidal and suicidal. His admission to a hospital is urgently advised." In response, Mailer said to the Magistrate, Reuben Levy:

> It is important for me not to be sent to a mental hospital because my work will be considered that of a disordered mind. My pride is that I can explore areas of experience that other men are afraid of. I insist that I am sane.

The other statement is excerpted from Mailer's testimony at the Superior Court of Boston in 1965, where he spoke as a defense witness at the obscenity trial of William Burroughs's *Naked Lunch:*

> . . . I found I had more respect for the reading of it this [the third] time. I haven't finished it. I had to read slowly and think about it a great deal, as to my respect for it. I have a feeling that it is much more of a literary work than I felt the previous time, even though the previous time I felt it was a work of high talent. The man has extraordinary talent. Possibly he is the most talented writer in America. . . .
> . . . I think he catches the beauty, at the same time the viciousness and the meanness and the excitement, you see, of ordinary talk, the talk of criminals, of soldiers, athletes, junkies.
> There is a kind of speech that is referred to as gutter talk that often has a very fine, incisive, dramatic line to it; and Burroughs captures that speech like no American writer I know. He also—and this makes it impressive to me as writer—he also has an exquisite poetic sense. His poetic images are intense. They are often disgusting; but at the same time there is a sense of collision in them, of montage that is quite unusual. And, as I say, all this together gives me great respect for his style. But I also began to feel that really this time there is

more to his intent than I had ever recognized before; that the work was more of a deep work, a calculated work, a planned work. In other words, the artistry in it was more deliberate and more profound than I thought before. So, as a matter of fact, after this case is over, I am looking forward to finishing it. . . .

. . . I found it absolutely fascinating because it draws me to read it further and further, the way *Ulysses* did when I read that in college, as if there are mysteries to be uncovered when I read it.

It has enormous importance to me as a writer.

. . . To me this is a simple portrayal of Hell. It is Hell precisely.

Yes, *Naked Lunch* had enormous importance to Mailer. We saw how badly *An American Dream* suffered from the conflict between his desire to play and his conception of himself as the apocalyptic conscience of his generation. Certainly Burroughs suggested that by using a partially dehumanized narrative voice one could combine humor and profundity, play and social criticism. The voice of *Naked Lunch,* which tells us that it is a writing instrument or a tape, profoundly anticipated the electronic yawp of Mailer's disc jockey in *Vietnam.* Mailer is careful to let us know this; D.J. tells us that he's a disciple of Burroughs, and the "friendLee voice at your service" in the very first sentence of the novel reminds us that Lee is the name of one of Burroughs's most important characters. In fact Burroughs's first novel, *Junkie,* was published under the pseudonym of William Lee.

Mailer played with punning—by and large successfully—much more than Burroughs did, and most of the time he wisely stayed away from the surreal, disassociated images that fill so much of *Naked Lunch.* As sharp as Mailer's visual sense can be, it cannot compete with something like:

> Pool covered with green slime in a ruined French Garden. Huge pathic frog rises slowly from the water on a mud platform playing the clavichord.

Mailer also rejected modeling any part of his novel after the most horrific extremes of *Naked Lunch.* Burroughs was not telling the whole story when he wrote in the introduction to that book:

> Certain passages in the book that have been called pornographic were written as a tract against Capital Punishment in the manner of Jonathan Swift's *Modest Proposal.* These sections are intended to reveal capital punishment as the obscene, barbaric and disgusting anachronism that it is.

For there are too many accounts told with too much relish of, for example, mutilating young boys, of how

> Aztec priests strip blue feather robe from the Naked Youth. They
> bend him back over a limestone altar, fit a crystal skull over his
> head, securing the two hemispheres back and front with crystal
> screws. A waterfall pour over the skull snapping the boy's neck. He
> ejaculate in a rainbow against the rising sun.

Part of Burroughs enjoyed this just as part of Mailer was stirred by
contemplations of all that action in those Dallas bathrooms, but however much he might appreciate the writing of the preceding quotation, it is inconceivable that the horror of the Aztec ceremony would
sexually stimulate Mailer. One of the greatest services Burroughs performed for Mailer is that he dramatized such monstrous extremes of
human possibility that Mailer could, however temporarily, concede
to him the title of the most far-out critic of American life, the man
"willing to explore areas of experience that other men are afraid of."
With what one feels was considerable relief, Mailer could then write
in four months the relatively charming, good-natured book that is
Why Are We in Vietnam? It was not the undiluted horror but the
burlesque horror of *Naked Lunch* that helped to shape Mailer's novel
—say, the antics of Doc Benway or the Latah, the monster who must
imitate but who switches hanging ropes so that he uses the trick,
rubber one and survives while his tormentor is hanged. At his funniest,
with the satire of Rusty and Middle Assholes Pete and Bill, Mailer
could not compete with such madly hilarious sections from *Naked
Lunch* as "The County Clerk" or "Islam Incorporated and the Parties
of Interzone." But then, neither could any other living American
writer.

Mailer's greatest debt, however, follows from Burroughs's use of
the vernacular with articles, verbs, and relative pronouns dropped;
with "ungrammatical" tense shifts, subject-verb agreements, and pro-
noun usage; with obscenity, the interjection of phrases of French,
German, Spanish (though Mailer has done this before), of "uh" or
"hurumph" or "heh-heh-heh," of words like "fright wig" or "Sender";
with all sorts of verbal quick cuts. *Vietnam* probably could not have
been written had Mailer not read passages like:

> So this elegant faggot comes to New York from Cunt Lick,
> Texas, and he is the most piss elegant fag of them all. He is taken
> up by old women of the type batten on young fags, toothless old
> predators too weak and too slow to run down other prey. Old moth-
> eaten tigress shit sure turn into a fag eater. . . .
> [Eventually the old women discover the costume jewelry he is
> making is filled with fake stones.] So a Sabbath is hastily called.
> (Lucy Bradshinkel, look to thy emeralds.) All those old witches ex-

amining their rocks like a citizen find leprosy on himself.
"My chicken blood ruby!"
"My bleck oopalls!" Old bitch marry so many times so many
gooks and spics she don't know her accent from her ass. . . .
"My stah sahphire!" shriek a *poule de luxe*. "Oh, it's all so awful."
"I mean they are strictly from Woolworth's. . . ."

Mailer's affection for what he called in the Boston trial "gutter talk"
is strong,* and at its best, so is his ability to use colloquial intonations
and obscenities as a sort of ground base and to heighten them with
the quick cuts of his own associative flashes. All of this is a vastly
easier undertaking than creating a prose that could turn Manhattan
into a Manichean romance ground. In the same way, he could let his
sharp, satiric eye record the posturings and intonations of the hunters
and let his great feeling for place create the beautiful descriptions of
the Brooks Range terrain. Even though the invocations of "now we're
stalking a mystery" during the last quarter of the book creaked a bit,
the boys' adventures were, even here, a joy next to the renderings of
Barney Kelly's Devil's Lair. If some of us did somewhat tire of D.J.'s
voice by the end, we are still left with one of the ten best American
novels of the decade and a palpable assertion that Mailer's novelistic
talents have not at all waned as much as many of his critics claim.

IV

It is quite possible that I have misread the ending of *Why Are We in
Vietnam?* Perhaps Mailer was suggesting that D.J.'s sensibilities were

* . . . during the course of the campaign I was to find out that he had a
one-way love affair with street types. If someone had been part of an
experience foreign to his own (being Black, a convict, a prize-fighter),
Mailer found in him occult powers bestowed only on the children of the
gutters. Their dreariness of thought and total lack of performance in any
function assigned to them made no difference to him. This enchantment had
to do with Mailer's high sense of intrigue and his romantic notion of the
streets. That the gutter was a spawning ground which produced dullness
far more than genius was never considered. [Flaherty, *Managing Mailer*,
pp. 64–65.]
A crucial policy letter printed in the New York Times in the closing weeks
of the 1969 Democratic primary campaign concluded with an inane slogan
that a resident of Bedford Stuyvesant had given Mailer, which he took
to his heart as a cobblestone of street genius. To wit: ". . . a Black,
middle-aged man with a round head, round belly and a big smile. He
shook our hand. 'We've had the rest,' he said, 'Now try the best. Vote
Mailer-Breslin.' " [*Ibid.*, p. 186.]

The characters in *Vietnam* are not from the gutter, but the energizing effect
of his decision to use the vernacular is clear enough.

irreparably damaged before the Alaskan trip and that the beastlike God who wanted him to go and kill was the Devil. However, all of the details which contrast the corruption of the hunting party that the boys have fled and the ensuing purity of their experience argue against this interpretation. All that argues for it is Mailer's increasing opposition to violence, but this shift in feeling is so significant that the author's 1968 comment of having traveled half the distance from Marx to conservatism is not as much of a smokescreen as it might appear. Perhaps a glance over his changing stances toward mass revolution will make this shift more graphic.

In 1951 (in *Barbary Shore*) Mailer argued that the continuation of humane value, indeed of civilization itself, could only be sustained by a victorious proletarian revolution. By 1957 ("The White Negro") he was thinking less of a unified mass, informed of their material interests, than of a quasi-revolutionary elite unintentionally altering the life style of the nation. If the hipster attracts enough converts and followers to make the revolt against conformist America a mass one, the effect will be more to permit general psychic expansion than to change the form of government or the ownership of the factories. By 1960 Mailer was ready to argue that the surface of Eisenhower America had broken open enough to allow growth by less desperate seekers than the hipsters and, as the cracks in the social fabric grew into fissures, his desire for social turmoil so ebbed that he approvingly included in his piece on the 1964 Republican convention quotations from that great work of political conservatism, Edmund Burke's *Reflections on the Revolution in France*. On the whole, the quotations serve to comment sarcastically about the radical conservatism of the Goldwater Republicans both by their matter and the quality of their thought, which strongly contrasts with the often ignorant, sometimes bloodthirsty tenets of Goldwaterism. Yet a part of Mailer hoped that Goldwater would be elected President:

> For if Goldwater were President, a new opposition would form, an underground—the time for secret armies might be near again. And when in sanity I thought, Lord, give us twenty more years of Lyndon Johnson, nausea rose in some cellar of the throat, my stomach was not strong enough to bear such security; and if true for me, true for others, true perhaps for half or more of a nation's vote. Yet what of totalitarianism? What of war? But what of war? And the answer came back that one might be better a little nearer to death than the soul dying each night in the plastic encirclements of the new architecture and the new city, yes better, if death had dimension and one could know the face of the enemy and leave a curse. What blessing

to know the face of the enemy by the second third of the twentieth century.

But this side is identified as the Devil's. The sane or cowardly side —"which is it?" Mailer wonders—wins out; it will not vote for Goldwater, and the closing anticipation of the piece is more to be dreaded than welcomed: "The wars are coming and the deep revolutions of the soul." By autumn, 1968, when Mailer wrote *Miami and the Siege of Chicago,* the fabric of the Republic had been so shredded that Mailer inveighed against all advocates of far-reaching disorder, no matter what their place on the political spectrum. The remark which John Updike made after the assassination of Robert F. Kennedy,

> that God might have withdrawn His blessing from America . . . gave insight to the perspectives of the Devil and his political pincers: Left-wing demons, white and Black, working to inflame the conservative heart of America, while Right-wing devils exacerbated Blacks and drove the mind of the New Left and liberal middle class into prides of hopeless position. And the country roaring like a bull in its wounds, coughing like a sick lung in the smog, turning over in its sleep at the sound of motorcycles, shivering at its need for new phalanxes of order. Where were the new phalanxes one could trust?

The part of the book which deals with the Republican convention of 1968 closes with the hope that Nixon is on the side of God and will bring order, that he is not a candidate of the Devil "to loose the fearful nauseas of the century." The idea that total upheaval might be the wish of God is never considered. In fact, the last quotation very sharply states the distance that Mailer has traveled. In the decade between the mid-fifties and the mid-sixties, he argued in hundreds of different ways that the nauseas must at all costs be loosed lest our souls be lost.

Yet the question of the depth of Mailer's commitment to preserving the best of the past remains a prickly one. If he came out against extreme solutions of right and left, he also irresponsibly collapsed the liberal center into a totalitarian force which was all for the new totalitarianism of plastic encirclements and the corruption of psyches through mass media. Irving Howe was right when he wrote in an important 1968 article on the New York intellectuals that Mailer bears a heavy responsibility for that aspect of the new sensibility which has no experience with true fascism or totalitarianism but recklessly calls contemporary American society totalitarian and too easily refers to "liberal fascism." In fact, after Howe attacked the new sensibility for its easy

contempt of all political, moral, and aesthetic complexity, he then proceeded to designate Mailer as its

> central and certainly most dramatic presence . . . thaumaturgist of
> orgasm . . . metaphysician of the gut . . . psychic herb-doctor
> . . . advance man for literary violence . . . dialectician of unrea-
> son . . . in his major public roles he has come to represent values
> in deep opposition to liberal humaneness and rational discourse.

Mr. Howe is a hard man to disagree with, but it must be said that
Mailer has always had great respect for the major art of the past and
had for the past few years been toning down his appeals for violence
and his exhortations for sexual experiment. His major public role in
1968 was as the protagonist in a book so filled with that humaneness
which represents the best of liberalism and a discourse between the
divided parts of himself and an equally divided America that *The
Armies of the Night* has accurately been described as "one of the most
anxiousy, sadly patriotic books in our literature." In the following
year, his major public role was as a candidate for the New York
mayoralty. Rather than representing some maddened mutant of
leftism, he ran in the primary of the Democratic party and was much
praised by responsible political analysts for the ideas he brought into
the political marketplace of open discourse.

Since Mailer so often delights, particularly in public, in confound-
ing what he feels the majority expects from him, one cannot speak
absolutely about his public roles any more than one can accurately
measure his political influence. We can say that he often takes an extreme tack in his attempt to bend a central position more toward
something he would like to see but that if he felt an excessive number
took the same extreme position he would try to bend it closer to the
center. His response toward violence and revolution is a case in point.
Many more of his sympathies are with the liberal center than appearances suggest. It is just that he cannot make literary capital from
a body committed to reasonable compromise; if he no longer feels
with quite the same intensity of ten years ago that life is a battle of
warring opposites, he still uses this approach as the basis of most of
his writing. Although he likes to take what he can use for his writing
from both sides, the two books he wrote during fifteen hugely productive weeks in 1967 and 1968—*Armies* and *Siege*—deal in varying
degrees with the possibility of his finding a home if the polarizing forces
in the country pull us into civil war. At his most hopeful, he argued that
the new army of the left could help bring into being a truly radiant
America. At his least optimistic he could not be fully sure, only a few

hours after seeing the young soldiers clubbed, gassed, and arrested by the rioting Chicago police, that his deepest loyalties lay with them, for it was quite possible that they no more represented the potential for the kind of revolution Mailer could approve of than the police stood for a commendable stability. Still, the books argue, if the crunch came he would join the young left—drug-ridden, promiscuous, somewhat maddened—a force which has lost so many nourishing connections with the past, has so far to go to become a true army of Being that "he could join . . . At what a cost! At what a cost!"

6
Up and Down the Endless Ladder

IN the preface to *Existential Errands* (1972), Mailer summarized the work of the past five years in this way:

> . . . *The Deer Park* as a play was given its last draft and then produced, *Why Are We in Vietnam?* was written and then *The Armies of the Night, Miami and the Siege of Chicago, Of a Fire on the Moon* and *The Prisoner of Sex*. Three movies were also made. So it is a period when, with every thought of beginning a certain big novel which had been promised for a long time, the moot desire to have one's immediate say on contemporary matters kept diverting the novelistic impulse into journalism. Such passing books began to include many of the themes of the big novel. On the way, shorter pieces were also written for a variety of motives and occasions, written in a general state of recognition that if one had a philosophy it was being put together in many pieces. Still a view of life was expressed in those books and those years.

Having one's immediate say, even putting together one's philosophy, made his motives all too declarative. Driven as he might have been by the hot economic whips of four wives, six children, several homes, an apparently high life style, the 1969 New York City mayoralty campaign, the cost of his movies; perhaps frightened by that successor to *Moby Dick* he promised back in 1959, one still feels that in the four journalistic efforts he hoped for more than the immediate appreciation of the reading public. The acceleration of energies, the opening of new questions, the testing of old answers—Mailer sought these and more in the writing. About eight years ago I was told that back in 1957 or 1958 a quaffer at some Manhattan bar could regularly find the solitary Mailer looking and looking for something in the faces of the other drinkers. Whether or not this is true, he has found a good deal (whether or not much of it exists) and he is still looking. But what else was he seeking in the four nonfiction works?

In *Of a Fire on the Moon* Mailer laments the absence of a true objective correlative for that "event of his lifetime," the flight of Apollo 11. The passage is a bit confused—it only makes sense if we regard the way Americans should have felt as a subjective correlative—but we can pick up Mailer's Eliotism for our own ends. Mailer has (only) half-jokingly referred to himself several times as a Renaissance man, and, with all differences of achievement allowed for, we might remember Michelangelo's statement that he tried with his sculpture to free the figure hidden in the stone. Hidden within the beating of the protesters before the Pentagon in the early hours of October 22, 1967, in the actions of Nixon in the 1968 convention, in the eight days that Apollo 11 was off the earth, and in the consequence of even the drabbest sex, Mailer was able to find the possibility of the rites of passage of the American middle class, Nixon Transfigured (God save the mark!), the vision of God or the Devil projected out among the stars, and the microscopic miracle of an ovum choosing that soul in the sperm cell which had swum so far so fast in its effort to be reborn. Although a fair amount of bluff is spread through these books, I believe that Mailer sought not just the raw materials which would enable him to meet contracts, expenses, and the publishing demands of his ego but sequences of gestures and actions which, if captured in incandescent prose, could serve as correlatives to his intimations of the way things secretly are or might publicly and/or secretly become, correlatives which would serve as the axis of major works. And with these works, with this approach to his version of Gatsby's green light, might come yet more acute perceptions, more skill, greater energy.

As much as Mailer could manage it, there is at or near the center of each book the tension created by the contrasting claims of creativity and dehumanizing technology. (In one case, with the events described in *Miami and the Siege of Chicago,* what he saw so little seized his imagination that this particular tension exists only as cursory hope, not driving animus.) If we think of this pull as one circle of light moving across a stage, we must allow for a second circle controlled by a different lightman which often seems to exist a good distance from the first. Sometimes the second circle encloses the first one, and sometimes it is smaller but inside the latter. Once in a while it's not on the stage at all but is wildly waving around on the ceiling; most of the time, however, the second circle partially coalesces with the first one, but with great variety of placement so that the commonly lit area varies considerably within each book. To at last free you of the metaphor, the second circle is the persona of Mailer in any particular book, for he has returned to that strategy of mythologizing himself which he employed with such mixed results in *An American Dream.* Since the events which the persona faces are often mythologized, does this mean that Mailer is finally only telling what Huck Finn gently calls "stretchers"? For what does that so casually dropped word *myth* mean? In answer to "is it true?"—for nonfiction is commonly supposed to be precisely nonfiction—the quite incomplete but nearest dictionary offers, among its six meanings for the word, five which apply in all their contradictions to the "truths" of the four mythologized works:

> *myth n.* 1. A traditional story, usually focusing the deeds of gods or heroes, often in explanation of some natural phenomenon, as the origin of the sun, etc. It purports to be historical, but it is useful to historians principally for what it reveals of the culture of the peoples it describes or among whom it was current. 2. A theme, motif, character type, etc. in modern literature that expresses or is felt to express significant truths about human life or human nature: the *myth* of the alienated man. . . . 4. An imaginary or fictious person, thing, event, or story. 5. A collective opinion, belief, or ideal that is based on false premises or is the product of fallacious reasoning. 6. An allegory or parable used to explain or illustrate a philosophic concept, as in Plato's dialogues —Syn. See FICTION.

If we ignore the common language philosophers with their criteria of "verifiability" and "univocalism" and appeal to such literary touchstones as the control of language, character, thought, and pace, or the ability to engage and move the reader, then by far the best of the four books is *The Armies of the Night*. It is also the book which, by the delicacy of its perceptions, contains the most significant truths about life and nature, dramatizes the longest imaginary story based on false premises (the rites of passage of the American middle class), and catalogs what is for Mailer the most traditional, Godlike story— the way in which one reconstructs the self. Thus, a philosophic concept is illustrated even if we deny the particular accuracy of the account of the particular reconstruction. I will therefore devote the most space to this so fictionalized winner of the 1969 National Book Award and the Pulitzer Prize for nonfiction.

II

Let us begin by looking coldly over the bare bones of *Armies*. The work is divided into two books. Book One, "History as a Novel: The Steps of the Pentagon," ran 213 pages in the hardcover edition, almost three times the length (and ten times the worth) of Book Two, "The Novel as History: the Battle of the Pentagon." Book One's primary claim for the use of the word *novel* in its title rests on its focus upon the inner life of the hero—though he did live and act in historical circumstances which the author renders as objectively as he can (which, for the existential historian, means the combination of the most vigorous accuracy in reporting what happened "out there" and in himself with the most enlightened subjectivity in order to discern the meaning of those happenings). Of the historic and the novelistic in Book Two I shall write in good time and instead list some of the events of a morning in September, 1967, and of four days in the following month—as a whole, the time span of *The Armies of the Night*. So much is written on what happened in those five days because I think that with the possible exception of the materials of *Why Are We in Vietnam?*, Mailer's fictional imagination was eventually more deeply and consistently moved by the events of those days than by anything it contemplated since the imagined events on Anopopei found form in the great stretch of writing in the third part of *The Naked and the Dead*.

On that September morning, a man in his Brooklyn home answered a phone call from an old friend (Mitchell Goodman) and, after resisting, agreed to participate in a demonstration at the Department of Justice Building in Washington, where a number of protesters of the American involvement in Vietnam were to turn in their draft cards on Friday, October 20. As large a group as could be gathered was to march to the Pentagon on the following day and disrupt some of the operations there. The man arrived in Washington on the afternoon of October 19, for two weeks after the first call he had agreed to speak that Thursday night at the Ambassador Theater with Paul Goodman, Robert Lowell, and Dwight Macdonald. He spoke, freely peppering his speech with obscenities and himself with the contents of a bourbon-filled coffee mug. He also so emphasized that fact that many would be arrested that he perceived he could not leave Washington without being arrested himself. On Friday he attended and spoke to a gathering in front of the Department of Justice Building. Nine hundred ninety-four draft cards were collected, and an attempt was made to present them to Attorney General Ramsey Clark, but Clark was not in his office and his assistant refused them. On Saturday the hero attended a rally at the Lincoln Memorial—where he was annoyed at not being asked to speak; he wanted to address between fifty and one hundred thousand people—and then marched with about fifty thousand others across the Potomac and into the vast north parking lot of the Pentagon. After a short time he walked out of the lot, then stepped over a restraining rope so that he could be arrested by one of the line of military police a few yards away. When the first MP refused to arrest him, he ran past another MP and sprinted down upon a group of United States marshals and told them, as he told the first MP, that he would go on to the Pentagon if he was not arrested. So he succeeded in being arrested, was the tenth of the thousand who were booked, and spent part of that Saturday in the jail above the United States post office in Alexandria. On the same day, he was moved twenty miles to a workhouse in Occoquan, Virginia, where he spent the night and much of Sunday. Late Sunday afternoon he was sentenced by a U.S. commissioner to a fifty-dollar fine and thirty days in prison, only twenty-five of which were to be suspended, but a wonderfully energetic and skilled lawyer named Hirschkop managed to get him released on his own recognizance, and he flew back to New York, where he had dinner with his wife.

There he also wrote the whole of Book One—which appeared in *Harper's Magazine* in March, 1968, as "The Steps of the Pentagon"— in less than three months, for the hero is, of course, Norman Mailer. Never does Mailer refer to his protagonist in the first person; he is usually "Mailer" or "he," sometimes "the Novelist," and very rarely something else—he turns up once each as "the Existentialist," "the Ruminant," and "the Participant." Even though the autobiography is told in the third person, we sometimes experience something not unlike that dizzying hallway-of-mirrors sensation gained from trying to decide how much "objective truth" there is in the narratives of, say, the slightly mad narrator of Ford's *The Good Soldier* or the quite mad narrator of Nabokov's *Pale Fire*. Here, however, the problem is usually not one of madness but of foolishness. The author's final judgment of his protagonist (offered on the last full page of Book One) is that he was "a simple of a hero and a marvel of a fool"; 150 pages earlier we learned that the hero was "an egotist of the most startling misproportions, outrageously and often unhappily self-assertive." In fact, perhaps the simplest way to describe the fable underlying Book One is to say that it is the story of how a famous man from the big city who thinks too highly of himself goes out to the provinces and sees that the little people whom he had held in contempt are in certain ways more admirable than he is. For a while the famous man fights against the humility which the perception forces upon him, but, by balks and starts, he accepts the fact that he's not quite as great a fellow as he had thought, and he returns to the big city a humbler and better man. So far it sounds like the favorite bedtime story of Richard Nixon or Uriah Heep, but since the egotistical fool is also "in command of a detachment classic in severity (for he was a novelist and so in need of studying every last lineament of the fine, the noble, the frantic, and the foolish in others and in himself)" he not only feels deeply and subtly but makes many wonderfully acute, on-the-spot observations.

We might judge with sureness (at least to ourselves) that certain passages of Book One are silly if we could ever be sure of just how much the writer back in Brooklyn is distanced from the talented fool in Washington. For example, it was clearly outlandish of the protagonist to believe that he could at all affect the American consciousness by giving quotable comments to reporters after he was arrested, and we might feel that three paragraphs which discuss whether or not the hero, by now imprisoned in Alexandria, should take a drink of water and so spoil his intimations of the years ahead are silly, but we've read enough Mailer to know that, well, that's Mailer—whether in Washington or New York. But what do we do with the hero's perception that he could not be

> in some final cataclysm . . . an underground leader in the city, or a guerilla with a gun in the hills . . . he would be too old by then, and too incompetent, yes, too incompetent said the new modesty, and too show-boat, too lacking in essential judgment. . . . No gun in the hills, no taste for organization, no, he was a figurehead, and therefore, he was expendable, said the new modesty—not a future leader, but a future victim: *there* would be his real value. He could go to jail for protest, and spend some years if it came to it, possibly his life, for if the war went on, and America put its hot martial tongue across the Chinese border, well, jail was the probable perspective, detention camps, dissociation centers, liquidation alleys, that would be his portion, and it would come about the time he had learned how to live.

If we were to have looked over the author's shoulder as he wrote this passage and complained that it drooled with pathetic self-pity, Mailer might have dodged over the hill into the next paragraph, calling over his shoulder, "Well I told you he was a fool"—though the disappearing artist might still have been savoring the self-pity. But so many pages are so well written with such delicate shifts of perception and emotion, and Book One as a whole is such a singular blend—funny, grim, joyous, despairing, ironic, alive—that one feels forgiving and regards it as an interesting tension. How pleasant it is to try to sift the writer from the protagonist next to that stupefying "where am I?" as Stephen Rojack dashes across Harvard Yard or continues unbelievable conversations with Barney Kelly. The hero's guilty contemplations of his desire to get out of prison are overdone and threaten to topple the strangely successful mixture of the romantic and the ironic which the author preserved, but he rights the balance with the courtroom scene and the protagonist's speech to the reporters upon his release.

Let us look at the fable more closely. When Mailer first heard from Goodman of the plan to occupy the Pentagon, he envisioned no vastly important symbolic attack upon so much he hated. No, "it sounded vaguely and uneasily like a free-for-all with students, state troopers, and Hell's Angels flying in and out of the reports—exactly the sort of operation they seemed to have every other weekend out on the Coast. He felt one little bubble of fear tilt somewhere about the solar plexus." This sole bubble was scarcely going to drive Mailer to get his head pounded in what seemed to be a habitual and futile activity. Even though the period when Mailer resembled John Garfield ended some years earlier, the primary demand of the bubble was that it be hidden. With a single verb, the author catches the gap between the fear and a facade which, in this case, was perhaps intended to be not unsimilar to Humphrey Bogart's " 'Yes, this sounds more interesting,' he growled."

And in a passage which captures as well as any in Book One the ironic control of the hero, he responded with peevishness to Goodman's request for participation in the draft-card ceremonies but agreed to go mostly from the embarrassment at sounding like an old fool before a friend with a better character than his own:

> . . . Mailer began to scold Goodman. He went on for a breath or two on the redundancy of these projects. When was everyone going to cut out the nonsense and get to work, do their own real work? One's own literary work was the only answer to the war in Vietnam. As he was talking, Mailer began to realize that he had not done any real writing in months—he had been making movies—but then it didn't matter, he had done as much in the way of protest about the war as anyone. . . . Mailer, filled with such righteous indignations, was therefore scolding Goodman at near to full pedal, when the organ came to a sudden stop. The thought that he was beginning to sound like a righteous old toot came just as suddenly into his head. Mailer had never had a particular age—he carried different ages within him like different models of his experience: parts of him were eighty-one years old, fifty-seven, forty-eight, thirty-six, nineteen, et cetera, et cetera—he now went back abruptly from fifty-seven to thirty-six.

On that third Thursday in October, then, Mailer blew into Washington, very much the grand author grudgingly giving his time to the unheroic activities of less talented men than himself (though with secret begrudgement, since it pleases his ego to belie his reputation and behave with charm and concern to the dull liberals at a pretheater dinner party). But (so goes the fable) the events of the three and one-half days pull him far from the easy contempt of the sterile houses of liberal academics of such literary logrolling as not being too charming with Dwight Macdonald, since the latter was at that time writing a review of *Why Are We in Vietnam?* (for if Macdonald liked Mailer too much, he would, as a proof of his integrity, be forced to bend over backwards to treat the book severely). Before he was in Washington twenty hours

> a deep gloom began to work on Mailer, because a deep modesty was on its way to him . . . he hated this because modesty was an old family relative, he had been born to a modest family, had been a modest boy, a modest young man, and he hated that, he loved the pride and the arrogance and the confidence and the egocentricity he had acquired over the years, that was his force and his luxury and the iron in his greed, the richest sugar of his pleasure, the strength of his competitive force.

No modesty came from his performance at the Ambassador, where he tried to energize the audience with opening lines like "I'm trying to say the middle class plus shit, I mean plus revolution, is equal to one big collective dead ass." Or with telling his listeners how he was Lyndon Johnson's dwarf alter ego or how he had, in the darkness of the men's room, just urinated on the floor, or with his scourging the press as "the silent assassins of the Republic." Steven Marcus wrote in the introduction to the 1963 *Paris Review* interview that Mailer clearly enjoyed being interviewed and behaved throughout with the large air of a secular prince. The Prince was a little eccentric at the Ambassador, but his eccentricity was expansive, *special*, or, if I may reach a bit, a part of the life style which the speaker in Dylan Thomas's "Lament" sums up in this way:

> Brandy and ripe in my bright, bass prime,
> No springtailed tom in the red hot town
> With every simmering woman his mouse
> But a hillocky bull in the swelter
> Of summer come in his great good time
> To the sultry, biding herds. . . .

Even Mailer's sudden, wrenching envy at the ease with which Robert Lowell gained the affection of the audience is a part of the grand style: "Mailer felt hot anger at how Lowell was loved and he was not, a pure and surprising recognition of how much emotion, how much simple and childlike bitter sorrowing emotion had been concealed from himself for years under the manhole cover of his contempt for bad reviews." (If there is self-pity there, it's poignant, *special* self-pity.) Later, however, the armored arrogance was endangered by the students who turned in their draft cards—for he was unsure if he, had he been twenty years old in 1967, would have turned in his—and pierced by the moral struggle of the teachers who began surrendering their cards when the students had finished:

> Unlike the students, they had not debated these matters in open forum for months, organized, proselyted, or been overcome by argument, no, most of them had served as advisers to the students, had counseled them, and been picked up, many of them, and brought along by the rush of this moral stream much as a small piece of river bank might separate from the shore and go down the line of the flood. It must have been painful for these academics. They were older, certainly less suited for jail, aware more precisely of how and where their careers would be diverted or impeded, they had families many of them, they were liberal academics, technologues, they were being forced to abdicate from the machines they had chosen for their life. Their decision to turn in draft cards must have come for many in the middle of the night; for others it must have come even last night, or as they stood here debating with themselves. Many of them seemed to stand irresolutely near the steps for long periods, then move up at last.

The protagonist did not at this time savor the revolutionary potential of men turning themselves away from the social machine (as he had not been able to turn himself away from the literary log-rolling machine the night before) but looked inward and explored this modesty which might be the herald of a permanently altered set of psychic alternatives. The modesty so deepened that he gave up perhaps his fondest revolutionary fantasy, the guerrilla with the gun in the hills. It's funny, but it's serious, and with this the stream of the fable turns into much more somber lands. The writer will sometimes continue to write humorously of others, of his protagonist, and, in those many cases where the two are inseparable, of himself, but now the fate of Norman Mailer is considered with no small seriousness, and the fate of the Republic is pondered with great gravity. Or, to put things in a way that will anticipate a bend this exposition will take, the fable now carries within its flow those metaphors of growth which have absorbed him for so long. And are not all myths metaphors or chains of metaphors?

This third-person autobiography by a man who ironically interrelates his own history with a collective history, who sees himself caught in a dying world and looks with anguish at the birthings of an unfamiliar one, reminds us of that most impressive of American autobiographies, *The Education of Henry Adams.* One can only guess at how much Mailer is counterpointing his book with implicit comparisons to Adams's great work; however much or little, it is much less overt than the piece on the Goldwater convention, with its quotations from Edmund Burke. Mailer does in Washington stay at the Hay-Adams hotel and slyly says, "One may wonder if the Adams in the name of his hotel bore any relation to Henry; we need not be concerned with Hay . . . other than to say that the hotel looked like its name, and was indeed the staunchest advocate of that happy if heavy style in Washington architecture which spoke of a time when men and events were solid, comprehensible, often obedient to a code of values, and resolutely nonelectronic." We do not know if the building reminded Mailer of any precise historical perod. He could not be referring to the eighteenth century, with its acceptance of natural law and natural rights, its commitment to the rational cultivation of the self, and its faith in the value and importance of the solitary, civilized self—that period in which Adams (who described himself as an eighteenth-century man who was born in the nineteenth and somehow lived on into the twentieth) wished he had been born.

We could wander about for a good many pages comparing and contrasting these two unconventional educators and autobiographers, drawing very indistinct distinctions between the dynamo and Virgin of Adams and Mailer's electronic circuits and Christ of mystery who turns up in *Armies* and seems to be contrasted with Mailer's existential God. Yet something should be said about some of the differences between Adams and the historian who describes himself in *Armies* as feeling at times that only Kennedy among the candidates for the presidency since World War II might have been more suited for the job than himself, or who, with eloquent bathos, laments "getting fat against [his] will, and turning into a clown of an *arriviste* baron when [he] would rather be an eagle or a count, or rarest of all, some natural aristocrat from these damned democratic states." Like Robert Lowell, whom Mailer treats in the book with considerable affection, envy, and very conscious and ironic pettiness, or like that great-grandson of one president, grandson of another, son of a great diplomat, and heir to what was believed to be at his maternal grandfather's death the greatest fortune in Boston, Henry Adams.

By 1900 (when he was sixty-two) Adams had decided that he could not understand the interrelationships of cause and effect (and thus write accurate history) by the humanistic methods he had been using:

> Where he saw sequence, other men saw something quite different, and no one saw the same unit of measure. He cared little about his experiments and less about his statesmen, who seemed to him quite as ignorant as himself and, as a rule, no more honest; but he insisted upon a relation of sequence, and if he could not reach it by one method, he would try as many methods as science knew. Satisfied that the sequence of men led to nothing and that the sequence of their society could lead no further, while the mere sequence of time was artificial, and the sequence of thought was chaos, he turned at last to the sequence of force; and thus it happened that, after ten years' pursuit, he found himself lying in the Gallery of Machines at the Great Exposition of 1900, his historical neck broken by the sudden irruption of forces totally new.

We should not, in our desire to contrast Adams with Mailer, underestimate the former's feeling that men and masses of men must be studied, but emphasize Adams's perception of the need to study the workings of force (by 1900, read "technology") as a starting point. After all, Adams talks in *The Education* of how much he learned from Marx, the only thinker he read who had some idea of how violently the nineteenth-century world would change, and it is in *Armies* that Mailer calls the mind of that prophet of power "perhaps the greatest single tool for cerebration Western man had ever produced." But we should bear down upon the two authors' responses to the new powers that had been unleashed. Adams was deeply disturbed at the gradual collapse of eighteenth-century virtues—perhaps most economically summarized by his grandfather Adams's "Resistance, Truth, Duty, Freedom." The average man already had no understanding of the forces that ruled his life, and Adams anticipated with horror the inevitable total replacement of the cathedral by the dynamo—the time when the vast mass of men would look with uncomprehending faith, with adulation, at those scientists who had replaced the priests, artists, and historians. Then their lives would be totally ruled by the arbiters of soulless, conscienceless power; the Atom King would then rule supreme, and the humane edicts communicated by Christian priests or by other humanists would be completely replaced by the imperatives of arbitrary force.

Adams's historical neck was broken because he could no longer discern cause-and-effect relationships. Since the new force of electricity was anarchical and incomprehensible, its source and form were not measurable. The historian's sequences of cause and effect had thus become meaningless in the twentieth century, and Adams had, to a great extent, lost his vocation. The nourishing unity of the past—which could be accurately studied—had been replaced by impersonal, incomprehensible twentieth-century multiplicity. As if to prove his ability to achieve even greater pessimism, Adams, in *The Degradation of the Democratic Dogma* (completed in 1909), came up with the lugubrious conclusion that our vital energy is declining and that humanity is doomed because all the energy of the solar system is being lost to the outer reaches of the universe through the laws of entropy. Yet if Adams is not being wholly ironic, here is his first response to what became for him the symbol of the amoral, technological age:

> To him [the scientist explaining the exhibit to Adams] the dynamo itself was but an ingenious channel for conveying somewhere the heat latent . . . in a dirty engine-house . . . but to Adams the dynamo became a symbol of infinity. As he grew accustomed to the great gallery of machines, he began to feel the forty-foot dynamos as a moral force, much as the early Christians felt the Cross. The planet itself seemed less impressive, in its old-fashioned, deliberate annual or daily revolution, than this huge wheel, revolving within arm's-length at some vertiginous speed, and barely murmuring. . . . Before the end, one began to pray to it; inherited instinct taught the natural expression of man before silent and infinite force.

So obvious is the historical movement from the dynamo and combustion engine to atomic power plants, resolutely electronic values, and men on the moon, and so much has been written in the last fifty pages of Mailer's hatred of the implosive order, so much written in the past two hundred of his belief in the potential of solitary, courageous self, that I need not belabor the obvious and rant on about Mailer's unwillingness to pray to amoral authority. Although he did not consciously go to Washington to war against the Pentagon, he did by the third day in Washington attack in his own way

> the symbol, the embodiment, no, call it the true and high church of the military-industrial complex . . . blind five-sided eye of a subtle oppression which had come to America out of the very air of the century (this evil twentieth century with its curse on the species, its oppressive Faustian lusts, its technological excrement all over the conduits of nature, its entrapment of the innocence of the best—for which young American soldiers hot out of high school and in love with a hot rod and his Marine buddies in his platoon in Vietnam could begin to know the devil of the oppression which would steal his soul before he knew he had one [as D.J.'s and Tex's souls were stolen] . . . the eye of the oppressor, greedy stingy dumb valve of the worst of the Wasp heart, chalice and anus of corporation land,

smug enclosed, morally blind Pentagon, destroying the future of its own nation with each day it augmented in strength. . . .

His actions in Washington constituted one small attack, but the book implicitly argues that the primary meaning of his adventures lay in the much larger attack he was able to perceive. He saw (or at least the most optimistic part of him saw) the meaning of the march expand beyond the protest of a war in Southeast Asia until it became what Adams never hoped for—a substantial portion of the American nation turning against and rejecting the blind, soulless power which had partially deranged their senses.

For Mailer, these rebellious sons and daughters of the middle class have none of the exquisite sense of self that he proclaimed a decade before for that other revolutionary vanguard, the hipsters. Yet the kids who, instead of purring muted hip argot, so often utter crude propaganda or chant slogans or sing songs still have a dim sense of what will cure their ills. Historic cause-and-effect relationships are not nearly so denied to Mailer as they were to Adams. The protesters sense, as Mailer has sensed for so long, that if we behave bravely things will get better and if we do not things will get worse.

Although six more decades of technology have made their awesome inroads between the times that *The Education* and *Armies* were written, Mailer does not see the promise of democracy as irrevocably doomed as Adams did. In fact, he offers utterance in the last paragraph of the book to his heightened sense of a new period in American life:

> Brood on that country who expresses our will. She is America, once a beauty of magnificence unparalleled, now a beauty with a leprous skin. She is heavy with child—no one knows if legitimate—and languishes in a dungeon whose walls are never seen. Now the first contractions of her fearsome labor begin—it will go on: no doctor exists to tell the hour. It is only known that false labor is not likely on her now, no, she will probably give birth, and to what?—the most fearsome totalitarianism the world has ever known? or can she, poor giant, tormented lovely girl, deliver a babe of a new world brave and tender, artful and wild? Rush to the locks. God writhes in his bonds. Rush to the locks. Deliver us from our curse.

The locks are the locks of our lives. If the will of the people permits them to turn so that we can become more than we were, then the collective will is the will of God. But, to quote the last line of the preceding paragraph, "Liars controlled the locks." Mailer's ideas and concerns did not so much change as deepen between *Cannibals and*

Christians and *Armies*. The liars are still the mass media, the whip hands in our homes of the totalitarian forces who, as Mailer has said so often, accelerate the growth of apathy in the nation by distorting reality. Even if television or the press correctly reports a sequence of facts or happenings, each medium cauterizes the events of their existential truth, of the ambience that surrounds or surrounded them.

Here we come to what will most likely be the most significant attack that Mailer's Washington days permitted—*The Armies of the Night*. As much as the author can, he offers reality to the soldiers of his army as he tries to push them to the locks. Life-sustaining reality flows from many sources. One small model of growth is offered by the October, 1967, adventures of Norman Mailer, who gained something and lost something but felt that he gained more than he lost. Then there is what seems to be—who knows?—the relatively uninhibited reporting of his responses to the events he lived through. The book opens with the *Time* account of his antics at the Ambassador Theater, and the chapter ends with Mailer's comment, "Now we may leave *Time* in order to find out what happened." Now we may move to an account of Mailer's actions which has not had all of the existential truth cut away from it by two or three rewritings by two or three editors—none of whom were at the Ambassador. Mailer also offers the collective history of the march in Book Two with an analysis of its importance. For if he regarded the protest activities with condescension when he came to Washington, by the time he left he felt that the Battle of the Pentagon was the first skirmish in a war that would last twenty years and that would determine nothing less than the future of America.

As you might have noticed, I have for the past few pages been juggling the second meaning of *myth* (how a character type in modern literature expresses significant truths about human life) with aspects of the fourth and fifth meanings (an imaginary or fictitious story based on false premises). That Norman Mailer was able for a while to connect new circuits in Washington is eminently possible; the prose of Book One provides reasonable evidence in itself. But Mailer argues in Book Two that (as Yeats wrote after the Easter, 1916, uprising in Dublin) "all [is] changed, changed utterly." Out of the Gethsemane the protesters endured, "a terrible beauty is born," and the American middle class can turn its back upon the death of sense and the technological appropriation of nature and human sensibility. As I write this, in March, 1973, the United States is finally bringing back the last troops from Vietnam, but then again, the middle class has helped to reelect by an immense majority a president who argued that one consequence of the 1972 arms limitation pact was the need for new weapons. Very little seems to have changed significantly, and if the country's attitude toward the war did shift in the past six years, it was much more the result of, say, the Tet offensive of 1968 than the apocalyptically reconstructed sensibilities of the protesters. As for Mailer's enlistment in the twenty-year war, if literal fighting broke out, his commitment—to borrow a distinction from Mordecai Richler —would still be with the shitheads (the drug-using youth) against the shits, but with *Armies* Mailer's affection for the New Left peaked, and even here the best that he can argue is that *some* part of "the spoiled children of a dead de-animalized middle class" was transformed. It did not take that much shift in intuition for him to tell Tom Hayden, not more than four months after he finished *Armies,* that he was for Kennedy "because I'm not so sure I want a revolution. Some of those kids are awfully dumb."

Correspondingly, there is little about the Chicago protesters in *Miami and the Siege of Chicago,* completed the same year as *Armies.* One feels that this lack results not as much from an unwillingness to rewrite the insights of less than a year before as from the dissipation of the ability to sustain the intimations of the "terrible beauty." There is no mention of the rites of passage. We are told the sense of honor of the protesters is developing every year, there is beauty in their vision, and they have somehow become an army in the ten months that have intervened since the Pentagon, but they are years away from becoming an effective fighting force, and, more important, they are still a bit too crazy. They "make jokes about putting LSD in drinking water . . . they talked of burning money . . . they believed in taking the pill and going bareass in the park." If Mailer claims in an argument that the protesters are his troops and that they are great, he also feels in August of 1968 (as he apparently did not in late October, 1967) that the plague is deepening.

Nevertheless, unless his conscious ability to write a parable to illustrate an existential possibility (a slight altering of the sixth meaning of *myth*) or his desire to write a readable, economically profitable book, no matter how faked, is much greater than I believe it to be, the most optimistic side of Mailer was able to believe that the rites of passage has occurred. Ever since the publication of *Advertisements,* it has been quite clear that Mailer has had the ability or disability to see in his own struggles the evolvement of the future of America. Call it egomania, realistic synecdoche, literary strategy; even if it was the last at the beginning of the writing, at a certain level, as Marx was fond of saying and Mailer of repeating, quantity becomes quality. In the tests and discoveries that the writing provided Mailer, sooner or later the most optimistic side was convinced that something in himself and in the collective middle class had altered as profoundly as the shift in the foundation of a building. Although Mailer has never admitted it, he must surely feel by now that the last thirty pages of Book Two, with their claims for the rites of passage for the American middle class, were quite simply a mistake. Yet this error made possible much of what is so fine in *The Armies of the Night.* Correspondingly, the weakest parts of Book One are the broodings about the nature of growth, but these, like the possible rites of passage, are essential parts of the double process that energized his imagination.

III

To finally close with our myths, Mailer's and America's counterforce against the blind, dumb authority, against the sterility and disproportion which the Pentagon symbolizes, is the same. Such terminology as soul, being, and spirit is happily omitted, as are, on the whole, God and the Devil. The protagonist of Book One is no inspired prophet but an energetic and imaginative, if sometimes contradictory or confused, man doing the best he can. So there is no metaphysical parlance; Mailer simply says that he accepted Hemingway's *"If it made you feel good, it was good.* That, and Saint Thomas Aquinas's 'Trust the authority of your senses,' were enough to enable a man to become a good working amateur philosopher."

As much as possible, the causes of the bad feelings must be fought down. Mailer's running in fear in the parking lot because he did not want his eyes sprayed with MACE when there was no such danger at the time must be atoned for by his immediately charging upon the MPs and marshals. But of course, it's more complicated than that. Sometimes the senses are simply wrong; when Mailer confronts the sentencing commissioner on Sunday afternoon, the novelist decides that he likes him as much as any man he has met in the past few days and immediately receives an unexpectedly severe sentence. But the moral drama of the individual myth, as in most myths (whether single or collective) which deeply engage us, turns on situations when imperfect goods collide and no single feeling can be permanently authoritative. Although Mailer in Brooklyn claims to report the subjective states of Mailer in Washington in all the certainty they had for him at the time, the retrospective author does add that his feelings about, say, America "tended to change a little every minute from the truth he detected in the last face he saw." Or the man who Friday was resigned to spending years in prison was by Saturday anxious to be released from custody so that he could attend a party in New York, where, it must be said, he hoped to begin the doubling and tripling of the richness of experience the Washington days offered him.

If this man who contained so many ages gave up in the convincing fiction that is Book One the last gasp of the White Negro—the twenty-three-year-old guerrilla leader in himself—he was still able by the next day to see himself as a warrior of sorts and to reap the sensuous benefits that combat has to offer. As Mailer and Lowell were on that Saturday morning walk with the other protesters towards the gathering at the Lincoln Memorial, both were silently comparing the streaming demonstrators with the green Union soldiers off to fight in their bloody, idealistic war. And as Mailer saw this army of the Left gathering, he experienced the certain "thin high breath of pleasure, like a child's anticipation of the first rocket to be fired on the Fourth of July," that he had not felt since walking toward his first confrontation with Japanese troops nearly twenty-four years before. Aside from the pleasure of the sensation, it sharpened his already heightened sense of reality: "If you were in . . . good shape for war . . . there was very little which was better for the senses."

To attack the last paragraph for what must flaw almost any rendering of the book except the book itself, it is totalitarian in its excision of ambience. It gives no sense of Mailer's relatively low position on the hill between the Washington Monument and the Lincoln Memorial, of his sense of seeing the hats of those in front and above him bobbing on the horizon, or of his being on an eye level with the feet of some protesters, which made them seen peculiarly animated, prancing and frolicking into battle. Added to his sense of going to battle is his recollection of the exhaustion, illness, and apathy that accompanied months of combat, and then the reflections about Hemingway and Aquinas and how the ambitious novelist needed to be "a good working amateur philosopher . . . since otherwise he is naught but an embittered entertainer, a story-teller, a John O'Hara!" There is so much more that contributes to the ambience of Mailer's going to war: "the clear bitter-sweet excitation of a military trumpet resounding in the near distance, one peal which seemed to go all the way back through a galaxy of bugles to the cries of the Civil War," and the hippies in fantastical uniforms—a hundred in the Confederate gray, several dressed like Arabian sheiks, some feathered Indians, a

Batman, a stalking knight without horse but in real armor, and many more "from all the intersections between history and the comic books, between legend and television, the Biblical archetypes and the movies."

It was after the seemingly endless speeches, after the herding of the milling protesters into a line, when he was significantly in the first row of that motley, ragtag, starting and stopping and starting column bound for the Pentagon, that Mailer's historical sense of the meaning of the march swelled into the broad, generalized perception that he was fighting for more psychic living space, as the eighteenth-century revolutionaries had in France and the Union soldiers had in this country seventy years later. It took the experiences of the next twenty-six or so hours—probably of the several months of those discoveries which history proved to be inventions as he wrote *Armies*—for him to work out the intricacies of the march's import. Book One deals with Mailer's personal journey, and it is apt that, though it will need testing and qualification, his accompanying perception of what the march meant to him will be more pointed. The sources of meaning are still the dynamics of growth and decline. If Mailer could no longer be a guerrilla chieftain, he could still feel that he had grown in the most important way:

> Mailer knew for the first time why men in the front line of a battle are almost always ready to die: there is a promise of some swift transit—one's soul feels clean; as we have gathered, he was not used much more than any other American politician, litterateur, or racketeer to the sentiment that his soul was not unclean, but here, walking with Lowell and Macdonald, he felt as if he stepped through some crossing in the reaches of space between this moment, the French Revolution, and the Civil War, as if the ghosts of the Union Dead accompanied them now to the Bastille . . . the sense of danger to the front, sense of danger to the rear—he was in fact in love with himself for having less fear than he had thought he might have —he knew suddenly that he had less fear now than when he was a young man; in some part of himself at least he had grown; if less innocent, less timid—the cold flames of a perfectly contained exaltation warmed old asthmas of gravel in the heart. . . .

His new conception of himself was threatened when he fled in the parking lot, but he pulled himself together and got arrested. He did not merely tell the arresting marshals to take their hands off him, "he roared, to his own distant pleasure in new achievement and authority." And in keeping with his new modest sense of the need to be useful, he concentrated in his statements to the press upon succinctness, not profundity, so that he could for once be quoted accurately. The reporters would distort what he said, but not knowing this, feeling that he was finally dealing with the mass media in an unqualifiedly effective way, pleased that he was finally being arrested for a real cause after twenty years of radical opinions, proud of the way he managed the arrest, Mailer felt the many disparate parts of his life—his many ages—come together:

> Mailer always supposed he had felt important and unimportant in about as many ways as a man could feel; now he felt important in a new way. He felt his own age, forty-four, felt it as if he were finally one age, not seven, felt as if he were a solid embodiment of bone, muscle, flesh, and vested substance, rather than the will, heart, mind, and sentiment to be a man, as if he had arrived, as if this picayune arrest had been his Rubicon.

He kept the pieces together as he stared down, heckled, but did not insist upon fighting a Nazi fellow prisoner who had called him a kinky-haired, dirty Jew as they waited in the Volkswagen bus that was to take them to Alexandria, and as he rode on another prisoner-filled bus—the one that took him from Alexandria to Occoquan—there came to him feelings which he had not experienced for years, ones which deepened and reinforced his sense of individual and interpersonal unity. If his sensations were of a deeper, more resonant timbre than the high, shrill pitch of pleasure, they had been lost to Mailer for just as long and were as irrevocably connected with being a good soldier in a just cause. In a particularly delicate passage, Mailer lyrically argues that a night journey on a bus never fails to bring American strangers together in a sense of common purpose. Yet the deep peace, the mutual suspension of anger and anxiety and unpleasant ambition which the night wind blowing through a bus window, the sound of tires, and the flash of passing lights brings to travelers, is experienced by the novelist against the background of going to or from battle, as "that restful silence of men traveling, that sense of security in their muscle and in their number, and in their patience, which he had not felt since old days in the Army moving in convoy along dark roads."

Nevertheless, on Sunday Mailer's conflicting loyalties began pulling the psychic unity apart. The sentencing commissioners were at that time offering a deal to most of the protesters who had been arrested Saturday afternoon—twenty-five-dollar fines and a five-day sentence, the latter to be suspended if the protester promised not to return to the Pentagon for six months. Mailer was not to get such a light sentence, and it took great agility by his lawyer to keep him from staying on in jail for five days, but what concerns us here is that he thought the deal "not unreasonable" until another prisoner, Tuli Kupferberg, told him that since Kupferberg had come to Washington to protest the government and not to collaborate with it, he had been forced to reject the bargain. Thus, Kupferberg was unhappily facing the possible consequences his long hair and beard might bring him from the regular prisoners. Of course Mailer was able to reason against Kupferberg's example—Mailer's purpose had been to receive not a stay in prison but a well-publicized arrest so that he could let "technology land . . . let Global Village hear today that [he] . . . had been arrested in protest of Uncle Sam's Whorehouse War"; nothing would happen in the next six months anyway; the required promise was unconstitutional, and one would only be collaborating with the illegality of the government by keeping it; each must do what was most important, and it was most important for himself to be in New York pondering the meaning of the march:

> Yes, his arguments were cogent, but his cool had most undeniably been cracked. There was the definite taint of an unholy desire to get out, as if to remain too long was dangerous. Seen from one moral position—not too far from his own—prison could be nothing but an endless ladder of moral challenges. Each time you climbed a step, as Kupferberg just had, another higher, more dangerous, more disadvantageous step would present itself. Sooner or later, you would have to descend.

Courage is concerned with the possible. The man who drops his rifle so that he can try to fell a charging grizzly with his fists is more foolish than brave. The tragic hero who is confronted with a choice between death and a degraded conception of himself (with no third choice offered) sees even death as a possible, indeed inevitable, moral solution. In more pertinent terms, out of the spectrum of confrontations the prison authority can hand the prisoner there are some the latter feels sure he can win and some he feels he might win. The rest he must surely lose. Mailer's interest has of course been with the second category, where the end is unknown; he has never been much interested in hopeless immolation. So far, there is nothing in the endless-ladder conjecture that runs counter to any of the author's favorite theories of human development, but the rest of the passage I began quoting above argues against the cult of courage that has nourished Mailer and his work for so many years:

> It did not matter how high you had climbed. The first step down in a failure of nerve always presented the same kind of moral nausea. Probably, he was feeling now like people who had gone to the Pentagon, but had chosen not to get arrested, just as such people, at their moment of decision, must have felt as sickened as all the people who should have marched from Lincoln Memorial to the Pentagon, but didn't. . . . One ejected oneself from guilt by climbing the ladder—the first step back, no matter where, offered nothing but immersion into nausea. No wonder people hated to disturb their balance of guilt. To become less guilty, then weaken long enough to return to guilt was somehow worse than to remain cemented in guilt.

Properly defined, then, the argument equates defeat not with "objective" consequences but with the agent's failure of nerve. It would seem to have followed from Mailer's intuition that, were he to remain in prison, before he was released he would suffer a much more severe failure than his flight in the parking lot or the more recent breaking of his determination not to count upon being released. His rejection of all the confrontations of the second category for fear of one in the third category, his fear of prison and his hatred of that fear, led Mailer to the consideration of an argument which was, for him, striking in its secularity. The possibility of being a soldier of God's embattled vision and of advancing the front lines of Being is wholly absent in this temporary collapse of Mailer's thought into a species of that leveling, absurd subjectivism from which his ontology had freed him. If all nausea is the same and the defeat which will cause the nausea is inevitable, then there is really no prevailing reason for behaving bravely, or, in fact, for not behaving in a consistently cowardly fashion. Even if a man succeeds by struggle in escaping his guilt for not trying to develop himself and the human community—for Mailer, the inseparable halves of the same process—he will eventually feel guilt for not struggling still higher. If the same nausea comes with the inevitable defeat, then Mailer's moral order is wiped from the universe, for, by the authority of the senses, if one feels equally bad one is equally bad. Since Being is the collective accumulation of growth, it is erased with the denial of all the individual accumulations.

In just a few hours, after Hirschkop's energy and ingenuity had gained him his freedom, Mailer was able, as he stood outside Occoquan, to assert more characteristically that "all effort was not the same, and to eject oneself from guilt might yet be worth it, for the nausea on return to guilt could conceivably prove less. . . ." Thus he could continue arguing that a man who had, let us arbitrarily say, worked his way through three victories and one failure of nerve between time one and time two could be at a higher psychic level after time two than he was before time one. So it was with Mailer:

> . . . standing on the grass, he felt one suspicion of a whole man closer to that freedom from dread which occupied the inner drama of his years, yes, one image closer than when he had come to Washington four day ago. The sum of what he had done that he considered good outweighed the dull sum of his omissions these same four days.

Or, to reach into Book Two, he will be able to claim that although the vanguard of the protesters at the Pentagon was forced from victory back into defeat, the level to which they were driven back was still a vastly important psychic distance above their pre-Pentagon level.

Mailer was able to utter to himself the assertion outside Occoquan because he obeyed the authority of his senses, in this case the senses of smell and touch:

> . . . in this resumption of the open air after twenty-four hours, no more, there was a sweet clean edge to the core of the substance of things—a monumentally abstract remark which may be saved by the concrete observation that the air was good in his lungs—not often could Mailer count on such sweet air. He felt a liberation from the unending disciplines of that moral ladder whose rungs he had counted in the dormitory while listening to Kupferberg, no, all effort was not the same. . . .

If he had done more good than bad in his Washington days, the surplus was not large enough to justify such feelings of pleasure about himself and sympathy for the prison guards and pride in his fellow prisoners, particularly since he had made no assertion since his morning doldrums and his freedom was gained through Hirschkop's efforts, not his own:

> . . . too much, much too much, it must come crashing soon, but still—this nice anticipation of the very next moves of life itself (and all for just an incredibly inexpensive twenty-four hours in jail) must mean, indeed could mean nothing else to Christians, but what they must signify when they spoke of Christ within them, it was not unlike the rare sweet of a clean loving tear not dropped. . . .

IV

The preceding pages might be "too much," since they excise so much that is striking from the last hundred pages of Book One: stunning, brief characterizations like the one of an escaped prisoner ("a red-bearded young goat with a red look in his eye and a lithe stubborn spring to his moves") or the marshal with the gray-green flaming ice cubes for eyes, stone larynx, and leather testicles ("And he had his Marshal's club in his hand as well. Brother! Bring back the Nazi!") or surprising shifts of feeling—the way in which Mailer clearly has more respect for Commissioner Scaife than for most of his fellow prisoners, or, indeed, his complex response to one prisoner's attempt to play a prank on the guards. Whether those Washington days did or did not permanently change Mailer as a man, they brought back to his work, after a twenty-year absence, the largeness of sympathy which enabled the twenty-four-year-old Mailer to characterize Gallagher so movingly and even render Stanley with some tenderness. In this case, Mailer lamented that the pranks worked to destroy the efforts of the guards and to remake, slowly and painfully, their nervous systems as they worked out, in their exchanges with the prisoners of kind and stingy gestures, "the long slow stages of a grim tableau—the recapitulation of that poverty-ridden rural childhood which had left them with the usual constipated mixture of stinginess and greed, blocked compassion and frustrated desires for power." The emphasis given to Mailer's surplus of feeling is a bit disproportionate, particularly since (in the terms of the fable) it was somewhat diminished by a fight with his wife when he returned to New York and (in terms of his career) was quite substantially diminished by the time he appeared in his next book as a depressed person. Modulations like this help Book One to feed powerfully our desire for "the real," particularly when we compare it with Book Two.

After the first forty pages of Book Two (with their careful delineation of the differing aspirations and potentials for actions of the protest groups and the countering efforts of the government), Mailer tells us that although Book One, with its single hero, seems more of a novel than the collective history of Book Two, the latter section partakes far more of the fictional. For, whatever happened to Norman Mailer between October 19 and October 22, it was less recondite to the author than what transpired in the conscious and unconscious minds of all the protesters and soldiers in the early hours of that last day. Mailer can then argue that with Book Two we "enter that world of strange lights and intuitive speculation which is the novel" far more profoundly than we did in Book One. For bluff, this reminds one of Mailer's claim that *An American Dream* was one of the best-written novels of the century. Even in this time of the breakdown of the "realistic" novel, fiction is still probably more than speculation and insight, and surely Mailer is juggling two meanings of "novelistic" or "fictitious." With its delicacy of tone, sharpness of characterization, and solidity of structure, Book One very much succeeds in terms of a fiction, a fable, which Mailer has quite obviously created. But the "truth" of Book Two depends on more than its own internal coherence; it depends on the behavior of groups which exist quite apart from the author. So do the characters of Book One, but Book Two seeks to be prophetic as well as reportorial; it is a fiction not only because a consciousness has arranged it but because it is a false prophecy. The account of the "objective" events is accurate enough; in fact, the sharpness of the reportage argues more than anything else that the confrontation would not have, as Josh Greenfield predicted, "the same musty feel of a May Day parade scuffle in Union Square thirty years past." But history has not justified Mailer's intuitive speculations, and our credence is weakened accordingly. Book Two became a fiction in a way that Mailer did not intend it to be.

In retrospect, the intuitions became a bit too predictable. For example, the great confrontation is all too simple. The generous Christian God who gave Mailer such a delicious if temporary emotional surplus is replaced by the more familiar embattled God, who has no easy benefactions for those several hundred protesters who broke through the restraining line of MPs and marshals to gain the plaza before the northwest entrance of the Pentagon or the several hundred more who joined them in the next hour. This multiformed (not uniformed) assemblage serves as a sort of elite batallion, representing as they do the best of that army of sons and daughters of the urban middle class who are at last openly rebelling against the degraded and degrading corporate center of American life. We begin to see that Mailer is turning the collective unconscious of America into the relative simplicities of a boxing match. In the near corner is the white hope of the middle class, still afraid of the champion, and in the far corner is the other army on the darkling plain of the asphalt plaza— their long lost cousins from the small towns and the urban working class now facing them with rifles and clubs. In keeping with the passage from "Dover Beach" from which the title of the book derives, both contenders, both armies, are ignorant, the invading one of the sources of life which have nourished their opponents:

> The sons and daughters of that urban middle class, forever alienated in childhood from all the good simple funky, nitty-gritty American joys of the working class like winning a truly dangerous fist fight at

the age of eight or getting sex before fourteen, dead drunk by sixteen, whipped half to death by your father, making it in rumbles with a proud street gang, living at war with the education system, knowing how to snicker at the employer from one side of the mouth, riding a bike with no hands, entering the Golden Gloves, doing a hitch in the Navy, or a stretch in the stockade, and with it all, their sense of élan, of morale, are the manna of the working class: there is a Godgiven indifference to school, morality, and job. The working class is loyal to friends not ideas. No wonder the Army bothered them not a bit.

It is petty to carp that "surely there were some soldiers there from the urban middle class"; what is more important is Mailer's almost painful mythologizing of the working class, of these sons of *his* old army buddies—all so solid and fun-loving? Do none of them try to describe their difficulties with that hopelessly inadequate explanation, "I have a terrible inferiority complex"? But let us continue with the fable as Mailer works collectively with processes that have obsessed him for so long.

In accordance with stern Maileresque justice, the protesters had to try to fill this hole in themselves to continue their protest against corporation, technology, and all arbitrary and barren organization—against the Pentagon. This could only be done by facing the defenders of the Pentagon and the consequent "fear and . . . profound respect in every middle class son for his idea of that most virile ruthless indifferent working class which would eventually exterminate them as easily as they exterminated gooks." Both of the forces facing each other across the charged psychic space between them are flawed; one is ignorant of struggle and given to surrealistic response, and the other is more used to combat but ignorant of any reason for rebellion against the Pentagon. It was not hard to fill them with "the small-town legends about the venality, criminality, filth, corruption, perversion, addiction and unbridled appetites of that mysterious group of city Americans referred to first as hipsters, then beatniks, then hippies; now hearing they are linked with the insidious infiltrators of America's psychic life, the Reds!"

If each group is confronting perhaps its deepest terror, the demonstrators' victory must lie closer to the conceptual than to the concrete. They have no more chance of physically defeating the soldiers than they had of occupying the Pentagon. A fellow prisoner was to tell Mailer the next morning that had they temporarily occupied the Pentagon they could have painted a wall and created confusion. Mailer reflected that "it was a battle conceived unlike any other, for in a symbolic war, victory had no tangible fruit." However, there is internal fruit, and the protesters reap some of it as, in the first hour of confrontation, they manage with their appeals to the soldiers and their own sense of solidarity to feel that the troops were more afraid of them than they were of the troops. Thus, they began doing what the White Negro and D.J. sought to do, what Rojack rather quickly did, and what the weary old prison guards at Occoquan were very slowly and surprisingly doing—rebuilding their nervous systems:

> . . . they were unbloodied, they felt secretly weak, they did not know if they were the simple equal, man for man, of these soldiers, and so when this vanguard confronted soldiers now, and were able to stare them in the eye, they were, in effect, saying silently, "I will steal your élan, and your brawn, and the very animal of your charm because I am morally right and you are wrong and the balance of existence is such that the meat of your life is now attached to my spirit, I am stealing your balls." A great exaltation arose among the demonstrators in that first hour. Surrounded on the plaza and on the stairs, they could have no idea of what could happen next, they could be beaten, arrested, buried in a stampede, most of them were on the mouth of their first cannon, yet for each minute they survived, sixty seconds of existential gold was theirs.

All of this was just the first hour. The next five or six hours seemed to be an existential standoff as the troops were constantly rotated to negate the attempts of the protesters to fraternize with the soldiers. One army characteristically asserted itself by burning draft cards, smoking marijuana, making love, and continuing to plead the justice of their cause. Some of the men offered their girls to the soldiers. Some of the girls unbuttoned their blouses for the soldiers; others put flowers in the rifle barrels. The other army protested not morality but force as they occasionally arrested randomly chosen protesters, but shortly after midnight, after the television crews had gone home and after the journalists had been called inside the Pentagon for a final press conference, a particularly fierce group of soldiers, paratroopers who had seen combat in Vietnam, appeared. They formed a wedge and drove down the middle of the plaza, clubbing, kicking, and dragging away those protesters who were seated in their path. Although the SDS leaders pleaded through bullhorns for the protesters to withdraw, they sat where they were, they sang the "Star-spangled Banner," they appealed to the paratroopers to join them, to be merciful to them, and they were beaten or saw those in the center beaten. To have fled from a hopeless situation would have been no failure of nerve, but the passive acceptance of a clubbing or the refusal to try to aid a girl a few feet away who was being struck with a rifle butt was a surrender to the

> dead nerveless area on the Left, comprised of the old sense of paralysis before the horror of the gas chamber. There are very few on the Left who do not live with the partial belief their own life someday will end in such a way—perhaps that is why they are hung like a string of fish on the power of public speech for all occasions. In a crowd listening to a speech, perhaps they are then farthest from the nightmare of retching upon one's last salts in the incredible ballooning suffocations of the last gas. Perhaps it is better to die each public evening by such an inch. One wonders why no musicians were playing as the clubs came down—just motherly legalistic injunctions from the bullhorn; motherly! the clubs of the Marshals, the butts of the rifles of the soldiers came down with more force. Kill the mothers! . . . Yes, it was a difficult hour—the working class had plucked all stolen balls back. Great cheer. With rifles and clubs they had plucked them back.

What a strange blend this is. On the one hand, the idiosyncratic rightness of some of the images—the protesters hung like a string of fish before a speaker—on the other, the obvious inflation of the last three lines. At any rate, if the protesters were forced part of the way down the moral ladder, they began climbing it again with every hour they remained after the troops had finished the clubbing separation of their ranks, for rumors were circulating that some of their number had been killed, that they were all to be killed. We have seen purer soldiers of growth than these spoiled, de-animalized children of the middle class, so dependent upon their gimmicks of jargon and drugs —Mailer attributes a large part of their passivity to the clubbing to their having just come down from a marijuana high. Yet Mailer brings us back to Croft and Rojack fighting their fear of the unknown on the heights above Anopopei and the parapet over midtown Manhattan. The author eloquently argues that though their refusal to flee was a mere simulacrum of the tenacity shown at Valley Forge, Gettysburg, and the Alamo, their holding their ground and opening themselves to the deepening levels of their fear kept alive some of the promise of their individual and national pasts. Now Mailer really lets go as the book moves deeper into the apocalyptic, and his theories about the transmigration of souls (and the implicit need to maintain one's purchase on eternity) emerge:

> . . . the rite of passage was invoked, the moral ladder was climbed, they were forever different in the morning than they had been before the night, which is the meaning of a rite of passage, one

has voyaged through a channel of shipwreck and temptation and so some of the vices carried from another nether world into life (on the day of one's birth) may have departed, or fled, or quit; some part of the man had been born again, and is better, just as some hardly so remarkable area of the soul may have been in some miniscule sweet fashion reborn on the crossing of the marchers over Arlington Memorial Bridge, for the worst of them and the most timid were moving nonetheless to a confrontation they could only fear, they were going to the land of the warmakers.

Perhaps, just perhaps, the hundreds who sat out the night were "changed, changed utterly," but the rest of the American Left and near-Left most certainly were not. However much the rich prose of the last thirty pages of Book Two works to lift Mailer's hopes above the barren ground of wild optimism, the events of the last five years bring the collective implications of the long night right back to that barren ground. As great as our admiration for some of the prose might be, our response is most likely our own equivalent of Jake Barnes's response to Lady Brett's claim that they could have had such a good life together, "Isn't it pretty to think so?"

V

The events of the Democratic and Republican conventions of 1968 clearly did not seize Mailer's imagination as did those of the Washington days. He was apparently able to believe, as he wrote Book One of *Armies,* that the speed with which he wrote so well followed from an expansion of self which followed in turn from some mysterious expansion of the collective psyche—thus, the gnostic optimism of Book Two. For all of the sea breeze freshness of so much writing in *Miami and the Siege of Chicago,* and even for the occasional small discoveries (like the toughness of Eugene McCarthy), there is an almost Eliotic strain in the book, a sort of "I have known them all already, known them all." Known the berserk policeman, the smell of marijuana in the park, the sight of Hubert Humphrey singing *"castrat' "* in Chicago; known the squealing Nixonettes and the law and order speeches in Miami. This is not to say that his days in Miami and Chicago were uninteresting—the arresting images and metaphors of the recounting speak for the sharp responses of the experiencing— but Mailer wondered with some weariness if he should join the protesters; he had deadlines to meet and there would be so many pitched battles to follow—forty years of them, he tells a daughter of Eugene McCarthy. A dull depression about the fate of the Republic seemed to be present even as his senses gratefully pulled in the vivid sights and smells of Chicago. The transcendent marching in the soaring vaults of history and the tender babe of America are a very long way off.

I could have substituted "the reporter" for Mailer; this, with "he," is the persona, a considerable dramatic remove from "the novelist," "Mailer," or "the existentialist." Only when the observing is finished, as the protagonist is about to go off drinking with friends and then leave Chicago for New York, is he referred to as "Mailer." Perhaps, for aesthetic reasons, the author made the reporter somewhat glummer than he actually was, but conjectures like this seem most irrelevant. The protagonist of *Siege* occupies only about one-tenth of the dramatic stage that he did in *Armies;* the reporting is so sharp and the authority of Mailer's voice is usually so strong and consistent that the reader does not often wonder if the author is distorting the protagonist. Much more than in *Armies* and *Of a Fire on the Moon,* one tends to see the two lights of the author and the protagonist coalescing.

The banality of Miami and the chaos of Chicago certainly did nothing to free the bright prophetic mood of the man who was able to argue eight years before that John Kennedy could set free the buried creativity of the nation, or who less than ten months before had argued that a radiant America was still possible. Added to the usual horrors of racism, addiction, and corporate power, the recent assassinations of Martin Luther King and Robert F. Kennedy did not help either. The only really extraordinary suggestion in the book is the megalomaniacal offering that Norman Mailer, who in the twelve hours before Senator Kennedy was assassinated did enjoy a dalliance and did not confess it to his wife, was somehow in part responsible.

The Republican convention offered the reporter no opportunity for dramatic action and so few for dramatic thought that except for a small crisis involving his feelings about Negroes, the most his inner drama could offer hung upon his ruminating about whether Nixon had really changed. Had the defeats in the 1960 presidential election and the 1962 California gubernatorial one brought compassion and true modesty to the shameless opportunism of the Checkers speech, to the man who Mailer saw in 1960 acting out "the apocalyptic hour of Uriah Heep"? Would not such a transformation herald hope for America? For all of the computerized banality of Nixon's acceptance speech, in spite of the tenth-rate Whitmanese of the "I see a day . . . I see a boy . . ." peroration, the reporter was still unable to decide whether Nixon was a "new and marvelously complex improvement of a devil, or angel-in-chrysalis, or both." So submerged was Nixon's personality beneath the systematic attempt to appeal to all and to offend none that the reporter

> was left by the television set with the knowledge that for the first time he had not been able to come away with an intimation of what was in a politician's heart, indeed did not know if he was ready to like Nixon, or detested him for his resolutely non-poetic binary system, his computer's brain, did not know if the candidate was real as a man, or whole as a machine, lonely in his sad eminence or megalomaniacal, . . . a rudder to steer the ship of state or an empty captain above a directionless void, there to loose the fearful nauseas of the century.

The writing is fine, but the attempt to enliven the reporting by the invocation of the system strains the credulities of all of us who are not party-line Manicheans. Even in 1968, we types who read Mailer might have felt that the defeats of the early sixties might have somewhat humanized Nixon, but to consider him as an angel-in-chrysalis! If this was all that puzzled the reporter, it was not all that struck so penetrating an eye that our way of seeing certain people is forever altered—Nelson Rockefeller, with his unnaturally wide, thin-lipped mouth, in the middle of which a smaller, thicker-lipped mouth talked, campaigning in the midst of the peculiar blend of surrealism that Miami Beach, with its sixty-year-olds in bikinis, has to offer; David Eisenhower, whose innocent, "near to yokel [face was] redeemed by the friendliest of simple smiles. An ambitious high school dramatics teacher might have picked him to play Billy Budd"; Ralph Abernathy of the Poor People's March, tasting and marveling over the sounds of the words he uttered, "a man from Mars absolutely fascinated with the resonance of earthly sound." The seventy pages of the Miami section are studded with such sharp little engravings, and Miami Beach appeals enough to Mailer's always strong sense of place to evoke vivid writing. The architectural triumph of the High Vulgarity style is nicely cataloged, but his most endearing image follows his explanation of how much of what had once been jungle was now covered by white buildings, white streets, and white sidewalks. "Is it so dissimilar from covering your poor pubic hair with adhesive tape for fifty years?" he then sweetly asks. Of course, the climate that helped to produce a jungle still exists, but with some seriousness Mailer attributes the disabling combination of temperature and humidity in Miami Beach in August to "vegetal memories of that excised jungle . . . ghosts of expunged flora, the never-born groaning in vegetative

chancery beneath the asphalt came up with a tropical curse. . . ."
For the leaders of a national political party, it is much more toler-
able for outraged vegetal nature to revenge itself in climate than for
outraged human nature to offer up the curse of riot. This riot the
Republicans largely prevented by holding the convention on a narrow
peninsula where the delegates and candidates could be protected from
any invading mob by sealing off the four viaducts across Biscayne Bay
and the one highway from the north. Richard Nixon could make his
perfect, computerized speech without worrying that any of the rioting
blacks from across the bay in Miami would spill into the convention
hall.

Chicago no more allows easy policing than it plasters over angry
nature with artifacts for vacationing pleasure seekers. The city is ma-
terialistic enough, but the love of commodities partakes much more
of the honest stench of the stockyards than of Miami Beach's odor-
less vaults where the temperature is air-conditioned down into the sixties so that women can wear fur coats in ninety-degree weather. The
Democratic convention was held in the Amphitheater, and nobody
ever described its location (the stockyard section of the South Side)
as a vacation spot. With the honest, primordial butchery of the cattle
and the stink of the excrement of the terrified animals, the stockyards
serve to remind us, claims Mailer, again invoking Aquinas, that we
are born between urine and feces. Even to the people in the half-mile-
wide veneer of civilization—the universities, expensive shops, elegant
apartment buildings—running along the lake, the blessings of the frequent southwest wind will bring with the stench of the yards the reminder of where their meat has come from (even if some dullard were
to state that most of it now came from Omaha). And if the Loop is
dying,

> what a dying! Old department stores, old burlesque houses, avenues,
> dirty avenues, the El with its nineteenth-century dialogue of iron
> screeching against iron about a turn, and caverns of shadow on the
> pavement beneath, the grand hotels with their massive lobbies, ba-
> roque ceilings, resplendent as Roman bordellos . . . red fields of
> carpet, a golden cage for elevator, the unheard crash of giant mills
> stamping new shapes on large and obdurate materials is always
> pounding in one's inner ear—Dreiser had not written about Chicago
> for nothing.

Between his desire to find a dialectical opposite for Miami Beach
and his tendency to romanticize the working class, Mailer has selected
from here and exaggerated from there. When I first read the Chicago

section in 1968, I found myself wishing that I could live in this city where the people were

> simple, strong, warm-spirited, sly, rough, compassionate, jostling, tricky, and extraordinarily good-natured because they had sex in their pockets, muscles on their backs, hot eats around the corner, neighborhoods which dripped with the sauce of local legend. . . .

I particularly wished this since I had been living in Chicago since 1959, and as the sixties proceeded so had the increase in the collective anxiety and frustration in most white neighborhoods, the dullness of all those white neighborhoods filled with bungalows with grotesque lamps in the middle of picture windows, and the upheavals in black neighborhoods.

Still, Chicago is a much more honest animalistic city than Miami Beach, and things instinctual were out in the open there. Both inside and outside the Amphitheater, the lust to maintain the prevailing alignments of power violently collided against the lust to alter them. What was most assured before the convention began was that Humphrey would be nominated; most important was just how much the nauseas of the century would be loosed in the process. The rival stage managers (the Yippie leaders and Mayor Daley) whetted anticipations by claiming on the one hand that Humphrey's nomination would have to be supported by rifles and on the other that nobody was going to take over Chicago, but it came as a shock to many to see or read about the Chicago policemen behaving like Terry Southern or William Burroughs creations as they pushed a crowd (many of them middle-aged onlookers) through the plate glass window of a restaurant, leaped through the glass, and began clubbing protesters, onlookers, and diners alike. With incidents like these outside the Amphitheater and Daley bellowing obscenities at Senator Ribicoff, or men apparently representing Daley's will punching delegates and reporters, inside it, Mailer had the war which is his central metaphor for experience and which has inspired so many fine pages. But although the various firefights call forth good writing, too much of him sees the literal and verbal versions of clubbing on one side and rock throwing on the other as the loosing of nausea to permit such a lyrical trip as *Armies* or one of such excited discovery as Part Three of *The Naked and the Dead.*

There is a small struggle within the reporter as his desire for dramatic action collides with and then rides over his caution and he promises to lead a protest march to the Amphitheater if three hundred delegates will join him. The effort is a fiasco, but later in the day he behaves well with the Chicago police as he is arrested twice and released twice. Not very much is made of it; the thematic bridge between the Chicago section and his next work is offered not by any expansion of self but in his perception that tired as he was he might still have gathered the delegates had the telephones at the hotels been working or had he a walkie-talkie: "He was always rushing or waiting in hallways—he learned the first lesson of a convention: nothing could be accomplished without the ability to communicate faster than your opponent." And earlier in the book he observed that a reporter now depended on television for a full coverage of a convention.

VI

On July 5, 1969, eleven days before the launch of Apollo 11, astronauts Armstrong, Aldrin, and Collins held a press conference at the NASA Manned Spacecraft Center in Houston. In the bland styles of "three young junior executives . . . announcing their corporation's newest subdivision," they answered questions "about a phenomenon which even ten years ago would have been considered material unfit for serious discussion." A bit more than ten years before—eleven years and three months to be precise—Norman Mailer was very seriously arguing with Richard Stern and claiming, perhaps for the first time to anyone besides himself, that it is our responsibility to carry God's embattled vision across the universe. A good deal of the intervening time was of course devoted to attacking different causes, aspects, and effects of that technology ironically so necessary for such a literally supramundane expansion of heroic activity.

In Stanley Kubrick's movie *2001,* the protagonist had to destroy the computer to reach a level of consciousness which was as far above man's as man's was above the ape's. Yet he could not have gotten "beyond Jupiter" were it not for technology in general and Hal the Computer in particular. In the fifties Mailer lamented that the poet had been replaced by the psychiatrist as the arbiter of society. As the sixties proceeded, the foe inflated itself into all of mystery-hating technology, but at least in *Of a Fire on the Moon* (1970) Mailer's implacable hostility to the dethroner of the poet was weakened when he was confronted in the last months of the decade by so much that impressed him—the vast, perfected power of the Saturn V booster rocket; the courage and abilities of the astronauts; the intricacy and perfection of the space module; the near miraculous blend of ingenuity, labor, and cooperation which in less than a decade enabled the

NASA physicists and engineers to overcome all of the thermal, gravitational, and spatial obstacles in the way of getting men to, on, and back from the moon. Then there was the possibility that—to use that flat first phrase uttered on the moon—the mission might be a giant step forward for mankind which could combine technological wizardry and great poetry, the computer and Shakespeare. Or perhaps there was a divine force behind the fact that "the heroes of the time were technologists, not poets, and the art was obliged to be in the exceptional engineering, while human communciation had become the routine function"; maybe "God, aghast at the oncoming death of man in man deviled pollution, was finally ready to relinquish some part of the Vision, and substitute a vision half machine, and half of man, rather than lose all."

These are the conjectures of a much different persona than the protagonist of *Miami and the Siege of Chicago*. If, as Mailer claims, the Apollo 11 mission is so representative of the final third of the twentieth century in its blend of technological complexity and faceless, interchangeable men operating the technology, then the conventional nonspecialized reporter—who can only describe the "reality" of relatively simple processes and recognizable human gestures—has been made obsolete. So Mailer sheds the hat of "the reporter" and dons that of "Aquarius," the cosmic detective who, for example, burrows beneath the corporate manners of the astronauts to offer Maileresque readings of their unconscious fears and desires. The cause of a bad joke by Aldrin can then become "perhaps some natural male anxiety at the thought of evil moon rays passing into one's private parts," or Collins, orbiting the moon alone after Aldrin and Armstrong had landed, might be wondering if a monkey which had died while orbiting the earth had begun "to sicken and die because of some drear but most recognizable message its animal sense had received from space, some message too fine for the insulated nerves of man to receive." Immediate reflection tells Aquarius that the mission is clearly the expression of God or of the Devil. Mediate doubts of the presence of the supernatural set in; perhaps the mission merely represents an attempt to plaster over our growing terror of our own imbalances with a massive assertion of technological control. But probably some kind of God or some kind of Devil are contributing mightily to the whole space program.

Mailer's underlying dramatic strategy is easy enough to grasp. The dominant force in America is still the corporate mind with its dependence upon technology. (Sometimes Mailer lumps together the corporation and technology, but usually he seems to regard the technological mind as the purest distillation of the corporate one.) All of this might be true enough, but now Mailer begins escalating. How wrong we are if we happen to think of corporate effort as being, in good part, a harnessing of irrational, aggressive energy. According to Mailer, the corporate son of that rough reckless plunger—the frontiersman of capitalism—sought like his father

> to make profit for the corporation, but neither he nor the corporation did it for profit, they did it for reason, did it to remove contradiction from the earth, remove problem and heartache from human interface; subtract germs, viruses, pests and bugs from the bounty of nature; subdue contradictory ideologies in foreign affairs; extirpate irrationality from conduct and inefficiencies from machines; and sometimes Aquarius would even suspect they wished to remove human activity from divine punishment.

Although the corporate mind manages to keep its knowledge of mystery and last judgment repressed (making for the schizophrenic collision of conscious and unconscious that Mailer has described for so long), the conscious mind has become a bit guilty about the shoddiness of so many of its products. Thus, it has recently turned to its technological vanguard, to NASA, for the technological perfection requisite for success in the Apollo program will reassure it of the excellence of the corporate way. As the purest expression of the "rational" corporate mind, the technologist is particularly opposed to mystery; "beautiful data was clear and thorough data. An engineer's idea of beauty was system perfection. Beauty was obviously the absence of magic." Now corporation-technology is simultaneously going to reassure itself of its worth and seize the moon—the symbol of inspiration and dream, of all the thrusts and tugs of the irrational. It was more than a symbol to Steve Rojack, and perhaps it is more than a symbol to us; if the differing gravitational pulls of the phases of the moon can affect something as massive as the seas, might they not affect structures as delicate as our psyches? So determined is technology to strip the moon of magic, particularly of the sinister, that the landing area is called Tranquility Base, and even the astronauts seem committed

> to make the moon a playground of the future. . . . "The moon was a very natural and very pleasant environment in which to work," Aldrin reports after what excessive expenditure of BTU's it has taken a strong man like himself to drive a narrow pipe all of six or eight inches into the ground when the flight plan had called for twelve.

. . . "I was sure," said Armstrong, "it would be a hospitable host.
It had been awaiting its visitors for a long time."

Well, they're not going to get the moon so easily from us acolytes
of poetic, mysterious Diana because we have Aquarius on our side.
He can argue that the mission did not kill mystery but added to it, for
it added to the holdings of some kind of God (who might have settled
for a new soldier—half man, half machine—or who might have gone
mad) or of some kind of Devil (who might be beautiful)—but
which? They are so determined to kill the language of Shakespeare
that they refer to man's first walk on the moon as the EVA, but
Aquarius can observe that the preparations for the EVA took such
disciplined men as Aldrin and Armstrong twice as long as they should
have and can then conjecture that moon rays altered one's sense of
time. He can even attribute purpose to the moon and suggest that it
might have been drawing us toward it for years to exact revenge for
the way we had tried to kill off the irrational. Or perhaps technology
did conquer the moon and it gave its now malign blessing to the dull
binary mind of Richard Nixon and its malign curse to the more
inspired Edward Kennedy, whose presidential hopes had just been
dashed by the Chappaquiddick disaster.

However much the astronauts might look and act like junior
executives, they are generals "of the church of the forces of technology," the foremost edge of the technological vanguard. As such,
they must be particularly subject to that schizophrenia between technology and the irrational which, according to Mailer, characterizes
the corporative psyche. If they "dwell in the very center of technological reality (which is to say that world where every question must
have answers and procedures)," we have Aquarius to assure us that
they also "inhabit—if only in . . . [their] dreams—that other world
where death, metaphysics and the unanswerable questions of eternity
must reside." Armed with his own post-Freudian dream theory—we
run through simulations of potential experiences in our dreams, they
are not just wish fulfillments—Aquarius can, for example, assure us
that the dreaming astronauts brooded over the different relationships
of the moon to the earth more than they consciously knew. In *The
Armies of the Night,* Mailer told us that he was well suited to specu-
late on the meaning of the march, since the imbalances of his psyche
fitted those of the time. Even synecdoche escalates in *Of a Fire on the
Moon.* Since these courageous, talented, but rather prosaic fellows so
combine technology and courage, and since they are the first to take
the corporate vision out toward the stars, they must be the last of an

old kind of man or the first of a new, just as man must be going to the moon to look for God or to destroy Him. Just as in spite of—perhaps because of—its curious dullness the flight was the event of the century and must presage the way the rest of the century would go; just as a whole new psychology is needed if we are to understand these amazingly complex astronauts.

New mysteries yet fresh mysteries beget. For not only is Aquarius a man to offer exotic explanations of man and moon, but he also received a degree from Harvard in aeronautical engineering, and, with the help of some books and manuals and much study, he can ride out on the horse of romance and joust with the technologues on what they thought was their own field. Whether or not the early effacements honestly describe the way Mailer felt as he set out to begin his coverage of the mission—he had just finished fourth in a field of five in the Democratic primary for the New York mayoralty and "was weary of his own voice, own face, person, persona, will, ideas, speeches and general sense of importance. . . . not unhappily, mildly depressed, somewhat used up, wise, tolerant, sad, void of vanity, even had a hint of humility"—they do not at all anticipate the man who could better than anyone else "brood about the chasm between technology and metaphysics." Perhaps Mailer's greatest single assertion of ego lies in this attempt to somehow combine the worlds of Bechuana warriors and Wernher von Braun, to tell us that gravity, indeed all energy, was a mystery and that to anticipate "every whim of a computer was equal to foreseeing the steps of a virgin whose heart was nymphomaniac." Then he goes on to proclaim that this was only to state the beginnings of mechanical mysteries, for machines might have minds of their own, and to offer as evidence more than a dozen examples of the unpredictable behavior of the electronic circuitry of machines.

Although most of the mysteries remain unsolved at book's end, Aquarius seems to conclude that the moon's powers have gone to Nixon against the Hemingways or the Kennedys: to the anti-mysterious corporate forces and against Aquarius and the rough-talking, free-drinking members of "his army"; to the boring suburbs around Houston and against Provincetown. Seemingly indestructible marriages broke up in Proivncetown that summer of 1969. Aquarius's fourth, then as before powerfully influenced by lunar emanations, conclusively collapsed about six weeks after the module splashed down in the Pacific. Two or three days after the splashdown, Aquarius, still committed to his theories of a cosmic interplay of forces, gave way to speculations and accusations as megalomaniacal as the confession that an unconfessed dalliance helped cause Bobby Kennedy's assassination. In one of the most simplistic dichotomies in his book of too many simplistic dichotomies, Aquarius laments that his army—big drinkers, "deep into grass and all the mind il-luminants beyond the grass, princelings on the trial of the hip, so avid to deliver the sexual revolution," roaring "at the blind imbecility of the Square, and his insulation from life"—had lost the moon to the much less self-indulgent WASP technocrats. His army (and the un-spoken, obvious implication is that he is at the head of it), "treach-erous, silly, overconfident and vain, haters and despisers of every-thing tyrannical, phony, plastic and overbearing in American life had dropped out, goofed and left the goose to their enemies." Yet mystery remains. Perhaps the victorious enemy is out to save the world and not to destroy it; perhaps WASP technology is "God's intended. Looking at his drunken own, Aquarius did not know. He was one judge who would write willy-nilly out of his desolations this year."

But Mailer is not finished having it both ways. Several months after his concession of defeat, desolate Aquarius confronts a piece of moon rock and tries to guess the future from it. This is really a tough problem because its rays and odors—its creative forces—are hermetically sealed behind two panes of glass, but he can still trust the authority of one of his senses: "there was something familiar as the ages of the bone in the sweet and modest presence of the moon rock, modest as a newborn calf, and so he had his sign, sentimental beyond measure . . . all worship the new science of smell! It was bound to work its way through two panes of glass before three and a half billion years were lost and gone." Was Aquarius justified in giving in to his quite possibly prejudiced visual sense? Would tech-nology force us into such awesome discoveries that we would again have to regard the world as poets, "behold it as savages who knew that if the universe was a lock, its key was metaphor rather than measure"? It's a mystery.

Buried among all the objections to the rising influence of scientific equation and the precipitous decline of compelling poetic metaphor is the possibility that technology has made poetic creation impossible. Of course, Mailer has tried to make use of that old strategy of turning personal or social loss into aesthetic gain. While lamenting the eclipse of language, the book is supposed to offer manifest proof that poetry is still possible, that language can still move us deeply. For all its faults, *Of a Fire on the Moon* frequently does this. No part of it is, as writing, as unsuccessful as the majority of scenes in which the Kellys appeared in *An American Dream,* and many parts are splendid. As Richard Poirier has written of *Fire:*

> His most impressive performances are descriptive ones, which isn't to join the tiresome chorus of those who step away from the difficulties of his achievement by saying that he is a great journalist and a lesser novelist. The distinction, not much good to begin with, is trivializing in the case of a writer who reveals here a genius for even the quickest characterizations (Frank McGee is said to have a "personality all reminiscent . . . of a coach of a rifle team"), for casual but packed analogies that Lowell might envy ("what if the moon were as quiet as the fisherman when he lays the fly on the water"), for Proustian social observation (as in the account of an evening at the Houston home of European friends). . . . Not in his intellectual superstructurings, but in these more open evidences of his powers as a writer is there assurance enough that the Machine has not yet collapsed the language or stilled the imagination. His magnificent description, the product of intense research, of the cratered fact of the moon excels anything made available in words or pictures by the machined men of the Apollo flights.

The extended observation is seldom as delicate and compelling as that in *Armies*—in fact, there is a fair amount of fakery in the scene in the Houston home *—but arresting figures and descriptions of many kinds and lengths swarm out from the book. Dancing alone, such an unimportant face in the crowd as a go-go dancer is "a round sullen country girl"; before friends, she is "full of relish for her work, slinging her breasts, undulating her belly on a river of cogitating promise—the voracity of her hip-sock suggested she was one real alligator." At first glance, Buzz Aldrin might look dull to most of us, but by the time Mailer finishes describing his mighty but subdued voice, large features, downturned samurai eyes, and downturned mouth corners—all of this giving him "the expression of a serious man at home on a field of carnage"—we applaud that serious-humorous admission that "the movie director in Aquarius would have cast him on the spot for Major in Tank Cavalry." As the rocket speeds away from the earth, the affectionate best wishes from the launch crew and thanks from the flight crew express the "confidence between them, the confidence of missionaries, the very air of mes-

---

* For example, as he is preparing for a dialogue between the creative time of Negroes and the deadening time of technology, Mailer tells us that he was delighted to have a black guest tell him that CPT was colored people's time. He knew this by 1959 when he wrote about Ralph Ellison's *Invisible Man,* in which CPT is discussed.

sianic love—that love which, like Robert Frost's cube of ice, traveled on its melting." Just as the rocket travels on its own burning.

Even the scientific analogies can be stunning, from wing shots (the module, orbiting the earth "fell forward like a ball thrown into an endless chasm, and as it fell forward it fell around the curve of the earth"; if the theory that the craters of the moon were created by meteoric bombardments is true, then the bombardments had "an occasional perfection of aim equal to shooting pearls onto the circular points of a crown") to the overwhelming pages in which Mailer lingers over the power and perfection of the Saturn V rocket like a lover over the body of the beloved. For as much as Mailer might have injected desolation, dread, and mysterious contemplations into Aquarius's head, one doubts if he doctored the protagonist's response to the launching. The sight of the rocket slowly rising, "white as a ghost, white as the white of Melville's Moby Dick," the immense roar of the sound as it reached him, the shaking of the ground under his feet, Aquarius repeating "Oh my God" again and again—these are in many senses the real thing. To use an analogy Mailer might appreciate, when a certain professional basketball player was after two or three years at forward moved back to center, a position much better suited for his singular blend of size, ferocity, and grace, he said, "It's like coming home." One feels that when Mailer confronted the rocket, he too, in a sense, came home—we might remember that he was thinking of the white whale when he described Mount Anaka. When he later describes the rocket, how deeply he is stirred by its power, how lovingly he caresses its bulk—363 feet tall, weighing more than six and one-half million pounds, developing a thrust of more than nine million pounds. We feel his nostrils flaring even as he runs through the accessories—the tractor which pulls the rocket to the pad has on each crawler treads which measure over seven feet in width and weigh a ton; the metal shield which deflects the mighty flames weighs one million three hundred thousand pounds. How great was his respect for the elegant simplicity of the plan to true the takeoff— eight pins at the base of the rocket are merely pulled through their own dies.

Small wonder the descriptions of the launching and the rocket are so effective, ribbed as they are with Aquarius's envy of the astronauts. *He* wants to have all that power ripping him beyond the earth; *he* wants to fly those hundreds of thousands of miles, to walk on the surface of the moon. To regard once again the mission from the writer's point of view, Mailer had, with rocket, flight, and moon, parts of the objective correlative he had sought since *The Naked and the Dead,* but the most important ingredient was missing. Instead of Croft silently, potently clinging to the crude unformed vision in his soul, there were those technocratic adventurers who refer to potential disasters as contingencies. Maintaining his search for adventure nonetheless, Mailer colonized unconsciouses and injected mystery at every turn until, for all of the intelligence and talent on so many pages, the book became top-heavy and turgid.

On the one hand *Of a Fire on the Moon* is a tremendous assertion of ego; on the other, it encourages one to entertain such a psychological platitude as "a man with a truly strong ego does not have to assert it so flamboyantly." For one thing, the excessive bulk, the repetition of the book, calls to mind Calder Willingham's observation, "It is a technical fact that when a writer is working under stress he is apt to write too much." Mr. Poirier has interestingly suggested that Mailer's mind has become enslaved by his belief in the dramatic efficacy of the God-Devil, Corporation-Mystery dichotomies and that we would do well to regard them not as the matter but the fuel, even the lubricants, of the books. Mailer needs them, he argues, to get him interested enough in his subject to do the fine straight reporting, but Mailer did not need the dichotomies for the fine straight reporting of the Chicago section of his preceding book. The repetitiveness argues for an uncertainty about his effectiveness, and then there are the apologies; several times Mailer tells us in different ways that it was somehow better for him to think the apocalyptic way he does. However, the way in which the book clearly needed to have at least eighty pages of suet boiled off might follow from more than excessive or deficient confidence in his approach or even from his obvious desire to assert his energy after his fourth marriage broke up.

It must also be said that the last two-thirds of the book have less cosmic blubber per page than the first third, which was published in three installments in *Life* and inflated accordingly. Mailer wrote a curious aside early in the first *Life* installment, one which he left in the book. After Aquarius tells us that his campaign contributions stopped the instant the *New York Times* erroneously reported that he would make a million dollars from the forthcoming moon book, we learn that he will be paid much less, and

> actually, Aquarius would be lucky if he were left with any real money at all, for he was in debt from having made three movies (for which he had put up the cash himself) and he calculated that with the restitution of consequent borrowings, and the payment of taxes,

he would have enough to live and think for a year. Not so bad. He had only to write a book about the moon shot.

Two years before, Mailer had announced in the *New York Times* that he had written *An American Dream* under the pressure of the *Esquire* deadlines because he had to make a good deal of money in a short time. Here he indirectly tells us, in the seventh paragraph of what was to become his second-longest consecutive work, that he is writing it so that he can pay his debts and do what he wants to do. This could be an arrogant declaration of independence to the habitual *Life* readers or the self-conscious apology of a man who had attacked the Luce chain for so long and was now going to make what he could from it. Certainly this announcement of his economic bind is a response to all those critics who had taken to calling him an opportunist, to all those readers who were going to feel that he regarded the moon venture as just another timely thing to write up for the quick financial harvest. Here is a sample of a cruel parody, written by Louis Grant in the third-person autobiographical style of *Armies* and *Siege,* probably before he even knew that Mailer was going to write about the moonshot for *Life:*

> Mailer had become a professional celebrity. For some time Grant had wondered when Mailer, like the former greats of all the professions, would begin making television commercials. Grant could envision Mailer selling Halo Shampoo for $5000 a minute. Perhaps in March that was Grant's vision of the Apocalypse: Norman Mailer pitching Halo Shampoo on NBC "Want a fuck? Try Halo," says Mailer, sticking his head out from behind the shower curtain. "All us novelists use it."

Perhaps Mailer's attempt to preserve his integrity by giving his readers their money's worth was as much the cause of the inflation of the book as his finally dazing attempts to find the romantic where it did not exist.

The apologies deepen with *The Prisoner of Sex,* originally a long article for *Harper's.* To put out a book on Women's Lib the year after the moon book was published—how trendy can one get! So Mailer quite openly admits that he cannot believe himself worthy to advocate revolution until "he had written the novel of his life and succeeded in passing judgment on himself"; he should not write this book because the themes of Women's Lib "also belonged to that huge novel he had promised to begin so many times. To trick some of these ideas forth now was to play danger with this book." Yet the valkyries of Women's Lib have been trying to destroy him; they are trying to take the mystery out of reproduction; he sometimes thinks that "to be in the center of any situation was . . . the real marrow of his bone . . . his genius was to mobilize on the instant." And so we come to *The Prisoner of Sex*.

A number of Mailer's earlier positions are sharpened in that book; for example, his 1965 complaint that he did not know if the orgasm or the family was more important is resolved (for himself at least) with his claim that one has to have good sex to have good children; he admits that some of his thinking about sex in the early sixties was melodramatic, but, using the liberated diction of the seventies, he was right to seize on the fact that "the fuck either had a meaning which went to the root of existence, or it did not" and still more right to argue that it did. We quickly perceive that the book is what more and more seems to be Standard Mailer. With their attempts to level out all differences between male and female, to divorce sex from truly creative possibility, and to destroy the reputation of any writer who argues for differences and/or creative possibilities, Women's Lib is the sexual vanguard of flattening totalitarianism. So the polarities are squared off again. In one corner is Kate Millett—to many of us merely the author of a best-selling book filled with some interesting ideas and many grating paragraphs, oversimplifications, and stunning dishonesties, but to Norman Mailer, the vanguard of the vanguard, someone who must be attacked—not merely because she wants to discredit every vision of life that has more grandeur, poetry, or possibility than her own mediocre one—but because

> she had all the technological power of the century in her veins, she was the point of advance for those intellectual forces vastly larger than herself which might look to the liberation of women as the first weapon in the ongoing incarceration of the romantic idea of men— the prose of future prisons was in her tongue, for she saw the differences between men and women as non-essential—excesses of emotion to be conditioned out. . . . She gave intimation by her presence that the final form of the city was nearer to the dormitory cube with ten million units and a perfect absence of children and dogs.

In the other corner is the Prisoner of Sex (née Norman Mailer), truly a prisoner since he argues that to be male is to be set against the world in a way that woman essentially is not, here setting out again against the technological way the world is going. Things are looking up. Since we had Aquarius on our side, "they" really had to struggle to get the moon; they know so much less about sex than they do about rocketry, and we still have the Prisoner on our side. Just as Aquarius could use physics texts and rocketry manuals to argue that energy was a mystery and machines had minds of their own, the Prisoner ballasts his own claims with statistics used by those totalitarian sexologues who actually claim that there is no magical attraction between the ovum and the sperm cells but that one can take advantage of predictable biological procesess and statistical possibility to choose in advance the sex of one's child with an eighty percent chance of success. But what of the conceptions of the remaining twenty percent—could they not also argue that the ovum can choose the cell it most desires? This is the quintessence of Standard Mailer; the couple might consciously think they want a daughter and so use an acidic douche which will kill the y-bearing male cells. But one heroic plumed knight of a y-bearing cell swims through the acid to the languishing princess of the ovum waiting to embrace him— just as Sergius O'Shaugnessy was supposed to have fought his way to artistry against "all power of good manners, good morals, the fear of germs, and the sense of sin." For the ovum might have a mind of its own or, perhaps, instead of the technological paraphernalia of douches, coital positions, and schedules a woman might choose at some unconscious level of herself what sex her child shall be—indeed, whether or not she will become pregnant.

All of this might sound as unconvincing to most of us as the claims for the conscious intents and unconscious terrors of the corporate mind in *Fire* except that the arguments are much more cleanly and sparsely made. If nothing in *The Prisoner of Sex* has the power of the best descriptive stretches of the preceding book, it is a much cleaner work, in good part because it is only about one-third the length of *Fire*. But there are other reasons: Mailer would seem to have perceived that extended God-Devil ponderings had to go, and so we merely see technology trying to operate on God's sexual body; the writing is crisp, with a consistently genial tone that never falls into the sodden maunderings of some of *Fire;* the literary criticism is fine, in particular the brilliant discussion of the interrelationships between Lawrence's childhood union with his mother, his later life, and his writings. Yet one overwhelmingly feels that the author is treading water with this new version of Mailer versus technology, and for all of the book's pluses one is reminded of the first lines of the "Sixth Advertisement for Myself": "After I left *The Voice,* I knew it was time to clean myself up. I had a novel in me, the novel which I have talked about in these prefaces, but if I were ever to do it, I had to start the slow and not encouraging work of learning how to work all over again."

The sense that Mailer himself must realize that his work is standing still or declining with his attempts to inject mystery into events which obdurately resist the transfusion was supported by the April, 1972, news that he was hard at a new novel. Consequently, the piece on the Democratic convention which appeared in the July 28 *Life* seemed to be a quick sidetrip for money to help finance the really great novel he might yet write. The piece did nothing to alter the feeling that the nonfiction strategems were wearing thin. Of course there were the arresting images and fine on-the-wing characterizations always present in Mailer's reportage. Here are two examples from a score of contenders: the ramp on the plane that the president had lent Governor Wallace "flew out in sections like an animated giant pterodactyl's tongue in a King Kong film"; Wallace's well-built, assured national campaign director, Charles Snider, "stood in front of the podium with his legs apart, as if at parade rest, weight on the balls of his toes. Wearing a pale cream suit, a yellow shirt and a well-chosen light-blue-and-brown figured tie, he suggested the aplomb of a marine who is wearing the world's best clothes." But what tired stuff so much of the rest was—the invocation of Mailer's God locked in cosmic battle with Mailer's Devil; the sense that a revelation was near; the suggestion that the average voter in the booth might be "engaged in some inarticulate transaction with eternity"; the wheezing start of the mystery-making machine in the first paragraph as Mailer writes that the convention offers so many questions and so little overt drama that he will have to rely on—most unconvincing modesty— his poor, slow brain; and the final conclusion that the peculiar quality of the convention followed from the "insufficient evil in the room." This seemed to be a smirking reminder of how familiar *he* was with evil, all too reminiscent of the very silly, black-velvet rustlings of those satanic Kellys in *An American Dream*. Well, perhaps evil will be worked up more palpably in the novel.

Three months later the news came that Mailer had a new book out. What energy; he's finished the novel already. Two more days, and there was a review of *St. George and the Godfather*. The piece was only an installment. Tricked again by his growing whorishness! So the book was picked up with the smug knowledge of why it was going to be as bad as it must be.

Tricked and retricked. The Manichean creakings of the piece fall away or show themselves as shrewd preparations for the main show, which is the coverage of the Republican convention. In fact, *St. George* ranks high among Mailer's nonfiction books. It is not as good a work as *The Armies of the Night,* but then none of the nonfiction is going to be until two conditions are simultaneously met: Mailer must again find an event in which the author's fascination with what is happening to Norman Mailer so wonderfully meshes with a more diffused drama of social discovery, and there must be the excitement generated by a sense of new stylistic possibility, as with his perception of the potential of the third-person autobiography in *Armies.* A recurrence of this happy blend does not appear imminent. But *St. George* is at least as good as the 1968 convention book, *Miami and the Siege of Chicago,* which is no small achievement, since the recent conventions offered Mailer nowhere near the reportorial possibilities of the Chicago holocaust. But what Mailer did with what he had gave *St. George* a depth of feeling that has been absent from his work since *Armies.*

In the book, Mailer fleshed out his account of the Democratic convention by adding about forty pages to the forty-five or so which had already appeared in *Life.* One of the new chapters deals with McGovern's extrication from his platform planks on welfare, abortion, homosexuality, and drugs—any one of which could be shaped by opponents into a political crucifix. For the support of any one of these points could drive to revenge that enormous number of potential voters who are defined less by their political allegiances than by their dissatisfactions and resentments. This group Mailer calls "the wad," and the most pleasant surprise of the book is the great subtlety with which he controls the very reasonable proposal that the evil absent from the Democratic convention is the cynical ability to manipulate the fears, hatreds, and sad assertions of the wad. This brings one back with the dismal, repetitive force of depression to the fact that shortly after *St. George* was released, Richard Milhous Nixon won reelection by one of the greatest majorities in the history of the presidency. The only silliness in *Siege* followed from Mailer's 1968 broodings over whether Nixon, resurrected after losses to JFK and Pat Brown, was a "new and marvelously complex improvement of a devil, or angel-in-chrysalis, or both." The Vietnam crop of Nixon's first term, with all its new deaths, mutilations torturings, refugees, and bomb craters, of course renders obscene any conjectures of the Good Angel Richard. In fact, at one point in *St. George* Mailer refers to his need to restore his powers as a witness. Restored they were; his loathing of the ease with which the majority of Americans were ready to settle for Nixon's Vietnam policy hovers over his account of the Republican doings like Banquo's ghost over Macbeth's groaning table. Yet there is no sanctimony, and the reasons for this are many: his fascination with the participants; the humor of so many observations; certain sympathies for some staunch Republicans and for the wad itself; even his own impurity as he is easily tempted in an interview with Kissinger to engage in the Establishment's schizophrenia of moral concealment.

But the best part of the book is a result of Mailer's confrontation with Nixon's manipulative genius. His treatment seems in part to follow from the ruminations of Rubashov, the imprisoned Old Bolshevik in Koestler's great study of the temptations of totalitarianism, *Darkness at Noon*. Rubashov wrote in his diary that *"we were neo-Machiavellians in the name of universal reason . . . history has taught us that often lies served her better than the truth, for man is sluggish and has to be led through the desert for forty years before each each step in his development."* The steps can be charted. In a temporary swing back to a justification of his own "utopian Machiavelliaism," Rubashov works out in his diary an addition to Marx's dogma of the interrelationships of the base and superstructure; thus he can "scientifically" argue that the masses must be totally manipulated after each new productive surge. Just as Rubashov claims that only the Marxists toiled with the masses in the mud of history, Mailer argues that

> Nixon was the artist who had discovered the laws of vibration in all the frozen congelations of the mediocre . . . only Nixon had thought to look for the harmonics of the mediocre, the miniscule dynamic in the overbearing static, the discovery that this inert lump which resided in the bend of the duodenum of the great American political river was more than just an indigestible political mass suspended between stomach and bowel but had indeed its own capacity to quiver and creep and crawl and bestir itself to vote if worked upon with unremitting care and no relaxation of control. . . . this was the major work of Nixon's intellectual life, to chart the undiscovered laws of movement in the glop of the wad.

Tracing Nixon and his laws, Mailer is again stalking a mystery, but his discoveries are sometimes compelling and, in one way or another, always arresting. The way in which Nixon has fused his own personality with the nausea potential of TV, his varied uses of the Jeanette Weiss principle ("wherever possible use a black lady with a German Jewish name doing a patriotic bit"), his perception that much of the wad feels that the bombs dropped in Vietnam somehow kill hippies at home, the ease with which he taught most of the Republican right wing "to take ten steps to the left and smile at the center"—all this is somehow true enough. Instead of Rubashov's diary, we have Nixon's Maxims, and their terse cynicism often creates an effective counterpoint. For example, the report of Daniel Ellsberg's searing indictment of our activities in Southeast Asia is immediately followed by:

> *From Nixon's Maxims:* The Silent Majority, while often accused of being non-political, actually prefer to have a definite idea and will often drift at surprising speed from one position to its opposite. May I point to the shift of opinion on the war in Vietnam. The American public once ready to get out is now ready to stay in and win provided no American blood is shed.

Sometimes the conjectures are outlandish, but Mailer covers his tracks well. The maxim which proclaims that the triple keynote speech by Brooke, Lugar, and Armstrong suggests images "of a tranquil brook, a World War II Luger and a fine body, which in turn will symbolize Peace, Military Might and a Healthy Economy" is hokum, but so is Nixon arranging his face and voice on TV hokum. Yet he gets all that power and all those votes *just the same.* Rubashov manipulated for the liberation of man, but for what goal does Nixon juggle the dazed electorate?

All of this is blended with reporting superior to that of the Democratic convention—what a job Mailer does on the Young Voters for the President, Goldwater, Pat Nixon, Agnew—and a subtle but pervasive moral point of view. In a 1969 interview, Mailer said that a writer can always try to confound his enemies, and *St. George* certainly strikes back at those readers (like myself) who had decided that the nonfiction was atrophying. But Mailer in good form acts upon me much as the possibilities of total electoral triumph act upon the half-hysterical gluttons of YVP's—I want more and better; *St. George* makes me yet more conscious (to borrow a phrase used to describe Eitel) of Mailer's unused artist's depths. Mailer probably could publish a nonfiction work filled with sharp observations, crackling writing, and interesting speculations each year. But for him to settle with reportage—however brilliant it might be—is to refuse to meet the demand he made for all writers to attempt to add to the house of literature, if only by an inch. To go beyond the reasonably inspired reportage in the nonfiction is most likely to fall into the inflations of *Of a Fire on the Moon.* This he did not do in *St. George* or *The Prisoner of Sex,* but as Mailer himself suggests, a book like *Prisoner* is a minor effort compared to a novel. The growing sense of just how difficult it is for Mailer to equal the nonfiction achievement of *Armies* has laid to rest the possibility of convincingly defending his total limitation of his talents to nonfiction.

This brings us back—as any discussion of Mailer finally does, as Mailer himself usually does—to the question of his talent. If he ever does get back to the new novel, one hopes that it is not the blockbuster, the descendant of *Moby Dick,* about orgy, violence, and time which he so portentously promised back in 1959 and still seemed to be promising twelve years later in *The Prisoner of Sex.* How far his sensibility seems to have moved from the gamecock posturings of the two segments of the promised work that did appear in *Advertisements*; how far his style has come from the clotted, narcissistic prose of "Advertisements for Myself on the Way Out"; how much more reasonable his sense of proportion is from that of the mournful braggart of the first paragraph of *Advertisements,* alas "imprisoned with a perception which will settle for nothing less than making a revolution in the consciousness of our time." However much he might have somewhat shifted a good many sensibilities, he did not create the revolution. But what tools he still has to create major fiction—immense energy; great memory; fine eye and ear; great stylistic facility; considerable charm; consuming curiosity; a quick, leaping imagination; striking intelligence. What has been missing in his fiction (but present in *Armies*) since *The Naked and the Dead* is what so much helped to make his first published novel, for all its faults, still his most compelling one. The most acute critic of Mailer pinned the missing element down for us in *Advertisements.* A depression set in once it was obvious that the war novel was going to be a best seller, for

> I probably had been hoping *The Naked and the Dead* would have a modest success, that everyone who read it would think it was extraordinary, but nonetheless the book would not change my life too much. I wished at that time to protect a modest condition. Many of my habits, even the character of my talent, depended on my humility—that word which has become part of the void of our time. . . . No surprise then if I was a modest young man when the war was over. I knew I was not much better and I was conceivably worse than most of the men I had come to know. At least a large part of me felt that way, and it was the part in command while I was writing *The Naked and the Dead.*

However tempting it is to say that Mailer can only write about himself, it is still true that he will only write major fiction when he cleans up not the sludge of his style—as he had to do when he left *The Vil-*

lage Voice—but his habit of subordinating the subject matter to his ego instead of his ego to the subject matter. Only in the war novel was there the happy combination of modesty and objective correlative which permitted a true surrender to the imaginative effort coming from himself. No megalomaniac wrote *Barbary Shore*; in fact, squarely in the middle of the book is the confused young author, wandering about in his attempt to grow up. He's still wandering in *The Deer Park,* except that now he is beginning to flex with self-conscious stylistic preenings and dogged profundities. At or near the center of Mailer's last two novels is a bright boy showing off, except that in *Why Are We in Vietnam?* Mailer found with D. J. a way to accommodate the pull between his exhibitionism and his acute social criticism. The novel is a brilliant *tour de force,* but it still does not engage us all that deeply; it is not for Mailer "the covenant of his worth," the great "novel which would lift him at a bound" to the creative plateau which *The Naked and the Dead* pointed toward. The quoted phrases are from "The Man Who Studied Yoga"—of all his fictional efforts the one which has, line for line, the most felt life. Since Sam "lacks energy and belief . . . it is left for him to write an article some day about the temperament of the ideal novelist." This is, of course, what I am doing here, and it seems particularly comical to insist that Mailer regain a certain modesty toward experience and toward his own fiction when the struggle to overcome that modesty was clearly necessary to free the energy without which major fiction cannot be written. Yet his two-decade-long obsession with the workings of his mind does seem to preclude imaginative efforts as compelling as Book One of *Armies.* Here, his fascination with Norman Mailer and his ironic control of that fascination stand in striking counterpoise to the larger social and historical moment, but Mailer has not approached this kind of success with the subsequent harnessings of his persona.

This explains in good part why Mailer's imagination can be so strong and yet so flighty and why for all of his control of physical, emotional, and verbal nuance it has become hard to imagine him creating a group of characters who interact with increasing intensity over hundreds of pages. Would they not eventually begin to bore him? And then—whether by forced insights or conjectures, zany intrusions or gratuitous stylistic pyrotechnics—there would be Norman Mailer running around in the book. With the possible exception of Croft, has any of his characters ever approached being as interesting as the protagonist of *The Armies of the Night*?

All of this is tied up with Mailer's need to present extreme characters in extreme situations. Perhaps this became in his last two novels not as much a need of offering (as he put it in a much different context) "the most extravagant amalgams of possibility," but of keeping himself interested. It is so easy to say that like Burroughs, Genet, and Céline, Mailer has become obsessed with the extremes of experience, and we cannot expect him now to concern himself with more extended versions of Sam Slavoda, to render with the same delicacy characters whose triumphs can only be small ones. He did this with himself (of course!) in *Armies,* but the same book gives ample testimony of how much more sympathy he has than Burroughs, Genet, or Céline ever seemed to possess. In a quite literal sense, it remains to be seen whether he will write really great fiction by adding to his formidable powers the generosity of spirit of the twenty-four-year-old who completed *The Naked and the Dead* or the forty-five-year-old who completed *The Armies of the Night.* What we shall almost certainly see, if Norman Mailer is granted long life, are a good many more books by him. But what will be the precise mixtures of discipline and self-indulgence, integrity and opportunism, passion and affectation, invention and repetition? Mailer has now had an international reputation for a quarter of a century, he is fifty, and at his most recent count he has published eighteen books, yet it is impossible to predict with even relative sureness what turns his literary career will take. But then it is altogether fitting that the future of a man who has for so long offered so many amalgams of possibility be an open question.

Notes

page
vii–viii. "At Matthausen . . . with it."—George Steiner, "Naked But Not
Dead," *Encounter,* December, 1961, p. 67.

viii. "the commonplaces . . . and Forlornness."—Saul Bellow, *Herzog*
(New York: The Viking Press, 1964), p. 75.

ix. "if Norman . . . his voice."—Susan Sontag, "On Paul Goodman,"
New York Review of Books, September 21, 1972, p. 10.

3. "he had . . . to do."—Philip Young, *Ernest Hemingway* (New
York: Rinehart and Company, Inc., 1952), p. 1.

4. "The captain . . . at it.' "—Norman Mailer, *Advertisements for
Myself* (New York: G. P. Putnam's Sons, 1959), p. 70 (hereafter
cited as *Advertisements*).

"The Pacific . . . PM editorials."—*Ibid.,* p. 28.

"His ears . . . a book?"—Louise Levita, "The *Naked* are Fanatics
and *The Dead* Don't Care," *New York Star Magazine,* August 22,
1948, p. 4 (hereafter cited as *Star* interview).

5. "By their . . . more insular"—Norman Mailer, *The Naked and the
Dead* (New York: Rinehart and Company, Inc., 1948), p. 72 (hereafter cited as *Naked*).

"People say . . . better world."—"Rugged Time," *New Yorker,*
October 23, 1948, p. 25. The word "proportions" was misprinted
"propositions" in the article. Mailer was kind enough to point out
the twenty-five-year-old misprint in his review of this manuscript.

6. "everybody, literate . . . be evident. . . ."—Norman Mailer, *Of a
Fire on the Moon* (New York: New American Library, 1970), pp.
143–46 (hereafter cited as *Fire*). There will be considerable discussion of the Navigator in chapters three and four.

7. "Beneath the . . . of violence. . . ."—Norman Mailer, *The Presidential Papers* (New York: Bantam Books, 1964), p. 136 (hereafter
cited as *Papers*). Since I will be writing of Mailer's responding to
his characters and of the novel itself as having an existence which is
to some extent independent of his wishes, it might be added that for
Mailer himself, this is indeed the case. The author has said that
novel writing is a relation and not an experience because "it may
consist of several experiences which are braided together; or it may
consist of many experiences which are all more or less similar, *or
indeed it may consist of two kinds of experiences which are an-
tagonistic to each other.* [Italics mine.] Throughout all of this I've

261

spoken of characters *emerging*. [Italics Mailer's.] Quite often they don't emerge; they fail to emerge. And what one's left with is the *dull compromise which derives from two kinds of experiences* warring with one another. . . . [Italics mine.] [Characters emerge not only from myself]; they are also emerging from the book. A book takes on its own life in the writing. . . . Very often I'll feel a certain shame for what I've done with a novel. I won't say it's the novel that's bad; I'll say it's I who was bad. Almost as if the novel did not really belong to me, as if it was something raised by me like a child" ("Writers at Work: Interview with Norman Mailer," *Paris Review*, No. 31 [Winter–Spring, 1964], p. 49 [hereafter cited as *Paris Review* interview]). The first line I italicized is clearly the case in *Naked,* and the second helps to explain the characterization of Hearn.

9. "there were . . . mold them."—*Naked,* p. 717.

"living like . . . fifteen months"—*Advertisements,* pp. 93–94.

10. "phenomenal talent . . . single gift."—Norman Podhoretz, "Norman Mailer: The Embattled Vision," in *Recent American Fiction,* ed. by Joseph J. Waldmeir (Boston: Houghton Mifflin Co., 1963), p. 185.

11. "The Naked . . . at the start."—Harris Deinstfrey, "The Fiction of Norman Mailer," in *On Contemporary Literature,* ed. by Richard Kostelanetz (New York: Avon Books, 1964), pp. 422–23.

"contained in . . . with terror."—Charles C. Walcutt, *American Literary Naturalism: A Divided Stream* (Minneapolis: University of Minnesota Press, 1956), p. 17.

12. "the interweaving . . . *Moby Dick.*"—This is from p. xvii of Chester Eisinger's introduction to the Holt, Rinehart & Winston paperback edition of the novel.

"work a spasm through Croft's fingers"—*Naked,* p. 530.

13. "Entrenched in . . . it all."—Ihab Hassan, *Radical Innocence: Studies in the Contemporary American Novel* (New York: Harper & Row, Publishers, 1966), p. 144.

14. "then all . . . years ago."—Hassan catches this closing and predominating effect of *The Naked and the Dead* with an interestingly similar image: "The last section of the novel removes us from all the characters we have got to know intimately, from their trials and tribulations, as if they had all been lost in an absurd cosmic shuffle. From the first moment of the invasion, "Wave," to the last, "Wake," effort is wasted and purpose lost. The ending brings no resolution; the camera simply fades off leaving bubbles on a scarcely rippled surface" (*ibid.,* p. 149).

"war . . . ultimate expression."—John Dos Passos, *Three Soldiers* (Boston: Houghton Mifflin Co., 1964), p. 310. The passage is quoted in John M. Muste's "Norman Mailer and John Dos Passos: The Question of Influence," *Modern Fiction Studies,* Vol. 17 (1971), p. 374. In the opening part of his article, Mr. Muste contrasts enough of the techniques and purposes of *U.S.A.* and *The Naked and the*

Dead to argue very convincingly that Mailer's novel is not—as so many have claimed—a rehash of Dos Passos' greatest work.

15. "it brings . . . jungle air."—Diana Trilling, "The Moral Radicalism of Norman Mailer," *Claremont Essays* (New York: Harcourt, Brace and World, Inc., 1964), p. 182.

15–16. ". . . from man's . . . of our existence."—*Naked*, p. 323.

16. "man is a . . . the Superman."—Willard Huntington Wright, ed., *The Philosophy of Nietzsche* (New York: The Modern Library, 1954), p. 8.
"to seek . . . crisis of modernity."—Werner Dannhauser, "Friedrich Nietzsche," in *History of Political Philosophy,* ed. by Leo Strauss and Joseph Cropsey (New York: Rand-McNally & Company, 1963), p. 742.

16–17. "society, the . . . circumstances castration."—The quoted phrases are from *The Will to Power* and are quoted in Conor Cruise O'Brien, "The Gentle Nietzscheans," *New York Review of Books,* November 5, 1970, p. 13.

17. "Nietzsche does . . . of nobility."—Dannhauser, "Friedrich Nietzsche," p. 742.
"like a large . . . be indefinable."—*Naked*, p. 182.

18. "he's been there."—Ralph Ellison," in *Writers at Work: The Paris Review Interviews, Second Series,* ed. by Malcolm Cowley (New York: The Viking Press, 1963), p. 321.

19. "There were . . . and mighty hunger."—*Naked*, p. 415.
"I want . . . in detail."—James Baldwin, "The Black Boy Looks at the White Boy," *Esquire,* May, 1961, p. 105.
". . . he couldn't escape . . . fascinated him."—*Naked*, p. 85.

20. "he is alone . . . her body."—*Ibid.*, p. 414.
"phallus-shell . . . into the earth."—*Ibid.*, p. 568.

20–21. "the natural role . . . is anxiety."—*Ibid.*, p. 177.

21. "a preview of the future."—*Ibid.*, p. 324.
"every man . . . turn it outward."—*Ibid.*, p. 176.
". . . they forgot . . . a human being."—*Ibid.*, p. 698.
"a man who . . . burn it out."—*Ibid.*, p. 323.

22. "I was sure . . . Moby Dick."—Harvey Breit, *The Writer Observed* (Cleveland: World Publishing Company, 1956), p. 199.
". . . death and . . . so baldly."—"Norman Mailer," *Current Biography: 1948* (New York: H. W. Wilson, 1948), p. 410.

22–23. "Gallagher stared . . . climax of words."—*Naked*, p. 447.

23. "Croft was . . . his feet."—*Ibid.*
"For an instant . . . unloading detail."—*Ibid.*, p. 28.

24. "opened to Croft . . . portents of power."—*Ibid.*, p. 40.
"numb throbbing . . . be the same."—*Ibid.*, p. 40.
"crude unformed . . . his soul."—*Ibid.*, p. 156.
"We you . . . Yank"—*Ibid.*, p. 49.

26. "Croft experienced . . . on his jaws."—*Ibid.*, p. 495.
"Croft had an . . . was traveling."—*Ibid.*, p. 634.
"innate or . . . to take."—*Ibid.*, pp. 634–35.

27. "He is that way . . . of adjustment."—*Ibid.*, p. 156.
    "ancestors pushed . . . endless hatred."—*Ibid.*, p. 164.
28. "Croft kept looking . . . Everything."—*Ibid.*, p. 709.
28–29. "The closer . . . reached it."—*Ibid.*, p. 699.
29. "annoyed at . . . the patrol"—*Paris Review* interview, p. 37. In this 1963 interview Mailer said that some war novels he had read stimulated his desire to write a short novel about a long patrol before he had even gone overseas: "And I began to create my characters. All the while I was overseas a part of me was working on this long patrol. I even ended up in a reconnaissance outfit which I had asked to get into. A reconnaissance outfit, after all, tends to take long patrols." But in the 1948 *Star* interview (p. 5) he said: "But I didn't see too much combat—a couple of fire fights and skirmishes. The platoon's most eventful patrol had occurred before I joined them. They had a three-day patrol behind the enemy lines, and I kept hearing about it the whole time I was with them. Everything in the book really happened somewhere in the war."
30. "That Croft was a *boy*, all right."—*Naked*, p. 459.
    "the existential . . . through action."—Edmond Volpe, "James Jones–Norman Mailer," in *Contemporary American Novelists,* ed. by Harry T. Moore (Carbondale, Ill.: Southern Illinois University Press, 1964), p. 116.
31. "has selected . . . real sacrifice."—James Scott, "The Individual and Society: Norman Mailer Versus William Styron" (Ph.D. diss., Syracuse University, 1965), p. 51.
    "blunted and . . . stupefied"—*Naked*, p. 673.
    "Israel is . . . the nations."—*Ibid.*, p. 483.
32. "rather than . . . this venture."—Scott, "Individual and Society," p. 50.
    ". . . he had carried . . . nothing mattered"—*Naked*, pp. 681–82.
33. "From time to . . . vast hopelessness."—*Ibid.*
    "the most . . . in America."—*Current Biography*, p. 408.
    "the bitterness . . . had followed"—*Ibid.*, p. 704.
    the lust for power and the longing for love—Hans Morgenthau, "Love and Power," *Commentary*, March, 1962, pp. 247–51.
    "I won't . . . from nobody"—*Naked*, p. 32.
33–34. " 'The only thing . . . your integrity"—*Ibid.*, p. 326.
34. "style without . . . the world"—Podhoretz, "Embattled Vision," p. 188.
    "everything is . . . touch it."—*Naked*, p. 350.
35. "a dilettante . . . sewers"—*Ibid.*
    "The trouble . . . the mountain."—Podhoretz, "Embattled Vision," p. 189.
36. "the desperate . . . their minds."—*Naked*, p. 174.
    "there was . . . the same."—Norman Mailer, *The Deer Park* (New York: New American Library, 1964), p. 294 (hereafter cited as *Deer Park*).
    "he would . . . or die."—*Naked*, pp. 326–27.

37. "the contest . . . the peak."; "the kind . . . few minutes."—*Ibid.,* pp. 497–98.
"Hearn, however . . . early morning."—*Ibid.,* p. 502.
"the unique . . . another Croft."—*Ibid.,* p. 580.
38. " 'It is . . . a value."—*Ibid.,* p. 584.
"the decisions . . . seemed unimportant"; "He was . . . the pass."
—*Ibid.,* p. 602.
39. "This morning . . . the mountain."—*Ibid.,* p. 601.
40–41. As Irving Howe . . . to Mailer.—Irving Howe, *Politics and the Novel* (Cleveland and New York: The World Publishing Company, 1962), p. 160. As is often the case, Howe's observations deserve repetition: "The growth of ideology, I would suggest, is closely related to the accumulation of social pressures. It is when men no longer feel that they have adequate choices in their styles of life, when they conclude that there are no longer possibilities for honorable maneuver and compromise, when they decide that the time has come for "ultimate" social loyalties and political decisions—it is then that ideology begins to flourish. Ideology reflects a hardening of commitment, the freezing of opinion into system."
41. "brought the . . . and privilege." Podhoretz, "Embattled Vision," p. 191.
"opportunity to . . . never achieve."—Norman Mailer, *Barbary Shore* (New York: New American Library, 1951), p. 205.
41–42. "the epitaph . . . lives in.'—Chester Eisinger, *Fiction of the Forties* (Chicago: University of Chicago Press, 1963), p. 93.
42. " 'existentialist' in . . . people involved."—Podhoretz, "Embattled Vision," p. 191.
43. "It seems . . . way it is.' "—*Advertisements,* p. 92.
"this divorce . . . of absurdity."—Albert Camus, *The Myth of Sisyphus and Other Essays* (New York: Random House, 1961), p. 5. The book's best single description of this process is found on pages 8–11. Mailer's statement on page 93 of *Advertisements,* "Willy-nilly I had had existentialism forced upon me," is meaningful in this context. For a good indication of the way in which the tone of Mailer's fiction was affected by this movement from intellection to emotional apprehension, compare Goldstein's perception of the absurd (quoted on page 33 of this study) with the half-mad Lannie's evocation of the behavior of the German guards in the death camps in her attempt to explain why she gave herself to the FBI agent (*Barbary Shore,* pp. 152–53).
"prominent and empty"; "scared, excited . . . gauche, grim"; "success had . . . the present"—*Advertisements,* pp. 92–93.
44. "This was . . . was unreal."—*Ibid.*
"the weird . . . all inhabit"—Podhoretz, "Embattled Vision," p. 193.
45. "a world . . . promised land."—Camus, *Sisyphus,* p. 5.
"represents and . . . social life."—Howe, *Politics,* p. 160.
"*Barbary Shore* . . . destroy itself."—*Advertisements,* p. 94.

46. "the insoluble . . . the Colossi"—*Ibid.*, p. 213. The essay was written in 1953.

"whose ultimate . . . enemy soldier"—*Ibid.*, p. 205.

47. "almost certainly . . . political life"; "the faint . . . socialist world."—*Ibid.*, p. 213.

"Yet, after . . . idea alive."—*Ibid.*, p. 203.

"as socialists . . . tragedy itself."—*Ibid.*, pp. 203–4.

48. "virtually a . . . the GI."—David Dempsey, "The Dusty Answer of Modern War," *New York Times Book Review*, May 9, 1948, p. 6.

49. "the choice . . . emotional control."—Anthony West, "East Meets West, Author Meets Allegory," *New Yorker*, June 9, 1951, pp. 108–9.

It is not . . . seventies deepens.—Two weeks after I first wrote this sentence I came across the following one: "No social scientist has yet come up with a theory of mass society that is entirely satisfying; no novelist has quite captured its still amorphous symptoms—*a peculiar blend of frenzy and sluggishness* [italics mine], amiability and meanness" (Irving Howe, "Mass Society and Post-Modern Fiction," in *A World More Attractive* [Freeport, N.Y.: Books for Libraries, Inc., 1963]).

50. "There are no . . . of it."—*Barbary Shore*, pp. 153–54.

"the falling rate"—*Ibid.*, p. 155.

"Barbary Shore . . . so unearthly."—*Paris Review* interview, p. 40.

51. "Today, the enemy is vague."—*Advertisements*, p. 188.

"subterranean river . . . the nation."—*Papers*, p. 38.

"a kind . . . and revolutionaries."—*Advertisements*, p. 94.

53–54. "embody his . . . seem significant"—Howe, "Mass Society," pp. 91–92.

54. "But in . . . to show."—*Ibid.*

"needed . . . evil genius."—*Paris Review* interview, p. 48.

55. "the experience . . . of my books."—*Advertisements*, pp. 232–33.

55–56. ". . . something broke . . . their passage."—*Ibid.*, pp. 234–35.

56. "the style . . . its air."—*Ibid.*, p. 235.

57. "Stores looked . . . cabin cruiser."—*Deer Park*, pp. 7–8.

58. "Like so . . . business operations."—*Deer Park*, p. 50.

"What he sees . . . considered 'good.' "—Podhoretz, "Embattled Vision," pp. 197–98.

"his trembling passage in Desert D'Or"—Dienstfrey, "Fiction of Norman Mailer," p. 433.

59. "he had begun . . . him fragile."—*Deer Park*, p. 91.

"Here is truly . . . *the Dead.*"—Trilling, "Moral Radicalism," p. 191.

59–60. "was his dream . . . the other."—*Deer Park*, p. 97.

60. ". . . the core . . . relatively so."—*Ibid.*, pp. 106–7.

62. "The past . . . create it."—*Ibid.*, p. 146.

"The essence . . . was not."—*Ibid.*, p. 220.

"For where . . . and death."—*Advertisements*, p. 324.

63. "I was . . . outside them."—*Ibid.*, p. 238.

"I used . . . a drug."—*Deer Park*, p. 85.

"wars and . . . burned orphans"—*Ibid.*, p. 45.

64. "of courage . . . changing proportion"—*Ibid.*, p. 276. The source for the last phrase in this sentence was McLeod's comment, "Action always gives ballast to theory" (*Barbary Shore*, p. 163).
"life is . . . to use"—*Deer Park*, p. 300.
"I had . . . concluded artifact."—*Ibid.*, p. 303.

65. "where orphans . . . simple fact."—*Ibid.*, p. 318.
"He'll kick . . . that kid."—*Ibid.*, p. 170.

66. "life is . . . the same. . . ."—*Advertisements*, pp. 349–50.

67. "Nobility and . . . the end."; "Slobs . . . to think."—*Deer Park*, p. 128.
"God-in-banishment . . . true Heaven."—*Ibid.*, p. 281.

68. "So let . . . dead dawn."—*Ibid.*, p. 139.
"it's all right. . . . More education."—*Ibid.*, p. 291.

69. *"The Deer Park* . . . his characters."—Bruce Cook, "Norman Mailer: The Temptation to Power," *Renascence*, Vol. 14 (Fall, 1965), p. 213. Fred W. Dupee very lucidly extends the observation. After describing Mailer's superb observation of the manners and comic conversations of the movie magnates, he continues: "The routines of the call-girls form a weird dance-like pattern within the slowly moving narrative. In the rendering of such things Mailer's passion for experience is matched by his expert knowledge of what he writes about. How does it happen, then, that his panorama of iniquity is constantly threatening to turn into a waxworks display? For one thing, Mailer's trio of heroes, Eitel, Faye, and O'Shaughnessy, are too sententious and loquacious and self-conscious. In their frequent colloquies they constitute a sort of committee interminably 'chewing on' . . . the agenda of the day. And with much help from the author, by way of his often intrusive comments on the action, they just about chew the hell out of it . . . they all but convert the experience of modern corruption into something inert, dry and abstract" (Fred W. Dupee, "The American Norman Mailer," *Commentary*, February, 1960, p. 132). When, in November, 1955, Mailer was asked what he was trying to say in *The Deer Park,* he replied, "Everything I know about life at the age of thirty-two" (*Advertisements*, p. 269). The novel would have been stronger had he left a few things out.
"I think . . . to altogether."; "God can . . . other Gods."—*Paris Review* interview, p. 42.
"It is . . . to maturity."—Dupee, "The American Norman Mailer," p. 131.

70. "But the . . . grow up."—*Ibid.* I do not see why this theme, which can be found in Western literature as far back as *The Odyssey,* should be designated as Freudian.
"against all . . . of sin."—*Deer Park*, p. 318. I do not mean that the novel is not schematic enough; *The Deer Park*, "The Time of Her Time," "Advertisements for Myself on the Way Out," and *An American Dream* all suffer from over-schematism. My point is that the schematism of this novel is confused.

71. "the assumption . . . the laity."—Marvin Mudrick, "Mailer and Styron: Guests of the Establishment," *Hudson Review*, Vol. 17 (Autumn, 1964), p. 356.
    "I was . . . my shoulder."—*Deer Park*, p. 114.
72. "Before I . . . too great."—*Advertisements*, p. 243.
    "into the . . . of chaos."—Norman Mailer, *Cannibals and Christians* (New York: The Dial Press, 1966), p. 108 (hereafter cited as *Cannibals*).
72–73. "he knew . . . hospital bed."—*Deer Park*, p. 294.
73. "the orgasm . . . our becoming."—*Papers*, pp. 199–200. In the October, 1962, *Realist* interview he said: "When you make love, whatever is good in you or bad in you goes out into someone else. I mean this literally. I'm not interested in the biochemistry of it, the electromagnetism of it, nor in how the psychic waves are passed back and forth. . . . All I know is that when one makes love, one changes a woman slightly and a woman changes you slightly" (*ibid.*, p. 140).
74. "flat and familiar dispirit"—*Advertisements*, p. 158.
    "as a covenant . . . bountiful complexity."—*Ibid.*, p. 183.
    "reality is . . . what it is."—*Ibid.*, p. 179.
    "One could . . . not exist."; "Destroy time . . . be ordered."—*Ibid.*, pp. 184–85.
    For one thing, . . . that night.—". . . the books would revolve around the adventures of a mythical hero, Sergius O'Shaugnessy, who would travel through many worlds, through pleasure, business, communism, church, working class, crime, homosexuality and mysticism. To thicken the scheme, I was going to twist and scatter Time, having many of the characters appear in different books, but with their ages altered" (*Advertisements*, p. 154). The first novel, which dealt with the world of pleasure, obviously became *The Deer Park*.
75. ". . . when Time . . . the future."—*Ibid.*, p. 521.
76. "his appetite . . . novel situations"—*Ibid.*, p. 158.
    "a little . . . fantasy triumphant."—*Ibid.*, p. 175.
    "Is it . . . make jokes."—*Ibid.*, p. 176.
77. "self-critical . . . breakfast eggs."; "Sam the . . . running cold." —*Ibid.*, pp. 181–82. This is the first example of Mailer's proclaiming his hatred of pornography. His tendency to oppose in print all sexual activity which does not bring with it meaningful conflict is treated more fully in the discussion of *Why Are We in Vietnam?*
    "the sword . . . new experience."—*Ibid.*, p. 278.
78. "the only . . . sexual revolution."—*Ibid.*, p. 325.
    "Rewriting . . . of it."—*Ibid.*, p. 265. The validity of both of Mailer's comments (cited above this quotation) about the nature and intensity of his new commitment is supported by the recollection of close friends. Daniel Wolf, the editor of *The Village Voice* and one of the two people to whom Mailer dedicated *The Deer Park*, has said, "he'd stopped being concerned about being a writer, and became much more concerned as a bringer of truth." Judith Feiffer, wife of the cartoonist, said that during this period "almost every-

body . . . was an actor in some Hip dream." Both quotations appear in Brock Brower, "Always the Challenger," *Life*, September 24, 1965, p. 111.

"with his brain full of marijuana"—*Advertisements*, p. 268.

"to keep . . . the temptations"—*Ibid.*, p. 269.

"is to be . . . as possible." *Ibid.*, p. 276.

79. "my self-analysis . . . a war."—*Ibid.*, p. 277.

"to give . . . upon us"—*Ibid.*, p. 278.

"I think . . . photograph me."—"Rugged Time," p. 25.

79–80. "the most . . . of view."—*Advertisements*, p. 238.

80. "Mailer's sense . . . I am."—John W. Aldridge, "Victim and Analyst," *Commentary*, October, 1966, p. 131.

"the column . . . the past"—*Advertisements*, p. 283.

"If I do not . . . *Voice*."—*Ibid.*, p. 284.

"seeking to . . . of existence"—*Ibid.*, p. 325. This is from "A Public Notice on Waiting for Godot," which Mailer published in *The Village Voice* a week after his seventeenth column. I have treated it as one of the columns.

81. "because I . . . pull it off."—*Ibid.*, p. 496.

"itself up . . . first night."—*Ibid.*, p. 495.

"weeks to . . . to win."—*Ibid.*, p. 500.

83. "neo-Marxist . . . human energy."—*Ibid.*, p. 357.

"a good working amateur philosopher"—Norman Mailer, *The Armies of the Night* (New York: New American Library, Hardcover Edition, 1968), p. 91 (hereafter cited as *Armies*).

"written in . . . many pieces."—Norman Mailer, *Existential Errands* (Boston: Little, Brown and Company, 1972), p. x.

"politicians, medicos, . . . endless communicatiors."—*Papers*, pp. 39–40.

84. "If we . . . some whisky."—*Advertisements*, p. 382.

"down sharp while others were passing me."—*Ibid.*, p. 477.

85. "But there . . . another's imposing."—Tony Tanner, *City of Words* (London: Jonathan Cape, 1971), p. 17.

86. ". . . it's no . . . get there."—*Paris Review* interview, p. 58.

89. "existentialism is . . . be nothing"—Carl Michaelson, *Christianity and the Existentialists* (New York: Harper & Row, Publishers, 1956), p. 10.

"Probably, we . . . a stop."—*Advertisements*, p. 338. Unless otherwise indicated, all citations between pages 89 and 104 of this chapter refer to quotations from "The White Negro," *Advertisements*, pp. 337–58.

89–90. "if our . . . the self."—*Ibid.*, p. 339. Mailer also places "the square's" terror of self in historical context: "The Second World War presented a mirror to the human condition which blinded anyone who looked into it. For if tens of millions were killed in concentration camps out of the inexorable agonies and contractions of super-states founded upon the always insoluble contradictions of injustice, one was then obliged also to see that no matter how crippled and perverted an image of man was the society he had

created, it was nonetheless his creation, his collective creation . . .
and if society was so murderous, then who could ignore the most
hideous of questions about his own nature?" (*ibid.*, p. 338).

90. "narcissistic detachment . . . the psychopath."—*Ibid.*, p. 343.
91. "the very . . . analyst himself."—*Ibid.*, pp. 345–46.
91–92. "two strong . . . candy-store keeper"—*Ibid.*, p. 347.
92. "to divorce oneself from society"—*Ibid.*, p. 339.
92–93. "If there . . . of nature."—*Fire*, p. 189.
93–94. "The psychopath . . . to murder."—*Advertisements*, pp. 346–47.
94. "incompatibles have come to bed"—*Ibid.*, p. 342.
94–95. "murders—if . . . imprisons him."—*Ibid.*, p. 347. This is the
seed of Mailer's idea that one should only love that which offers
growth.
97. "to be . . . next orgasm."—*Ibid.*, p. 351. In keeping with the
theory of reality to be discussed on pages 101–3, Mailer admitted
that this was his own hypothesis.
a long note—The breakneck speed which the sentence develops is
impressive, but the problems created in the easy equation of a univocal "good" for markedly different views are quickly evident even
for the reader who has made no attempt to unearth the bases of
Mailer's positions. For example, Reich's orgone belongs in its human
manifestations to a closed system with an inner final cause, the
satisfaction of *our* needs. Shaw's life force is transcendent, and its
end lies outside the individual in the creation of a higher biological
organism. As Mailer gradually extended his transcendent positions
he, for example, agreed with Shaw that sex primarily exists for
reproduction and did not regard reproduction (as Reich did) as a
by-product of our sexual needs.

We seem to have here the statement that the ultimate reality, the
nature of man, is a mighty instinctual lover of pleasure and power.
It is buried within us and we can best realize our nature by freeing
this trapped God and experiencing the benefits of power, pleasure,
and perception He would bring to us. (This metaphorical immanent
God is not to be confused with the literal, transcendent God who
plays such an important role in Mailer's post-1957 thought. Although
this latter God manifests part of himself in our unconscious, it is
precisely a part—he is far more than one person's instincts.)

Although His nature cannot be fully liberated, it is still the fixed
core of our being, and inasmuch as we are not acting to free it we
are unnatural. This regaining of our immanent, primal essence seems
to me to be what Lawrence urged (and Eitel sought to achieve),
and were this clearly and simply Mailer's only position, those critics
would be justified who have called him a romantic primitivist—
an essentialist and not an existentialist at all. But later in "The
White Negro," Mailer asserted the familiar existentialist position
that a man's nature is not a set entity, but that with every action he
creates a new self and a new truth about what it means to be a
particular human being. When Mailer writes that in Hip "each man

is glimpsed as a collection of possibilities" (*Advertisements*, p. 354), he is stating an existential view of man as surely as Heidegger was when he stated that possibility is higher than and prior to actuality or as Sartre was when he claimed that man is the future of man.

George Schrader has claimed that Mailer was an essentialist who advocated having "orgasm over and over again, each time more than the last and with no development" and that "he seeks to live only in the *instant* which is unchanged in being repeated" ("Norman Mailer and the Despair of Defiance," *Yale Review*, Vol. 51 [December, 1961], p. 274) when Mailer's emphasis was on how unattainable the ultimate orgasm and perpetual instant was. What Schrader attributed to Mailer was something very close to Eitel's noble savage theory, one which Mailer never really accepted and certainly did not in "The White Negro." Schrader correctly accused the latter of being a romantic but said that "European existentialists have been considerably opposed to all varieties of romanticism" (*ibid.*, p. 270). Mailer's romanticism centers not in his belief that perfection can be achieved only in the art object—he has too didactic a view of art for that—but in his emphasis upon the quest for an ever-receding goal. In contrast to Schrader's claim of the existential opposition to romanticism, this quest bears a strong resemblance to Sartre's description of the inevitably futile attempt to fuse the *en-soi* and the *pour-soi* except that for Mailer the quest is a less "romantically" hopeless one (see pages 110–13 of this study). If it is argued that Sartre objects to this inevitable romanticism and Schrader's claim is thus still valid, we might turn to the obvious comparisons that might be drawn from William Barrett's acute comments on the quest for Being in Wordsworth (William Barrett, *Irrational Man* [Garden City, N.Y.: Doubleday and Co., Inc., 1962], pp. 125–26; and Heidegger: *Being and Time,* tr. by John Macquarrie and Edward Robinson [New York: Harper & Row, Publishers, 1962], pp. 304–11). As the discussion of Mailer's later writings proceeds, we will see the hipster's desire to grow fused with a quest for Being, though from what I can make out of *Being and Time,* Mailer's conception of Being is much different from Heidegger's.

would go to a Reichian one—*Advertisements*, p. 301. On page 424 of the same book, Mailer claims that "Wilhelm Reich as a mind" is hip but "Wilhelm Reich as a stylist" is square.

98. "incompatibles have . . . into death."—*Ibid.*, p. 342–43.

"the universe . . . the center"—*Ibid.*, p. 352.

"the hip . . . *with it*"—The quotation is found in Mailer's reply to a criticism of "The White Negro" by Ned Polsky, both of which were printed in the Winter, 1958, *Dissent* and collected in *Advertisements* (p. 369).

100. "Hip abdicates . . . with it."—*Ibid.*, p. 353.

101. "This I . . . larger whole."—William Barrett, *What is Existentialism?* (New York: Grove Press, Inc., 1964), pp. 41–42. This is from an ingenious imaginary monologue that Barrett constructs for the young Hegel. In keeping with Hegel's belief in a logical progression

of character and historical development, the quotation suggests that man does indeed consistently evolve for the better. The emphasis on context is existential; the belief in a process which is consistently ameliorative in its relation to man is not.

102. "What dominates . . . the present."—*Advertisements*, p. 354. Anticipating the charge that his theory of the subjective nature of reality is undermined by the fact that it is *his* theory, limited by his energy and perception level, Mailer admits on page 351, "What I have offered above is an hypothesis, no more, and there is not the hipster alive who is not absorbed in his own tumultuous hypotheses." "reality is . . . by man."—Howard M. Harper, Jr., *Desperate Faith* (Chapel Hill: University of North Carolina Press, 1967), p. 127.

103. "It's not . . . their actions."—*Deer Park*, p. 171.
"in the deepest . . . against them."—Podhoretz, "Embattled Vision," p. 186.

104. "the psychopath . . . back again."—*Advertisements*, p. 347.
"has been . . . conventional psychopath."—*Ibid.*, p. 343.

105. "If there . . . a sonofabitch."—*Naked*, p. 607.

106. That novel's . . . in print again.—The Christ of the end of Book One of *The Armies of the Night*, who gave Mailer so much for so little, is quickly replaced by the usual embattled God in Book Two.
"For I . . . man's efforts."—*Advertisements*, p. 324.
". . . there is . . . to His."—*Ibid.*, p. 380.

108–9. "In Hip . . . beautiful mystic."—*Ibid.*, p. 381.

109. ". . . if there . . . over God."—*Papers*, p. 193.
"a monumental bureaucrat of repetition"; "If the world . . . overthrow him."—*Papers*, p. 194.

110. "I don't . . . deadening influence."—"*Playboy* Interview: Norman Mailer," *Playboy*, January, 1968, p. 74. The quotation continues: "I don't know who or where the enemy is. In fact, I don't have the remotest notion of who or what I'm working for. Sometimes I think I'm unemployed. That's despair, son." The joking tone of the last two sentences gives Mailer away. Most of the time that he is able to believe in the God-Devil struggle, he most certainly believes he is working for God.

111. "that we . . . useless passion.' "—Samuel Hux, "American Myth and Existential Vision: The Indigenous Existentialism of Mailer, Bellow, Styron and Ellison" (Ph.D. diss., University of Connecticut, 1966), p. 206.
"that hole . . . of Being"—Jean-Paul Sartre, *Being and Nothingness*, tr. by Hazel E. Barnes (New York: New Philosophical Library, 1956), p. 617. Sartre's position is perhaps most clearly stated in Orestes' speeches to Zeus in *The Flies* (Jean-Paul Sartre, *No Exit and Three Other Plays* [New York: Vintage Books, 1956], p. 120): "You are the king of gods, king of stones and stars, king of the waves of the sea. But you are not the king of man. . . . you should not have made me free." And again (p. 122): "Foreign to myself—I know it. Outside nature, against nature, without excuse, beyond

remedy, except what remedy I find within myself. But I shall not return under your law; I am doomed to have no other law but mine. Nor shall I come back to nature, the nature you found good; in it are a thousand beaten paths all leading up to you—but I must blaze my trail. For I, Zeus, am a man, and every man must find out his own way. Nature abhors man. . . ."

112. ("part of . . . of 1962")—*Papers,* p. 308.
113. "It was . . . the universe."—*Fire,* pp. 410–11.
     "has an . . . their being."—*Advertisements,* p. 386.
114. "when, in anticipation . . . by anything."—Heidegger, *Being and Time,* p. 355.
     "a being. . . a situation."—Jean-Paul Sartre, *Anti-Semite and Jew,* tr. by George J. Becker (New York: Schocken Books, Inc., 1948), p. 90.
     "Thus we . . . to ourselves. . . ."—Sartre, *Being and Nothingness,* p. 545.
     "although there . . . the bargain."—*Ibid.,* p. 548.
114–15. ". . . the reluctance . . . into Eternity."—*Papers,* pp. 213–14.
116. "the onanisms . . . born again"—*Advertisements,* p. 526.
     ". . . already on . . . empty waters."—*Ibid.,* p. 532. The quotation suggests the interrelations between Mailer's theory of time (see pages 74–75 of this study), God, soul, spirit, and excrement. The connections are schematically presented in the footnote on page 108, and more is said about the theory of excrement on pages 190–91.
117. "he is still . . . weak today."—*Fire,* p. 85.
     "a philosophy of hugely paranoid proportions"—*Cannibals,* p. 366.
118. "are not mathematical, . . . a scientist."—*Ibid.,* p. 307.
119. "with the poetic . . . pioneer observations."—*Ibid.,* p. 308.
120. "the devil . . . contemplate it."—*Ibid.,* p. 334. The following paragraph helps to explain this comment in the 1960 dialogue, "The First Morning's Interview": "Nothing in one's metaphysical scheme is as important as one's sense of the present" (*ibid.,* p. 252). Compare Mailer's theory that drugs are Devilish with the discussion of gimmicks on pages 139–42 of this work.
121. "he is . . . his 'talent')."—Wilfred Sheed, "One Man Dance Marathon," *New York Times Book Review,* August 21, 1966, p. 1.
     "had built . . . finally knowable?"—*Fire,* p. 13.
     "once, how . . . found the mark. . . ."—Norman Mailer, "The Evil in the Room," *Life,* July 28, 1972, p. 36.
     "comfortable middle-aged Aquarius"—*Ibid.,* p. 26.
122. "it was . . . scientific work."—Sigmund Freud, *Civilization and Its Discontents* (New York: W. W. Norton & Co., 1961), p. 66.
     "Mailer has . . . of ideas."—Aldridge, "Victim and Analyst," p. 131.
125. "there weren't . . . my armies."—"An Interview with Norman Mailer," *Mademoiselle,* February, 1961, p. 161 (hereafter cited as *Mademoiselle* interview).
126. "INTERVIEWERS: Does . . . be authentic. . . ."—*Ibid.,* pp. 161–63.

127. "a combination . . . Mayoralty campaign."—*Papers*, p. 63.
  "with a funny look on his face"; "I felt . . . wasn't me."—Brower, "Always the Challenger," p. 100.
  "moved out . . . orgiastic linkage."—*Ibid.*, p. 111.
127–28. "he had . . . own creature."—*Ibid.*, p. 112. As for the problems in Brower's account, he argues that the Mailers' deteriorating marriage was the model for the relationship of Eitel and Elena in *The Deer Park*, but the marriage occurred in 1954, the same year that the second draft was finished. Furthermore, Brower writes that the knife just missed Adele Mailer's heart, whereas the *New York Times* account of November 22, 1960, states that she was stabbed in the back and abdomen. One wonders if the two-and-one-half-inch blade Mailer used could have reached the heart from the back.
128. he might say in 1965 that—Brower, "Always the Challenger," p. 112. The statement continues, "I know God and the Devil are on opposite sides in this, but I don't know which side is which." In a few years he will not be able to feel the presence with as much sureness as this.
  "lying in . . . royal balls."—Norman Mailer, *Deaths for the Ladies (and other disasters)* (New York: G. P. Putnam's Sons, 1962), no pagination.
129–30. ". . . Roth is . . . not *dig*."—*Cannibals*, p. 122.
130. "for every . . . lacked courage"—Norman Mailer, "The Big Bite," *Esquire*, June, 1963, p. 28.
  "To have . . . moral coward."—Brower, "Always the Challenger," p. 102.
  "about someone . . . Liston-Patterson fight."—*Ibid.*, p. 100.
  "he found his trade ready to hand."—*Deer Park*, p. 18.
  "felt weak without a drink"—*Existential Errands*, p. 198. This was originally written in the preface to a later edition of *Deaths for the Ladies*. Mailer here describes the difficult two years following the stabbing.
131. "of existential . . . of motivation."—Norman Mailer, *An American Dream* (New York: The Dial Press, 1965), p. 8 (hereafter cited as *Dream*).
  "career seems . . . his books."—Anatole Broyard, "A Disturbance of the Peace," *New York Times Book Review*, September 17, 1967, p. 1.
  "You have a big brother somewhere."—*Dream*, p. 159.
131–32. ". . . I lay back . . . the moon."—*Ibid.*, p. 162.
132. "Let me say . . . wasn't insane."—Brower, "Always the Challenger," p. 112.
  "Hell's Angels . . . against poverty"—*Fire*, p. 137.
  "not only . . . of them."; "the dialectic . . . to themselves"—Norman Mailer, *The Prisoner of Sex* (New York: New American Library, 1971), pp. 101–3 (hereafter cited as *Prisoner*).
134. "by taking . . . unexpectedly provides."—Leo Bersani, "The Interpretation of Dreams," *Partisan Review*, Vol. 32 (Fall, 1965), p. 606.

"God was not love but courage"—*Dream*, p. 204.

"in order . . . dare insanity."—*Papers*, p. 128.

135. "There was one . . . was running."—*Dream*, p. 58.

136. " 'Are you . . . a contest."—*Ibid.*, p. 60.

"the quixotic . . . false teeth' ")—*Papers*, p. 27.

"the Messianic . . . himself with."—Dwight Macdonald, "Politics," *Esquire*, May, 1968, p. 94.

137. "Since the First . . . not die."—*Papers*, pp. 38–40.

138. "Which of . . . Judgement cease."—*Ibid.*, pp. 159–60.

139. "doing something . . . to win"—*Mademoiselle* interview, p. 161.

"which entered . . . irrevocable battle."—*Papers*, p. 238.

140. "Patterson was . . . corporation executive."—*Ibid.*, pp. 241–42.

141. "the forces . . . his people."—*Ibid.*, p. 258.

"the place for magic"; "bossland"—*Ibid.*, p. 237.

142. "Kennedy's most . . . of others."—*Ibid.*, p. 48.

143. "the moment . . . must do."—*Mademoiselle* interview, p. 160.

143–44. "a stiff . . . even scared."; "danger withdraw . . . the sand."—*Dream*, pp. 2–3.

144. "all of it . . . And missed."—*Ibid.*, p. 5.

145–46. "an older . . . more deadening."—*Papers*, p. 245.

147. "Where many . . . for politics."—*Dream*, p. 7.

"We even . . . his girl."—Norman Mailer, "The Harbors of the Moon," *Esquire*, January, 1965, p. 77.

148. "had made . . . times before."—*Dream*, pp. 1–2.

the Devil's vicar—John William Corrington, "American Dreamer," *Chicago Review*, Vol. 18 (Fall, 1965), p. 65.

"the money man inside the golden room"—Alfred Kazin, "Imagination and the Age," *The Reporter*, May 5, 1966, p. 34.

149. "upstart, whereas . . . at twenty-three."—*Dream*, p. 240.

"God and . . . the top."—*Ibid.*, p. 246.

150. ". . . God has . . . we waste. . . ."—*Papers*, p. 275.

" 'Well, B. Oswald . . . good luck."—*Dream*, pp. 240–41.

"includes a lion . . . *Caelo Terraque*."—Corrington, "American Dreamer," p. 65. *Victoria in Caelo Terraque*: "Victory on Heaven and Earth."

151. "Lying in . . . of power."—*Dream*, pp. 243–44.

"a spider . . . *York Times*."—*Ibid.*, p. 237.

"the armature . . . like clay."—*Ibid.*, p. 17.

"come to believe . . . and succubi."—*Ibid.*, p. 37.

"ready to blow the rails"—*Ibid.*, p. 28.

"certain nights go leaden with dread"—*Ibid.*, p. 8.

152. "it's just that evil has power."—*Ibid.*, p. 36. Deborah's flight from the snake rustling in Rojack's heart presumably occurred before she conclusively chose to follow the Dream of Power.

"evacuate my . . . other hooks."—*Ibid.*, p. 9.

152–53. "She had . . . his drug. . . ."—*Ibid.*, pp. 18–19.

153. "soft now . . . Portuguese man o' war."—*Ibid.*, p. 26.

154–55. "So I stood . . . to die."—*Ibid.*, pp. 11–12.

156. "The logic . . . a child."—*Papers*, p. 198. As for the retreat from

Freudian assumptions, we learn in *Dream* that Rojack "would like
to blow up poor old Freud by demonstrating that the root of neurosis
is cowardice rather than brave old Oedipus" (*ibid.*, p. 251). The
year after the novel was published, Mailer said to Brock Brower,
"The bourgeois world says life consists of solving problems. Suppose
that isn't the case. . . . Suppose life consists entirely of a series
of gambles . . . what if only cowards have problems?" (Brower,
"Always the Challenger," p. 96).

157. "Do you . . . snap."—*Dream*, p. 133.
"The soul . . . never repeats."—*Papers*, p. 194.
"Which instinct . . . my torso."—*Dream*, pp. 12–13.
158. "the only . . . a time."—*Cannibals*, p. 91.
158–59. "if the liberal . . . of peace."—*Papers*, pp. 246–47.
160. "like carrying . . . cast-iron hill"—*Dream*, p. 8. Like Reich, Mailer
believes that cancer is caused by suppressed violence.
160–61. "I had . . . of salts"; ". . . my flesh . . . to please."—*Ibid.*,
pp. 31–32.
161–62. "My hands . . . such calm."—*Ibid.*, pp. 37–38.
162. "particularly loathsome and ridiculous."; "the excremental, the sadistic, the hideous"—"Bad Boy," *Partisan Review*, Vol. 32 (Spring,
1965), p. 292.
"Postulate a . . . sensuous desires."—*Cannibals*, pp. 269–70.
163. "had a desire . . . that I knew."; "a raid . . . the Lord"; "the
monomaniacal . . . the world"; "a host . . . great thief."; "mendacity, guile . . . trick authority."—*Dream*, pp. 44–45.
164. "only in . . . and evil."—Philip Rahv, "Crime Without Punishment," in *The Myth and the Powerhouse* (New York: Farrar,
Straus and Giroux, Inc., 1965), p. 237.
165. "Tony and . . . his discomfort."—*Dream*, pp. 116–17.
166. "having psychic . . . next table"—Norman Mailer, *Miami and the
Siege of Chicago* (New York: New American Library, Signet Paperback Edition, 1968), p. 215 (hereafter cited as *Siege*).
"long, mad . . . of logomachy."—Brower, "Always the Challenger," p. 96. To turn once more to this crucial interview: ". . . if
you get marvelous sex when you're young, all right; but if you're not
ready to make a baby with that marvelous sex, then you may also be
putting something down the drain forever, which is the ability that
you had to make a baby; the most marvelous thing that was in you
may have been shot into a diaphram, or wasted on a pill. One
might be losing one's future.
"The point is that, so long as one has a determinedly atheistic and
rational approach to life, then the only thing that makes sense is
the most comprehensive promiscuous sex you can find" (*Papers*, p.
142). Eight years later, in *The Prisoner of Sex*, Mailer made a much
more sustained effort to preserve romantic possibility in procreation,
but the last sentence of the quotation argues as well as any in
Mailer's writing what he claims is his detestation of purposeless intercourse.

167. "Perversity is . . . of villainy."—Richard Poirier, "Morbid Minded-ness," *Commentary*, June, 1965, p. 91.
    "One has to . . . make life?"—*Papers*, p. 139.
    "Go to . . . is time!"—*Dream*, p. 208.
169. ". . . tropical people . . . proliferate *being*."—*Papers*, pp. 146–47. This is quite consistent with the neoprimitivist distrust of civiliza-tion which was so strong from 1955 to 1965. Mailer's Reichian proclamation that the orgasm was the inescapable existential moment continues: "Every lie we have told, every fear we have indulged, every aggression we have tamed arises at that instant to constrict the turns and possibilities of our becoming. If we gain the world and our timing is dulled—as was Stalin's and Eisenhower's—then the world is deadened, and damn our revolution, we were better without it, better to be banging away like jungle bunnies in the brush. What is at stake in the twentieth century is not the economic security of man —every bureaucrat in the world lusts to give us this—it is, on the contrary, the peril that they will extinguish the animal in us" (*Papers*, pp. 199–200). The quotation traces his opposition to the welfare state to its root.
    "caught the . . . go on."—*Dream*, pp. 268–69.
170. "in feats . . . younger men"—Rahv, "Crime Without Punishment," p. 242.
    "tending toward . . . of Hell"—Corrington, "American Dreamer," pp. 64–65.
172. "When I . . . realistic novel."—Vincent Canby, "When Irish Eyes Are Smiling, It's Norman Mailer," *New York Times*, October 27, 1968, p. 15.
173. "She was . . . was dead."—*Dream*, p. 32.
    "That blew it out."—*Ibid.*, p. 30.
    "Not Central . . . by half."—*Ibid.*, p. 51.
    "a champion sight"—*Ibid.*, p. 195.
174. "I could . . . enough, what!"—*Ibid.*, p. 12.
    "Let woman . . . a cigar."—*Prisoner*, p. 168.
174–75. ". . . 'choose now!' . . . her cunt."—*Dream*, p. 128.
175. "But I'm . . . I fear"—*Ibid.*, p. 174.
    "some rich . . . to stuff"—*Ibid.*, p. 97.
    "I know . . . little fear"—*Ibid.*, p. 179.
    " '. . . I always . . . sending up,' "—*Ibid.*, p. 197.
177. "Don't I know it, honey one"—*Ibid.*, p. 23.
    "I mean, *figure-toi*, pet . . ."—*Ibid.*, p. 25.
    "I got . . . don't complain"—*Ibid.*, p. 213.
178. "I don't . . . for me."—Joseph Roddy, "The latest Model Mailer," *Look*, May 27, 1969, p. 28.
    "He told . . . for timbre."—Conrad Knickerbocker, "A Man Des-perate for a New Life," *New York Times Book Review*, March 14, 1965, p. 39.
179. "the clue . . . one's attack."—*Armies*, p. 25. Mailer says that he learned this from Dwight Macdonald.

179–80. "Yet every . . . the night?"—*Cannibals*, p. 4.
180. "He came . . . been passed."—*Armies*, p. 188.
181. "Disc Jockey . . . over again."—Norman Mailer, *Why Are We in Vietnam?* (New York: G. P. Putnam's Sons, 1967), p. 24 (hereafter cited as *Vietnam*).
181–182. ". . . Big Luke . . . a dyke."—*Ibid.*, pp. 114–16.
182. "come to . . . good temper."—*Armies*, p. 47.
"suffers from . . . through shit."—*Vietnam*, p. 49.
183. "I'm afraid . . . of genius."—Norman Mailer, "Mr. Mailer Interviews Himself," *New York Times Book Review*, September 17, 1967, p. 48.
"own wandering . . . programmed out"; "out there in all that implosion land"—*Vietnam*, p. 8.
"wholeness, empathy and depth of awareness"—Marshall McLuhan, *Understanding Media: The Extensions of Man* (New York: New American Library, 1965), p. 21.
"huge seamless web"—*Ibid.*, p. 20.
184. "The twentieth . . . the imagination. . . ."—*Papers*, pp. 38–39.
"help to keep America insane"; "notions which . . . say, monotonous."—*Ibid.*, p. 218.
"corporation land's whip . . . at home"—*Armies*, p. 252.
"Fascism is . . . little further."—*Papers*, p. 134.
185. "their hate . . . within it."—*Armies*, pp. 86–87.
"Any play . . . technological matters."—Quoted in Neil Compton, "The Paradox of Marshall McLuhan," *New American Review*, Vol. 2, p. 93. Readers of Compton's brilliant article will realize how heavily I have leaned upon it.
"The authority . . . mysterious reasons."—*Armies*, pp. 86–87.
186. "in a modern . . . accelerating rate"; "we believe . . . go hungry."—*Cannibals*, pp. 3–4.
187. "there is . . . second rate."—*Ibid.*, p. 4.
"I am not . . . of war."—*Papers*, p. 167. Mailer is speaking here of the Right Wing, but the Cannibals are largely members of the Right Wing.
". . . they believe . . . mass graves."—*Cannibals*, p. 4.
188. "the American consciousness . . . fifty years."—*Ibid.*, p. 102.
188–89. "Then they . . . of Vietnam."—*Ibid.*, p. 103.
189–90. "Tex is . . . fuck tastefully. . . ."—*Vietnam*, pp. 17–20.
190. "closet fucks"; "cliff-hanging menopause types"; "a two minute . . . cunt fuck."—*Ibid.*, pp. 155–56.
"innocent, decent-spirited . . . of love."—*Armies*, p. 14.
190–91. "plus ghoul . . . year ago."—*Vietnam*, p. 157.
191. "is that America . . . of thoughts."—*Ibid.*, p. 36.
"committees do . . . the corporation."—*Papers*, p. 43.
"the American corporation . . . world today."—*Armies*, p. 49.
191–92. "Mailer's grasp . . . and ruthless."—Joseph Epstein, "Mailer Rides Again: Brilliant, Idiosyncratic, Unquotable," *Book World*, September 10, 1967, pp. 1, 34.
192–93. "all the minions . . . Luke's boots."—*Vietnam*, p. 46.

193. "if you . . . a *man!*"—*Ibid.*, p. 47.
"the cream of corporation corporateness"—*Ibid.*, p. 29.
". . . let Rusty . . . that deer."—*Ibid.*, p. 55.
"the commercial. . . . altogether believe."—*Cannibals*, p. 4.
194. "the highest . . . to suffocate"—*Vietnam*, p. 37.
"shedding those . . . ass beast."—*Ibid.*, pp. 127–28.
"a secret . . . a crow."—*Ibid.*, pp. 132–33.
". . . when D.J. . . . burial march. . . ."—*Ibid.*, p. 147.
195. ". . . Rusty, wetting . . . forgiveness gone."; ". . . D.J., in . . .
one father."—*Ibid.*, p. 147.
"half-fouled . . . natural hunter. . . ."—*Ibid.*, p. 175.
195–96. "Rusty, in his . . . it is."—Epstein, "Mailer Rides Again," p. 34.
196. ". . . mixed shit . . . white as a sheet!"—*Vietnam*, pp. 177–78.
"(1) the King . . . you, whoo-ee. . . ."—*Ibid.*, pp. 186–87.
197. "D.J. your . . . the night. . . ."—*Ibid.*, p. 170.
"a secret . . . of things."—*Ibid.*, p. 196.
198. "And they . . . and squeeze. . . ."—*Ibid.*, p. 202.
"Tex Hyde . . . *and kill.* . . ."—*Ibid.*, p. 203.
199. "North America . . . static charge."—*Ibid.*, pp. 205–6.
200. "We are martyrs these days."—*Cannibals*, p. 3.
201. "Next to . . . other humans."—*Armies*, p. 185.
202. "It is . . . am sane."—*New York Times*, November 23, 1960, p.
26. The court doctor, Conrad Rosenberg, was not a psychiatrist, but
Magistrate Levy still denied Mailer's request: "Your recent history
. . . indicates that you cannot distinguish fiction from reality. In
your interest and the public interest I must commit you." After
seventeen days in Bellevue, Mailer was declared legally sane and
released.
202–3. ". . . I found . . . Hell precisely."—"Naked Lunch on Trial,"
in William S. Burroughs, *Naked Lunch* (New York: Grove Press,
Inc., Paperback Edition, 1966), pp. xi–xiii.
203. "Poor covered . . . the clavichord."—*Ibid.*, p. 118.
"Certain passages. . . it is." *Ibid.*, p. xliv.
204. "Aztec priests . . . rising sun."—*Ibid.*, p. 80.
204–5. " 'So this . . . from Woolworth's. . . .' "—*Ibid.*, pp. 128–29.
206–7. "For if . . . twentieth century."—*Cannibals*, p. 41.
207. "The wars . . . the soul."—*Ibid.*, p. 45.
"that God . . . could trust?"—*Siege*, p. 15.
208. "central and . . . rational discourse."—Irving Howe, "The New
York Intellectuals," *Commentary*, October, 1968, p. 50. Joseph Roddy
quoted Howe's comment to Mailer and seemed to be paraphrasing
the latter's immediate response with: "Liberal humaneness is not
far from middle-class inhumanity in Mailer's mind. And the rational
discourse Howe believes in is, to Mailer, just the language of the
techni-structure." But after suggesting that Howe stuck these labels
on him in an attempt to get a firm hold on his (Howe's) own past,
Mailer said, "It is not that I am against what Irving Howe means by
liberal humaneness and rational discourse—as a practical matter he
means hardly anything more than courteous manners. But what

he is really looking for is a world he has lost, and I would remind him that I didn't kill it. I just saw that it was going because it was inadequate" (Roddy, "The Latest Model Mailer," p. 25). The contradiction—liberalism is close to inhumanity, and what's wrong with well-meaning liberalism is its ineffectuality—captures some of the caprice of Mailer's stances toward liberalism. Had Roddy attacked both Howe as a secret commissar and the fundamental inhumanity of contemporary liberalism, Mailer would probably have defended both vehemently.

"one of . . . our literature."—Richard Poirier, "The Ups and Downs of Norman Mailer," *New Republic,* January 23, 1971, p. 24.

209. "he could join . . . a cost!"—*Siege,* p. 198.

210. ". . . *The Deer Park* . . . those years."—*Existential Errands,* pp. ix–x.

"event of his lifetime"—*Fire,* p. 119.

212. the best of the four books is *The Armies of the Night.*—I have not tried to check out whether Mailer accurately reported what objectively happened, but I settle with Dwight Macdonald's word: " 'Curious,' Lowell said to me after reading it, 'when you're with another novelist, you think he's so sensitive and alert and you find later he wasn't taking in anything, while Norman seems not to pay attention but now it seems he didn't miss a trick—and what a memory!' What a memory indeed—he took no notes that I observed and yet he reproduces, with few errors or omissions I detected, the scenes and dialogues of the weekend; doubtless he reconstructed them by ear, but his reconstructions ring true, and sometimes they border on the prodigious, as that play-by-play account, at the end, of the duel between the W.A.S.P. Commissioner Scaife, and the scrappy, indefatigably ingenious Jewish civil-liberties lawyer, Hirschkopf [sic]—a real hero—over Mailer's release on bail. I wasn't there but, as an amateur of legal processes, it sounds right; the technical jockeying back and forth is reproduced with the expertise and verve of a Dickens . . ." (Macdonald, "Politics," p. 42).

241. "a simple . . . a fool"—*Armies,* pp. 215–16.

"an egotist . . . unhappily self-assertive."—*Ibid.,* p. 54.

214–15. "in command . . . in himself"—*Ibid.*

215. "in some . . . to live."—*Ibid.,* p. 78.

216. "it sounded . . . solar plexus."; " 'Yes, this . . . he growled.";
". . . Mailer began . . . to thirty-six."—*Ibid.,* p. 9.

217. "a deep . . . competitive force."—*Ibid.,* p. 77.

"I'm trying . . . dead ass."—*Ibid.,* p. 37.

"silent assassins of the Republic."—*Ibid.,* p. 51.

217–18. "Mailer felt . . . bad reviews."—*Ibid.,* p. 45.

218. "Unlike the . . . at last."—*Ibid.,* pp. 76–77.

219. "One may . . . resolutely nonelectronic."—*Ibid.,* p. 54.

"getting fat . . . democratic states"—*Ibid.,* p. 41.

220. "Where he . . . totally new."—Henry Adams, *The Education of Henry Adams* (New York: Random House, Modern Library College Edition, 1931), p. 382.

221. "To him . . . infinite force."—*Ibid.*, p. 380.
221–22. "the symbol . . . in strength. . . ."—*Armies*, pp. 113–14.
222. "Brood on . . . our curse."—*Ibid.*, p. 320.
224. "the spoiled . . . middle class."—*Ibid.*, p. 280.
    "because I'm . . . awfully dumb."—Jack Newfield, "On the Steps of a Zeitgeist," *The Village Voice*, May 30, 1968. Mailer said this at a fund-raising party for the SDS at which he easily promised to speak to GI's at a coffeehouse in Columbia, South Carolina, and contributed one hundred dollars in cash and a check for a loan of nine hundred dollars against the receipts of a benefit showing of *Wild 90*—at a time when he was in debt. After giving the money, he said to Newfield: "I don't agree with SDS. I gave them money because they are an active principle. They are taking chances and they just might be right. I have some sympathies with them, but not intimate agreement. I'm not a left hard-on. I'm a left conservative." The SDS might have been right (with the advocacy of violence) or they might do good and stop short of violence. But if, let us say, they blew up a university building and killed a faculty member within it, Mailer—who supported and encouraged the movement—would surely withdraw his support. Or there are times when he seems one step away from turning such a drama of irresponsibility into a quick moneymaker.
    Irving Howe has attacked Mailer for encouraging illegality and then washing his hands of the consequences, and most of the public evidence is on Howe's side. As far back as 1959, Mailer spoke of the conflict between his strong desire to exhaust the emotions of others (*Advertisements*, p. 92) and his attempt to repress that desire. His co-founder of *The Village Voice*, Daniel Wolf, said in the mid-sixties: "Norman likes people but never for the good, right reasons. . . . he likes them for their hidden combustibility. . . . He wants to do good. But he likes to kick off things in the unconscious" (Brower, "Always the Challenger," p. 111). Mailer would have been an immoral primitivist not to have done this, but then again, primitivism might not be too moral. Certainly Mailer has been more generous with the New Left than they have been with him. See Louis Grant's "Dialogue with a Non-Mayor," *Ramparts*, December, 1969, pp. 44–46, and Robert Merideth's "The 45-Second Piss: A Left Critique of Norman Mailer and *The Armies of the Night*," *Modern Fiction Studies*, Vol. 17 (1971), pp. 433–49. There is a characteristic passage from Grant's attack on page 251 of this chapter.
    "make jokes . . . the park."—*Siege*, p. 214.
225. *"If it made . . . amateur philosopher."—Armies*, pp. 90–91.
226. "tended to . . . he saw."—*Ibid.*, p. 77.
    "thin high . . . of July"; "If you . . . the senses."; "a good . . . John O'Hara!"; "the clear . . . Civil War"—*Ibid.*, pp. 90–91.
226–27. "a hundred . . . the movies."—*Ibid.*, p. 92.
227. "Mailer knew . . . in the heart. . . ."—*Ibid.*, p. 113.
    "he roared . . . and authority."—*Ibid.*, p. 131.

228. "Mailer always . . . his Rubicon."—*Ibid.*, p. 138.
"that restful . . . dark roads."—*Ibid.*, p. 174.
229. "technology land . . . Whorehouse War"—*Ibid.*, p. 97.
"Yes, his . . . to descend."—*Ibid.*, p. 195.
230. "It did not . . . in guilt."—*Ibid.*
"all effort . . . prove less. . . ."—*Ibid.*, p. 212.
231. ". . . standing on . . . four days."; ". . . in this . . . the same . . .";
". . . too much . . . not dropped. . . ."—*Ibid.*, pp. 212–13.
232. "a red-bearded . . . his moves"—*Ibid.*, p. 197.
"And he . . . the Nazi!"—*Ibid.*, p. 144.
"the long . . . for power."—*Ibid.*, p. 197.
"enter that . . . the novel."—*Ibid.*, p. 255.
233. "the musty . . . years past."—Josh Greenfield, "The Line Between Journalism and Literature: Thin, Perhaps, But Distinct," *Commonweal*, June 7, 1968, p. 362.
233–34. "The sons . . . a bit."—*Armies*, p. 258.
234. "fear and . . . exterminated gooks."—*Ibid.*
"the small-town . . . the Reds!"—*Ibid.*, p. 256.
234–35. "it was . . . tangible fruit."—*Ibid.*, p. 199.
235. ". . . they were unbloodied . . . was theirs."—*Ibid.*, pp. 258–59.
236. "dead nerveless . . . them back."—*Ibid.*, p. 277.
236–37. ". . . the rite . . . the warmakers."—*Ibid.*, p. 280–81. Mailer enhances their courage by reminding us that he "had made haste to refuse" (*ibid.*, p. 279) that moral ladder which the protesters agonizingly accept. Since their change is proportionate to the amount of courage they displayed, the quotation also argues against the leveling pessimism of the first articulation of the endless-ladder theory.
237. "*castrat'* "—*Siege*, p. 126.
238. "the apocalyptic hour of Uriah Heep"—*Papers*, p. 58.
238–39. "new and . . . or both."—*Siege*, p. 50.
239. "was left . . . the century."—*Ibid.*, pp. 81–82.
"near to yokel . . . Billy Budd"—*Ibid.*, p. 30.
"a man from . . . earthly sound."—*Ibid.*, p. 54.
"Is it so . . . fifty years?"—*Ibid.*, pp. 1–2.
240. "What a dying! . . . for nothing."—*Ibid.*, p. 85–86.
241. "simple, strong . . . local legend. . . ."—*Ibid.*, p. 87. It must be said that Mailer admits that he is sentimental about Chicago because it reminds him of the Brooklyn of his youth. His description might capture the latter city; it misses the former.
242. "He was always . . . your opponent."—*Ibid.*, p. 198.
"three young . . . newest subdivision"; "about a . . . serious discussion."—*Fire*, pp. 25–26.
243. "the heroes . . . routine function"—*Ibid.*, p. 48.
"God, aghast . . . lose all."—*Ibid.*, p. 411.
"perhaps some . . . private parts"—*Ibid.*, p. 42.
"to sicken . . . to receive."—*Ibid.*, p. 370.
244. "to make profit . . . divine punishment."—*Ibid.*, p. 166.
"beautiful data . . . of magic."—*Ibid.*, p. 275.
244–45. "to make the moon . . . long time."—*Ibid.*, pp. 360–61.

245. "of the church . . . of technology"—*Ibid.*, p. 165. Here Mailer is specifically describing Neil Armstrong.
     "dwell in . . . and procedures)"; "inhabit—if . . . must reside."
     —*Ibid.*, p. 48.
246. "was weary . . . of humility"—*Ibid.*, p. 11.
     "brood about . . . and metaphysics."—*Ibid.*, p. 187.
     "every whim . . . was nymphomaniac."—*Ibid.*, p. 319.
247. "deep into . . . sexual revolution"; "at the blind . . . from life";
     "treacherous, silly . . . their enemies."; "God's intended . . . this year."—*Ibid.*, pp. 385–86.
     "there was . . . and gone."; "behold it . . . than measure"—*Ibid.*, pp. 413–14.
248. "His most . . . Apollo flights."—Poirier, "Ups and Downs," pp. 25–26.
     "a round . . . real alligator."—*Fire,* p. 19.
     "the expression . . . of carnage"; "the movie . . . Tank Cavalry."
     —*Ibid.*, pp. 27–28.
248–49. "confidence between . . . its melting."—*Ibid.*, p. 184.
249. "fell forward . . . the earth"—*Ibid.*, p. 202.
     "an occasional . . . a crown"—*Ibid.*, p. 257.
     "white as . . . Moby Dick"—*Ibid.*, pp. 92–93.
250. "It is . . . too much."—Calder Willingham, *Geraldine Bradshaw* (New York: Dell Books, 1964), p. 6.
250–51. "actually, Aquarius . . . moon shot."—*Fire,* p. 12.
251. "Mailer had . . . use it.' "—Grant, "Dialogue with a Non-Mayor," p. 44.
     "also belonged . . . this book."—*Ibid.*, p. 26.
252. "to be in . . . the instant."—*Ibid.*, p. 17.
     "the fuck . . . did not"—*Ibid.*, p. 136.
     "she had all . . . and dogs."—*Ibid.*, p. 161.
253. "all power . . . of sin."—*Deer Park,* p. 318.
253–54. "After I . . . over again."—*Advertisements,* p. 331.
254. "flew out . . . Kong film"—Mailer, "Evil in the Room," p. 28.
     "stood in front . . . best clothes."—*Ibid.*, p. 40.
     "engaged in . . . with eternity"—*Ibid.*, p. 27.
     "insufficient evil in the room."—*Ibid.*, p. 41.
256. *"we were . . . his development."*—Arthur Koestler, *Darkness at Noon* (New York: Bantam Books, 1968), pp. 78–80.
     "Nixon was . . . the wad."—Norman Mailer, *St. George and the Godfather* (New York: New American Library, Signet Books, 1972), p. 138.
     ("wherever possible . . . patriotic bit")—*Ibid.*, p. 180.
257. "to take ten . . . the center"—*Ibid.*, p. 190.
     "From Nixon's . . . is shed."—*Ibid.*, p. 196.
     "of a tranquil . . . Healthy Economy"—*Ibid.*, p. 192.
258. "imprisoned with . . . our time."—*Advertisements,* p. 17.
     "I probably . . . the Dead."—*Ibid.*, p. 91.
260. "the most extravagant amalgams of possibility"—*Armies,* p. 17.

Index

285